an introduction to

Sociology

For Eirene

an introduction to
Sociology

SECOND EDITION

Ken
Browne

polity

First edition published 1992
Reprinted 1992, 1993, 1994, 1995, 1996, 1997

This edition published in 1998 by Polity Press in association with Blackwell Publishing Ltd

Reprinted 2000, 2001, 2002, 2003 (twice), 2004

Editorial office:
Polity Press
65 Bridge Street
Cambridge CB2 1UR, UK

Marketing and production:
Blackwell Publishing Ltd
108 Cowley Road
Oxford OX4 1JF, UK

Published in the USA by
Blackwell Publishing Inc.
350 Main Street
Malden, MA 02148, USA

ISBN 0-7456-2020-5
ISBN 0-7456-2021-3 (pbk)

A catalogue record for this book is available from the British Library and has been applied for from the Library of Congress.

Typeset in 10.5 on 12.5 pt Sabon by Wearset, Boldon, Tyne and Wear.
Printed in Great Britain by TJ International, Padstow, Cornwall.

This book is printed on acid-free paper.

CONTENTS

Contents

Contents

Contents

PREFACE

How pleasant it is to be proved right. In the original preface to this book I confidently suggested that it deserved to be highly popular among all those who were just beginning to ask about the nature of sociology. I wrote enthusiastically about Ken Browne's unusual capacity to be straightforward without being simplistic, and praised his ability to move gently from common-sense ideas towards sociological explanations in a language which was refreshingly free from jargon, pedantic academic references and lengthy quotations. I also commended the manner in which he managed to blend data, concepts, theories and methods, and wrote glowingly about his capacity to arouse the reader's imagination and curiosity. Above all I lauded the author's ability to convey the sense that sociology mattered, that its commitment to unmasking and demystifying our taken-for-granted social and cultural arrangements made it not only an exciting and challenging subject but one which might even help to make the world a better place.

And now I have solid proof of my prescience. Teachers and students have repeatedly told me that this is indeed an ideal introductory text for all those in schools, colleges and evening classes who are just beginning to ask about the nature of the subject, and now comes news from the publishers that the book has already become so well established that there is an urgent demand for a second edition.

It is typical of Browne's conscientious approach to his subject matter that this new edition is much more than a modernized version of the original. Everyone will welcome the updated statistics (many of which are derived from primary sources rather than already outdated publications), the section on the death of Diana, and an analysis of the 1997 General Election, together with the wide range of references to new Labour policies on education and welfare to work.

But the most valuable additions to the text are the two brand new chapters on Health and Illness and Ethnicity and Race. These both display the author's typical concern with establishing the details of the subject matter (patterns of immigration, rates of mortality) before going on to provide insightful sociological explanations of existing inequalities. As in all the other chapters, there is a wealth of illustrative material (cartoons, photographs, graphics and suggestions for possible student projects and activities).

In my preface to the first edition of this book, I suggested that the future of sociology in this country might well be far more dependent upon the quality of introductory textbooks than upon some of the more esoteric debates about the nature of the subject which fill the pages of the academic journals. Nothing has happened in the intervening years to change my mind. Indeed, it might be salutary if some of those professional sociologists who continue to wrangle indulgently about the proper content of their discipline were to sit down quietly one evening and read this splendid text. It might at least remind them of the origins of the enthusiasm for their subject which they see written upon the faces of those they eventually get to teach.

Laurie Taylor

INTRODUCTION TO THE SECOND EDITION

This book is intended as an elementary introduction to sociology for both the general reader and those studying at GCSE and GNVQ level. No previous knowledge of sociology is assumed. All the key issues and areas included in GCSE and other introductory sociology courses are covered, with each chapter closely modelled on the syllabus content of the major GCSE examining boards.

The second edition has been completely revised and updated, including a range of new material reflecting more contemporary social changes and social trends. Two new chapters on health and ethnicity have been added, along with new cartoons, photographs and graphics.

The book is particularly suited to further education students studying for GCSE on one-year courses, who require a clear and concise account of each topic area. It is also suitable for use by students on other introductory courses which have a sociological component, such as nursing, social work and GNVQ health and social care courses. This book will enable the content of such courses to be covered easily and thoroughly, and allow time for students and teachers or lecturers to discuss, pursue the acquisition of skills and carry out the coursework assignments which are often important aspects of such courses. Students studying at home or on other distance-learning courses will find the book a valuable companion to their studies. Those who are taking an A-level or Access sociology course or an Advanced GNVQ in Health and Social Care will find the book very useful both as preparatory reading and as an easy-to-read foundation text.

Reading about sociology is no substitute for getting involved in the fascination and difficulties of doing an actual piece of research. Chapter 18 provides a comprehensive guide to sociological research methods and the way to tackle project work. Suggestions on appropriate research topics are included at the end of every chapter except chapters 1 and 18.

ACKNOWLEDGEMENTS

Writing a book is, like any other productive enterprise, very much a social process. Particular thanks go to my students at North Warwickshire and Hinckley College who, over several years, have been used to 'road test' much of the material in the pages that follow. They have helped me to keep my feet firmly on the ground in terms of the accessibility of both the text and the level, and have prevented me from flying off into intellectual and academic hyperspace. I must also thank Eirene Mitsos, who suffered enormously from my manic workaholism during the preparation of this second edition. Ken Pyne did fine work in producing the new cartoons, and Ted Fussey was very helpful in producing photographs to order. Many thanks are owed to Laurie Taylor for his generosity in writing the preface to both the first and second editions. Ian Bottrill, Eirene Mitsos, Danny Owen, Phil Whitehead, and Ronnie White provided useful tips and advice. I'd like to thank Rebecca Harkin, Pamela Thomas, Lin Lucas and Jane Rose for their energetic efficiency, support, and encouragement, Fiona Sewell – once again – for her informed and professional copy-editing, and all the other staff at Polity Press.

I am grateful to all those who gave permission to reproduce copyright material, particularly the Department of Health, the Department of the Environment, Transport and the Regions, the Department for Education and Employment, the Home Office, and the Office for National Statistics for permission to reproduce data from Crown Copyright publications. Other thanks must go to Blackwell Publishers, British Gas, the Child Poverty Action Group, Christian Research, the Commission for Racial Equality, the Equal Opportunities Commission, Phil Evans, Gower Publishing, the *Guardian*, David Haldane, HarperCollins Publishers, JBP/House of Viz, Liberty, London Weekend Television, Loughborough University's Communication Research Centre, Macmillan, National Readership Surveys Ltd, the NSPCC, R.R.C. Penfold, Penguin Books, Barrie Percival and Loughborough Grammar School, Peugeot-Talbot, Philip Allan Publishers, *Punch*, Routledge, Rover Group, David Solomons, and Clara Vulliamy. The source of copyright material is acknowledged in the text. Should any copyright holder have been inadvertently overlooked, the author and publishers will be glad to make suitable arrangements at the first possible opportunity.

HOW TO USE THIS BOOK

Most chapters in this book are fairly self-contained, and it is not necessary to read them in any particular order or to read all of them. Select chapters according to the course you are studying. Those not familiar with the interpretation of statistical data will find it useful to study the appendix fairly early on. Those doing research projects of various kinds should read chapter 18. When issues are discussed in more than one chapter, cross-references are made in the text.

Throughout the book, a range of activities and discussion topics is included. These provide valuable exercises to develop your skills and understanding, and should be attempted whenever possible, though they are not essential for understanding each chapter. Important terms are printed in **bold type** when they first appear. These are normally explained in the text, and listed at the end of the chapter. They are also included in a comprehensive glossary at the end of the book. Unfamiliar terms should be checked in the glossary or index for further clarification or explanation. The contents pages or the index should be used to find particular themes or references.

Chapter summaries outline the key points that should have been learnt after reading each chapter. These should be used as checklists for revision – if you cannot do what is asked, then refer back to the chapter to refresh your memory. The glossary at the end of the book also provides both a valuable reference source and a revision aid, as you can check the meaning of terms.

A last word: do not look on this book as your final and absolute source of authority. Much of sociology is controversial and the subject of intense and heated debate. Discuss with others what you read in this book, and bring to your studies a questioning mind and an unwillingness to accept uncritically statements or assertions that are frequently advanced. Take nothing for granted and do not accept things at face value. Above all, enjoy sociology.

INTRODUCING SOCIOLOGY

1

```
KEY ISSUES IN THIS CHAPTER
```

- What is sociology?
- Sociology and science.
- Key introductory ideas and important terms.

Newcomers to sociology often have only a vague idea as to what the subject is about, though they frequently have an interest in people. This interest is a good start, because the focus of sociology is on the influences from society which mould the behaviour of people, their experiences, and their interpretations of the world around them. To learn sociology is to learn about how human societies are constructed, and where our beliefs and daily routines come from; it is to re-examine in a new light many of the taken-for-granted assumptions which we all hold, and which influence the way we think about ourselves and others. Sociology is above all about developing a critical understanding of society. In developing this, sociology can itself contribute to changes in society, for example by highlighting and explaining social problems like divorce, crime, and poverty. The study of sociology can provide the essential tools for a better understanding of the world we live in, and therefore the means for improving it.

WHAT IS SOCIOLOGY?

Sociology is the systematic (or planned and organized) study of human groups and social life in modern societies. It is concerned with the study of **social institutions**. These are the various organized social arrangements which are found in all societies. For example, the family is an institution which is concerned with arrangements for marriage, such as at what age people can marry, whom they can marry and how many partners they can have, and the upbringing of children. The education system establishes ways of passing on attitudes, knowledge, and skills from one generation to the next. Work and the economic system organize the way the production of goods will be carried out, and religious institutions are concerned with people's relations with the supernatural.

Sociology tries to understand how these various social institutions operate, and how they relate to one another, such as the influence the family might have on how well children perform in the education system. Sociology is also concerned with describing and explaining the patterns of inequality, deprivation, and conflict which are a feature of nearly all societies.

Sociology and Common Sense

Sociology is concerned with studying many things which most people already know something about. Everyone will have some knowledge and understanding of family life, the education system, work, the mass media, and religion simply by living as a member of society. This leads many people to assume that the topics studied by sociologists and the explanations sociologists produce are really just common sense: what 'everyone knows'.

This is a very mistaken assumption. Sociological research has shown many widely held 'common-sense' ideas and explanations to be false. Ideas such as that there is no real poverty left in modern Britain; that the poor and unemployed are inadequate and lazy; that everyone has equal chances in life; that the rich are rich because they work harder; that men are 'naturally' superior to women; that it is obvious that men and women will fall in love and live together – these have all been questioned by sociological research. The re-examination of such common-sense views is very much the concern of sociology.

A further problem with common-sense explanations is that they are tightly bound up with the beliefs of a particular society at particular periods of time. Different societies have differing common-sense ideas. The Hopi Indians' common-sense view of why it rains is very different from our own – they do a rain dance to encourage the rain gods. Common-sense ideas also change over time in one society. In Britain, for example, we no longer burn witches when the crops fail, but seek scientific explanations for such events.

Not all the findings of sociologists undermine common sense, and the work of sociologists has made important contributions to the common-sense understandings of members of society. For example, the knowledge which most people have about the changing family in Britain, with rising rates of divorce and growing numbers of single parents, is largely due to the work of sociologists. However, sociology differs from common sense in two important ways:

- Sociologists use a sociological imagination. This means that, while they study the familiar routines of daily life, sociologists look at them in unfamiliar ways or from a different angle. They ask if things really are as common sense says they are. Sociologists re-examine existing assumptions, by studying how things were in the past, how they've changed, how they differ between societies, and how they might change in the future.
- Sociologists look at evidence on issues before making up their minds. The explanations and conclusions of sociologists are based on precise evidence which has been collected through painstaking research using established research procedures.

Sociology and Naturalistic Explanations

Naturalistic explanations are those which assume that various kinds of human behaviour are natural or based on innate (in-born) biological characteristics. If this were the case, then one would expect human behaviour to be the same in all societies, as people's biological make-up doesn't change between societies. In fact, by comparing different societies, sociologists have discovered that there are very wide differences between societies in customs, values, beliefs, and social behaviour. For example, there are wide differences between societies in the roles of men and women and what is considered appropriate 'masculine' and 'feminine' behaviour. This can only be because people learn to behave in different ways in different societies. Sociological explanations recognize that most human behaviour is learnt by individuals as members of society, rather than being something with which they are born. Individuals learn how to behave from a wide range of social institutions right throughout their lives. Sociologists call this process of learning **socialization**.

Sociology and Science

Sociology is one of a group of subjects, including economics, psychology, and politics, which are known as the social sciences. The idea that sociology might be considered a science poses a number of problems. This is because the term 'science' is usually associated with the study of the natural world, in subjects like physics, chemistry, and biology which make up the natural sciences.

However, the study of society by sociologists presents a range of problems which do not exist in the natural sciences, as the following comparison suggests.

Natural science

- Experiments can be carried out to test and prove ideas and it is possible to isolate causes in laboratory conditions.

- As a result of experiments, natural scientists can accurately predict what will happen in the same circumstances in the future. For example, the chemist can predict with certainty, as a result of experiments in laboratory conditions, that some combinations of chemicals will cause explosions.

- In the natural sciences, the presence of the scientist doesn't affect the behaviour of chemicals or objects.

- The natural scientist does not have to persuade objects, chemicals, or, usually, animals to cooperate in research.

Sociology

- Human beings have rights, and might well object to being experimented upon. For example, the idea of removing children from their parents and raising them in isolation to test the influence of society on human behaviour would be regarded by most people as outrageous. Sociology also wants to study society in its normal state, not in the artificial conditions of an experiment.

- Human behaviour cannot be predicted with such certainty: in two similar situations, people may react differently, and people can change their minds.

- Sociologists studying people may change the behaviour of those being studied, who may become embarrassed, be more defensive and careful about what they say, or act differently because they have been selected for study. If this happens, then the results obtained will not give a true picture of how people behave normally.

- People may refuse to answer questions or otherwise cooperate, making sociological research difficult or impossible. They can lie or otherwise distort and conceal the truth when they are being researched, making the findings of research suspect.

Natural science   Social science

Photos: Michael Dyer LRPS

Is Sociology Scientific?

The differences between the natural sciences and sociology mean that sociologists cannot follow exactly the same procedures or produce such precise findings as those in the natural sciences. Despite this, sociology might still be regarded as adopting a scientific approach to the study of society as long as it has the following features:

- **Value freedom** – the personal beliefs and prejudices of the sociologist should not be allowed to influence the way research is carried out and evidence interpreted. Obviously the personal interests and beliefs of the sociologist will influence the choice of topic he or she studies, but the research itself should not be distorted by these beliefs. In other words, sociologists should not 'cook the books' to make their point.
- **Objectivity** – the sociologist should approach topics with an open mind, and be prepared to consider all the evidence in a detached way.
- The use of systematic research methods – sociologists collect evidence about topics using planned and organized methods. These are discussed fully in chapter 18.
- The use of evidence – sociological descriptions of social life, and the

explanations and conclusions drawn, are based on carefully collected evidence.

- The capacity for being checked – the findings and conclusions of sociological research are open to inspection, criticism, and testing by other researchers. 'Bad' sociology, using inadequate evidence to reach unjustifiable conclusions, is likely to be torn to shreds by others interested in the topic.

SOME KEY INTRODUCTORY IDEAS

Socialization and Culture

Socialization is the life-long process of learning the **culture** of any society. The term 'culture' refers to the language, beliefs, **values** and **norms, customs, roles,** knowledge, and skills which combine to make up the 'way of life' of any society. This culture is socially transmitted (passed on through socialization) from one generation to the next.

Roles and Role Conflict

Roles are the patterns of behaviour which are expected from people in different positions in society – they are very much like the roles actors

Role conflict for working women

play in a television series. People in society play many different roles in their lifetimes, such as those of a boy or girl, a child and an adult, a student, a parent, a friend, and work roles like factory worker, police officer, or teacher. People in these roles are expected by society to behave in particular ways. The police officer who steals, or the teacher who is drunk in the classroom, shows what these expectations of behaviour are!

One person plays many roles at the same time. For example, a woman may play the roles of woman, mother, worker, sister, and wife at the same time. This may lead to **role conflict**, where the successful performance of two or more roles at the same time may come into conflict with one another, such as the conflict between the roles of full-time worker and mother which some women experience.

ACTIVITY

1 List all the roles you play, and briefly outline what others expect of you in each of these roles. For example, how are you expected to behave as a student, and what activities are you expected to carry out which you wouldn't have to if you were not a student?
2 From your list of roles, try to pick out those which conflict with each other, as suggested in the cartoon opposite.

Values and Norms

Values are ideas and beliefs about what is 'right' and 'wrong', and the important standards which are worth maintaining and achieving in any society. They provide general guidelines for behaviour. In Britain, values include beliefs about respect for human life, privacy, and private property, about the importance of marriage and the importance of money and success. There are often strong pressures on people to conform to a society's values, which are frequently written down as **laws**. These are official legal rules which are formally enforced by the police, courts, and prison, and involve legal punishment if they are broken. Laws against murder, for example, enforce the value attached to human life in our society.

Norms are social rules which define correct and acceptable behaviour in a society or social group to which people are expected to conform. Norms are much more specific than values: they put values (general guidelines) into practice in particular situations. The rule that someone should not generally enter rooms without knocking reflects the value of privacy, and rules about not drinking and driving reflect the value of respect for human life. Norms exist in all areas of social life. In Britain, those who are late for work, jump queues in supermarkets, laugh during funerals, walk through the streets naked, or never say hello to friends are likely to be seen as annoying, rude, or odd because they are not following the norms of accepted behaviour. Norms are mainly informally enforced – by the disapproval of other people, embarrassment, or a 'telling off' from parents.

Customs are norms which have existed for a long time and have become a part of society's traditions – kissing under the mistletoe at Christmas, buying Easter eggs, or lighting candles at Divali are typical customs found in Britain.

Values and norms are part of the culture of a society, and are learned and passed on through socialization. They differ between societies – the values and norms of an African tribe are very different from those of people in modern Britain. They may also change over time and vary between social groups in the same society. In Britain, living together without being married is much more accepted today than it was in the past, and wearing turbans – which is seen as normal dress among Sikh men – would be seen as a bit weird among white teenagers.

Social Control

Social control is the term given to the various methods used to persuade or force individuals to conform to those social values and norms which have been learnt through socialization, and to prevent **deviance** – a failure to conform to social norms.

Sanctions are the rewards and punishments by which social control is achieved and conformity to norms and values enforced. These may be either *positive sanctions*, rewards of various kinds, or *negative sanctions*, various types of punishment. The type of sanction will depend on the seriousness of the norm: positive sanctions may range from gifts of sweets from parents to children, to merits and prizes at school, to knighthoods and medals; negative sanctions may range from a feeling of embarrassment, to being ridiculed or gossiped about or regarded as a bit eccentric or 'a bit odd', to being fined or imprisoned.

DISCUSSION

Discuss the various positive and negative sanctions which affect the way you behave in your daily life.

CHAPTER SUMMARY

After studying this chapter, you should be able to:

- Explain why sociology is different from common-sense and naturalistic explanations.
- Explain some of the problems sociologists face compared with those working in the natural sciences.
- Explain why sociology is scientific.
- Define the meaning of socialization, culture, roles, role conflict, values, laws, norms, social control, deviance, and positive and negative sanctions, and explain their importance in understanding human behaviour in human society.

KEY TERMS

culture	sanctions
customs	social control
deviance	social institutions
laws	socialization
norms	sociology
objectivity	value freedom
role conflict	values
roles	

2 SOCIAL STRATIFICATION

KEY ISSUES IN THIS CHAPTER

- The meaning of social stratification and key terms.
- The caste, feudal, and social class systems of stratification.
- Social class and status.
- The Marxist theory of social class.
- Defining class by occupation.
- An outline of the class structure of Britain.

SOCIAL STRATIFICATION

Most people would agree that few societies are really equal. The study of social stratification is of central concern to sociologists, because modern societies display such a wide range of inequalities. These include inequalities between rich and poor, between social classes, between men and women, and between black and white. Inequalities exist in a wide range of areas of social life, such as in job security, leisure opportunities, health, housing, income, and the power to influence events in society. Much of this book is concerned with describing and explaining these inequalities, so an understanding of social stratification provides a necessary starting point for the newcomer to sociology.

The word 'stratification' comes from 'strata' or layers, as in the way different types of rock are piled on top of one another to form rock strata. **Social stratification** refers to the division of society into a pattern of layers or strata made up of a hierarchy of unequal social groups. These stand in relations of advantage and disadvantage to one another in terms of features such as income, wealth, occupational status, race, or sex, depending on the stratification system. Those at the top of the stratification hierarchy will generally have more power in society than those at the bottom.

ACTIVITY

Make a list of what you consider to be the most important inequalities in society today. Explain in all cases why you think they are important in people's lives and how they affect the chances people get in life.

Key Terms Used in the Study of Social Stratification

- *Economic inequality* refers to all those material things which affect the lives of individuals, such as their wealth, their income, and the hours they work. These inequalities can be measured, and continue to exist regardless of whether people recognize them as important or not.
- **Life chances** are the chances of obtaining those things defined as desirable and of avoiding those things defined as undesirable in any society. Life chances include the chances of obtaining things like good-quality housing, good health, holidays, job security, and educational success, and avoiding things like ill-health and unemployment.
- **Status** refers to the differing amounts of prestige or respect given to different positions in a group or society by other members of that group or society. Status involves people's social standing in the eyes of others. Status inequalities only exist so long as other people in a group or society continue to recognize them. For example, a vicar in a Christian society is generally given high status, but is unlikely to be given such status in a society practising witchcraft or voodoo.
- **Status groups** are groups of people sharing a similar status. For example, teachers generally share the same status.
- *Ascribed status* is status which is given to an individual at birth and usually can't be changed. Examples of such status include a person's age, race, sex, or place or family of birth. Members of the royal family in Britain have ascribed status.
- *Achieved status* refers to status that individuals have achieved through their own efforts, such as in education, skill, or promotion at work and career success.
- *Status symbols* are things that 'show off' people's status to others, such as the kind of job they have, the way they spend their money, the sort of house they live in, the car they drive, and their general lifestyle. All these things may be highly or lowly rated by other members of society.
- **Social mobility** is the term used to describe the movement up or down the social hierarchy between levels of a stratification system. For example, a

person who came from a working-class family but became a middle-class doctor would have achieved upward social mobility. An **open society** is one where social mobility is possible; a **closed society** is one where no social mobility is possible.

SYSTEMS OF STRATIFICATION

Sociologists have identified three major types of stratification system, which have important differences between them: the caste system, feudal estates, and social class.

The Caste System

The **caste system** is the most rigid system of stratification and is associated with India. The levels of the social hierarchy are called castes, and this hierarchy is fixed and clearly defined. The social position of individuals is ascribed at birth in accordance with Hindu religious beliefs and customs. Hindus believe in reincarnation – that people are born again after death. Hinduism suggests that people's behaviour in their previous life will decide the caste they are born into after rebirth. Since people believe the social position they are born into (their caste) is god-given, they generally accept their ascribed caste position.

A caste society is a closed society, with no social mobility possible from one caste to another. Each caste is completely closed off from others by religious rules and restrictions, which ensure that very little social contact occurs between members of different castes. The purity of each caste is maintained by **endogamy**. This means that marriage is only permitted to a person of the same caste. Besides the choice of marriage partner, caste membership also determines social status and occupation.

In the Indian system, the Hindu religion divides the population into five major castes:

1 Brahmins – the highest caste of priests and religious people.
2 Kshatriya – rulers and administrators.
3 Vaisya – merchants and farmers.
4 Sudras – manual workers.
5 The 'Untouchables' – literally, a group without a caste: social outcasts.

Despite recent attempts by the Indian government to remove the inequalities of the caste system, the system still continues, as many people still accept the Hindu religious beliefs on which it is based.

It has been suggested that the apartheid regime in South Africa showed some similarities with the caste system. Here people were stratified according to ascribed racial characteristics (white, coloured, and Bantu or black populations), with legal restrictions on mixing/marriage between different races, and with an almost 'religious' ideology of white supremacy. However, changes in the late 1980s in South Africa weakened some of the traditional features of the apartheid regime, and the system was abolished in the 1990s.

Feudal Estates

Feudalism was typically found in medieval Europe. The levels of the social hierarchy were called estates, and based on ownership of land. There was no legal equality between estates, and people in higher estates had more legal rights and privileges than those in lower ones. The lower estates had obligations and duties to those higher up the hierarchy, which were backed up by laws. For example, there was an obligation for serfs to work one day a week on the master's land. Membership of any estate was determined largely by birth, with social position, power, and status all ascribed at birth.

Feudalism was, like the caste system, a closed society, with social mobility from one estate to another extremely limited. However, some upward mobility to a higher estate was possible, for example through gifts of land as a reward for outstanding military service. In general, estates were preserved by endogamy, and inter-marriage was only rarely allowed between individuals of different estates.

The feudal system of stratification looked something like the diagram below:

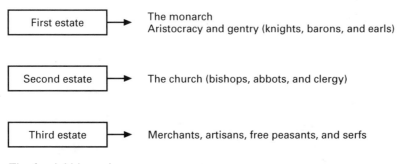

The feudal hierarchy

Social Class

Social class is the form of stratification found in industrial societies, like modern Britain. Social classes can be defined as broad groups of people who share a similar economic situation, such as occupation, income, and ownership of wealth. Often, these criteria are closely related to each other and to other aspects of individuals' lives, such as their level of education, their status and lifestyle (for example, housing, car ownership, and leisure activities), and how much power and influence they have in society.

The main differences between the social class system and the caste and feudal systems are:

- Social class is based not on religion or law, but mainly on economic criteria such as occupation, wealth, and income.
- The levels of the social hierarchy (social classes) are not clearly separated from one another: the divisions between social classes are frequently quite vague – it is hard to say, for example, where the working class ends and the middle class begins.
- Social class differences are not backed up by legal differences. All members of society in theory have equal legal rights, and those in higher social classes do not have legal authority over those in lower classes.
- There are no legal or religious restrictions on inter-marriage between people of different social classes. In theory people can marry whom they like; in practice people tend to marry someone in their own social class.
- Social class societies are open societies. There are no legal or religious restrictions on the movement of individuals from one social class to another, and social mobility is possible.
- The social class system is generally meritocratic. A **meritocracy** is a

'Look. Don't judge me by the clothes I wear, the car I drive, the books I read, the food I eat, the music I like, the friends I see, the money I earn, the place I live, the job I have, the things I say or the way I act. OK?'

Reproduced by permission of *Punch*.

society where social positions are generally achieved by merit, such as educational qualifications, talent, and skill, rather than ascribed from birth. However, the social class of the family into which a child is born can have an important effect on his or her life chances. Entry into the propertied upper class is still mainly through inherited wealth, and therefore social positions here remain mainly ascribed rather than achieved.

Social class and status

An individual's social class and status are often closely linked, and a member of a high social class will usually have high status as well. This is because the amount of social respect individuals get is often influenced by the same factors as their social class – their wealth, their income, and their occupation.

However, while an individual can only belong to one social class, he or she may have several statuses. For example, a person with a low-status, working-class job such as a refuse collector may achieve high status as a local councillor. Similarly, it is quite possible for two people to share the same social class but to have different statuses. For example, a white semi-skilled manual worker will find it easier to achieve status in a group of racially prejudiced white workers than a black or Asian immigrant, who may be given lower status simply because of his or her race, even if he or she has the same occupation and income as the white worker.

ACTIVITY

1 If you were trying to decide a person's social class, what features would you take into account? Think about issues such as her or his job, speech, dress, housing, leisure activities, level of education, and car ownership. List all the features you can think of.
2 Now put your list into order of importance, with the most important features first. Explain why you have put them in that order.

TWO VIEWS OF SOCIAL CLASS

In the last activity, you listed the most important features that you would take into account in deciding a person's social class. The features you think important, though, may not be the same as those chosen by others. A similar dispute exists among sociologists. While most sociologists would agree that social classes consist of groups of people who share a similar economic situation, there are different views regarding exactly which aspect of that economic situation is the most important in defining a person's social class. The following discussion deals with two of the most common definitions of social class which are used by sociologists: the Marxist view of class, and the definition of class by a person's occupation.

The Marxist Theory of Social Class

Much sociological discussion about social class has been influenced by the writings of Karl Marx (1818–83), who based his ideas on industrial capitalism in nineteenth-century England.

Ownership of the means of production

For Marx, an individual's social class was defined by whether or not she or he owned the **means of production**. By this Marx meant factories and land – the key resources necessary for producing society's goods, whose ownership brought to their owners an unearned income in the form of profit.

Bourgeoisie and proletariat

Marx argued there were two basic social classes in capitalist industrial society: the class of owners of the means of production (whom he called the **bourgeoisie** or capitalists) and the class of non-owners (whom he called the **proletariat** or working class). The proletariat, since they owned no means of production, had no alternative means of livelihood but to work for the bourgeoisie. The bourgeoisie exploited the proletariat, making profits out of them by keeping wages low and paying them as little as possible instead of giving them the full payment for their work.

Karl Marx, 1818–83

The ruling class

The class of owners was also a ruling class, according to Marx. For example, because they owned the means of production, the bourgeoisie could decide where factories should be located and whether they should be opened or closed down, and they could control the workforce through hiring and firing. Democratically elected governments could not afford to ignore the power of the bourgeoisie, otherwise they might face rising unemployment and other social problems if the bourgeoisie decided not to invest its money.

The ruling ideas

The ruling ideas in society – what Marx called the 'dominant ideology' – were those of the owning class, and the major institutions in society reflected these ideas. For example, the laws protected the owning class rather than the workers; religion acted as the 'opium of the people', persuading the proletariat to accept their position as just and natural (rather than rebelling against it), by promising future rewards in heaven for putting up with their present suffering; the bourgeoisie's ownership of the mass media meant only their ideas were put forward. In this way, the working class were almost brainwashed into accepting their position. They failed to recognize they were being exploited and therefore did not

A Marxist view of false consciousness and class consciousness

rebel against the bourgeoisie, because they thought their position was 'natural' and they could see no alternative to it. Marx called this lack of awareness by the proletariat of their own interests **false consciousness**.

Exploitation, class conflict, and revolution

Marx predicted the working class would become poorer and poorer and society would become divided into two major social classes: a small, wealthy, and powerful bourgeoisie and a large, poverty-stricken proletariat. The exploitation of the proletariat by the bourgeoisie, Marx believed, would eventually lead to major class conflict between the poverty-stricken proletariat and the bourgeoisie. The proletariat would struggle against the bourgeoisie through strikes, demonstrations, and other forms of protest. The proletariat would then develop **class consciousness** – an awareness of their common working-class interests and their exploitation – until eventually they would make a socialist revolution and overthrow the bourgeoisie.

Communism

After the revolution, the proletariat would nationalize the means of production (which were formerly the private property of the bourgeoisie) by putting them in the hands of the state. The means of production would therefore be collectively owned and run in the interests of everyone, not just of the bourgeoisie. Capitalism would be destroyed and a new type of society would be created, which would be without exploitation, without classes, and without class conflict. This equal, classless society Marx called **Communism**.

A summary of Marx's theory of class

Marx's theory of social class is based on a model of two social classes, defined by whether or not they own the means of production. The bourgeoisie (the owning class) is a ruling class which exploits the proletariat (the non-owning class). This exploitation gives rise to class conflict between these two major classes. The proletariat will eventually overthrow the bourgeoisie in the socialist revolution, and create an equal, classless society called Communism.

The strengths and weaknesses of Marx's theory of class

There has been much discussion of the Marxist view of social class, particularly whether it can still be applied in modern industrial societies like Britain. One of the more obvious criticisms of Marx is that the revolution he predicted has not happened in Britain or any of the Western industrialized societies. While many of the class inequalities and conflicts which

DISCUSSION

1 Discuss the strengths and weaknesses of Marx's theory of class given above. Do you think Marx's ideas are still relevant in any way in the modern world, or do you think they are basically old-fashioned and out of date? Try to think of other evidence and examples to back up your viewpoint besides those given above.

2 To what extent do you think there are conflicts between groups of people in modern Britain, such as conflicts between rich and poor, managers and workers, and the unemployed and people with jobs? Why do you think these conflicts might exist? How might society be made more equal, with reduced conflicts between people?

Marx identified remain in modern capitalist industrial societies, the communist solutions he proposed do not seem to be working in the way he foresaw. In those countries where revolutions have occurred, like the countries of Eastern Europe, the Soviet Union, and China, Communism did not succeed in creating an equal society, and there emerged a new 'ruling class' of people who were better off than the majority. From 1989 onwards, a major wave of popular revolts shook Eastern Europe and the Soviet Union, and swept away the former Communist regimes. There is now no communist country left in Europe. Some other competing arguments over Marx's theory of social class in relation to Britain are shown below:

Strengths

- The means of production remain mostly privately owned in the hands of a small minority of the population. There are still great inequalities of wealth and income in modern Britain, and widespread poverty: 10 per cent of the population own 51 per cent of the wealth, and about 23 per cent of people are living in poverty.

- There remains much evidence of major social class inequalities in life chances, such as in health, housing, and levels of educational achievement and job security.

- Unemployment is an on-going problem, and affects most severely those in working-class occupations.

- The owners of the means of production still have much more power and influence than the majority. For example, the major positions in the state, industry, and banking are held by the privileged rich who have attended public schools, and they own the mass media.

Weaknesses

- While great inequalities in wealth and income continue to exist, the working class has not got poorer as Marx predicted. Living standards have improved vastly since Marx's day, and the welfare state and compulsory state education have given the working class a better lifestyle than Marx predicted.

- Compulsory education has given the working class more chances of upward social mobility, and the welfare state provides a safety net guaranteeing a minimum income for all. Housing, health, and educational standards are much improved compared with the nineteenth century.

- Unemployment benefits help to reduce the more severe hardships which were associated with unemployment in Marx's day.

- Voting rights and the formation of trade unions have given the working class more power and influence in society than when Marx was writing.

Strengths

- The laws still favour the bourgeoisie, such as those which try to weaken trade unions and make it difficult to take legal strike action against employers. In a *Guardian* ICM survey, 67 per cent of the population agreed that there was 'one law for the rich and one for the poor'. The 1997 British Social Attitudes survey found that two thirds of the population thought that the poor were more likely to suffer miscarriages of justice than rich people.
- There is still evidence of opposing class interests and class conflict, such as strikes and industrial sabotage in the workplace. The British Social Attitudes Survey has reported that over half of the population of modern Britain still believe there are strong conflicts between rich and poor and between managers and workers.

Weaknesses

- The laws are passed by a democratically elected Parliament, chosen in free elections. The laws therefore may be said to represent the will of the majority.

- Marx suggested only the two opposing classes of bourgeoisie and proletariat would emerge. In fact, the past century has seen the emergence of a new middle class of professionals, managers, and office workers between the bourgeoisie and proletariat. While these groups do not own the means of production, they benefit from exercising authority on behalf of the bourgeoisie and have higher status and better income and life chances than the working class. They generally have no interest in overthrowing the bourgeoisie. Trade unions are basically concerned with improving pay within the system rather than promoting revolution.

Defining Class by Occupation

Max Weber (1864–1920) was opposed to the Marxist theory of social class. He argued that the most important factors defining social class were the skills and qualifications which people possessed when competing for work in the job market. Employers were willing to give some people higher pay and status than others because they possessed the scarce skills and qualifications necessary for some occupations. This meant there were many social classes, consisting of people in different occupations requiring different types of skill and qualification. This view of Weber's has been generally accepted by most sociologists, and occupation has become a widely used definition of class.

Occupation is certainly the most common definition of social class used by governments, by advertising agencies when doing market research, and by sociologists when doing surveys. This is because a person's occupation is an easy piece of information to obtain, and people's occupation is generally a good guide to their skills and qualifications, their income, their life chances, and other important aspects of their lives. Occupation is also a major factor influencing status in society, and most people judge the social standing of themselves and others by the jobs they do.

ACTIVITY

List all the ways you can think of that a person's occupation might affect other aspects of his or her life, such as family life, status in society, housing, health, leisure activities, beliefs and values, future planning, and so on. Make sure you explain precisely how the effects you mention are linked to a person's job.

The Registrar-General's Scale

There is a wide range of occupational scales in use, but one of the best known and most widely used definitions of class by occupation is that of the Registrar-General. The Registrar-General is in charge of the government statistical department, and is responsible for carrying out the census and registering births, marriages, and deaths, among other things.

The Registrar-General's Scale divides the population into five social classes based upon occupation and employment status, with a division of class III into manual and non-manual workers (the division between working class and middle class). Non-manual (middle-class) occupations are those of people who work primarily in offices, doing mainly mental rather than physical work. The manual (working-class) occupations are those of people who work mainly with their hands (sometimes called **blue-collar workers**). The term **white-collar workers** refers to non-manual clerical workers and sales personnel in class III.

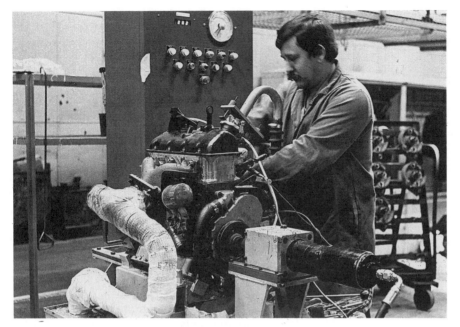

Manual work

Non-manual work
Photos: Michael Dyer LRPS

The Registrar-General's Scale

This occupational scale ranks occupations according to employment status (the general standing within the community of the occupations concerned) and occupational skill.

Social class	Commonly called:	Examples of occupations
Class I Professional	Upper middle class	Architects, doctors, dentists, opticians, solicitors, accountants, surveyors
Class II Intermediate	Middle class	Airline pilots, MPs, nurses, teachers, farmers, managers
Class III (Non-Manual) Skilled non-manual	Lower middle class	Clerical workers, estate agents, receptionists, sales assistants, secretaries
Class III (Manual) Skilled manual	Upper working class	Bus drivers, bricklayers, electricians, cooks, hairdressers, police constables
Class IV Semi-skilled manual	Semi-skilled working class	Postal workers, bar workers, agricultural workers
Class V Unskilled manual	Lower working class	Road sweepers, refuse collectors, labourers, window cleaners

The Standard Occupational Classification

The Registrar-General's Scale was largely replaced in the 1990s by the Standard Occupational Classification, which contains a wider range of occupational groups. There are nine major groups of occupations, classified according to their similarity of qualification, training, skills, and experience.

The Standard Occupational Classification

This occupational scale ranks occupations according to their similarity of qualification, training, skills, and experience.

Social class	*Examples of occupations*
Class 1 Managers and administrators	Police inspectors and above, managers and administrators in national and local government and large companies
Class 2 Professional	Teachers, doctors, solicitors, architects, vicars, social workers, librarians
Class 3 Associate professional and technical	Surveyors, computer programmers, nurses, youth workers, journalists
Class 4 Clerical and secretarial	Clerical workers, secretaries, receptionists
Class 5 Craft and related	Bricklayers, electricians, plumbers, car mechanics, butchers, bakers
Class 6 Personal and protective services	Traffic wardens, police officers (sergeant and below), hairdressers, nursery nurses, waiters/waitresses
Class 7 Sales	Sales reps, sales assistants, supermarket check-out operators
Class 8 Plant and machine operatives	Assembly line workers, packers, bus/lorry/taxi drivers
Class 9 Other occupations	Coal miners, farm workers, refuse collectors, postal workers, road sweepers, cleaners, hospital porters

The Institute of Practitioners in Advertising (IPA) Scale

The IPA Scale

Advertisers are mainly interested in selling things to people, so their scale ranks occupations primarily on the basis of income. They obviously want to know how much money people have so they can target their advertising at the right people.

Social class	Commonly called:	Examples of occupations
Class A Higher managerial, administrative, or professional occupations	Upper middle class	Opticians, judges, solicitors, senior civil servants, surgeons, senior managers (in large companies), accountants
Class B Intermediate managerial, administrative, or professional occupations	Middle class	Airline pilots, MPs, nurses, teachers, social workers, middle managers
Class C1 Supervisory or clerical and junior managerial, administrative, or professional occupations	Lower middle class	Clerical workers, computer operators, receptionists, sales assistants, secretaries
Class C2 Skilled manual workers	Upper working class	Carpenters, bricklayers, electricians, cooks, plumbers
Class D Semi-skilled and unskilled manual workers	Semi-skilled and lower working class	Postal workers, bar workers, office cleaners, road sweepers, agricultural workers
Class E Those on the lowest levels of income	The poor	Pensioners (on state pensions), casual workers, long-term unemployed, and others on income support and the lowest levels of income

> **ACTIVITY**
>
> The Registrar-General's Scale ranks occupations according to the status of the job (employment status); the Standard Occupational Classification ranks occupations according to their similarity of qualification, training, skills, and experience; and the IPA scale ranks occupations primarily on the basis of income. Examine some of the occupations listed in the three scales. Do you agree with the categories they are placed in? Do you think some should be placed in higher or lower classes? Give reasons for your answers.

The problems of defining class by occupation

While occupation is very commonly used to define social class, the use of occupation and occupational scales presents a number of problems for the sociologist:

- The use of occupation excludes the wealthy upper class, who own property and have a great deal of power but often don't have an occupation. Occupational scales therefore do not reveal major differences in wealth and income within and between social classes.
- Groups outside paid employment are excluded, such as housewives and the never-employed unemployed. Housework is not recognized as an occupation.
- Social class is based primarily on the occupation of the 'head' of the household – this is usually assumed to be the man. While this makes such scales blatantly sexist, it is also out of date now that so many households have both male and female partners as major bread-winners.
- The use of a single head of household ignores dual-worker families, where both partners are working. Such families have much better life chances than single-income households in the same class. Their combined incomes might even give them the lifestyle of a higher social class.
- The classes on occupational scales tend to be very broad, and disguise major differences within each class. For example, professionals (Class I on the Registrar-General's Scale and Class 2 on the Standard Occupational Classification) include both poorly paid junior NHS doctors and rich Harley Street private specialists. Similarly, teachers, architects, and solicitors are all put in Class 2 on the Standard Occupational Classification. There are major differences in income and life chances between such people, yet they are placed in the same class.

THE CLASS STRUCTURE OF BRITAIN

Often, when talking of social class, sociologists will refer to terms quite loosely. Figure 2.1 illustrates which groups of occupations are generally being referred to when particular social classes in modern Britain are mentioned. Note that the main division between working class and middle class is generally accepted as being that between manual and non-manual occupations. The controversial idea of the underclass is discussed in chapter 4.

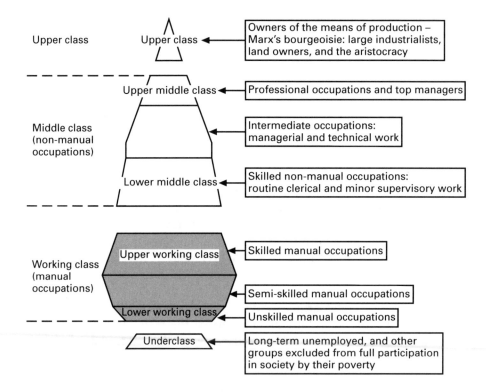

Figure 2.1 The class structure

CHAPTER SUMMARY

After studying this chapter, you should be able to:

- Explain what is meant by social stratification.
- Describe the main features of the caste, estate, and class systems, and the differences between them.
- Explain what is meant by the term 'status'.
- Define the term 'social class'.
- Describe the main features of the Marxist theory of class, and discuss some of its strengths and weaknesses.
- Explain why sociologists often use occupation as an indicator of social class, and explain the problems in the use of occupation and occupational scales.
- Outline the five classes on the Registrar-General's Scale, and briefly describe the Standard Occupational Classification and the Institute of Practitioners in Advertising Scale.
- Outline the main social classes in Britain today.

KEY TERMS

blue-collar workers	means of production
bourgeoisie	meritocracy
caste system	open society
class consciousness	proletariat
closed society	social class
Communism	social mobility
endogamy	social stratification
false consciousness	status
feudalism	status groups
life chances	white-collar workers

PROJECT SUGGESTIONS

1 Ask a sample of people about their attitudes to social class – what they think it is, what is the most important factor defining it, whether it is still important, whether everyone has the same chances in life. Ask them to describe themselves as middle or working class, and to say why.

2 Make a list of occupations drawn from all classes on the Registrar-General's Scale and ask a sample of people to put them into order of importance. Ask them how they decided the order. Do your results coincide with the Registrar-General's Scale?

SOCIAL CLASS IN MODERN BRITAIN 3

KEY ISSUES IN THIS CHAPTER

- Social class inequalities in wealth, income, health, life expectation, and employment in modern Britain.
- Changes in the class structure.
- Embourgeoisement and the new working class.
- The proletarianization of white-collar work.
- Social mobility.

Many people assume that social class is not really very important today, often blaming sociologists for highlighting class inequalities which don't really have much impact on people's lives. However, pretending that social classes don't exist will not make them go away, any more than not being able to see a plate glass door will stop you from hurting yourself when you walk into it. Ask yourself why you don't buy expensive clothes, houses, and cars, or travel first class by train. Why don't you go to exotic foreign countries three times a year? Why don't you eat out at restaurants all the time instead of cooking? Why don't you try to skip National Health Service waiting lists by paying for private medicine?

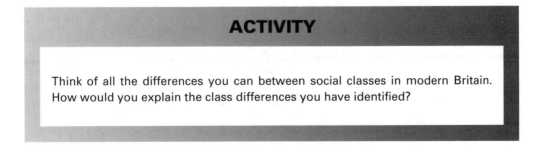

ACTIVITY

Think of all the differences you can between social classes in modern Britain. How would you explain the class differences you have identified?

The point is that social classes do not exist merely in the mind of the sociologist: there are wide, measurable differences in life chances between social classes. The higher the social class of an individual, the more access she or he will have to society's resources – such as better housing, cars, food, holidays, income, and job security – and the more influence he or she will have in society. The following section examines some examples of these class differences, and further examples are discussed in other parts of this book (see particularly chapter 13 on inequality in education).

CLASS INEQUALITIES

Wealth and Income

In 1994, 5 per cent of the population owned 38 per cent of the UK's wealth, and 10 per cent of the population owned over half of the wealth. The poorest 50 per cent of the population owned just 7 per cent of the UK's wealth. The top 20 per cent of income earners got about seven times the share of the bottom 20 per cent, and in the mid-1990s, there was a wider gap between the high-paid and the low-paid than at any time since records began in 1886. A 1996 United Nations report revealed Britain to be the most unequal country in the Western world. Poverty remains widespread, with 32 per cent of the population of Britain – about 18 100 000 people – living in or on the margins of poverty in 1994/95. These issues are discussed in the next chapter.

Health and Life Expectation

Despite the welfare state and the National Health Service, major differences in health continue to exist between social classes. A man from social class I on average lives seven years longer than a man from social class V. As shown in figure 3.1, nearly twice as many babies die at birth or in the first week of life (a **perinatal death**) or in the first year of life (**infant mortality**) in social class V as in social class I. Figure 3.2 shows how chronic sickness and acute sickness rise as one moves down the social class hierarchy (chronic sickness is long-standing illness or disability; acute sickness refers to restriction of normal activity due to illness or injury in the previous two weeks before interview). A survey in the early 1990s showed the death rate from heart disease was about one half higher than average for people in social class V, compared with one half lower than average for those in social class I. This is just part of a mass of evidence which shows that lower-working-class people suffer more from almost all diseases than those in the upper middle class.

These issues of health and illness are discussed further in chapter 17.

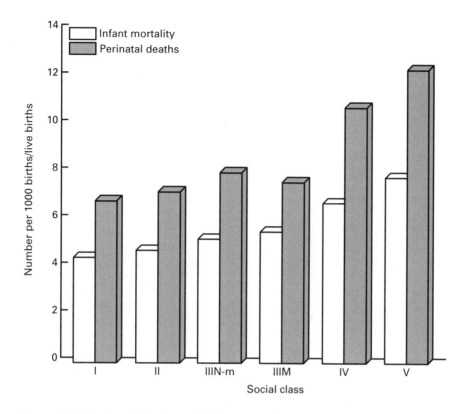

Figure 3.1 Perinatal deaths and infant mortality (for births within marriage only): by social class of father, England and Wales, 1995
Source: Adapted from *Population and Health Monitor* (Office for National Statistics, November 1996)

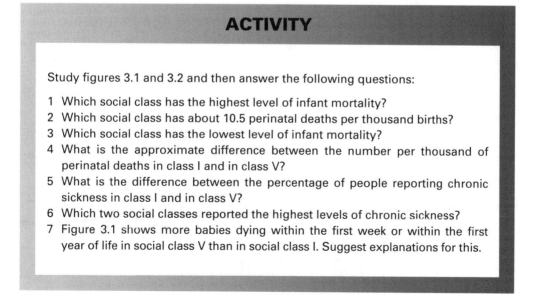

ACTIVITY

Study figures 3.1 and 3.2 and then answer the following questions:

1 Which social class has the highest level of infant mortality?
2 Which social class has about 10.5 perinatal deaths per thousand births?
3 Which social class has the lowest level of infant mortality?
4 What is the approximate difference between the number per thousand of perinatal deaths in class I and in class V?
5 What is the difference between the percentage of people reporting chronic sickness in class I and in class V?
6 Which two social classes reported the highest levels of chronic sickness?
7 Figure 3.1 shows more babies dying within the first week or within the first year of life in social class V than in social class I. Suggest explanations for this.

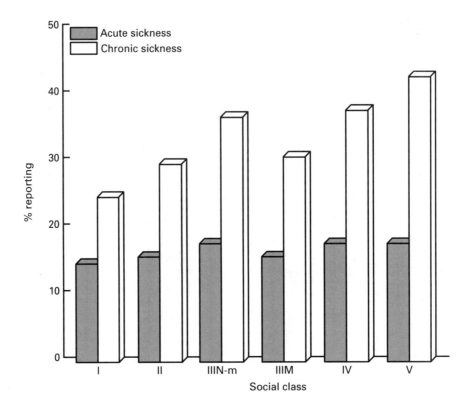

Figure 3.2 Chronic and acute sickness: by social class, Great Britain, 1995
Source: Calculated from *General Household Survey* (1995)

Explaining class differences in health and life expectation

These differences are often explained by the following features of working-class life, which are less likely to be experienced by those in middle-class occupations:

- Longer working hours, with shiftwork and overtime.
- Poorer conditions at work, with more risks to health and safety through accidents and industrial diseases.
- Less time off work with pay to visit the doctor.
- Lower income, leading to poorer diets and housing.
- More likelihood of working-class areas being at risk through industrial and traffic pollution.
- Poorer medical care in working class areas, with long hospital waiting lists and overworked GPs, and lack of enough income to make use of private medicine.

- Lower levels of education, which often mean less awareness of health and the services which are available.
- Poverty in old age, due to the lack of an occupational pension and inadequate earnings while working to save for old age.
- Smoking, which tends to be more common in the working class.
- Higher levels of unemployment and poverty, and therefore more stress-related illnesses.

Class Differences in Employment

The different status of occupations is backed up by different terms and conditions of employment under which people work. These improve with movement upward through the social class hierarchy.

Even the lowest level of non-manual workers, routine clerical workers, often have better terms and conditions of employment than manual workers, although they don't always earn more. In general, manual workers, compared with the non-manual middle class:

- Get lower pay, despite working longer hours with shiftwork and over-time (see table 3.1).
- Have shorter holidays.
- Work in more dangerous and less hygienic conditions, with greater risks of accident and disease.
- Are more supervised at work, having to clock in, getting pay 'docked' for lateness, and not being allowed time off with pay for personal reasons.

Table 3.1 Levels of average pay and hours: full-time employees on adult rates, April 1997

	Males		Females		All employees (males and females)	
	Manual	Non-manual	Manual	Non-manual	Manual	Non-manual
Average gross[a] weekly earnings (£ before deductions)	£314	£484	£201	£318	£293	£407
Of which (%):						
Overtime payments	14%	3%	7%	2%	13%	3%
Incentive, etc., payments	5%	5%	5%	3%	5%	4%
Shift, etc., premium payments	4%	1%	3%	1%	3%	1%
Average total weekly hours	45.1	39.1	40.2	37.1	44.2	38.2
Of which overtime hours (%)	12%	3%	5%	2%	11%	3%

[a] Gross earnings are those before deductions of income tax, national insurance, pensions, etc.
Source: Data adapted from *New Earnings Survey* (1997)

- Receive less training in their work.
- Are less likely to receive full pay during sickness, or to belong to an employer's pension scheme.
- Have much less job security: the risk of unemployment is seven times greater for an unskilled manual worker than for someone in social class I.

DISCUSSION

How might the terms and conditions of employment of manual workers affect their attitudes to work, their leisure activities, and their plans for the future?

ACTIVITY

Refer to table 3.1 on the previous page.

1 Which occupational group of males and females worked the shortest hours?
2 Which occupational group of males and females worked the most overtime?
3 Which group of all employees had the largest percentage of their pay made up of incentive payments?
4 Which group of all employees had the lowest percentage of their pay made up of payments for working shifts?
5 Which occupational group of males and females had the lowest gross weekly earnings in April 1997?
6 What differences does the table show between male and female full-time employees? Suggest possible explanations for the differences you identify.

Explaining class differences in employment

Class differences in employment are often explained or justified by the higher education, training, and increased management responsibility of many non-manual workers, and the need to retain their commitment and loyalty to the firm and thus protect the firm's interests and investment. Even routine office workers often have some knowledge of the firm's 'secrets', such as profit levels, accounts, sales, and orders, and the management might want to conceal these 'secrets' from manual workers, particularly if they are submitting a pay claim. It is therefore in the firm's interest to try to retain the loyalty and commitment of non-manual staff. The tighter control and poorer conditions of work of manual workers suggest they are not trusted by management, are considered more dispensable, and can be more easily replaced. The generally poorer pay of women, whether manual or non-manual, compared with males (illustrated in table 3.1) is fully discussed in chapter 6.

CHANGES IN THE CLASS STRUCTURE

The Changing Occupational Structure

In nineteenth-century Britain, the majority of people were working in manual working-class occupations, with less than a quarter being considered upper or middle class. However, in the last hundred years, changes in the economy have occurred which have changed the occupational structure. These changes include:

- A growth in the tertiary sector of the economy, which is concerned with the provision of services, such as administration, sales, finance and insurance, transport, distribution, and the running of government services (like the welfare state and education). This has created more middle-class jobs, particularly routine, low-level, non-manual jobs.
- A decline in semi-skilled and unskilled manual work, as technology takes over these tasks, and creates more skilled jobs.
- A steady increase in the percentage of the workforce engaged in non-manual occupations, especially white-collar occupations such as routine clerical work.
- An increase in lower professional occupations, like teachers and social workers.
- The growth of long-term unemployment.

These developments have led to a change in the shape of the social structure, with unskilled and semi-skilled manual occupations getting smaller and skilled manual and lower-middle-class occupations getting larger. There has also emerged a growing 'underclass' of long-term unemployed and other groups who are excluded by their poverty from full participation in society. The underclass is discussed more fully in the following chapter. As shown in figure 3.3, the social structure has changed from the pyramid shape that existed in the nineteenth century to the shape of a diamond.

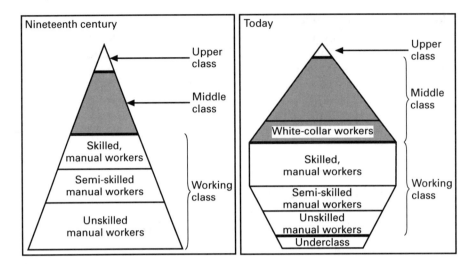

Figure 3.3 The changing shape of the class structure in Britain

Embourgeoisement and the Growth of the New Working Class

Embourgeoisement is the idea that the differences between the middle class and working class are disappearing, with well-paid manual workers merging into the middle class.

In the 1960s, the wages and living standards of skilled manual workers improved greatly, often exceeding those of some of the middle class. These highly paid manual workers were known as **affluent workers**. They could afford to buy their own homes and live in middle-class areas, and to buy the consumer goods like cars which previously only the middle class could afford. This gave rise to the idea of embourgeoisement.

The embourgeoisement thesis was tested by Goldthorpe, Lockwood et al. in 1969 among highly paid manual workers in three firms in Luton, including the Vauxhall car factory, in a piece of research called *The Affluent Worker in the Class Structure*. This research found that many differences still separated manual workers from the middle class, and that embourgeoisement was not occurring.

They found the following differences still separated affluent manual workers from the middle class:

- Their high wages were only obtained at the cost of overtime and shift-working – working conditions which were rarely experienced by non-manual workers.

- They lacked 'fringe benefits' which non-manual workers received, such as employers' pension and sick pay schemes.
- They had more limited promotion opportunities and less job security than non-manual workers.
- They had an instrumental attitude to work. This means their main concern was with money. The purpose of work was not to achieve status, promotion, or job satisfaction (as in the middle class), but to get money to enjoy life outside work.
- Even though they lived on the same estates as non-manual workers, manual workers did not mix with them, preferring the company of other manual workers like themselves.

The Changing Working Class: The 'Traditional' and 'New' Working Classes

While the Luton research suggested well-paid manual workers were not merging into the middle class, Goldthorpe and Lockwood did consider affluent workers to be part of a new working class, because they had a much more affluent lifestyle and a more privatized family life than the traditional working class. There was also evidence to suggest they had an instrumental attitude to the Labour Party and trade unions, supporting them only for selfish motives of personal gain rather than out of a sense of loyalty to their workmates. In the 1980s, many of these affluent workers in fact switched to voting Conservative because they thought the Conservatives offered them more personal benefits than the Labour Party.

In the 1970s and 1980s, the 'new' working class that Lockwood and Goldthorpe discussed expanded, and the traditional working class grew smaller. The main features of these two sections of the working class are summarized in figure 3.4.

The Changing Nature of Clerical Work: The Proletarianization of White-Collar Workers

Proletarianization is the opposite of embourgeoisement. It is the suggestion that, rather than affluent workers becoming middle class, the lower middle class (mainly clerical workers) are descending into the working class.

The proletarianization of clerical work can only really be understood by examining the changing position of clerical workers (sometimes referred to as 'clerks', white-collar workers, or even, for the old-fashioned, as black-coated workers) since the last century.

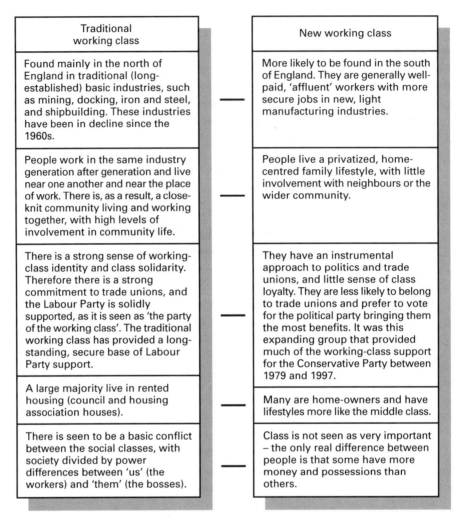

Traditional working class	New working class
Found mainly in the north of England in traditional (long-established) basic industries, such as mining, docking, iron and steel, and shipbuilding. These industries have been in decline since the 1960s.	More likely to be found in the south of England. They are generally well-paid, 'affluent' workers with more secure jobs in new, light manufacturing industries.
People work in the same industry generation after generation and live near one another and near the place of work. There is, as a result, a close-knit community living and working together, with high levels of involvement in community life.	People live a privatized, home-centred family lifestyle, with little involvement with neighbours or the wider community.
There is a strong sense of working-class identity and class solidarity. Therefore there is a strong commitment to trade unions, and the Labour Party is solidly supported, as it is seen as 'the party of the working class'. The traditional working class has provided a long-standing, secure base of Labour Party support.	They have an instrumental approach to politics and trade unions, and little sense of class loyalty. They are less likely to belong to trade unions and prefer to vote for the political party bringing them the most benefits. It was this expanding group that provided much of the working-class support for the Conservative Party between 1979 and 1997.
A large majority live in rented housing (council and housing association houses).	Many are home-owners and have lifestyles more like the middle class.
There is seen to be a basic conflict between the social classes, with society divided by power differences between 'us' (the workers) and 'them' (the bosses).	Class is not seen as very important – the only real difference between people is that some have more money and possessions than others.

Figure 3.4 The 'traditional' and 'new' working classes

Clerical work in the nineteenth century

In the nineteenth century, clerks were closely associated with management decision-making, and were often left to work on their own initiative and responsibility. They generally received higher pay than factory workers, had a good career structure, and could eventually expect to take on management positions after long service. They had much better working conditions than factory workers, frequently working in small-scale offices. They had higher status than manual workers, because they had a more middle-class lifestyle and a higher level of education.

Clerical work in the twentieth century

Throughout this century, the position of the clerical worker has changed in a number of important ways.

- The relative pay of clerical workers has declined dramatically, and generally is little better (and often worse) than that of manual workers.
- Promotion opportunities have been reduced. There is little chance of a clerical worker today 'working his or her way up' into management, as managerial jobs are often filled directly by graduates of universities and colleges.
- Clerical workers have lost their close association with management and they face increased supervision of their work by managers.
- Office technology such as calculators, computers, and word-processors has reduced the skills of clerical work – this is called **deskilling** – and much clerical work has become more like routine and repetitious factory work.
- With compulsory education, the skills required for clerical work are far more common today, so the educational differences between clerical and manual workers have been eroded and many more people can do clerical work. This has contributed to the decline in pay.

These changes have brought about a relative decline in status, and in terms of educational level, housing, and living standards there are few differences between clerical and manual workers. A further factor contribut-

Technology is changing clerical work
Source: Ken Pyne, *Labour Party News*, no. 23, (1991).

ing to this decline in status has been the 'feminization' of clerical work – it has become more defined as 'women's work', and in a world dominated by men, women's jobs are often seen as less important simply because they are done by women. In the face of these changes, clerical workers have turned more to trade unions to protect their position, and this brings them more in line with working-class strategies for defending pay and conditions.

DISCUSSION

Do you agree that clerical work has become more defined as 'women's work'? Why are women more likely than men to take up such work?

Are clerical workers now working class?

While there is no doubt that the position of clerical workers has declined dramatically during the twentieth century, clerical workers still have a number of differences from manual workers.

- They have more job security (though this is rapidly disappearing).
- They work shorter hours, have better fringe benefits, such as pension schemes and sickness benefits, and have longer holidays.
- They are still less supervised at work than manual workers: many do not have to clock in, have no pay knocked off for lateness, and have more flexibility in working hours (flexitime).
- They often share canteen and other facilities with management, and they generally cooperate with management, rather than display the mistrust of management shown by manual workers.
- Despite the growth of white-collar trade unions, these unions often maintain a separate identity from manual unions, and they are often concerned with 'staying ahead' of manual workers in terms of pay and conditions and maintaining status differences, rather than recognizing shared or common interests with manual workers.

These differences continue to separate clerical workers from manual workers, and so clerical workers cannot be regarded as part of the working class. However, proletarianization is an on-going process and their social position may continue to decline as changes in office technology make office work more and more like factory work.

SOCIAL MOBILITY

Modern industrial societies are said to be open societies because social mobility is possible, and people can move up or down the social class hierarchy. The study of social mobility enables sociologists to find out how open society is – how much people move from the social class into which they were born, and how much they improve their social position during their adult lives.

Measuring Social Mobility

Sociologists use the criterion of occupation to measure mobility, using occupational scales like the Registrar-General's Scale. This means that there are problems with the measuring 'tools' used in social mobility studies. For example, social mobility studies often exclude women, and sociologists differ in the occupational scales they use – some rank occupations according to their status, others by income – so the results of different mobility studies are often hard to compare. Also, the status of occupations changes over time and new occupations (like computer programmers) may emerge. As we saw earlier, clerical work has changed dramatically over the course of the twentieth century, so someone doing a clerical job in the 1930s may actually have had a much higher-status job than someone doing a clerical job today. Social mobility is usually studied in one of two ways:

- **Inter-generational social mobility** compares an adult's present occupation with that of the family she or he was born into (usually measured against the father's occupation). It therefore shows social class mobility between two generations. For example, a refuse collector's daughter who becomes a doctor has experienced upward social mobility compared with the class into which she was born.
- **Intra-generational social mobility** compares a person's present occupation with her or his first occupation, therefore showing how much mobility she or he has achieved in his or her lifetime. An example would be the person who began her or his working life as a small shopkeeper, but who eventually built up a massive supermarket empire.

How Much Social Mobility is There in Britain?

Social mobility in modern Britain is relatively limited. Most people stay in the broad social class they were born into. Over half of the adults in the working class and the middle class were born to parents of the same class. There are fairly high levels of inter-generational mobility, but most of this is short-range mobility, such as movement from class V to class III, and there is relatively little long-range mobility across several occupational classes, such as from class V to class I.

There is a high level of self-recruitment at the two extremes of the class hierarchy. This means many children born into class I themselves enter class I, and many children born into class V themselves enter class V.

Despite more social mobility today, the propertied upper class still remains largely closed, as most wealth is inherited rather than achieved through work or talent. The best way to get rich in modern Britain is still to be born to rich parents.

ACTIVITY

Go through the following list, writing down for each one 'upward mobility', 'downward mobility', or 'no change', *and* 'inter-generational mobility' or 'intra-generational mobility'. Refer to the occupational scales in the previous chapter if you find any difficulty.

1 A nurse who decides to become a labourer on a building site.
2 The daughter of a miner who becomes a bank manager.
3 A teacher who decides to retrain as a social worker.
4 A doctor's son who becomes a taxi driver.
5 An immigrant from a poor farming background in Africa who gets a job in Britain as a farm labourer.
6 The daughter of a skilled manual worker who becomes a routine clerical worker.
7 A postal worker who becomes a traffic warden.
8 A pilot whose son becomes a police constable.
9 The owner of a small shop whose daughter becomes the manager of a large supermarket.
10 A sales assistant in a shop who becomes a priest.

Women and Social Mobility

Studies of social mobility have generally ignored women, because of the mistaken assumption that most women are married, work as housewives, and depend on their husbands for their income. Women have therefore been seen as having their class decided by their husband's occupation. However, this is a wildly outdated view, and ignores the large number of

The 1:2:3 pattern of unequal opportunity

Whatever the chance a boy from a working-class background has of reaching social class I or II, a boy from a lower middle-class family has about twice the chance and a boy from an upper middle-class family has about three times the chance of entering class I or II as an adult. This clearly shows an inequality of opportunity in the chances of upward mobility in Britain.

non-married working women and the large increase this century in the numbers of working married women.

What is known is that women have far poorer chances of mobility than men, with women being mainly concentrated in semi-skilled manual occupations, routine clerical work, and the lower professions such as teaching and nursing. Women face major difficulties in entering skilled manual and managerial, technical, and top professional occupations. There are very few women compared with men in the top **elite** positions in society – those small groups of people holding a great deal of power in society, such as judges, leaders of industry, top civil servants, and MPs and government ministers. Women have less chance of promotion than men, and many women experience downward mobility as they abandon careers with bright futures to take care of children, only to return to work at a lower status than when they left. The reasons for this pattern are discussed more fully in chapter 6.

Explanations for Social Mobility

This century has seen a relative decline in the proportion of semi- and unskilled manual occupations and an expansion in non-manual professional, managerial, and routine clerical occupations. This has increased the opportunities for upward mobility for the working class, as there is more room at the top. There are fewer middle-class children than extra top jobs. This means that, even if all middle-class children go into middle-class jobs, there are still higher-level job vacancies to be filled by 'promoting' people from lower down the social scale.

Free and compulsory secondary education since 1944, and the development of comprehensive education in the 1960s, has enabled more working-class children to obtain the educational qualifications required for upward mobility. This is particularly important as intra-generational mobility is generally achieved through promotion at work, which increasingly depends on educational qualifications, and inter-generational mobility is also achieved mainly through educational qualifications.

Some people may achieve upward mobility through marrying a partner from a higher social class. It is mainly women who achieve upward mobility through marriage, but such cross-class marriages are uncommon and most people marry within their own social class.

Exceptional talents, such as in sport or entertainment, or luck, like winning the lottery, provide a route for upward mobility, but only for an extremely small number of people.

Obstacles to Social Mobility

While levels of social mobility have grown a little this century, there remain a number of obstacles to social mobility and the development of a truly 'open' society. The issues summarized below are discussed further in chapters 6, 7, and 13.

- Despite free and compulsory state education, there remains widespread inequality of educational opportunity. Many working-class children face a number of obstacles and disadvantages to success in education, which mean they do not do as well as their ability should allow them to, and this restricts their chances of upward mobility. Middle-class families are generally in a better position to secure for their children a middle-class occupation, as they are more able to afford to support their children in further and higher education.

- There remain biases in recruitment to the upper-middle-class elite jobs. For example, judges and top civil servants are recruited almost exclusively from people who have attended very expensive boys' public schools and then gone to Oxford or Cambridge university. This is a major obstacle for children from working-class backgrounds, who can't afford these schools and are therefore often denied the chance of getting into these top jobs.
- Women face a range of obstacles in achieving upward mobility, because of a range of factors which hinder their ability to compete in the labour market on equal terms with men (see chapter 6).
- Disadvantages in education, and **racism** (see glossary) in education, training, and employment, often present obstacles to the upward social mobility of some ethnic minority groups. Consequently, a high percentage of people of Afro-Caribbean and Pakistani/Bangladeshi origin are represented in the working class.

DISCUSSION

Do you think everyone who has intelligence, initiative, and skill can make it to the 'top' in modern Britain if they really try? Are those at the top and the bottom of the social class hierarchy there because they deserve to be?

This chapter has shown that social class differences persist as major features of life in contemporary Britain, and most people do not achieve much upward social mobility from the family into which they are born. These class inequalities become even more apparent when the two extremes of the social class hierarchy are studied: the rich and the poor. These themes are explored in the following chapter.

CHAPTER SUMMARY

After studying this chapter, you should be able to:

- Describe and explain a range of social class differences.

- Describe and explain the main changes in the class structure this century.
- Explain and criticize the suggestion that embourgeoisement has occurred.
- Describe the differences between the 'traditional' and 'new' working classes.
- Describe and explain the changing position of clerical workers this century.
- Describe and explain the patterns of social mobility in Britain this century, and outline the obstacles to social mobility.

KEY TERMS

affluent worker	inter-generational social mobility
deskilling	intra-generational social mobility
elite	perinatal death
embourgeoisement	proletarianization
infant mortality	racism

PROJECT SUGGESTIONS

1 Using secondary sources, do a study of some aspect of social class inequality, such as in health, at work, or in education.
2 Interview a sample of manual and non-manual workers and try to discover what differences exist in their terms and conditions of employment and their experience of work.

WEALTH, INCOME, AND POVERTY 4

KEY ISSUES IN THIS CHAPTER

- The meaning of wealth and income.
- The distribution of wealth and income.
- Absolute and relative poverty.
- The measurement and extent of poverty in Britain.
- The welfare state.
- Voluntary organizations.
- Why the poor remain poor.
- The debate over the underclass.

Many believe that large differences in wealth and income and the contrasts between the very rich and the very poor have largely disappeared in modern Britain. Surely the welfare state has got rid of poverty? However, a walk through the streets of any large city will reveal stark contrasts between the mansions, the luxury cars, and the expensive lifestyle of the rich, and the poverty and hardship of many of those who are unemployed, sick, or old, who are lone parents, who are homeless or living in decaying housing, and who are faced with a future of hopelessness and despair. This chapter will show the common assumption that the welfare state has resolved the problem of poverty to be misguided, and demonstrate that massive inequalities in wealth and income and widespread poverty remain in modern Britain.

WEALTH AND INCOME

- **Wealth** refers to property which can be sold and turned into cash for the benefit of the owner. The main forms of wealth are property such as homes and land, stocks and shares in companies, and personal possessions. **Productive property** is wealth which provides an unearned income for its owner, for example houses which are rented, factories and land, or stocks and shares which provide dividends. **Consumption property** is wealth for use by the owner, such as consumer goods like fridges, cars, and stereo systems, or owning your own home, which do not produce any income.

- **Income** refers to the flow of money which people obtain from work, from their investments, or from the state. This may be earned income, received from paid employment (wages and salaries), or unearned income, which is received from investments, such as rent on property, interest on savings, and dividends on shares.

The Distribution of Wealth and Income

Figure 4.1 shows that in 1994 the poorest 50 per cent of the population owned only 7 per cent of the wealth, while the richest 5 per cent owned 38 per cent. A quarter of the population possessed nearly three-quarters of the nation's wealth. This pattern becomes even more unequal when

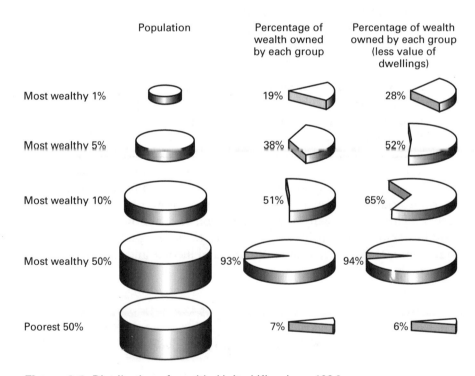

Figure 4.1 Distribution of wealth: United Kingdom, 1994
Source: Inland Revenue, 1997

you exclude the value of people's homes with over half of wealth owned by just 5 per cent of adults. These figures are official figures from the Inland Revenue (the government's tax collectors), and they therefore under-estimate the inequalities of wealth, as the wealthy have an interest in concealing their wealth to avoid taxation.

As figure 4.2 shows, income is also unequally distributed, with the richest fifth of income earners getting about 43 per cent of all income in 1994/5 – more than twice their 'fair share' if income were equally distributed, and more than the bottom three-fifths of income earners got between them. The poorest fifth got only about 6.3 per cent, less than a third of their 'fair share'.

Who Are the Rich?

The rich are:

- The aristocracy. They are major land owners, such as the Duke of Westminster, who owns sizeable chunks of London, Cheshire, the Scottish Highlands, Vancouver, and Hawaii, and whose wealth amounts to an estimated £1.7 billion, according to the *Sunday Times* 1997 'Rich List'.
- The owners of industry and commerce – the 'corporate rich' of the business world. This includes Richard Branson of Virgin, Britain's fifth-richest person in 1997 with estimated assets of £1.7 billion.
- Stars of entertainment and the media, such as Paul McCartney (£420 million), Elton John (£150 million), and the (relatively impoverished!) Sean Connery on £50 million.

The first two of these groups make up Marx's bourgeoisie.

Most wealth is inherited, with those inheriting doing nothing to earn their wealth. Most of the rich live on unearned income from investments rather than from employment.

High-income earners do not necessarily put in more work than those who receive low pay; it is simply that society places different values on people in different positions, and rewards them more or less highly. A senior executive in a large company or a rock star will probably not have to work as hard for his or her high income as an unskilled manual labourer working long hours in a low-paid job. Whenever one hears about 'hard-working royalty', it is worth bearing in mind that Britain's queen is one of Britain's richest women, with personal assets estimated at £250 million. If the queen were to pop this into her local building society, she would receive in unearned income each year (after tax!) an amount that would take a manual worker on average wages about 575 years to earn.

ACTIVITY

Study figure 4.2 and answer the following questions:

1 Which group increased its share of income the most between 1979 and 1994/5?
2 Which two groups suffered the least cut in their income share between 1979 and 1994/5?
3 By how much did the percentage share of the poorest fifth of the population fall between 1979 and 1994/5?
4 How might the evidence in figure 4.2 be used to show that the rich were getting richer between 1979 and 1994/5 while the poor, in comparison, were getting poorer?
5 Draw a pie chart to illustrate the distribution of income in 1994/5. Round the numbers up or down to the nearest whole number; for example, make 9.6 per cent = 10 per cent and 14.4 per cent = 14 per cent.

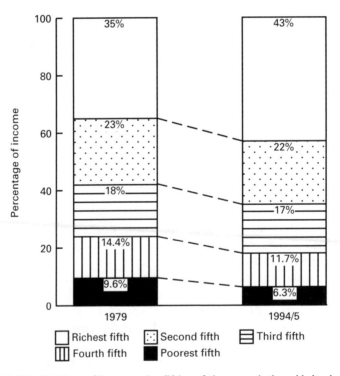

Figure 4.2 Distribution of income: by fifths of the population, United Kingdom, 1979–1994/5
Source: Households Below Average Income: A Statistical Analysis 1979–1994/95 (Department of Social Security 1997)

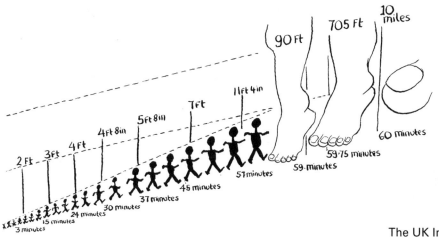

The UK Income Procession

Imagine that everyone's height was based on their income, so the more you earned, the taller you were. Suppose the entire population of Britain marched past you in one hour, ranked in order of their income. This is what you would see.

For the first 30 minutes, you would be greeted by a parade of very small people, between two and four feet high. The first person of average height (income) – 5' 8" – wouldn't go by until 37 minutes had passed. After 57 minutes, mini-giants of 11' 4" appear. In the last minute, super-rich giants of 90 feet appear, but these are dwarfed by the unbelievably rich super-giants (705 feet tall) who go by in the final few seconds. The last person is so rich that his or her 10-mile height makes all the others look tiny.

Attempts to Redistribute Wealth and Income

The massive inequalities in wealth and income which have existed this century, and the inequalities in life chances these have caused, have provoked various measures by governments to redistribute wealth and income more equally. Some of these measures are:

- Inheritance tax, which is a tax payable when people give gifts of wealth either before or after death, and is intended to limit the inheritance of vast quantities of wealth from one generation to the next.
- Capital gains tax, which is intended to reduce profits from dealing in property or shares, and is payable whenever these are sold.
- Income tax, which is payable on unearned and earned income, and rises as earnings increase.
- Social welfare benefits from the state, like income support, which are attempts to divert the resources obtained through taxation to the needy sections of society.

Why Have these Attempts Failed?

Despite these measures, attempts to redistribute wealth and income have been largely unsuccessful. Little real redistribution has occurred, and what redistribution has taken place has mainly been between the very rich and the already well off. This is because their investments often mean the wealthy can make their wealth grow at a faster rate than the rate at which it is taxed.

The state allows tax relief, money normally used to pay income tax, on a wide variety of things such as business expenses, school fees, private pensions, and mortgages. These are expenses which only the better off are likely to have. This means that they pay a smaller proportion of their income in tax than a person who is poorer but who does not have these expenses.

Tax avoidance schemes, which are perfectly legal, are often thought up by financial advisers and accountants to find loopholes in the tax laws and beat the tax system, thereby saving the rich from paying some tax. Such schemes involve things like living outside of Britain for most of the year, investing in pension schemes to avoid income tax, investing in tax-free or low-tax areas like the Channel Islands, giving wealth away to kin well before death to avoid inheritance tax, or putting companies in other people's names, such as those of husband/wife, children, or other kin.

Tax evasion is illegal, and involves people not declaring wealth and income to the Inland Revenue. This is suspected to be a common practice among the rich.

A final reason for the failure of attempts at wealth and income redistribution is that many people fail to claim the welfare benefits to which they are entitled. Some reasons for this are discussed later in this chapter.

During the Conservative government between 1979 and 1997, the trend which existed throughout the twentieth century towards the redistribution of wealth and income from the rich to the less well off was reversed. Wealth and income became more concentrated in the hands of those who were already rich. The highest rate of income tax paid by top earners was reduced from 83 per cent in 1979 to 40 per cent by 1991, other tax concessions were made to the rich, and the value of welfare benefits to the poor was severely reduced.

POVERTY

While there are great inequalities in the distribution of wealth and income in Britain, with a small section of the population possessing large amounts, there is at the other extreme the continued existence of wide spread poverty.

Much of the early sociological research into poverty was a reaction against the idea that poverty was the poor's own fault. Charles Booth's study of poverty in London between 1891 and 1903, and Rowntree's studies of poverty in York in 1899, 1936, and 1950, found that the poor were in fact 'deserving' – decent, hard-working families who had fallen into poverty through circumstances beyond their control. Such research helped to overcome the myth of the poor as 'idle scroungers'.

One of the key issues in discussing poverty, and certainly the most controversial, is the problem of defining what poverty is.

Absolute Poverty

Absolute poverty or subsistence poverty refers to a person's biological needs for food, water, clothing, and shelter – the minimum requirements necessary to subsist and maintain life, health, and physical efficiency. A person in absolute poverty lacks the minimum necessary for healthy survival. While the minimum needed to maintain a healthy life might vary, for example, between hot and cold climates and between people in occupations with different physical demands, absolute or subsistence poverty is roughly the same in every society. People in absolute poverty would be poor anywhere at any time – the standard does not change much over time. The solution to absolute poverty is to raise the living standards of the poor above subsistence level. Absolute poverty is most associated with the countries of the Third World, where it remains a widespread problem. It is unlikely many people live in absolute poverty in Britain today, where poverty is basically relative poverty.

The extent of absolute poverty

In 1997, 1.3 billion people were living on a dollar (about 60p) a day or less; 160 million children were moderately or severely malnourished; and one-fifth of the world's population were not expected to live beyond the age of 40.

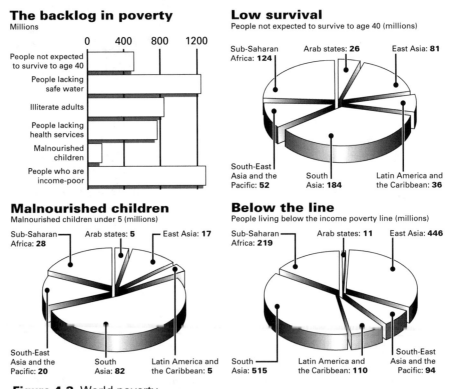

Figure 4.3 World poverty
Source: Guardian (12 June 1997); United Nations Human Development Report

Absolute poverty
Photo: Gordon Browne

Relative Poverty

Relative poverty involves defining poverty in relation to a generally accepted standard of living in a specific society at a particular time. This takes into account social and cultural needs as well as biological needs. Townsend has provided the classic definition of relative poverty:

Individuals . . . can be said to be in poverty when they lack the resources to obtain the types of diets, participate in the activities and have the living conditions and amenities which are customary, or at least widely encouraged or approved, in the societies to which they belong. Their resources are so seriously below those commanded by the average individual or family that they are, in effect, excluded from ordinary living patterns, customs or activities.

P. Townsend, *Poverty in the United Kingdom* (Penguin 1979)

This type of poverty is a condition where individuals or families are deprived of the opportunities, comforts, and self-respect which the majority of people in their society enjoy. Minimum needs are then related to the standard of living in any society at any one time, and will therefore vary over time and between societies, as standards of living change. For example, those living in slum housing in Britain would be regarded as poor here, but their housing would appear as relative luxury to poor peasants in the Third World. Similarly, running hot water and an inside bathroom and toilet would have been seen as luxuries one hundred years ago in Britain, but today are seen as basic necessities, and those without them would be regarded as poor by most people.

ACTIVITY

1 Either alone or through majority agreement in a group, go through the following list, ticking those items which you think are necessities, which all adults should be able to afford, and no one should have to go without.

1 An annual week's holiday away, not with relatives
2 A bath, not shared with another household
3 Beds for everyone in the household
4 A 'best outfit' for special occasions
5 A car
6 Carpets in living rooms and bedrooms
7 Celebrations on special occasions such as Christmas
8 Children's friends round for tea/snack fortnightly
9 A damp-free home
10 A decent state of decoration in the home
11 A dishwasher
12 A dressing gown
13 Fares to visit friends in other parts of the country four times a year
14 Fresh fruit and vegetables every day
15 A fridge
16 Friends/family for a meal monthly
17 Heating to warm living areas of the home if it's cold
18 Hobby or leisure activity
19 Holidays abroad annually
20 A home computer
21 An inside toilet (not shared with another household)
22 Insurance of house contents
23 Leisure equipment for children (sports, bicycle etc.)
24 Meat or fish or vegetarian equivalent every other day
25 New, not second-hand, clothes
26 A night out fortnightly
27 Out of school activities, e.g. sports, orchestra, Scouts
28 An outing for children once a week
29 Pack of cigarettes every other day
30 Presents for friends or family once a year
31 Regular savings of £10 a month for 'rainy days' or retirement
32 Restaurant meal monthly
33 A roast or vegetarian equivalent once a week
34 Separate bedrooms for every child over 10 of different sexes
35 Special lessons (for children) e.g. music, dance or sport
36 A telephone
37 A television
38 Three meals a day (for children)
39 Toys for children e.g. dolls or models
40 Two meals a day (for adults)

41 Two pairs of all-weather shoes
42 A video
43 A warm waterproof coat
44 A washing machine

(*Breadline Britain 1990s Study Pack*, London Weekend Television)

2 Compare your list with another person or group. How do your decisions compare with others? Were some items clear-cut and others borderline?
3 Now compare your list of necessities with those of the national survey conducted for *Breadline Britain 1990s*, presented below. How far does your list agree or disagree with these national findings? What conclusions might you draw from any differences or similarities between the two?
4 Do you think if you were in a very poor country you would have the same list of necessities? Give reasons for your answer.
5 What does this exercise tell you about the ways of measuring poverty in modern Britain?

The public's perception of necessities in Britain in the 1990s

Research carried out in the early 1990s tried to establish what the public regarded as necessary for a minimum standard of living in Britain in the 1990s. This research provides a useful guide to public perceptions of relative poverty. At least two out of three members of the public classed the following items as necessities which no one should have to go without:

- Self-contained damp-free accommodation, with an indoor toilet and bath.
- Carpets and heating.
- Beds for everyone in the household.
- A decent state of decoration in the home.
- A refrigerator.
- A warm, waterproof coat.
- Three meals a day (for children).
- Two meals a day (for adults).
- Insurance.
- Fresh fruit.
- Toys for children.
- Enough bedrooms for every child over 10 of different sex to have his or her own.
- Meat or fish or vegetarian equivalent every other day.
- Enough money for celebrations on special occasions such as Christmas.
- Two pairs of all-weather shoes.
- A washing machine.
- Presents for friends or family once a year.

- Out-of-school activities, such as sports, orchestra, Scouts.
- Regular savings of £10 a month for 'rainy days' or retirement.
- A hobby or leisure activity.

This research estimated that in Britain:

- 11 million people – 1 in 5 of the population – lacked three or more of these necessities.
- 10 million people lacked adequate housing.
- 7 million people went without essential clothing.
- $2\frac{1}{2}$ million children lacked at least one of the things they need, such as three meals a day, toys, or out-of-school activities.
- 5 million people were not properly fed.
- 31 million people – over half the population – lacked minimal financial security, being unable to insure the contents of their homes or save £10 a month.

Source: Harold Frayman, *Breadline Britain 1990s*, booklet accompanying Domino Films and London Weekend Television's series *Breadline Britain 1990s*.

The Controversy over Poverty

The idea of relative poverty and its measurement has been particularly controversial. In 1989, the Conservative social security minister, John Moore, made a speech attacking the idea of relative poverty and the suggestion that many people in Britain were poor. Item A below presents John Moore's view. Item B presents an alternative view put forward by the Child Poverty Action Group, with which many sociologists would agree.

ACTIVITY

Read item A and item B and then answer the questions which follow.

Item A

A former Conservative social security minister, John Moore, made a speech attacking the idea of relative poverty and the view that many people in Britain were poor. He argued that poverty 'in the old absolute sense of hunger and want' had been wiped out, and it was simply that some people today were 'less equal'. He claimed the lifestyle of the poorest 20 per cent of families represented 'affluence beyond the wildest dreams' of the Victorians, with half having a telephone, car, and central heating and virtually all having a refrigerator and television set. 'It is hard to believe that poverty stalks the land when even the poorest fifth of families with children spend nearly a tenth of their income on alcohol and tobacco.' He said it was absurd to suggest that a third of the population was living in or on the margins of poverty. Starving children and squalid slums had disappeared. He claimed that the idea of relative poverty amounted to no more than simple inequality, and argued that the use of the concept of relative poverty meant that however rich a society became, the relatively poor would never disappear. 'The poverty lobby would, on their definition, find poverty in Paradise.'

Item B

The Child Poverty Action Group (CPAG) supports the view that poverty should be seen in relation to minimum needs established by the standard of living in a particular society, and all members of the population should have the right to an income which allows them to participate fully in society rather than merely exist. Such participation involves having the means to fulfil responsibilities to others – as parents, sons and daughters, neighbours, friends, workers, and citizens. Poverty filters into every aspect of life. It is about not having access to material goods and services such as decent housing, adequate heating, nutritious food, public transport, credit, and consumer goods.

But living on the breadline is not simply about doing without things; it is also about experiencing poor health, isolation, stress, stigma and exclusion:

> Poverty curtails freedom of choice. The freedom to eat as you wish, to go where and when you like, to seek the leisure pursuits or political activities which others accept; all are denied to those without the resources ... poverty is most comprehensively understood as a state of partial citizenship. (P. Golding, ed., *Excluding the Poor* (CPAG 1986)).

The gradual raising of the poverty line simply reflects the fact that society generally has become more prosperous and therefore has a more generous definition of a minimum income. The poor should not be excluded as the general level of prosperity rises.

Source: Adapted from Carey Oppenheim, *Poverty: The Facts* (CPAG 1988)

1 With reference to item A, explain briefly in your own words Moore's objections to the idea of relative poverty.
2 Explain in your own words what Moore meant when he said 'The poverty lobby would, on their definition, find poverty in Paradise.'
3 On the basis of what you have studied so far in this chapter, what definition of poverty do you think Moore supports? Give reasons for your answer.
4 With reference to item B, identify four factors apart from material goods and services which the CPAG thinks should be taken into account when defining poverty.
5 What definition of poverty does the CPAG support? Give reasons for your answer.
6 How do you think the CPAG might respond to Moore's comment that 'It is hard to believe that poverty stalks the land when even the poorest fifth of families with children spend nearly a tenth of their income on alcohol and tobacco'?
7 Imagine you are a supporter of the CPAG. Write a response to John Moore's speech.

DISCUSSION

Do you think poverty really exists in modern Britain, given the starving populations in Africa?

The Measurement of Poverty in Britain: The Poverty Line

The **poverty line** is the dividing point between those who are poor and those who are not. There is no official poverty line in Britain today, but there are two separate measures which are widely used as poverty lines:

- The level of income at which income support (supplementary benefit or SB until 1988) becomes payable. The number of poor is calculated as all those claiming, or eligible to claim, income support.
- Fifty per cent of average income – the definition of poverty used by the European Union.

Most sociologists also take into account those who are living on the margins of these poverty lines, as those whose incomes are low often slip between being on or below the poverty line and just above it. The margins of poverty include anyone living on between 100 per cent and 140 per cent of income support or between 50 per cent and 60 per cent of average income. The statistics on poverty in the rest of this chapter are based on the 50 per cent of average income figure, and are updated from research originally done by Carey Oppenheim and Lisa Harker in *Poverty: The Facts*, 3rd edition (CPAG 1996).

The extent of poverty in Britain

In 1994/5 in Britain:

- 18 100 000 people were living in or on the margins of poverty (below 60 per cent of average income) – 32 per cent of the population.
- 13 400 000 were living on or below the poverty line (50 per cent of average income) – 23 per cent of the population.
- Over a third (35 per cent) of all children were living in or on the margins of poverty (below 60 per cent of average income). Over a quarter of all children were living on or below the poverty line.
- There were more children living in poverty than in any other European country, according to Eurostat, the European Union statistics agency.

The numbers of the poor, and the changes between 1979 and 1994/5 are shown in figure 4.4.

ACTIVITY

Study figure 4.4 and answer the following questions:

1 By how much did the percentage of the population living below 50 per cent of average income increase between 1979 and 1994/5?
2 What percentage of the population had between 50 per cent and 60 per cent of average income in 1994/5?
3 How many more people had below 50 per cent of average income in 1994/5 than in 1979?
4 What percentage of the population were living below 60 per cent of average income in 1994/5?
5 Identify two trends between 1979 and 1994/5 shown in figure 4.4.
6 Suggest possible reasons for the increase in the numbers of those living in poverty between 1979 and 1994/5.

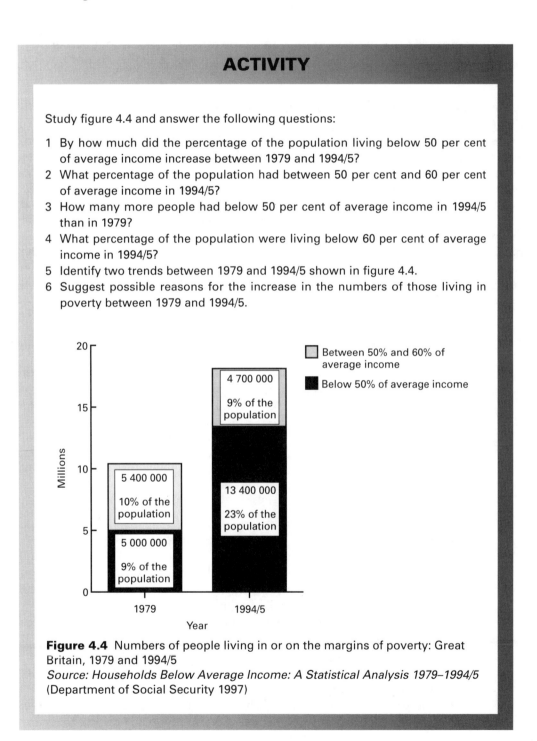

Figure 4.4 Numbers of people living in or on the margins of poverty: Great Britain, 1979 and 1994/5
Source: Households Below Average Income: A Statistical Analysis 1979–1994/5 (Department of Social Security 1997)

The feminization of poverty

Women are far more likely than men to experience poverty. In 1997, about 60 per cent of adults receiving income support were women. Women face a higher risk of poverty than men because:

- Women are more likely to be in low-paid and part-time work. In 1997, around two-thirds of low-paid workers were women.
- They are more likely than men to be lone parents with sole responsibility for children, leading to reduced possibilities for employment and dependence on inadequate state benefits.
- Women live longer than men and retire earlier, and therefore spend a greater proportion of their lives beyond retirement age. However, because of low pay throughout their lives they are less likely than men to have savings, and are less likely than men to be entitled to employers' pensions.
- In many low-income households, it is often mothers rather than fathers who bear the burden of trying to make ends meet, and in the face of poverty sacrifice their own standard of living to provide food, clothing, and extras for the children.

Who are the poor?

Poverty is essentially a problem of the working class, because other classes have savings, occupational pensions, and sick pay schemes to protect them when adversity strikes or old age arrives. The identity of the major groups in poverty suggests that poverty is caused not by idleness, but by social circumstances beyond the control of the poor themselves. The unemployed, the low-paid, and pensioners account for most of the poor. Of those living in poverty (50 per cent of average income) in 1994/5:

- 19 per cent were unemployed.
- 33 per cent were in full-time or part-time work. Many of the poor work long hours in low-paid jobs.
- 22 per cent were pensioners. Many elderly retired people depend on state pensions for support, and these are inadequate for maintaining other than a very basic standard of living.
- 20 per cent were lone parents. Lone parents are often prevented from getting a full-time job by the lack of childcare facilities, or only work, at best, part-time, which generally gets lower rates of pay. The costs of childcare often mean lone parents cannot afford to work. The majority of lone parents are women, who in any case get less pay than men.
- The sick and disabled are likely to be highly represented among the poor, particularly in the unemployed and low-paid sectors. Disability

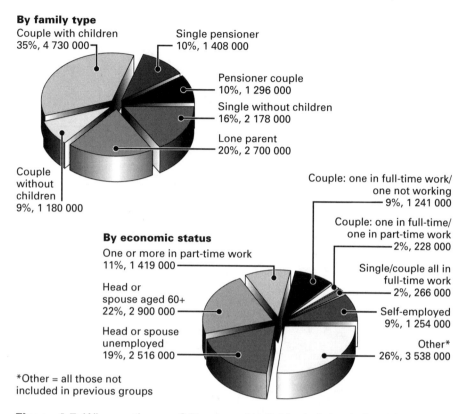

By family type

Couple with children
35%, 4 730 000

Single pensioner
10%, 1 408 000

Pensioner couple
10%, 1 296 000

Single without children
16%, 2 178 000

Lone parent
20%, 2 700 000

Couple without children
9%, 1 180 000

By economic status

One or more in part-time work
11%, 1 419 000

Head or spouse aged 60+
22%, 2 900 000

Head or spouse unemployed
19%, 2 516 000

Couple: one in full-time work/ one not working
9%, 1 241 000

Couple: one in full-time/ one in part-time work
2%, 228 000

Single/couple all in full-time work
2%, 266 000

Self-employed
9%, 1 254 000

Other*
26%, 3 538 000

*Other = all those not included in previous groups

Figure 4.5 Who are the poor? Number of individuals living below 50 per cent of average income after housing costs, 1994/5
Source: Households Below Average Income: A Statistical Analysis 1979–1994/5 (Department of Social Security 1997)

brings with it poorer employment opportunities, lower pay, and dependence on state benefits.

Figure 4.5 illustrates which groups make up most of those living in poverty in 1994/5, by family type and by economic status.

Criticisms of the Poverty Line

Many people are critical of the definition of poverty simply in terms of income, because it takes no account of all the extras most of the population take for granted, such as coping with household emergencies, going on holiday, going out for a drink with friends, and taking part in other leisure activities. Poverty is not simply a matter of how much income someone has, but can also involve other aspects of life such as the quality of housing and the quality and availability of public services like transport, hospitals, schools, and play areas for children.

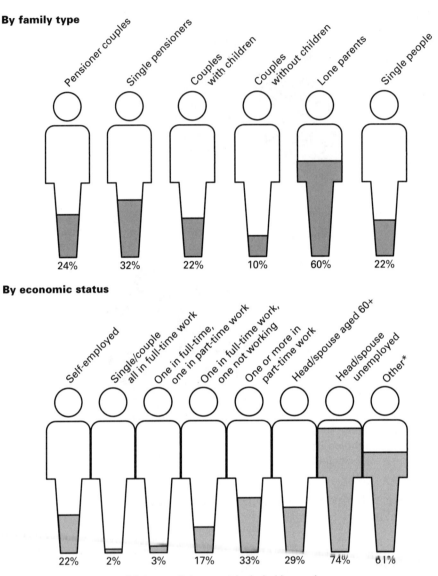

By family type

Pensioner couples 24%
Single pensioners 32%
Couples with children 22%
Couples without children 10%
Lone parents 60%
Single people 22%

By economic status

Self-employed 22%
Single/couple all in full-time work 2%
One in full-time, one in part-time work 3%
One in full-time work, one not working 17%
One or more in part-time work 33%
Head/spouse aged 60+ 29%
Head/spouse unemployed 74%
Other* 61%

*Other = all those not included in previous groups

Figure 4.6 The risk of poverty: proportion of individuals in particular groups living in poverty (below 50 per cent of average income after housing costs), 1994/5
Source: Households Below Average Income: A Statistical Analysis 1979–1994/5 (Department of Social Security 1997)

Poverty means going short materially, socially and emotionally. It means spending less on food, on heating, and clothing than someone on an average income. But it is not what is spent that matters, but what isn't. Poverty means staying at home, often being bored, not seeing friends, not going out for a drink and not being able to take the children out for a trip or treat or a holiday. It means coping with the stresses of managing on very little money, often for months or even years. It means having to withstand the onslaught of society's pressure to consume. It impinges on relationships with others and with yourself. Above all, poverty takes away the tools to build the blocks for the future – your 'life chances'. It steals away the opportunity to have a life unmarked by sickness, a decent education, a secure home and a long retirement. It stops people being able to take control of their lives.

Carey Oppenheim, *Poverty: The Facts* (CPAG 1990)

Let us briefly outline some aspects and consequences of poverty apart from shortage of income. While not all of those in poverty will experience all of these multiple deprivations, the list below shows how poverty can be like a spider's web, trapping the poor in a deprived lifestyle in many aspects of their lives.

- Homelessness.
  — In 1996/7, 116 180 households were officially accepted as intentionally or unintentionally homeless and in priority need by local authorities in England.

ACTIVITY

Refer to figure 4.6 and answer the following questions:

1 What percentage of self-employed people were living in poverty in 1994/5?
2 What percentage of couples with children were living in poverty?
3 What evidence is there in figure 4.6 that might be used to show that low pay is a cause of poverty?
4 What difference is there between the proportion of single pensioners and pensioner couples living in poverty?
5 Which two groups overall have the highest risk of poverty?
6 Which group overall has the least risk of being in poverty?
7 Suggest how the evidence in figure 4.6 might be used to show that the poor are victims of unfortunate circumstances rather than being themselves to blame for their poverty. Could any of the evidence in the figure be used to support the opposite view?

Britain in the 1990s: homeless young people prepare for another day after spending the night in the doorway of Burton's in the Strand, central London. Some prefer the street to sometimes frightening hostels
Source: Guardian (19 December 1990)

- — An estimated 77 000 single people were homeless in London alone in 1995.
- — Around 2000 people were estimated to be sleeping rough in London each night in 1991.
- Poverty in health care.
  - — There are few doctors practising in inner-city areas (where many of the poor live), and those who do are often overworked, because the poor have more health problems.
  - — The poor are less likely to get time off work with pay to visit the doctor.
  - — They face long hospital waiting lists.
  - — Many are not fully aware of what health services are available to them, and the poor tend to be less vocal in demanding proper standards of care from doctors.
- Poverty at school.
  - — Inner-city schools often have older buildings and poorer facilities.
  - — There is often a concentration of social problems in these schools, such as drugs and vandalism, and consequently a higher turnover of teachers.
  - — Parents are less able to help their children with their education, and have less money than non-poor parents to enable the school to buy extra resources.
- Poverty at work.
  - — Poor working conditions. These include a neglect of health and safety standards and a high accident rate; working at night and

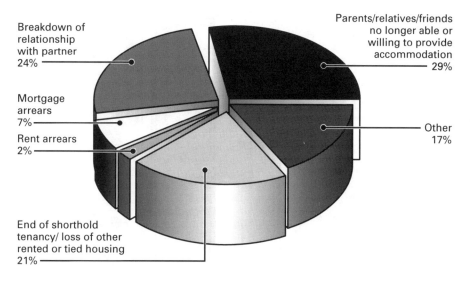

Parents/relatives/friends no longer able or willing to provide accommodation 29%

Breakdown of relationship with partner 24%

Mortgage arrears 7%

Rent arrears 2%

End of shorthold tenancy/ loss of other rented or tied housing 21%

Other 17%

Figure 4.7 Reasons for homelessness: households officially accepted as homeless in priority need, England, 1996/7
Source: Department of the Environment, Transport, and the Regions

long periods of overtime because the pay is so low; lack of trade union organization to protect the workers' interests; lack of entitlement to paid holidays; and no employers' sick pay or pension schemes.

— Insecure employment, often with very short notice of dismissal.

• Poor health, such as respiratory problems like asthma and infectious diseases, as a result of poor diet and damp, overcrowded housing.

• Going short of food, clothing, and heating, and not being able to replace household goods or carry out household repairs and decoration. A 1991 report by the National Children's Home found that 1 in 10 children under the age of 5 from low-income families went without enough food to eat at least once a month because their parents couldn't afford it, while 1 in 5 low-income parents denied themselves food on a regular basis. All the families in the study had an unhealthy diet, not because they didn't know or care about a nutritionally healthy diet, but because they couldn't afford it.

• Isolation and boredom. Making friends may be hard because there is no money to get involved in social activities.

• Stress, in the face of mounting bills and debts, perhaps leading to domestic violence, family breakdown, and mental illness.

• Low self-esteem, brought on by dependence on others, the lack of access to the activities and facilities others have, and difficulties in coping with day-to-day life.

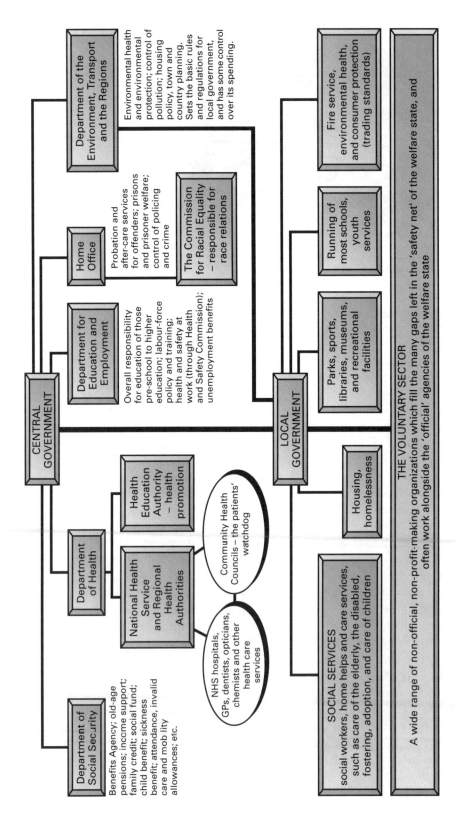

Figure 4.8 'Womb-to-tomb' care: the structure and key services of the welfare state

THE WELFARE STATE AND POVERTY

The main measures taken to help the poor have largely developed with the welfare state, which began with the Beveridge Report of 1942. This recommended the development of welfare services aimed at the destruction of the 'five giants' of want, disease, squalor, ignorance, and idleness, and the creation of a society where each individual would have the right to be cared for by the state from womb to tomb. The welfare state as we know it today came into effect on 5 July 1948 – the date of the foundation of the National Health Service.

The welfare state provides a wide range of benefits and services including:

- A range of welfare benefits through the social security system for many groups such as the unemployed, those injured at work, the sick and disabled, widows, the retired, expectant mothers, lone parents, and children.
- A comprehensive and largely free National Health Service, including ante- and post-natal care, hospitals, GPs, dentists, and opticians (although some charges are payable – for example to dentists and opticians).
- A free and compulsory state education for all to the age of 16.
- Social services provided by local councils, such as social workers, and special facilities for the mentally and physically handicapped, the elderly, and children. Local councils are also responsible for housing the homeless, and for the adoption and fostering of children. The structure and key services of the welfare state (as they were in early 1998) are shown in Figure 4.8.

Voluntary Organizations

Voluntary organizations are non-official, non-profit-making organizations which are 'voluntary' in the sense that they are neither created by, nor controlled by, the government. They employ both salaried staff and voluntary helpers, and are funded by donations from the public and grants from central and local government. Voluntary organizations try to fill some of the gaps left by the 'safety net' of the welfare state, by providing help and information in areas where state assistance is too little or non-existent. They also play important roles as **pressure groups**. These seek to put pressure, through public campaigns, on those in positions of power in society to improve welfare benefits for the poor and deprived. Voluntary organizations play a major role in highlighting the weaknesses of the welfare state, and keeping problems such as poverty, homelessness, and the care of the mentally ill in the public eye. They frequently provide expert knowledge and make recommendations to governments for changes to improve social welfare.

Table 4.1 Three voluntary organizations in Britain

Organization	Aim	Activities
NSPCC (National Society for the Prevention of Cruelty to Children)	To protect children from abuse in all its forms	• Taking action to protect children who are deprived, neglected or at risk of abuse, through a network of Child Protection Teams providing a 24-hour service • Working with parents, children, and social service departments to provide advice, support, counselling, and practical help to overcome family problems and prevent further child abuse • Providing education and training for professional and voluntary organizations, such as local authority social workers, the police, health visitors, and doctors
NACRO (National Association for the Care and Resettlement of Offenders)	To work towards a more effective approach to preventing crime and more humane treatment of offenders	• Running a housing association providing some 700 places for ex-offenders • Running employment training to help unemployed ex-offenders find work • Running youth training, education, and advice projects for offenders and people at risk of offending • Working with others locally and nationally to provide new approaches to criminal justice • Working with local communities to develop crime prevention and community safety schemes

		• Providing research, information, and training services
Shelter (National Campaign for the Homeless)	To fight for the right of everyone to a decent home	• Providing housing aid centres throughout the country which give advice and help
		• Working with local authorities to find solutions to the housing problems of young people leaving the care of the local authority
		• Campaigning for change and improvements in housing policy by acting as a pressure group on people in positions of power in society – primarily the government
		• Providing research and information on the problems of homelessness

Voluntary organizations include groups such as the Salvation Army, which provides hostel accommodation and soup kitchens; Shelter, which campaigns for the homeless and helps with finding accommodation; Help the Aged and Age Concern; the NSPCC (the National Society for the Prevention of Cruelty to Children); and NACRO (the National Association for the Care and Resettlement of Offenders). Much of the information on poverty in this chapter has come from one such organization, the CPAG, which promotes action for the relief of poverty among children and families with children.

THE PERSISTENCE OF POVERTY: WHY THE POOR REMAIN POOR

The welfare state in Britain was originally seen as a way of providing 'womb-to-tomb' care, and of eradicating poverty. However, while it may have removed the worst excesses of absolute poverty, widespread deprivation remains in modern Britain. The welfare state, as this chapter suggests, has failed to solve the real problems of relative poverty. Why is this?

A good way to remember the various explanations of poverty is to think of them as 'blaming theories' – where is the blame placed for poverty?
The explanations below variously:

- Blame the *generosity* of the welfare state (the 'nanny state').
- Blame the *inadequacy* of the welfare state.
- Blame the culture of the poor.
- Blame the cycle of deprivation.
- Blame the unequal structure of power and wealth in society.

Blaming the Generosity of the Welfare State: The Dependency Culture and the Underclass (Version 1)

Some conservatives argue that poverty arises because the welfare state is too generous in the benefits it hands out. The generosity of 'handouts' from the 'nanny' welfare state has, they say, created incentives for staying unemployed, leading to a situation where people learn to become dependent on others. This discourages the poor from taking action to help themselves, and undermines self-help and self-reliance. This is what has been called a **dependency culture** – a set of values and beliefs, and a way of life, centred on dependence on others.

Universal versus selective, means-tested benefits

Such writers believe that universal welfare benefits (which are available to everyone, regardless of income, such as child benefit, the state pension, free education, and health care) should be withdrawn from all those who are capable of supporting themselves. These benefits should instead be targeted only on those who genuinely need them, such as the disabled and the long-term sick. Universal benefits should therefore be replaced by selective benefits, targeted by means-testing. In other words, before people received any benefits they would have to pass a test of their income and savings (their 'means'), and only if these were low enough would they receive any benefits.

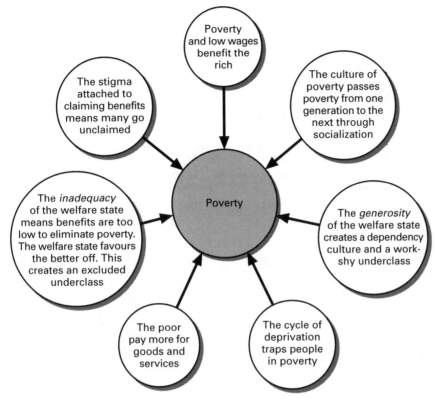

Figure 4.9 Why the poor remain poor

Unclaimed benefits

Welfare benefits have been cut in recent years by inflation and government policies, and they are not high enough to lift people out of poverty. Nevertheless, many people do not claim the welfare benefits to which they are entitled. Each year, around 800 000 families fail to claim state benefits to which they are entitled. According to the Department of Social Security's own statistics, published in 1997, an estimated £3 billion of benefits went unclaimed in 1994/5. This is often because of the complexity of the benefits system, the inadequate publicity, and the obscure language of leaflets, which means people often do not know what their rights are or the procedures for claiming benefits. This is particularly important as the poor are among the least educated sections of the population. The mass media periodically run campaigns about social security 'scroungers'. Headlines such as 'How to be a failure and get paid for doing nothing' (*Daily Telegraph*, 1976), 'End of the "something for nothing" society' (*Daily Mail*, 1992) and 'Stuff the spongers' (*Daily Star*, 1992) help to attach a stigma to claiming benefits which may deter some people from doing so. The establishment of the Department of Social Security's 'Beat-A-Cheat' hotline in 1996 gave such a stigma official support.

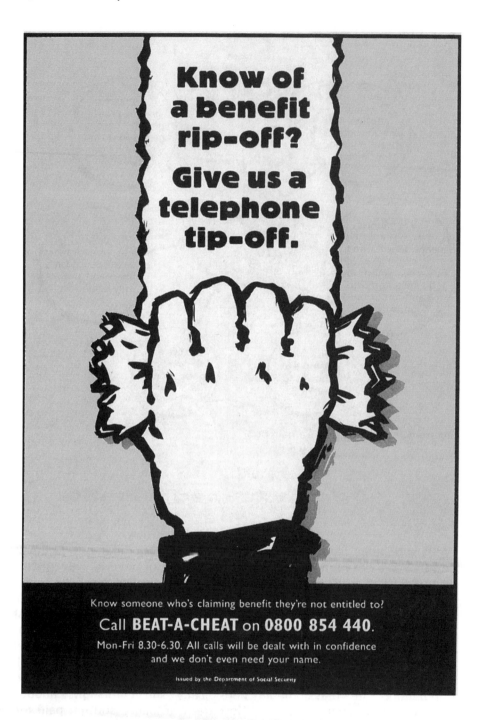

However, selective means-tested benefits tend to attach a stigma to those who claim them, and many who are entitled to benefits do not claim them (see 'Unclaimed benefits' box). There is also a danger that means-tested benefits which are received only by the very poor may lead some people to be worse off if they get a low-paid job. For example, they may lose housing benefit, family credit, and reductions in council tax. They may then find the extra they earn by getting a job is not enough to offset the loss of these means-tested benefits. This may stop people wanting to get a job at all. Universal benefits avoid this 'poverty trap'.

Are the poor an underclass? (version 1)

Some have argued that the generosity of the welfare state, and the dependency culture, have created an **underclass** of people – right at the bottom of the social hierarchy – who have developed a lifestyle and set of attitudes which make them reluctant to take jobs. They are willing simply to live off the welfare state. Supporters of this view of the underclass also point to their lack of morality, taking as evidence high crime levels, cohabitation, and large numbers of lone parents. However, many sociologists reject this view, arguing that the attitudes of the poor are no different from those of the non-poor: they want the same things as the rest of society, but just lack the means to achieve them. This alternative view of the underclass is explored below in version 2.

These ideas of the dependency culture and the underclass are also implied in the later 'culture of poverty' explanation.

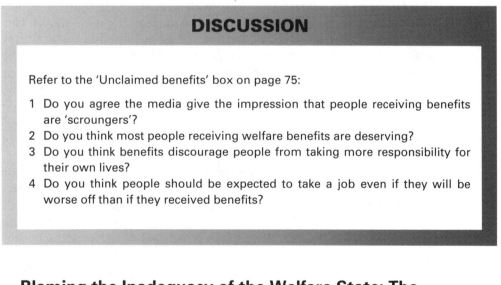

DISCUSSION

Refer to the 'Unclaimed benefits' box on page 75:

1 Do you agree the media give the impression that people receiving benefits are 'scroungers'?
2 Do you think most people receiving welfare benefits are deserving?
3 Do you think benefits discourage people from taking more responsibility for their own lives?
4 Do you think people should be expected to take a job even if they will be worse off than if they received benefits?

Blaming the Inadequacy of the Welfare State: The Underclass (Version 2)

An alternative explanation of the persistence of poverty is offered by those who argue that benefit levels are too low to lift people out of poverty. From this viewpoint, the welfare state is not generous enough, and middle-class people gain more from the welfare state than the poor. For example, the middle class gain more from state spending on education, because they keep their children in education longer (in further and higher education). The middle class also gain more from the health service, partly because they are more demanding and assertive in their dealings with doctors, and partly because the middle class are generally healthier. This means that doctors in middle-class areas are less overworked, and so are able to spend more time dealing with patients and their problems. Poor people, by contrast, get less time with their doctors and face longer hospital waiting lists. Tax relief on mortgages and private pensions also benefits the middle class more, as they are more likely to be home-owners and to have private pension schemes. In general, then – and it was particularly true during the Conservative government years between 1979 and 1997 – the middle class gain more from the welfare state than the poor. This bias towards the middle class has been called the **inverse care law** – that those whose need is greatest get the least resources, and those whose need is least get the greatest resources. This is discussed more in chapter 17 on health.

The underclass (version 2)

This failure of the welfare state to provide sufficient help to the poor has led to an alternative view of the underclass to that discussed above. This alternative view suggests the underclass consists of disadvantaged groups whose poverty means they are excluded from taking part in society to the same extent as the non-poor. This excluded underclass consists of groups such as the disadvantaged elderly retired, lone-parent families, and the long-term unemployed. These groups are forced to rely upon inadequate state benefits which are too low to give them an acceptable standard of living. This prevents them from participating fully in society, and gives them little opportunity to escape the poverty trap.

This view of the underclass suggests it is not the attitudes of poor people which are to blame for their poverty, but the difficulties and misfortune they face which are beyond their control (like unemployment). The poor live depressingly deprived lifestyles, and want many of the things most of society already has, like secure and decently paid jobs and opportunities. In this view, it is government policies which have neglected to tackle unemployment, failed to improve the living standards of those on some benefits, and failed to give the poor the opportunities and incentives needed to get off benefits. It is this, not the attitudes of the poor, which leaves them excluded from full participation in society. This view suggests government policies should tackle unemployment, improve the living standards of those on benefits (e.g. through higher pensions and child benefits), and give incentives to the poor to get off benefits by ensur-

ACTIVITY

Two views of the underclass

Version 1

A group who have developed a lifestyle and set of attitudes which means they are no longer willing to take jobs. They have evolved a dependency culture, which means they are not prepared to help themselves but are prepared to live off the welfare state. Lack of morality, high crime levels, cohabitation, and large numbers of single parents are associated with this view of the underclass. Their work-shy 'sponging' attitudes and lack of social responsibility are responsible for their poverty. Most of the poor have only themselves to blame.

Version 2

A group whose poverty means they are excluded from taking part in society to the same extent as the non-poor do, even though they want to. They consist of groups like the disadvantaged elderly retired, one-parent families, and the long-term unemployed. Their attitudes are the same as the rest of society's, but they are forced to rely upon inadequate state benefits which are too low to give them an acceptable standard of living. This prevents them from participating fully in society, and gives them little opportunity to fulfil their ambitions and escape the poverty trap.

Compare the two models of the underclass above:

1 Which view do you think provides the most accurate picture of poor people?
2 What solutions to the problem of the underclass would you adopt for each version?

ing decently paid jobs. Only in this way will the excluded underclass disappear in our society.

Blaming the Culture of the Poor: The Culture of Poverty

Another explanation for the persistence of poverty is the theory of the **culture of poverty**. This suggests it is the characteristics of the poor themselves, their values and culture, that cause poverty. It is suggested the poor are resigned to their situation, that they seldom take opportunities when they arise, are reluctant to work, and don't plan for the future. They seem, in this view, to make little effort to change their situation or

Trapped in poverty: the poor pay more

One of the great ironies of poverty is that the cost of living is higher for the poor than the non-poor, and this hinders the poor in their attempts to escape poverty. The poor pay more because:

- They often live in poor-quality housing, which is expensive to heat and maintain.
- They live mainly in inner-city areas, where rents are high.
- The price of goods and services is higher in poorer areas, owing to factors like shoplifting and vandalism.
- They have to buy cheap clothing, which wears out quickly and is therefore more expensive in the long run.
- They have to pay more for food as they can only afford to buy it in small quantities (which is more expensive), and from small, expensive corner shops as they haven't cars to travel to supermarkets. They also lack storage facilities like freezers for buying in bulk.
- The poor pay more for house and car insurance, owing to higher levels of theft and vandalism in poor areas.
- They pay more for credit; banks and building societies won't lend them money as they consider them a poor risk. Loans are therefore often obtained from 'loan sharks' at exorbitant rates of interest.
- They suffer more ill-health, and so have to spend more on non-prescription medicines.

to help themselves by taking the initiative and trying to break free of their poverty. Children grow up in this culture, and learn these values from their parents, and so poverty continues from one generation to the next.

The weakness of this type of explanation is that it tends to blame the poor for their own poverty, and implies that if only the poor would change their values, then poverty would disappear. However, if the poor do develop a culture of poverty – and this is hotly disputed – it may well be a result of poverty rather than a cause of it. For example, the poor cannot afford to save for a 'rainy day', planning for the future is difficult when the future is so uncertain, and it is hard not to give up and become resigned to being unemployed after endless searching for non-existent jobs.

The culture-of-poverty explanation, and the earlier 'dependency culture' one, are convenient ones for those in positions of power, as they put the blame for poverty on the poor themselves. If these explanations are adopted, then the problem of poverty will be solved by policies such as cutting welfare benefits to the poor, to make them 'stand on their own two feet', and job training programmes to get them used to working. Such a view of the poor seemed to lie behind many of the Conservative government's social security reforms between 1979 and 1997, and the cuts in welfare benefits these produced.

Blaming the Cycle of Deprivation

A further explanation for poverty is what has been called the cycle of deprivation. This suggests that poverty is cumulative, in the sense that one aspect of poverty can lead to further poverty. This builds up into a vicious circle which the poor find hard to escape from, and it then carries on with their children. Figure 4.10 illustrates examples of possible cycles of

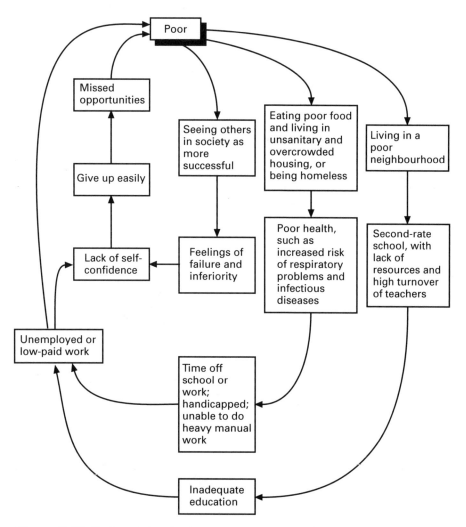

Figure 4.10 Cycles of deprivation

deprivation. The problem with this explanation is that, while it explains why poverty continues, it does not explain how poverty begins in the first place. The final type of explanation does try to do this.

Blaming the Unequal Structure of Power and Wealth in Society

These are structural explanations, which explain poverty in terms of the structure of society, with its unequal distribution of wealth and income and the inadequate assistance given to the poor. These are mainly Marxist arguments, which suggest that the reason the poor remain poor is because they are exploited by the rich. The owners of society's key resources make profits by paying low wages – and their wealthy position depends on poverty. Poverty ensures the dangerous, menial jobs are done, and the poor help to limit the wage demands of those who are non-poor by providing a threat to their jobs. The poor lack power to change their position, because they do not have the financial resources to change public opinion. In this view, it is not being unemployed, a lone parent, long-term sick, disabled, or old that causes poverty. Rather, it is government policy and the structure of society which mean people facing misfortune, through no fault of their own, are penalized for it by inadequate benefits.

Structural explanations suggest that any serious attempt to abolish poverty would involve a widespread redistribution of wealth and income. This would mean the creation of improved social services, higher welfare benefits, and more and better-paid jobs, with the introduction of higher taxes on the rich to pay for these reforms.

ACTIVITY

You have become the prime minister, with a huge majority in Parliament enabling you to carry through a successful campaign against poverty. Think carefully about all the explanations for poverty you have read of in this chapter, and the groups in poverty. Devise a series of policies which would help to reduce poverty. Explain in each case why you think your proposed policy would help to reduce poverty.

CHAPTER SUMMARY

After studying this chapter, you should be able to:

- Explain the difference between wealth and income.
- Describe the attempts made to redistribute wealth and income, and explain why these measures have failed.
- Explain the difference between absolute and relative poverty.
- Describe the poverty line in Britain, and make criticisms of it.
- Describe aspects of poverty apart from lack of income.
- Identify the main groups in poverty in modern Britain, and explain why each of them is poor.
- Explain why women are more likely to be in poverty than men.
- Outline the main features of the welfare state.
- Explain, with examples, the role of voluntary organizations.
- Explain why the cost of living is higher for the poor than for those who are not poor.
- Give a number of explanations why the poor remain poor, despite the welfare state.
- Discuss the different versions of the view that the poor are an underclass.

KEY TERMS

absolute poverty	poverty line
consumption property	pressure groups
culture of poverty	productive property
dependency culture	relative poverty
income	underclass
inverse care law	wealth

PROJECT SUGGESTIONS

1 Carry out a survey asking people about poverty in Britain today. Do they think it still exists? What do they mean by 'poor'? Draw up a list of items and ask people whether they think they are essential for a basic standard of living. You could use the list of items earlier in this chapter to help you. Try to draw some conclusions about the idea of relative poverty.

2 Interview a sample of people generally thought to be living in poverty, such as the unemployed or lone parents, and try to discover what difficulties they experience compared with those who aren't poor.
3 Do a case study of the activities of a local voluntary organization.

GENDER ROLE SOCIALIZATION

5

⬭ KEY ISSUES IN THIS CHAPTER ⬭

- The difference between sex and gender.
- Gender stereotyping.
- The roles of the family, the school, the peer group, and the mass media in gender stereotyping.
- Some consequences of gender stereotyping.

Stratification by sex is a feature found in most societies, with men generally being in a more dominant position in society than women. Our sex has major influences on how we think about ourselves, how others think about us, and the opportunities and life chances open to us. Men have traditionally been seen in a wide range of active and creative roles – as warriors, hunters, and workers, as political leaders or successful business executives, as scientists, engineers, inventors, or great artists (how many famous women scientists, engineers, inventors, or artists can you name?).

And what roles have women been traditionally seen in? As housewives and mothers confined to the home and caring for their husbands and children. Even when working outside the home, women's jobs often seem to be an extension of their caring role in the home, looking after others as receptionists, secretaries, nurses, teachers, social workers, shop and kitchen assistants, or cleaners. We might almost be forgiven for thinking that men and women exist in two different worlds, united only by belonging to the same species. Are these differences simply an extension of the biological make-up of males and females, or are they a product of the ways that males and females are brought up in society? This chapter will examine this question, and discuss how the social differences between men and women are constructed by socialization in modern Britain. The following chapter examines some of the particular inequalities facing women, which are, in part, a product of this socialization.

SEX AND GENDER

The term **sex** (whether someone is male or female) refers to the natural or biological differences between men and women, such as differences in genitals, internal reproductive organs and body hair.

Gender (whether someone is masculine or feminine) refers to the cultural, socially constructed differences between the two sexes. It refers to the way a society encourages and teaches the two sexes to behave in different ways through socialization.

A **gender role** is the pattern of behaviour and activity which society expects from individuals of either sex – how a boy/man or girl/woman should behave in society. Gender roles may sometimes be referred to as sex roles.

The difference between the terms 'sex' and 'gender' is best illustrated by the case of transsexuals – people who biologically belong to one sex, but are convinced they belong to the opposite sex, for example a woman 'trapped' in a man's body. When these people try to change their biological sex, through surgery and hormone treatment, they also have to learn to act in a different way and adopt new masculine or feminine gender roles. The *Independent on Sunday* (16 December 1990) reported the case of a man who changed sex twice: from male to female and back again. On taking on the female role, he had to adopt a new feminine gender identity, like changing his name from Colin to Cathy, wearing a dress and high-heeled shoes, putting on a black wig as his hair was too masculine in texture, and shaving off his beard. However, the importance of gender identity meant that, while he was losing his male friends, barriers remained in forming close relations with female friends. He felt he was simply changing from acting as a man to acting as a woman, and that the only group with which he could find full acceptance was that of other transsexuals. After three years of living as a woman, the pressures of being accepted as neither male nor female meant he stopped hormone treatment, reverted to his former male identity, and started dressing as a man again. It is experiences such as these that show the fundamental importance of gender identities, and how influential they are, not only in how we see ourselves, but in how others see us too.

GENDER AND BIOLOGY

It is sometimes suggested that the different gender roles played by women and men are 'obvious' extensions of the biological differences between the sexes. Therefore women are thought to be 'natural' mothers, with a maternal and caring 'instinct' and a biological inclination towards child rearing and domestic tasks. Men, on the other hand, it is suggested are 'naturally' assertive and dominant members of society, inclined towards the 'breadwinner' role of supporting the family.

If this argument were correct, then one would expect the typical roles played by men and women in Britain to be the same in every society: after all, the biological differences between men and women are the same everywhere. However, the comparative study of other societies suggests this is not the case.

Three Tribes in New Guinea

Margaret Mead described three tribes in New Guinea (*Sex and Temperament*, 1935) where the roles of men and women were quite different from those found in modern Britain.

- Among the *Mundugumar*, both sexes showed what we in Britain would regard as masculine characteristics – both sexes were aggressive, both hated childbirth and child rearing, and both treated children in an offhand way.
- Among the *Arapesh*, there were few 'natural' differences between the behaviour of the sexes. Both sexes were gentle and passive; women did the heavy carrying; the men tried to share the pains of childbirth with their wives by lying with them during it. Both sexes shared equally the tasks of bringing up children (women's traditional role in Britain).
- In the *Tchambuli* tribe, the traditional gender roles found in modern Britain were reversed – it was the men who displayed what we would regard as 'feminine' characteristics, such as doing the shopping and putting on make-up and jewellery to make themselves attractive. Women were the more aggressive, practical ones, who made the sexual advances to men and did all the trading.

These three examples suggest that gender roles are not natural, since they differ between societies even though biological differences remain the same. Further evidence that our biology does not decide our gender identity comes from studies of children who, although biologically male, have been brought up as females and developed feminine forms of behaviour. For example, there is the case of a seven-month-old boy whose penis was accidentally cut off. In response to this, his parents and doctors decided that the best thing to do was to transform him by surgery and hormone treatment into a female, and raise him as a girl. Within a few years he had a completely feminine gender identity, despite being entirely male biologically. It is evidence like this which has led sociologists to conclude that masculine and feminine gender identities are primarily constructed through socialization, rather than a product of the biological differences between men and women.

GENDER STEREOTYPING IN BRITAIN

A **stereotype** is a generalized, over-simplified view of the features of a social group, allowing for few individual differences among members of the group. The assumption is made that all members of the group share the same features. Examples of stereotypes include views such as 'all women are lousy drivers', 'all young people are vandals and layabouts', or 'the unemployed are all on the fiddle'.

A gender stereotype is a generalized view of the 'typical' or 'ideal' characteristics of men and women. In modern Britain, for example, girls and women are expected to show the 'feminine' characteristics of being pretty, slim, gentle, caring, sensitive, submissive, non-competitive, and depen-

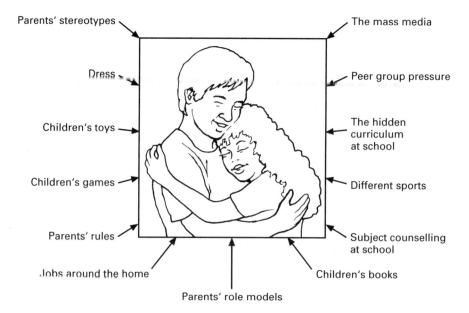

Figure 5.1 The social construction of gender differences through socialization

dent. The masculine stereotype, on the other hand, emphasizes characteristics like physical strength, aggression and assertiveness, independence, competitiveness, and ambition. Girls and women who fail to conform to the feminine stereotype are liable to be seen as 'tomboys', while men and boys who fail to conform to the masculine stereotype are likely to be seen as 'cissies' or 'wimps'. It is still the case that one of the worst taunts a male child can face is to be called 'a girl' by his peer group.

Some jobs and activities are also stereotyped as more suitable for men or women; housework and childcare, for example, are still seen as predominantly 'women's work', while 'men's work' is predominantly seen as something that takes place outside the home in paid employment.

ACTIVITY

1 What other groups of people tend to get stereotyped in the world today apart from men and women?
2 What are the main features of these stereotypes?
3 Do you consider these stereotypes to be flattering or insulting to the groups concerned? Give reasons for your answer.
4 Look at the following list of words, and divide them into three groups: those you might use to describe women, those you might use to describe men, and those you might use to describe both men and women.

clever	aggressive	sulky	thoughtful
powerful	gentle	caring	attractive
emotional	beautiful	pretty	soft
cold	assertive	kind	clinging
sweet	logical	quiet	ruthless
sly	delicate	brave	active
muscular	weak	handsome	competitive
slim	submissive	bitchy	bastard
bachelor	spinster	tart	blonde
domineering	hysterical	frigid	elegant
raving	plain	cute	slag
hideous	passive	tender	gracious

5 Now compare the two lists of words used to describe men and women. Do they present gender stereotypes? You will probably have found there are some words in both lists that have a similar meaning. Discuss why these words are not used to describe both sexes, and how they show stereotyped assumptions about women and men.

Gender stereotyping of the worst kind. This was how Mr Justice Harman responded in 1991 when someone explained to him the difference between Miss, Mrs, and Ms

There is a wide range of social institutions which influence the socialization of males and females into their gender roles in modern Britain, but here the family, the education system, the peer group, and the mass media will be focused on.

The Role of the Family

Children begin to learn their gender roles at a very early age, and by the time children start school they have already learnt much about masculine and feminine roles. For example, a survey conducted in 1991 for the National Association of Schoolmasters/Union of Women Teachers (NAS/UWT) and the Engineering Council among 5-year-olds found that car-repairing, woodwork, fire-fighting, mountain-climbing, and seeing war films were seen by most children to be mainly for men, and 73 per cent of the boys and 66 per cent of the girls thought that only men could be scientists. The family plays a very important part in this primary socialization.

Parents' stereotypes

Parents and relatives tend to hold stereotyped views of the 'typical' or 'ideal' characteristics of boys and girls, and they often try to bring up their children in accordance with this view of 'normal' masculine or feminine behaviour. Lee Comer argues in *Wedlocked Women* (Feminist Books 1974) that girls are expected and encouraged to show dependence, obedience, conformity, and domesticity, while boys are encouraged to be dominant, self-reliant, active, and outward looking. Young children soon learn that approval from parents and relatives often depends on conforming to these stereotypes, and as Michelle Stanworth noted in *Gender and Schooling* (Hutchinson 1983), 'parents may scarcely be aware that they praise their daughters for being pretty and loving, their sons for being courageous and resourceful.'

From birth, girls and boys are frequently dressed in different clothes and colours – 'blue for a boy and pink for a girl' – and parents generally buy girls clothes which are more colourful and 'pretty', and boys more practical clothing. Such different forms of dress continue, of course, right throughout life.

Children's toys

Children are generally given different sorts of toys to play with according to their sex. This increases the pressure on them to follow at an early age the different roles to which they will be expected to conform in adult life. Table 5.1 on the next page illustrates the way toys tend to be stereotyped according to their suitability for either boys or girls.

Boys tend to be given (and choose to play with), for example, Meccano sets, cricket bats, footballs, chemistry sets, electronic toys, guns, cars, aeroplanes, and computers: more active and technical toys, which take them outside the home, both physically and in their imagination. On the other hand, girls are generally given toys like sewing machines, dolls, prams, toy hoovers, cookers, tea sets, and drawing books – toys which are often played with inside the home, and serve to restrict girls to the domestic situation.

Children's games

Children's games frequently involve practising adult gender roles, such as girls playing the role of nurse to their brothers' doctor, or girls playing at being mothers or housewives by playing with dolls, trying on make-up, cooking, or serving tea to brothers with toy tea sets. A short time in a nursery shows that by the age of 3 most little girls are already acting out the stereotyped female gender role. Boys play more aggressive and dominant games, such as war games or cowboys and Indians.

ACTIVITY

Table 5.1 Sex-stereotyping of toys

Masculine toys		Either sex		Feminine toys	
Toy	Rating	Toy	Rating	Toy	Rating
Football	1.5	Banjo	4.5	Skipping rope	7.0
Plane	1.7	Rocking horse	4.6	Sewing machine	8.2
Toolset	2.0	Alphabet ball	4.9	Dish cabinet	8.3
Racing car	2.2	Paddling pool	5.0	Cleaning set	8.4
Dumper truck	2.5	Blackboard	5.3	Dolls' pram	8.5
Construction set	2.7	Rollerskates	5.3	Dolls' wardrobe	8.7
Tractor	3.0	Telephone	5.6	Cosmetics	8.8
Wheelbarrow	3.2	Teddy bear	5.8		
Sports car	3.6				

The ratings were made by 20-year-old psychology students, and were found to correspond strongly with the choices made by children of either sex.
1 = strongly masculine, 5 = appropriate for both sexes, 9 = strongly feminine.
Source: Data adapted from A. Oakley, *Sex, Gender and Society* (Gower)

1 Look at the two lists of strongly masculine and strongly feminine toys in table 5.1, and add any other toys to the lists you can think of.
2 Explain all the main differences you can between the masculine and feminine toys, and suggest how these differences might encourage boys and girls to learn different skills and behave differently as adults. Make sure you refer to examples of particular toys and particular adult roles in your answer.

Parents' rules

Research has suggested that girls face different rules to boys of the same age, and are more strictly supervised by parents. Girls are more likely to be collected by parents from school than boys, and are less likely to be allowed to play outside or in the street. Girls are also more likely to be told to be in at a certain time, and to have to tell their parents where they are going.

Jobs around the home

As table 5.2 shows, participation by children in household duties shows a

ACTIVITY

Table 5.2 11-year-olds' participation in household duties

Duty	Boys %	Girls %	Both %
Washing up	40	63	51
Indoor housework (tidying, vacuum cleaning, dusting, bedmaking, etc.)	19	44	32
Miscellaneous dirty/outside jobs (gardening, sweeping, cleaning car or windows, making or mending fires, peeling potatoes, shoecleaning, emptying bin, etc.)	36	8	22
Going on errands	39	21	30

Source: Adapted from J. Newson, E. Newson, D. Richardson, and J. Scaife, 'Perspectives in Sex Role Stereotyping', in J. Chetwynd and O. Hartnett (eds), *The Sex Role System: Psychological and Sociological Perspectives* (Routledge & Kegan Paul)

Study table 5.2 and answer the following questions:

1 What household duty is most likely to be performed by both sexes?
2 What household duty is least likely to be performed by (a) boys and (b) girls?
3 How do you think the divisions in household duties among 11-year-olds could be seen as preparation for adult gender roles? Give examples of particular adult roles.

marked difference between the sexes, with girls more likely to do indoor housework, generally helping their mothers with domestic jobs, while boys are more likely to do outdoor jobs with their fathers, like cleaning the car, sweeping the paths, and being shown how to do repairs and make things.

Watching and imitating parents

Small children mainly learn by watching and imitating the **role models** provided by others. A role model is simply a pattern of behaviour which others model their behaviour on. Children often observe their parents carrying out their respective gender roles every day. If children see their mothers spending more time in the home while their fathers go out to

Little girls' dreams? More than one billion Barbies (and members of her family) have been sold worldwide since 1959. If all the Barbies sold were placed head to toe, they would circle the world more than eleven times. But do such toys make girls over-concerned with their own bodies and image?
Photo: Ted Fussey

work, their mothers spending more time doing cooking, cleaning, and other housework than their fathers, and their mothers, rather than their fathers, taking time off work to look after them when they are sick, or taking them to the doctor, then children may well begin to view these roles as the 'normal' ways for men and women to behave. In general, small children are brought up by women, surrounded by women, and it is women who nearly always care for them, whether mothers, child-minders, or teachers. It is perhaps not surprising, then, that many girls still grow up today seeing childcare as being a major part of their role in life.

The Role of the School

The process of gender socialization begun in the home often carries on through schooling, and this has been excellently documented in Michelle Stanworth's study *Gender and Schooling* (Hutchinson 1983). Much of this socialization goes on through the school's **hidden curriculum**. This consists of the hidden teaching of attitudes and behaviour, which are taught at school through the school's organization and teachers' attitudes but which are not part of the formal timetable. This is discussed in more detail in chapter 12. The hidden curriculum emphasizes the differences between males and females, and encourages different forms of behaviour. Three examples help to illustrate this.

Teachers' attitudes

Teachers have also been socialized into gender roles, and there is evidence suggesting that teachers have traditionally had higher expectations of boys than girls, encouraging them more (especially in sciences and computing), and placing more emphasis on their progress than that of girls, because they expect boys to be the main future 'breadwinners'. Teachers may also give different career advice to boys and girls, such as steering girls towards nursing and clerical work, and boys towards a much wider range of occupations.

Boys demand more of the teacher's time, and disruptive, unruly behaviour from boys is more likely to be tolerated than the same behaviour from girls. Girls fighting in the playground, for example, are likely to be punished far more severely than boys fighting, since girls are not expected to show such 'unfeminine' behaviour.

Schoolbooks

Reading books in infant schools have often shown women and little girls in the housewife/mother role, such as helping mother in the home, or watching their brothers climbing trees, mending the car, and 'getting into mischief'. Boys are more likely to be portrayed as playing with cars or trains, playing football, exploring, building things, climbing trees, and so on. Schools are now tackling such stereotypes, but the effects of these changes will take time, and of course schools alone cannot reverse the stereotyping that goes on in a wide range of areas.

In secondary school, gender differences are reinforced by the illustrations in textbooks for different subjects – science books rarely show girls doing science, and boys rarely appear in home economics books, suggesting that some subjects are more suited to one sex rather than the other.

Subject choice

Girls and boys have traditionally been counselled by parents and teachers into taking different subjects. Girls have been more likely to take arts subjects (like English literature, history, and foreign languages) and study home economics, commerce, and 'keyboard skills', while boys have been more likely to take sciences, technical drawing, and design and technology – subjects which are more likely to lead to more skilled and technical occupations after school. This gender division is also found in sport, with football and cricket for the boys and hockey and netball for the girls. Under the National Curriculum introduced in 1988 (see chapter 12), *all* 11–14-year-olds have to take technology, which includes home economics, business studies, and design and technology. This means that these gender divisions between subjects have been breaking down during the 1990s, but some subject divisions still remain, as chapter 13 on education shows.

DISCUSSION

On the basis of your own experiences at both primary and secondary school, discuss any difficulties or pressures you might have experienced at school because of your sex in choosing subjects and options that you wanted to do. Take into account factors such as the views of your parents, friends, and teachers, and the advice of careers and subject teachers.

The Importance of the Peer Group

A **peer group** is a group of people of similar age and status with whom a person mixes socially. Generally, people try to gain acceptance among their peers by conforming to the norms of their peer group. These norms frequently involve stereotyped masculine and feminine roles. For example, among male peer groups, interests and norms often centre on activities like football, music, cars, motor-bikes, stereo equipment, and computers. Female interests often centre on things such as fashion, make-up, and dancing. The peer group can exert strong pressure to conform to these interests: a boy, for example, who collected soft toys would be quite likely to find himself ridiculed by his peer group; a girl who played football might be seen as a bit of a 'tomboy'. Such pressures can help to discourage participation in activities which don't conform to gender stereotypes.

Double standards

Among teenage boys (and often adult men too) sexual promiscuity and sexual 'conquest' are often encouraged and admired as approved masculine behaviour, and are seen as a means of achieving status in the male peer group. However, males will condemn this same promiscuity among women – promiscuous girls and women are likely to be called 'slags' or some other insulting term. This attitude is often reinforced even by the female peer group, where sexual relations by girls are only approved in the context of a steady, close relationship. Girls and women who have sex outside some 'steady relationship' are therefore likely to find themselves condemned by men and women alike. In short, promiscuous men are seen as 'stags' or 'studs'; promiscuous women are seen as 'slags' or 'sluts'. This double standard helps to encourage conformity to separate gender identities for men and women, with the stereotyped man as 'sexual athlete' and woman as the passive and faithful lover, wife, or 'girlfriend'.

DISCUSSION

Do you believe that there is a 'double standard' applied to the behaviour of males and females when it comes to sexual activity?

The Role of the Mass Media

The mass media include films, videos, television, newspapers, CDs and tapes, radio, advertising, books, comics, and magazines. The mass media create and reinforce gender stereotypes in a number of ways.

Comics, for example, present different images of men and women: girls are usually presented as pretty, romantic, helpless, easily upset, and dependent on boys for support and guidance, and boys and girls are often presented in traditional stereotyped gender roles such as soldiers (boys) or nurses (girls). A similar pattern is shown on children's television. Belotti argues that many traditional fairy tales, indeed much children's fiction, often portray females as either evil or fairly stupid and dependent on men for their ultimate safety, as the following suggests:

'Little Red Riding Hood' is the story of a girl, bordering on mental deficiency, who is sent out by an irresponsible mother through dark wolf-infested woods to take a little basket full to the brim with cakes to her sick grandmother. Given these circumstances her end is hardly surprising. But such foolishness, which would never have been attributed to a male, depends on the assurance that one will always find at the right moment and in the right place a brave huntsman ready to save grandmother and granddaughter from the wolf. (E.G. Belotti, *Little Girls* (Writers and Readers Publishing Co-operative 1975), quoted in A. Oakley, *Subject Women* (Fontana 1982), p. 109)

ACTIVITY

1 Do you agree with the view that female figures in children's fairy stories are mainly portrayed as either good but fairly stupid or evil and wicked? Try to think of evidence drawn from stories, other than the one given above, which either confirms or denies your view.
2 Examine some children's reading books, comics, or male or female adult magazines and see if you can identify any pattern in the different roles and interests allocated to boys and girls or men and women. Provide evidence for your conclusions.

You may have found from the previous activity that there are often very different types of story and magazine aimed at males and females. Romantic fiction is almost exclusively aimed at a female readership. A glance at the magazine shelves of any large newsagents will reveal a 'Women's interests' section, consisting almost exclusively of magazines on cooking, homecare and housekeeping, health and slimming, lifestyle, fashion and haircare, knitting, mother and baby, and weddings. This shows very clearly the way the media both encourage and cater for a particular view of a woman's role. There is no similar 'Men's interests' section. However, men (and not women) can often be seen queuing up to read magazines (classified as of 'general interest') concerned with photography, stereos, computers, DIY, and all manner of transport: cars, motor-bikes, aircraft, trains, and boats. The 'top shelf' soft-porn magazines are aimed exclusively at men.

Images of men and women

When women appear in the mass media, it is usually in one of two main roles (and rarely any other):

- *As a 'sex object'* – the image of the slim, sexually seductive, scantily clad figure typically found on page 3 of the *Sun* newspaper is used by the advertising industry to sell everything from peanuts to motor-bikes and newspapers. 'Supermodels' are the beauty queens of today, at a time when Miss World contests are seen by many as unacceptable.

or:

- *In the housewife/mother role* – as the content, capable, and caring housewife and mother, whose constant concern is with the whiteness of clothes, the cleanliness of floors, and the evening meal.

When men appear in the media, it is in a very wide range of roles which have no particular reference to their gender. Women's roles involve being women first – that is, women play limited roles restricted to their gender. The masculine stereotype of the physically well-built, muscular, handsome, brave, non-domestic male still often appears. These differing roles of men and women are most evident in advertising, even when

ACTIVITY

In 1997, a psychological study of the 'lonely heart' personal columns found that gender stereotyping was still the norm. Putting together the main features of the advertising, the study drew up the 'typical' male and female lonely hearts advertisements.

Male advert	*Female advert*
Male, high wage earner, own home, with caring genuine nature, attractive, with sense of humour and interested in home building, seeks attractive, loving young woman for genuine partnership.	Female, attractive, slim, tall shapely blonde, loving and sensitive, seeks financially secure caring man with good sense of humour and own home for genuine relationship.

1 What are the differences between the two advertisements in the qualities expected of a male and female?

2 Look at the personal columns of a local or national newspaper, and see if you can spot any common themes in the qualities men look for in women, and that women look for in men. Link your findings, if you can, to gender stereotyping.

1 What do the two cartoons on the opposite page suggest are the main forces which contribute to the gender socialization process?
2 Study the result of the socialization of men shown in the cartoons, and describe the stereotype of a 'typical male'.
3 Do you think the cartoons give an accurate impression of masculine behaviour? Back up your view with evidence of both child and adult male behaviour.

young children are used. For example, television advertisements for washing-up liquid or washing powder nearly always show mothers and small daughters working together, and boys are usually the ones who come in covered in dirt. While men and small boys hardly ever appear in such advertisements, when they do appear in a domestic role it is nearly always made clear it is an exception, or that they are not very good at domestic tasks.

Some consequences of media stereotyping

The images of men and women presented in the mass media in most cases do not conform to the reality of people's everyday lives. However, they may succeed in inducing feelings of guilt, inadequacy, and lack of self-confidence among the majority of women who don't 'measure up' to the 'sex object' or the 'happy housewife' images. A 1995 report on the mental health of teenagers found girls were very sensitive about their appearance. They continually sought reassurance about their hair, weight, and skin, and felt put down when this was not forthcoming. This may partly explain why so many women are concerned with slimming and dieting, why anorexia is an illness affecting mainly teenage girls, and why many housewives in this country are on tranquillizers.

With men, the consequences may take a more sinister turn, and it is possible that the rising number of violent crimes against women might in part be traced back to these media stereotypes, as the following writer argues:

> The only image the media will accept of a male is muscle-bound and dominant to the extent that when Prince Edward left the marines not even the pacifists applauded his rejection of a military lifestyle and he became Prince Wimp – a wimp in media terms being anyone incapable of fighting off alligators while delivering a box of chocolates. Many young men's heroes now include movie-star figures

like Arnold Schwarzenegger, who have made fortunes out of having bodies built like tanks, and who solve problems with relentless and ruthless violence. These images do not represent the reality for most men, and men may react to this imagery with feelings of inadequacy. An inadequate male will try to emulate screen heroes and then feel even more rejected when his life is not filled immediately with women who look like centre-folds. These men may react in the only way the media has taught them – aggressively. Possibly towards other men but more probably towards women, who are an easier target.

The rising number of violent crimes against women might not be because they are portrayed as sex objects but because men are shown to be all-powerful, irresistible and capable of solving problems with a karate kick or a Kalashnikov [Russian assault rifle]. The proof might turn out to be the number of rapists who, when caught, are found to be bodybuilders trying to conform physically, if not emotionally, to the male image as it is portrayed. (Based on R.R.C. Penfold, 'Image fakers', *Guardian* (15 June 1988))

ACTIVITY/DISCUSSION

1 In the passage above, list all the features which make up the mass media stereotype of men.
2 Suggest ways that each of these features might affect adult male behaviour.
3 Do you agree with the writer's view in the passage above that there is a link between male stereotyping in the media and violence against women?

THE SEXUAL DIVISION OF LABOUR

The processes of gender role socialization outlined in this chapter often mean that women and men have different experiences and expectations of life. Socialization has the general effect of emphasizing the domestic responsibilities of girls, limiting their self-confidence, and pushing them towards marriage and the roles of housewife and mother as their primary aims in life. Boys, on the other hand, are more likely to grow up conforming to the stereotype of the non-domestic, practical, independent, and assertive male, whose role in life is that of worker and main 'breadwinner'.

These patterns of socialization are changing, for example through less gender stereotyping in schoolbooks and by teachers, and more role models of female success in education and in the labour market. Nevertheless, the narrow, stereotyped gender roles of thirty years ago are still held by many of today's children.

The different socialization of males and females still shows itself in the **sexual division of labour** in the job market, with jobs being divided into 'men's jobs' and 'women's jobs', and with young men and women choosing different types of work. The 1995 report on the mental health of teenagers referred to earlier in this chapter found that girls had a strong awareness that they would one day have to balance work and a family. Many coped with this idea by aspiring only to undemanding careers. These divisions in the labour market, and the inequalities which women face in a number of areas of social life as a result of the socialization process, are examined in the following chapter.

CHAPTER SUMMARY

After studying this chapter, you should be able to:

- Explain the difference between sex and gender.
- Argue against the view that gender roles are biologically based.
- Describe the main features of gender stereotypes in modern Britain.
- Explain how gender socialization is carried out through the family, the school, the peer group, and the mass media.
- Explain some of the effects of the gender socialization process on both men and women.

KEY TERMS

gender
gender role
hidden curriculum
peer group

role model
sex
sexual division of labour
stereotype

PROJECT SUGGESTIONS

1 Observe children in a playgroup and see if boys and girls play different types of game or play with different toys. Interview their mothers or fathers about the types of toy they had for birthday or Christmas presents. Try to reach some conclusions about gender role socialization.

2 Study children's comics for a week (or reading books in an infant school, daily newspapers, children's books, television programmes and films, etc.), and see if boys/men and girls/women are presented in stereotyped ways. Give some detail on what the various stereotypes are and explain how they might contribute to gender role stereotyping.

3 Examine subject or option choices, or exam entries, at your school or college and see if there are differences between males and females. Interview male and female students about why they chose their options, and interview teachers about your findings.

WOMEN

6

KEY ISSUES IN THIS CHAPTER

- The changing status of women in Britain.
- Women and domestic labour (housework).
- Women in paid employment and the inequalities facing women at work.

The theme of the previous chapter was the way our ideas about masculinity and femininity, and the different roles expected of men and women in Britain, are constructed through the influence of a wide range of agencies of socialization. A popular assumption today is that throughout the twentieth century our ideas about women and the traditional housewife/mother role allocated to them have been changing. Women, it is often assumed, have achieved both full participation in society beyond the confines of the home, and equal status with men in most areas of social life.

The primary concern of this chapter is to examine this assumption. To what extent has the position of women in society improved, and what explanations are there for any changes? To what extent do women still face barriers to their full participation in society on an equal footing with men? The major focus here will be on identifying and explaining the continuing inequalities which women face in the world of work, both inside and outside the home, but other aspects of the inequalities confronting women are discussed in chapters 4, 5, 11, and 17.

THE CHANGING STATUS OF WOMEN IN BRITAIN

Women in the Nineteenth Century

In nineteenth-century Britain, most women lacked many of the legal and political rights which men had. Women were in most cases dependent on men for money and support, and faced major discrimination at work and in education, with a wide range of jobs and opportunities barred to them. Women's main role in life was expected to be that of a housewife and mother, and a typical working-class woman could expect to be pregnant about ten times, and spend many years of her life bearing and nursing children.

Women in the Twentieth Century

During the twentieth century, there has been a gradual improvement in the status of women in Britain, the outlines of which it is useful to list here. However, as will be seen later, women still face major inequalities with men, particularly the conflicting demands of family life and career success.

- Women have achieved more political equality with men, beginning with the powerful and often violent campaign waged by the Suffragette Movement at the beginning of this century. This won the right for women to vote in parliamentary elections. By 1918, all women over age 30 could vote, and this was lowered to age 21 in 1928. This put women in the same position as men for the first time in relation to voting rights.
- Women today have equal rights with men in education. It is now illegal to discriminate against women or men by denying them access to certain subjects and courses at school or in further and higher education because of their sex.
- More types of job are seen as suitable for women today, and many more women are going out to work in paid employment. Women now make up about half of the workforce in Britain, which gives them more financial independence.
- Equal opportunity laws have helped women to get a better deal and overcome prejudice and discrimination. For example, the Equal Pay Act of 1970 made it illegal for employers to offer different rates of pay to men and women doing the same or similar work. The Sex Discrimination Act of 1975 made it illegal to distinguish between men and women in work, leisure, and educational opportunities, and the Equal Opportunities Commission has been formed to help enforce the Sex Discrimination Act and the Equal Pay Act, and to promote equality of opportunity between men and women.
- Women have won equal rights with men in property ownership. The Married Women's Property Acts of 1880 and 1882 gave married women the right to own their own property, and the 1970 Matrimonial Proceedings Act established that all property was to be divided equally between husband and wife in the event of a divorce.

Equal Opportunities
the law is on your side – and so are we

The Equal Opportunities Commission was established by Parliament in 1975 to ensure effective enforcement of the Sex Discrimination Act and the Equal Pay Act.

It is the responsibility of the Commission to work towards the elimination of sex discrimination in employment, in education and training opportunities and in the provision to the public of goods, facilities services and accommodation.

As well as investigating areas of inequality between the sexes, the Commission has a duty to make recommendations to the Government about the operation of existing law.

One important function of the Commission is to advise you of your rights under the Sex Discrimination Act and the Equal Pay Act – rights which could have an effect on your career prospects as well as your pay packet.

Send second class stamp for free catalogue of publications, dealing with all aspects of sex discrimination.

Publicity Section

Equal Opportunities Commission

Overseas House, Quay Street, Manchester M3 3HN.

- Women have had equal rights with men in divorce since the 1923 Matrimonial Causes Act.
- The welfare state has provided more support for lone-parent families, the majority of whom are headed by women, and for women caring for dependent husbands and the elderly in the home.

Figure 6.1 Why has the status of women changed in twentieth-century Britain?

Why has the status of women changed in twentieth-century Britain?

The changing status of women in twentieth-century Britain outlined above can be explained by a number of factors.

The Suffragette Movement

The Suffragette Movement, which started at the turn of the twentieth century and lasted until 1918, aimed to achieve equal voting rights for women with men in parliamentary elections. This involved a long and often violent struggle against men's ideas about a woman's role. It was the first major struggle by women for equality with men, and began to change the ideas held by both men and women about a woman's role. The success of this campaign gave women political power for the first time in elections, and MPs had to begin to take women's interests into account if they were to be elected.

ACTIVITY

Go to a library and find out what you can about the kinds of actions carried out by the suffragettes in their campaign to achieve 'Votes for Women'. (You may find this information in a good encyclopedia, or in the history or sociology sections.) How do you think these activities might have changed both men's and women's views on women's traditional roles?

The two world wars

During the First (1914–18) and Second (1939–45) World Wars, women took over many jobs in factories and farms which were formerly done by men, as the men went off to be soldiers. Women showed during these war years that they were quite capable of doing what had previously been seen as 'men's jobs', and this began to change people's ideas about a woman's role.

Smaller family size

The declining size of families is both a cause and a consequence of the improving status of women. This has reduced the time spent in child rearing and given women greater opportunities to enter paid employment. A typical mother today spends about four years bearing and nursing children, and she can expect to live much longer than her nineteenth-century counterpart. This means once a woman has had children today, she still has a long life stretching ahead to pursue a career.

More jobs for women

There are more types of job seen as suitable for women today, and legal obstacles to the employment of women have been removed in most cases. Although there still remains a lot of prejudice and discrimination by employers about the suitability of some jobs for women, the way women took over men's jobs during the world wars, the pressures of the Suffragette Movement, and more recently the women's movement have helped to erode hostility to female workers among male bosses and workers.

This increase in employment opportunities for women has come about with the expansion of light industry, manufacturing, and the tertiary sector of the economy. The tertiary sector is concerned with services, finance, administration, distribution, transport, and government agencies, such as the NHS, the social services, and education. The expansion of this sector has increased the number of routine clerical and secretarial jobs which are overwhelmingly done by women. There has also been an increase in the number of jobs in the lower professions, such as teaching, social work, and nursing, which employ many women.

Maternity benefits and maternity leave now provide additional encouragement and opportunity for women to return to work after childbirth, as their jobs are kept open for them while they are absent having children. The fact that more women are working gives them greater financial independence and therefore more authority in both the family and society.

The compulsory education of children

Compulsory schooling since 1880, and particularly since 1944, has reduced the time necessary for the care and supervision of children in the family. This has given women with children a greater opportunity to go out to work than earlier in the twentieth century.

Technology in the home

Advances in technology have brought many improvements to the home environment, including better housing standards like central heating, labour-saving devices like freezers, washing machines, microwave cookers, food processors, and vacuum cleaners, manufactured foodstuffs such as canned and frozen foods, and 'instant meals'. It has been suggested that these improvements have reduced the time spent on housework. However, others argue that these developments have simply meant higher standards are expected, and therefore more housework has to be performed. For example, automatic washing machines mean that washing is done several times a week instead of just once on 'washing day', and people change their clothes more often. This also creates, of course, more ironing. Similarly, vacuum cleaners mean that houses are expected to be kept cleaner than they used to be.

The women's movement

The women's movement is concerned with the fight to achieve equality with men in a wide range of areas. This movement is not a single group, but consists of a large number of different women's groups with various aims, both in Britain and abroad. These groups are united by the need to improve the status and rights of women, and are concerned with ending **patriarchy**, which is the dominance of men in society. Since the 1960s, the women's movement has challenged many ideas about the traditional role of women, particularly the stereotype that 'a woman's place is in the home'. It has campaigned for:

- Better nursery facilities.
- Free contraception and free abortion on demand, and 'a woman's right to choose' whether to have an abortion or not.
- Equal pay and job opportunities.
- The removal of tax and financial discrimination against women.
- Freedom from violence against women.
- The right of women to define their own sexuality.

The women's movement has challenged many people's ideas about women, and has created a 'climate of expectation' where women expect to be treated equally and not simply as lovers, housewives, and mothers. It is mainly because of pressures from the women's movement that equal opportunity laws have been passed, and that **sexism**, or prejudice and discrimination against people because of their sex, is increasingly seen as unacceptable behaviour.

DISCUSSION

Do you think that women are treated more equally today? What obstacles and problems do women still face that men don't?

WOMEN AT WORK

Unpaid Work: Domestic Labour

When talking about women at work, many people assume this refers to paid employment. However, it is important to remember there is one job which is performed full-time almost exclusively by women – unpaid housework or **domestic labour**. This domestic labour of women is hardly recognized as 'real work' at all, and carries little status compared with paid employment. This is partly because housework involves women in cleaning up their own and their families' self-generated dirt, doing their own and their families' washing, etc. It is also because no qualifications are needed, and housework is 'private', with no recognition by others and no praise, only complaints if the work is not done. Many women who are housewives themselves often undervalue the status of their job, as is summed up in the phrase 'I'm only a housewife.'

Women with a child under 5 spend about 65 hours a week on housework, childcare, and related tasks – far more than most people spend in paid employment. Data published in 1997 by the Office for National

ACTIVITY

Table 6.1 The experience of monotony, fragmentation, and speed in work: housewives and factory workers compared

Workers	Percentage experiencing:		
	Monotony[a]	Fragmentation[b]	Speed[c]
Housewives	75	90	50
Factory workers	41	70	31
Assembly line workers	67	86	36

[a] Monotony refers to the feeling that the work is boring and repetitive.
[b] Fragmentation refers to the feeling that the work is divided into a series of unconnected tasks not requiring the worker's full attention.
[c] Speed refers to the feeling that the worker has too much to do, with too little time to complete the task, and so has to work at too fast a pace.
Source: A. Oakley, *The Sociology of Housework* (Martin Robertson)

Table 6.1 compares housewives' experience of their work with that of factory and assembly line workers.

1 Which group experiences the most monotony in their work?
2 Which group experiences the least speed in their work?
3 In which group did 31 per cent complain of too much speed in their work?
4 Suggest ways the evidence shown in table 6.1 might explain the finding that women who are exclusively housewives suffer more mental health problems than many of the population.
5 What differences are there between working exclusively as a housewife in the home and working in a factory which might make factory workers better able to cope with the monotony, fragmentation, and speed of their work?
6 Suggest reasons why housework is often not seen by many people as 'real work'.

Statistics (ONS) showed that women spent on average nearly five hours a day cooking, cleaning, shopping, washing, and looking after the children. However, domestic labour has none of the advantages of paid employment, like regular working hours, 'clocking off' after work, chances of promotion, holiday pay, or sick pay. As table 6.1 shows, housewives experience far more monotony, fragmentation, and speed in their work than workers on even the most gruelling assembly line, but without the compensation of being paid for it.

The ONS in 1997 calculated that if the time spent on unpaid work in the home was valued at the same average pay rates as equivalent jobs in paid employment (for example, if cooking were paid as it is for chefs, or childcare as for nannies and child-minders), it would be worth £739 billion a year.

Housework and childcare are still seen as primarily the responsibility of women. As shown in table 6.2, even when both partners are working full-time outside the home in paid employment, it is still women who are in most cases expected to take the major responsibility for housework and childcare. In the 1990s, 70 per cent of women in marriages or cohabiting couples where both partners were working full-time have responsibility for general domestic duties. This means, of course, that many full-time working women have two jobs to their male partners' one!

Women in Paid Employment

Many of the factors discussed above explaining the changing status of women have brought about a large increase in the employment of women in the twentieth century. In 1997, women made up about half of the workforce, compared with less than 30 per cent at the beginning of the twentieth century. Nearly 70 per cent of women of working age were in employment in 1997. Much of this increase has been among married women: less than 10 per cent of married women were working in the early twentieth century, but this had increased to about 70 per cent in 1997, with around 1 in 10 of these wives being the sole breadwinners in their families.

The inequality of women in paid employment

Although during the twentieth century the role and status of women have gradually improved, and women have obtained job opportunities and rights previously denied to them, women still have an unequal position with men at work. Much of this inequality arises because the central role of women is still seen by a male-dominated society as primarily that of housewife and mother. The following section summarizes the key features

ACTIVITY

Table 6.2 Who performed jobs in the home? Married or cohabiting couples with both partners working full-time, 1990s

Domestic job	Mainly man %	Mainly woman %	Shared equally %
Household shopping	8	45	47
Making evening meal	9	70	20
Washing evening dishes	28	33	37
Household cleaning	4	68	27
Washing and ironing	3	84	12
Repairing household equipment	82	6	10
Organizing household bills/money	31	40	28
Looking after sick children	1	56	40
Teaching children discipline	10	6	81
Summary: is responsible for general domestic duties	8	70	22

Source: Adapted from British Social Attitudes Survey

Table 6.2 looks at the way work is divided in the home where both husbands and wives, or cohabiting partners, have full-time jobs.

1 Which household task is most likely to be performed mainly by women?
2 Which household task is least likely to be shared equally?
3 Which household task is shared equally by 81 per cent of couples?
4 In the light of table 6.2, list each of the following statements as true or false:

Mostly men alone wash up the evening dishes.
Looking after sick children is most likely to be shared by men and women today.
When their partners work full-time as well, men are most likely to make the evening meal.
Even when they work full-time, women are still mainly responsible for general domestic duties.
The only thing that men still seem to take the main responsibility for is repairing household equipment.

5 How does the evidence in table 6.2 support the view that women do two jobs compared with men's one job? Refer to particular examples to back up your case.
6 How might sociologists explain the division of household tasks shown in table 6.2?

of women's employment situation, and describes and explains the main inequalities women face in the labour market.

The sexual division of labour

The sexual division of labour simply means that jobs are divided into 'men's jobs' and 'women's jobs', with women's jobs often having lower pay, poorer promotion prospects, and lower status than men's.

As shown in figure 6.2, fewer women than men are employed in the top professional and intermediate groups, and table 6.3 shows that few women in this group are in the top professional jobs. Figure 6.2 also shows that women are mainly employed in jobs which are concentrated at the lower end of the occupational scale: in unskilled and semi-skilled manual jobs and in routine, low-level clerical jobs like filing and typing, which require little or no training.

Women are also spread over a far narrower range of jobs than men. Figure 6.3 shows that nearly 70 per cent of women are concentrated in four main occupational groups: professional and related in education, welfare, and health; clerical and secretarial; sales; and catering, cleaning, hairdressing, and other personal services.

Women are mainly employed in low-grade and low-paid jobs which are seen as 'female occupations'. These are often extensions of the traditional domestic roles of housewives and mothers into which many women continue to be socialized. These involve serving and waiting on people, caring for them, cleaning and clearing up after others – all jobs that women have traditionally done in the home. Such jobs include nursing,

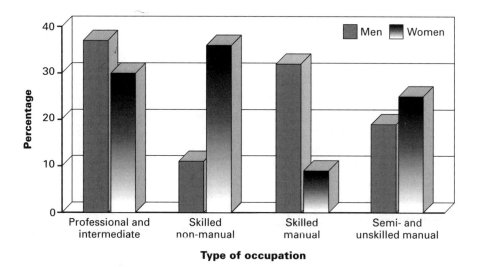

Figure 6.2 The occupations of men and women: Great Britain, 1996
Source: Data from Labour Force Survey

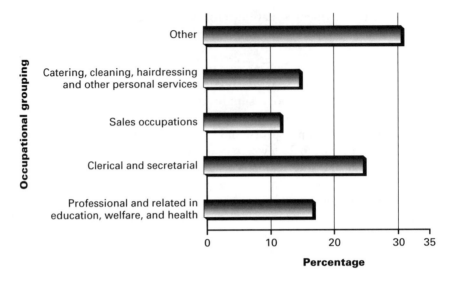

Figure 6.3 Occupational distribution of working women: Great Britain, 1996
Source: Data from Labour Force Survey, 1996

primary school teaching, secretarial and routine clerical work, low-grade catering work, such as that of waitresses and canteen assistants, and working as shop assistants, supermarket 'shelf-fillers', and check-out operators. For example, typists and secretaries serve their (still usually male) bosses, organizing the office to make things easier for them, making them coffee, and providing papers for and clearing up after their meetings; primary school teaching involves childcare; nursing is caring for the sick; catering involves cooking, serving, and clearing up meals.

Part-time work

In 1996, more than four out of five part-time workers were women, and about 44 per cent of women in paid employment worked only part-time compared with 8 per cent of men. Surveys suggest this is closely related to women's responsibilities for children and other domestic tasks. Many working women are limited in the jobs they can do and the hours they can work because they are still expected to take responsibility for housework and childcare, and to be at home for the children leaving for and returning from school. There are still few workplaces today with childcare facilities which would allow working mothers to take full-time jobs. The presence of dependent children (under the age of 16), and the age of the youngest child, are the most important factors related to whether or not women are in paid employment, and whether they work full or part-time. Figure 6.4 illustrates the importance of this link between dependent children and part-time status.

ACTIVITY

Table 6.3 Women and men in top professional jobs: 1990s

Job	Women %	Men %
Senior civil servant (top three grades)	9	91
Senior police officer (superintendent and above)	3	97
MP (1997)	18	82
Cabinet minister (1997)	23	77
Local government chief executive/chief officer	8	92
High court judge	8	92
Lord Justice of Appeal	3	97
Circuit judge	6	94
QC	6	94
Barrister	18	82
Solicitor	31	69
University professor	7	93
Full-time university lecturer	31	69
Nursery and primary school deputy head/head	62	38
Secondary school deputy head/head	32	68
University chancellor/vice-chancellor	6	94
NHS chief executive/general manager	28	72
General medical practitioner (GP)	32	68
Opportunity 2000 Company director	6	94
Director and senior manager in top 2300 UK companies	4	96

Sources: Labour Research (January 1997); *Price Waterhouse Corporate Register; Women at the Top* update (Hansard Society); *Separate Tables* (Department for Education and Employment 1997); Department of Health, 1997

Table 6.3 shows that there are very few women in top professional jobs.

1 Why do you think this might be the case? What obstacles prevent women from getting into these jobs?
2 What steps might be taken to overcome these obstacles?

While a lot of the expansion in the labour force in recent years has been among women, with men more likely to be unemployed, much of this has been because many new jobs are temporary or part-time, which fit more with women's needs for flexibility due to the demands placed on them in the home. Much part-time work is particularly vulnerable to economic recession, and therefore involves higher risks of unemployment.

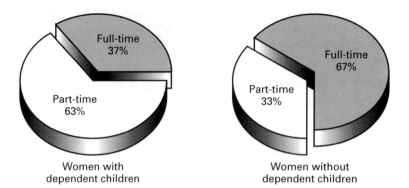

Women with
dependent children

Women without
dependent children

Figure 6.4 Women in employment: by dependent children and full- or part-time employment status, Great Britain, 1996
Source: Data from Labour Force Survey, 1996

Source: *Part-time Workers,* Labour Research Department

1 What does the cartoon suggest might be some of the reasons why women are less likely to attend trade union meetings than men?
2 How might more women be encouraged to attend union meetings?
3 Women are less likely to belong to trade unions than men. Suggest possible reasons for this.

Many employment protection laws still do not apply to part-time workers, and often part-time workers do not belong to trade unions and so lack trade union protection. These factors mean many women often face high risks of redundancy and unemployment.

Limited career opportunities

Women have more limited career opportunities than men for a number of reasons. Because of gender stereotyping at school and the wider gender-role socialization process, women, even when they have the necessary educational qualifications for the 'top jobs', often lack the self-confidence and assertiveness to apply for them.

There is widespread male prejudice about women in career jobs and senior positions. There is evidence that some men are reluctant to be supervised by female managers, and there is a common male belief that men make better bosses. It is often assumed single women will eventually leave paid employment to marry and have children, and married women, particularly, are often seen as 'unreliable' because of the assumption they will be absent to look after sick children – although research has shown there is little difference in absence from work between men and women who share the same circumstances. Three-quarters of all complaints of sex discrimination to the Equal Opportunities Commission come from women. A 1996 report by the Commission found that more than 1 in 4 women had experienced discrimination when applying for a job. Almost 1 in 5 had been a victim of sexism in their current employment. Even successful women in career jobs often find they come up against what has been called the **glass ceiling** – an invisible barrier of discrimination which makes it difficult for women to reach the same top levels in their chosen careers as similarly qualified men. These factors mean women are often overlooked for training and promotion to senior positions by male employers.

In addition, women with promising careers may have temporarily to leave jobs to have children, and therefore miss out on promotion opportunities. Top jobs require a continuous career pattern in the 20–30 age period – yet these are the usual childbearing years for women, so while men continue to work and get promoted, women miss their opportunities.

Finally, married or cohabiting women are still more likely to move house and area for their male partner's job promotion rather than their own. This means women interrupt their careers and have to start again, often at a lower level, in a new job, which means the men are getting promotion at the expense of lost opportunities for their partners.

Limited access to training

Women are less likely than men to enter training for better-paid and more secure skilled work. Often women are denied training, and therefore promotion opportunities, because employers, parents, teachers, and

119

sometimes the women themselves see training as 'wasted' on women. Employers, as a result of gender socialization, may assume women will leave work to produce and raise children. They may therefore be unwilling to invest in expensive training programmes for women. Rather, they prefer to employ women in low-skilled jobs where they can be easily and quickly trained and replaced. Of the small number of women who do obtain training, the vast majority are employed in 'feminine occupations' such as hairdressing, beauty, and clerical work, which are generally low paid with limited career prospects.

ACTIVITY

Many employers still ask women discriminatory questions

Do you agree with the suggestion in the cartoon above that the questions being asked at the interview discriminate against women, or do you think employers have a right to ask such questions? Do you think discrimination against women is still a problem in education, work, and leisure activities?

The ten worst-paid jobs in Britain . . .

Kitchen porter
Waitress
Catering assistant
Laundry worker
Supermarket shelf-filler
Cleaner/Domestic
Bar staff
Childcarer
Retail check-out operator
Hairdresser

. . . and they're nearly all done by women!

Source: TUC and Low Pay Unit, 1997.

Lower pay

While the Equal Pay Act gives equal pay to women if they do the same or similar work as men, it has been shown above that women often do not do the same work as men, and consequently have no one to claim equal pay with. The average pay of women is only about 80 per cent of the average male wage, and in 1997 women made up around two-thirds of all low-paid workers. Women have fewer opportunities to increase their pay

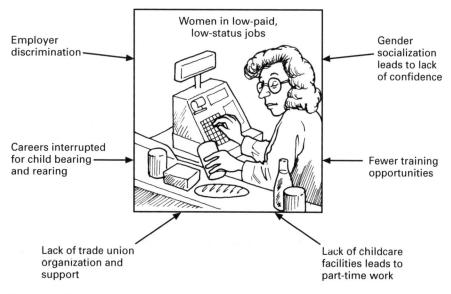

Figure 6.5 Why are women concentrated in lower-paid and lower-status jobs than men?

through overtime, shift payments or bonuses. Female part-time workers earn less than half the hourly pay of women in full-time employment. The ten worst-paid jobs in Britain are all performed mainly by women. In a nutshell, this is because many women are concentrated in low-skilled and part-time work, which lacks promotion prospects, trade union protection, and often sick pay, holiday pay, and redundancy payments – a situation which does not apply to the majority of men.

CONCLUSION

There have been great improvements in the position of women in the twentieth century, particularly from the 1970s onwards under the impact of the women's movement. Attitudes have changed, and sexism has become less acceptable. Women have become more self-confident and assertive. They are now outstripping males at every level in education, and they are beginning to achieve more success and influence in society.

However, it is still women who are most likely to face poverty, and women alone head 1 in 5 families with dependent children. Women still earn less than men and have poorer career opportunities, and there are still few women in any of the top positions of power and influence in society. Housework and childcare remain the primary responsibility of women, undermining their ability to compete with men on equal terms in paid employment, reducing their financial independence, and restricting their power in society. While women have gained much this century, there still remains some considerable distance to travel before women achieve equality with men in many areas of life in modern Britain.

DISCUSSION/ACTIVITY

1 This chapter has mainly focused on the inequalities facing women at work. What other inequalities do women face in their daily lives compared with men? Think about things like going into pubs alone, fear of attack and sexual assault, politics, and so on.

2 In the light of the issues raised in this and the previous chapter and your responses to the activity above, consider what steps might be taken to break down these inequalities. To help you do this, draw three columns. In the first column, list all the inequalities you can think of that women still face today compared with men; in the second column, list the causes of these inequalities; in the third column, list the changes that would need to be made in society to remove these inequalities.

CHAPTER SUMMARY

After studying this chapter, you should be able to:

- Describe how and explain why the position of women has changed in Britain this century.
- Describe the main features of domestic labour.
- Explain why more married women are entering paid employment.
- Describe and explain a range of inequalities facing women in paid employment.
- Explain why women get only 80 per cent of the average male wage and are poorly represented in top jobs.

KEY TERMS

domestic labour patriarchy
glass ceiling sexism

PROJECT SUGGESTIONS

1 Interview a sample of married or cohabiting women in paid employment who have small children, and try to discover any problems or role conflict they experience at work and in the home.
2 Interview a sample of full-time housewives and try to discover what they enjoy most and dislike most about being full-time housewives, how much time they spend each week on housework, and how much help, if any, they get from their male partners.
3 Do a survey among men and women of different age groups asking about their attitudes to the growing equality of women.

7 ETHNICITY AND RACE

KEY ISSUES IN THIS CHAPTER

- The meaning of race and ethnicity.
- The pattern of immigration.
- Who are the ethnic minorities?
- Some inequalities facing ethnic minority groups.
- The causes of racism.
- Are relations between ethnic groups improving?

RACE, ETHNICITY, AND ETHNIC MINORITIES

The idea of **race** refers to the attempt to divide humans according to physical characteristics (like skin colour) into different racial groups, such as Caucasians (white), Negroid (black African) or Mongoloid (Chinese). Sociologists generally regard this as a rather pointless exercise, as it has no value in explaining human culture. This is because human behaviour is largely a result of socialization, and cannot be explained by purely biological characteristics.

Ethnicity is a more valuable idea. This refers to the common culture shared by a social group, such as language, religion, styles of dress, food, shared history and experiences, and so on. An **ethnic group** is any group

Race refers to the divisions of humans according to physical characteristics (like skin colour) into different racial groups, such as Caucasian (white) or Negroid (black African).
Ethnicity refers to a common culture, such as language, religion and beliefs.
An **ethnic group** is a group of people who share a common culture. An **ethnic minority group** is a group which shares a cultural identity which is different from that of the majority population of a society.

Progressing or standing still? An attendant at the Tate Gallery
Photo: David Solomons

which shares a common culture, and an **ethnic minority group** is a group which shares a cultural identity which is different from that of the majority population of a society. This means that groups such as gypsies, New Age travellers, and the Irish are all ethnic minority groups in Britain.

There is a wide range of ethnic groups who have emigrated to Britain over the years, such as the Irish, the Chinese, the Jews, the Poles, and more recently the Asians and Afro-Caribbeans (West Indians). However, when most people think of 'ethnic minority groups' they think of people of a different racial origin – of a different skin colour – and white people in Britain tend to think mainly of those of Afro-Caribbean or Asian origin. It is important to recognize that all ethnic minority groups do not share the same cultural features. For example, Asians and Afro-Caribbeans show especially strong cultural differences, and Indian Asians may be Sikhs (the largest group in Britain) or Hindus, while Pakistanis and Bangladeshis are more likely to be Muslims.

THE PATTERN OF IMMIGRATION

It is only since the Second World War (1939–45) that there has been a sizeable non-white population in Britain. Black people entering Britain from the British Commonwealth in the twenty years after 1945 were actively encouraged ('pulled') to come here by the British government. This was due to the serious labour shortage in the period of economic expansion following the Second World War. This 'invitation' to come to Britain was often to fill unskilled and poorly paid jobs white people refused to do. These included jobs in the NHS, London Transport, and the textile industry. Families reuniting with other relatives became an important factor in later migration. 'Push' reasons for migration included unemployment and poverty at home. Most of the early Commonwealth immigrants came from the West Indies, but later the numbers of Indians, Pakistanis, and Bangladeshis grew. The scale of this immigration has been exaggerated, and in recent years a series of racist Immigration Acts have all but ended immigration by non-white people.

WHO ARE THE ETHNIC MINORITIES?

Only about 6 per cent of the population of Britain are non-white (see table 7.1 and figure 7.1), and these make up a small minority of all immigrants. Asians and Afro-Caribbeans together form about 4 per cent of the population of Britain. Over half the ethnic minority population were

Table 7.1 Ethnic origins of the British population: Great Britain, 1996

Ethnic group	Total (thousands)	% of the population
White	52 942	94.1
Black Caribbean	477	0.8
Black African	281	0.5
Other black	117	0.2
Indian	877	1.6
Pakistani	579	1.0
Bangladeshi	183	0.3
Chinese	126	0.2
Other Asian	161	0.3
Other ethnic minorities	506	0.9
All ethnic groups*	56 267	100

*Includes those who did not state their ethnic group.
Source: Derived from *Labour Force Survey*

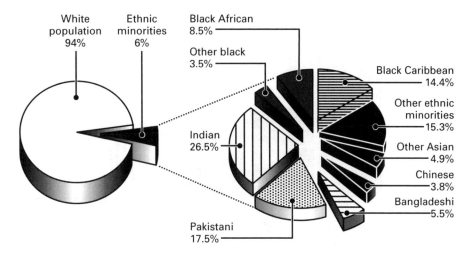

Figure 7.1 Ethnic minority population: Great Britain, 1996
Source: Data from Labour Force Survey

actually born here, so it is misleading to regard them as immigrants, while over half of those who really are immigrants have lived here for more than twenty-five years.

SOME INEQUALITIES FACING ETHNIC MINORITY GROUPS

While some ethnic minorities are doing very well in Britain, black and Asian people often face a series of disadvantages and poorer life chances that their white counterparts do not encounter. Pakistanis, Bangladeshis, and Afro-Caribbeans in particular face a series of disadvantages in Britain compared with the white majority, although there are differences within each group. Some of these disadvantages are discussed in the chapters on education, health, and the mass media, but they also exist in a range of other areas.

Employment and Unemployment

- Afro-Caribbeans, Pakistanis, and Bangladeshis are less likely than white people to secure the best jobs. These groups are under-represented in non-manual occupations, particularly in managerial and professional work. They are hugely under-represented in Parliament and the top elite occupations.

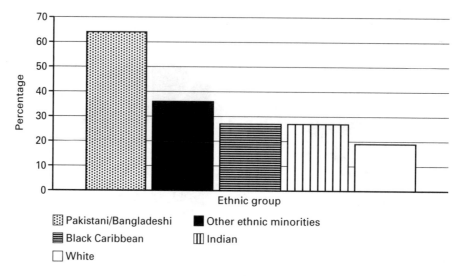

Figure 7.2 Percentage of each ethnic group in the poorest fifth of the population: Great Britain, 1995
Source: Department of Social Security, adapted from *Social Trends 27* (1997)

- They are over-represented in semi-skilled and unskilled manual occupations, and often work longer and more unsociable hours (shiftwork and night work) than white people.
- Black and Asian people are less likely to get employed when competing with whites with the same qualifications for the same job.
- Black and Asian people have lower average earnings, even when they have the same job level as white people. Small-scale surveys have shown that male Afro-Caribbeans earn 15 per cent less and Asians 18 per cent less than whites. As figure 7.2 shows, ethnic minority groups are far more likely to be in the poorest fifth of the population.
- People from ethnic minorities are more likely to face unemployment, especially those of Afro-Caribbean and Pakistani/Bangladeshi origin (as figure 7.3 shows).

ACTIVITY

Ethnic minority working-class women are frequently the most disadvantaged social group of all. Drawing on your knowledge of gender, ethnic, and class divisions, suggest possible explanations for this.

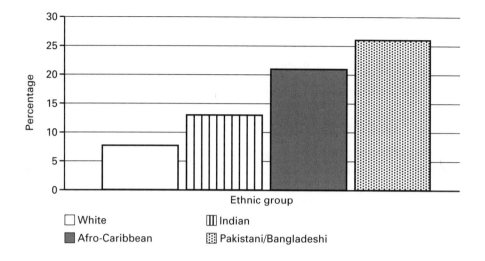

Figure 7.3 Unemployment rates: by ethnic group, Great Britain, 1996
Source: Data from *Labour Market Trends*

- Skilled and experienced ethnic minority women are twice as likely as white women to be unemployed, according to the Equal Opportunities Commission. Black and Asian women frequently work longer hours in poor conditions than white women or men, and receive roughly three-quarters of white women's pay, even though they are on average better educated.

Your country needs you – but not if you're black

Black and Asian people make up 1.1 per cent of the Royal Navy, 1.5 per cent of the army and 1.4 per cent of the Royal Air Force. In all services, black and Asian people are over-represented at or below corporal level. In 1994 only 13 per cent of black applicants for the army were accepted, compared with 27 per cent of white applicants. In recent years, there has been a string of cases of soldiers leaving the army because of racial abuse, violence, and the denial of opportunity by fellow soldiers.

Housing

ACTIVITY

Refer to figure 7.4 and table 7.2.

1 Which ethnic group is most likely to own their home outright?
2 Which ethnic group is most likely to rent their home privately?
3 Which ethnic group is most likely to own their home with a mortgage?
4 Which ethnic group has the highest percentage in overcrowded homes?
5 Suggest explanations for the patterns of housing ownership/renting and overcrowding shown in figure 7.4 and table 7.2.

- Black and Asian people tend to live in inferior housing to white people and in the 'less desirable' areas of towns and cities.
- They tend to live in older properties than whites, and are more likely to live in a terraced house or flat.
- They face much higher levels of overcrowding than white households (see figure 7.4).
- As table 7.2 shows, black people are more likely to live in rented

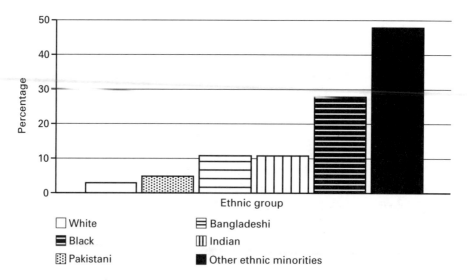

Figure 7.4 Percentage of households living in overcrowded accommodation: by ethnic group, England, 1994/5
Source: Data from Survey of English Housing, Department of the Environment

Table 7.2 Ethnic group of head of household: by tenure, England, 1995–6

	Owned outright %	Owned with mortgage %	Rented from social sector %	Rented privately %	All tenures (=100%) (thousands)
Ethnic minority group					
Black	8	29	49	15	412
Indian	20	60	12	8	281
Pakistani	19	41	16	24	104
Bangladeshi	12	37	37	14	25
Other ethnic minorities	11	40	29	20	245
All ethnic minority groups	13	41	31	15	1 067
White	26	42	22	10	18 844
All ethnic groups	25	42	22	10	19 918

Source: Social Trends 27 (1997)

accommodation, particularly in social housing (council or housing association properties), where they are often allocated the least desirable homes. Indian Asians, however, are more likely to be owner occupiers than whites are, although the quality of the Indian Asians' housing is often poor, and tends to be in the least desirable and cheaper areas.

- It is often the case that the ethnic minorities live in areas that are different from, and poorer than, those where the white population live.
- Black and Asian households, and single black and Asian people in particular, are more likely than whites to be homeless.

Explaining Racial Disadvantage in Employment and Housing

The following explanations for racial disadvantage should be considered together, as they are cumulative, in that one aspect of discrimination or disadvantage can lead to further disadvantage in other areas.

Social class

Many of the black and Asian population are working class, and therefore face the problems encountered by all working-class people, regardless of their ethnic origin. This would explain their disadvantage compared with the population as a whole. However, there is also evidence of additional racial prejudice and racial discrimination.

Racial prejudice and discrimination

- **Racial prejudice** is a set of assumptions about a racial group which people are reluctant to change even when they receive information which undermines those assumptions.
- **Racial discrimination** is when people's racial prejudices cause them to act unfairly against a racial group. For example, a racially prejudiced police officer might use his or her power to pick on black or Asian people more than white people, perhaps by stopping them in the street and asking what they're up to.
- **Racism** is believing or acting as though an individual or group is superior or inferior on the grounds of racial or ethnic origins, usually skin colour or other physical characteristics, and suggesting that groups defined as inferior have lower intelligence and abilities. Racism involves both racial prejudice and racial discrimination, and encourages hostile feelings towards groups defined as inferior.

The 1965 Race Relations Act made it illegal to discriminate on the grounds of race in employment and housing, and to 'incite racial hatred', and this was strengthened by the establishment of the Commission for Racial Equality in 1976.

However, there is widespread evidence that racial discrimination in

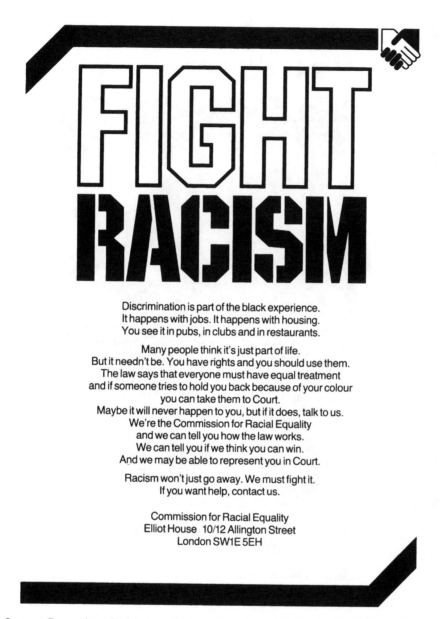

FIGHT RACISM

Discrimination is part of the black experience.
It happens with jobs. It happens with housing.
You see it in pubs, in clubs and in restaurants.

Many people think it's just part of life.
But it needn't be. You have rights and you should use them.
The law says that everyone must have equal treatment
and if someone tries to hold you back because of your colour
you can take them to Court.
Maybe it will never happen to you, but if it does, talk to us.
We're the Commission for Racial Equality
and we can tell you how the law works.
We can tell you if we think you can win.
And we may be able to represent you in Court.

Racism won't just go away. We must fight it.
If you want help, contact us.

Commission for Racial Equality
Elliot House 10/12 Allington Street
London SW1E 5EH

Source: Reproduced with permission of the Commission for Racial Equality

employment, housing, and other areas continues. For example, complaints of racial discrimination coming to the Commission for Racial Equality have more than doubled in the past ten years. Part of the problem is that it is difficult to prove racial discrimination. A black or Asian person who is turned down for promotion at work in favour of a white person may be told the white person was simply more suited to the job in some way.

THERE ARE LOTS OF PLACES IN BRITAIN WHERE RACISM DOESN'T EXIST.

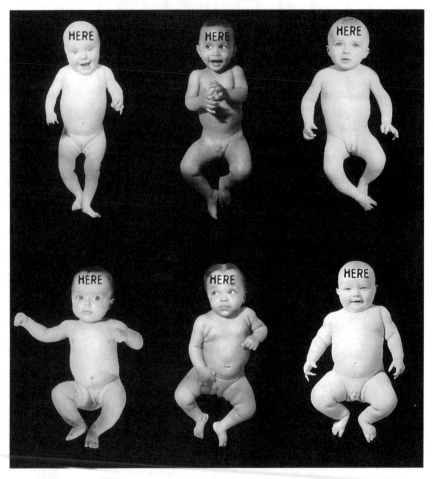

1997 EUROPEAN YEAR AGAINST RACISM CRE

Source: Reproduced with permission of the Commission for Racial Equality

ACTIVITY/DISCUSSION

Refer to the 'Babies' poster from the Commission for Racial Equality. What point is the poster making? What do you think the causes of racism might be?

ACTIVITY

1 Complete the following questionnaire by interviewing a group of people in your school or college. Try to get answers from people from a variety of ethnic backgrounds.
2 Analyse the results.
3 Discuss the answers in your class, considering how much racial prejudice you think might exist.
4 Suggest reasons why people might feel the way they do as shown by your interviews, taking into account any differences you found between ethnic groups.

SURVEY ON RACIAL PREJUDICE

1 To which of these groups do you consider you belong?......	White Pakistani Black–Caribbean Bangladeshi Black–African Chinese Black–other Other Indian
2 Do you think Britain as a society is?......	Very racist Fairly racist Fairly non-racist Completely non-racist
3 How much prejudice is there against black and Asian people in Britain today?......	A lot A little Hardly any Don't know
4 How prejudiced are you yourself against people of other races?......	Very prejudiced A little prejudiced Not prejudiced at all
5 How prejudiced do you think people are in your street or community?......	Very prejudiced A little prejudiced Not prejudiced at all Don't know
6 Do you think non-whites are treated better, worse or the same as whites by?......	Employers: better/worse/same The police: better/worse/same Schools: better/worse/same The courts: better/worse/same

7 Do you agree or disagree with the following statements?

• people should only marry within their own ethnic group......	Agree/disagree
• People of different races should keep to themselves......	Agree/disagree
• I would happily have people of a different race living next door to me......	Agree/disagree
• Immigration has made the variety of life better in Britain......	Agree/disagree
• White people are more intelligent than black people......	Agree/disagree

Source: Adapted from the *Independent on Sunday*, 7 July 1991, and the *Guardian*, 20 March 1995

The most straightforward explanation for disadvantages in employment is that they result from racism and prejudice by employers, who either refuse to employ some ethnic minority groups, or employ them only in low-status and low-paid jobs, or refuse to promote them. This view has been confirmed by a number of surveys in which it was found that white workers received more positive responses in job applications than similarly qualified ethnic minority applicants. For example, a 1997 survey by the Commission for Racial Equality found that white people were five times more likely to get interviews for jobs than black and Asian people with the same qualifications.

In January 1997 the Ford Motor Company, one of Britain's largest employers which claims to have a commitment to equal opportunities policies, agreed to pay compensation to seven black and Asian workers. They had claimed racial discrimination as they were denied the chance of getting highly paid jobs as lorry drivers in Ford's Dagenham factory. Of the factory's workforce, 45 per cent were from ethnic minorities, but less than 2 per cent of the 300 truck drivers were.

Education

Underachievement in education, with some ethnic minorities performing below their ability in GCSEs, A levels, GNVQs, and university entry (ethnicity and education are discussed in chapter 13), may partly explain why some ethnic minorities are under-represented in managerial and professional work, and more likely to be found in unskilled and semi-skilled occupations. These occupations tend to be those most at risk in times of recession, which helps to explain the higher levels of unemployment among black and Asian people. However, discrimination might well mean that they are more likely to be singled out for redundancy when the axe falls.

The generally lower pay of Asian and Afro-Caribbean minorities which follows from these explanations might explain their inferior housing. However, there is evidence of discrimination among landlords and council officials in allocating housing to black and Asian people.

Policing and the Law

How the police go about their work – what they look out for – is guided by their ideas about who 'troublemakers' or criminals are. Black and Asian people (especially black and Asian youths) fit the police stereotype of 'troublemakers'. Black and Asian areas are therefore subject to heavier policing, and black and Asian people are more likely to be stopped and searched than white people. For example, nearly 700 000 people were stopped and searched by police in England and Wales in 1996, according to Home Office statistics. Twenty-two per cent were from the ethnic minorities, even though they make up just 5 per cent of the population. In London, ethnic minorities make up about 20 per cent of the population, but 37 per cent of those stopped and searched. People from ethnic minorities are more likely than white people to be charged with offences such as obstruction or breach of the peace – offences which the police themselves can decide have been committed or not.

Evidence suggests that black and Asian people are more likely to be arrested than whites for the same offence. That they are more heavily policed and stopped and searched means that the police are likely to discover more crime among black and Asian people than among white people. In some cases, resentment at this treatment may actually provoke trouble and cause offences to be committed.

A 1995 survey in the *Weekly Journal* showed 92 per cent of black and Asian people felt that the police treated white people better. This confirmed the findings of a 1991 study by the National Association for the Care and Resettlement of Offenders (NACRO), 'Black People's Experience of Criminal Justice'. This suggested there was evidence of police misconduct towards black and Asian people, who faced more unnecessarily rough treatment and abusive language than white offenders. According to the government's own British Crime Survey, almost 60 per cent of young Afro-Caribbean men in inner cities said they had been stopped or questioned by the police in the previous twelve months. Forty-two per cent of Afro-Caribbeans with a car had been stopped, compared with just 18 per cent of white people with a car. Black and Asian people were far more

ACTIVITY

In 1994, an Asian man in Bradford won £18 million on the National Lottery. The article below is a response to the way the popular press, in particular the *Sun* newspaper, reacted. Read it, then answer the questions that follow.

Misdemeanour of the week. . .

Chasing the Lottery winner

IF THE lottery winner had not been "Asian" and/or "Muslim" would the tabloid press reports have been as bold and as ugly in their reaction? We are not here discussing the ethics of gambling, an activity that Islamic law does not permit, but whether the tabloids should have treated the religion of the winner in this odious manner.

VINDA LOOT!

Indian dad winner of £18 million takeaway

"We're Hindi money", "Vinda Loot", "The Happy Chap-ati" . . . These are just some of the pernicious headlines that appeared.

As a British Muslim, I felt that my religion was being held up to ridicule and wondered where this Islamophobic tendency would lead, particularly now that certain countries in Europe are heading towards ethnic and racial intolerance.

The tabloids, willingly or unwillingly, are playing into the hands of those few racist elements in society who question "why a Paki should get all this money". What if it was a good "white" family man from Durham? If the lottery itself is based on greed then its net result brings out the worst in people, such as envy, jealousy and further greed.

The tabloid reports urging individuals and "groups" to bounty-hunt for the family do not speak of a tolerant and pluralist 20th century society. The tabloid newspapers were, in effect, encouraging the establishment of "witchfinder generals" and urging posses of fascists to search out this individual and his family, like a turkey-shoot.

Surely what was ultimately relevant here was the prize? One would have hoped that the tabloids would be in the vanguard of promoting racial harmony rather than giving fuel to a minority of bigots.

Sayyed Nadeem A Kazmi
The author is editor of the Islamic monthly, Dialogue

Source: The *Guardian*, 16 December 1994

1 What are the main objections of the writer to the way the story of the lottery winner was reported in the press?
2 How do you think the story might have been different if the winner had been 'a good "white" family man from Durham'?
3 Do you agree or disagree with the objections raised by the writer? Give reasons for your answer, and discuss it with your fellow students.

likely than white people to be detained after being charged, and less likely to be allowed to make contact with friends, relatives, or a lawyer.

Black and Asian people are therefore more likely to get caught, arrested, and charged, and the original police stereotype is confirmed by the activities of the police themselves. Judges and magistrates hold similar stereotypes, and the evidence suggests that they crack down harder on black and Asian people than on whites, giving them heavier fines and sentences than white offenders committing similar offences.

- Black and Asian offenders are more likely to be charged where white offenders are cautioned for similar offences.
- Black and Asian people are more likely to be remanded than released on bail.
- Black and Asian people are more likely than whites to be given prison sentences rather than probation or community service.
- Black and Asian people make up only about 5 per cent of the population, but account for 18 per cent of those in prison, with black women making up 24 per cent of the female prison population.

Racist Attacks

Black and Asian people are the victims of more crimes of violence than white people, usually motivated by racism and organized by fascist groups like the British National Party and Combat 18. In some areas with high concentrations of ethnic minorities, these racial attacks are reaching almost epidemic proportions. The British Crime Survey found that both Afro-Caribbeans and Asians were more likely to be victims of assault than whites, and estimated there are around 140 000 racially motivated incidents each year in Britain, including harassment, abuse, threats, intimidation, and violence, with only around 9700 being officially recorded. Between 1993 and 1996, there were believed to be more than a dozen racist murders, such as that of 18-year-old Stephen Lawrence, who was stabbed to death in 1993 by white youths while waiting at a bus stop in London. In 1993, the minister of state at the Home Office told a Home Affairs Select Committee on racial violence that there might be between 130 000 and 140 000 racial attacks a year, and that the 'true figure' could be as high as 330 000 a year – over 900 every day of the year. In September 1995, *The Times* newspaper reported on one estate in the West Midlands where people from ethnic minorities had been shot at, beaten with metal bars, and had their cars set on fire in a campaign of 'ethnic cleansing' by white racists. Asian victims were particularly vulnerable to random attacks and harassment by passing groups of strangers unknown to them.

This means black and Asian people often live in fear of being attacked in the streets or in their homes.

ACTIVITY

Table 7.3 Ethnic minorities and the law: 1990s

Position	White %	Ethnic minority %
Law Lord	100	0.0
Court of Appeal judge	100	0.0
High Court judge	100	0.0
Circuit judge	99.2	0.8
Recorder	98.7	1.3
Practising barrister	94.0	6.0
Practising solicitor	98.5	1.5
Police force	98.5	1.5

Source: 'Human Rights and Racial Discrimination' (Liberty, 1996)

Refer to table 7.3 and then answer the following questions:

1 Suggest reasons why the ethnic minorities are so poorly represented, or not represented at all, in the law and the police force.
2 What difficulties do you think people from ethnic minorities might face in joining or staying in the police force?
3 Explain carefully, with examples, how the evidence above might be used to explain the unequal treatment of black and Asian people by the law, and the high proportion of black and Asian people among those in prison.

THE CAUSES OF RACISM

There is no simple explanation of racism, but there are four factors which help to explain it:

1 *History*. Our society has a long history of white domination of African and Asian countries. Slavery and colonization were often justified on the basis of ideas about the supposed superiority of white people to

those of other ethnic origins. These ideas still tend to linger on. For example, in the European Youth Survey, published by MTV in 1997, almost 30 per cent of 16–24-year-olds in Britain disagreed that all races were equal, and 26 per cent said they would never consider dating someone of a different colour.

2 *Stereotyping.* A stereotype is a generalized, over-simplified view of the features of a social group, allowing for few individual differences between members of the group. Often the media portray degrading and insulting stereotypes of ethnic minority groups which fuel racism (see for example the newspaper article earlier in this chapter).

3 *Scapegoating.* Scapegoats are individuals or groups blamed for something which is not their fault. When unemployment, poverty, and crime rates rise, it becomes easy to find simple explanations by scapegoating easily identifiable minorities, such as young people or ethnic minorities.

4 *Cultural differences.* Some argue that in any society where there are cultural differences between groups, such as in religious beliefs, food, dress, and so on, there are bound to be conflicts from time to time between the minority cultures and the majority culture.

ARE RELATIONS BETWEEN ETHNIC GROUPS IMPROVING?

Grounds for Optimism

Being black or Asian in Britain is often portrayed as a story of racial inequality, prejudice, and discrimination. Yet the news is not all bad. National and local government and some large private companies in Britain are trying to improve the under-representation of black people in important areas of social life. Methods adopted include the provision of training for all staff, and measures designed to increase the numbers of ethnic minority group members who apply for jobs, and to remove recruitment, selection, and promotion procedures which might discriminate against black and Asian people. These measures include advertising jobs in ethnic minority newspapers, and race awareness courses for recruiting staff. Monitoring of job applications for ethnic bias is becoming increasingly common, and equal opportunities policies to combat discrimination are being adopted by schools, colleges, and private and public sector employers. Many schools now include multicultural education as an important part of the curriculum, in an attempt to promote understanding between different ethnic groups and help to overcome prejudice and discrimination based on ethnic differences.

Key parts of British society have begun to respond well to the fact that Britain is a multiracial society. According to the largest survey of ethnic minorities ever carried out in Britain, by the Policy Studies Institute in 1997, around half of British-born Caribbean men, a third of Caribbean women, and a fifth of Indian and African Asian men now have a white partner, and about 80 per cent of 'Caribbean' children now have one white parent. A report by the Institute of Public Policy Research in 1997 found about 70 per cent of white people said they wouldn't mind if a close relative married a black or Asian person.

Racism is less acceptable than it once was. Initiatives such as the European Union's European Year Against Racism in 1997 brought home the message that racial prejudice has no place in a Europe of the second millennium. In some areas, such as education, some ethnic minority groups are doing better than their white counterparts. Some ethnic minorities are much more likely to continue their education beyond the age of 16 than white people, and around 12 per cent of British university students come from ethnic minorities – about double their proportion in the population as a whole. This might eventually lead to improved career prospects and bigger breakthroughs into high-status jobs. In a survey in 1997 for the *New Nation*, a newspaper targeted at Britain's black and Asian population, the outlook for race relations was described as positive, and over 60 per cent said things had improved in the previous five years.

Grounds for Pessimism

Despite these reasons for optimism, this chapter has shown that major problems of inequality still confront the ethnic minorities of Britain. Racist attitudes are still widespread. One in three Britons admitted to being a racist in a survey released in December 1997 by Eurostat, the European Union's statistical office. There has never been a non-white member of the Cabinet in Downing Street; there are no black or Asian chiefs of the armed forces or of the police force; and there are few black or Asian people in high-status positions of power in society. There are more black and Asian university students, but black and Asian graduates face a higher unemployment rate than both graduate and non-graduate white people. A Pakistani with a university degree is as likely to be living below the poverty line as a white person with no educational qualifications. Many black and Asian people are worse off than white people with similar qualifications. More than four out of five Pakistani and Bangladeshi households are living below the poverty line. Opportunities for Britain's ethnic minorities, whether they be in education, jobs, or housing, are still far fewer than for white people. Black and Asian people are still worse off than white people as victims of crime and in their dealings with the law. As one writer put it, there still 'ain't no black in the Union Jack'.

ACTIVITY

1 Discuss the explanations given in this chapter, and any others you can think of, for why people from ethnic minorities, particularly Afro-Caribbean and Asian minorities, often face racial prejudice and discrimination. Give examples to illustrate each explanation.
2 For each explanation, suggest ways in which the causes of the prejudice and discrimination might be removed.

CHAPTER SUMMARY

After studying this chapter, you should be able to:

- Explain what is meant by the terms 'race', 'ethnicity', 'ethnic group', and 'ethnic minority group'.
- Identify the main ethnic minority groups in Britain.
- Explain how and why ethnic minorities face inequalities in employment, housing, and the law.
- Explain what is meant by 'racial prejudice', 'racial discrimination', and 'racism'.
- Suggest some explanations for racism.
- Identify steps being taken to improve the position of the ethnic minorities, with examples.

KEY TERMS

ethnic group	race
ethnic minority group	racial discrimination
ethnicity	racial prejudice

PROJECT SUGGESTIONS

1 Devise a survey to question people about their attitudes to people of other ethnic groups. You might find the questionnaire included in this chapter a useful starting point.

2 Using secondary sources (see chapter 18), try to do a small-scale survey of local employment patterns to see if there is any evidence of discrimination against people from the ethnic minorities.

3 Investigate in your school, college, or workplace any efforts that are being made to create more equal opportunities for ethnic minority groups. For example, see if there are any equal opportunity policies in place or ethnic monitoring of job or student applications. Find out what steps are taken to analyse the effects of such policies, and how these findings change the actions of the institution.

POWER AND POLITICS

8

When most people in Britain think about politics, they usually think about voting and elections, councillors and MPs, and often boring party political broadcasts on television. This is quite a narrow view of politics, and of course in many parts of the world people are unable to vote in elections, and don't even have the right to be bored by the television broadcasts of competing political parties. Politics is not simply about councils and governments, but more widely about the exercise of power.

Power is the ability of people or groups to exert their will over others and get their own way, even if sometimes others resist this. **Politics** is concerned with the struggle to gain power and control, by getting in a position to make decisions and implement policies. This means that when partners in a personal relationship argue about decisions affecting them, we can talk about the 'politics of the personal'. In family life, disputes between husbands and wives, and parents and children, can be considered part of the 'politics of family life'. The power differences between men and women can be considered 'sexual politics'.

In this chapter, the focus will be on the political system in society as a whole – the extent to which individuals can influence the decisions of governments, the polices of the political parties, and the factors which affect the way people vote. A key question will be to what extent Britain can be regarded as a democratic society.

A distinction is often made between two types of power:

- **Authority** is power which is accepted as legitimate (fair and right) by those without power. We obey those with authority because we accept they have the right to tell us what to do.
- **Coercion** is that type of power which is not accepted as legitimate by those without power, as the power-holders rule without the consent of those they govern. People only obey because they are forced to by violence or the threat of violence.

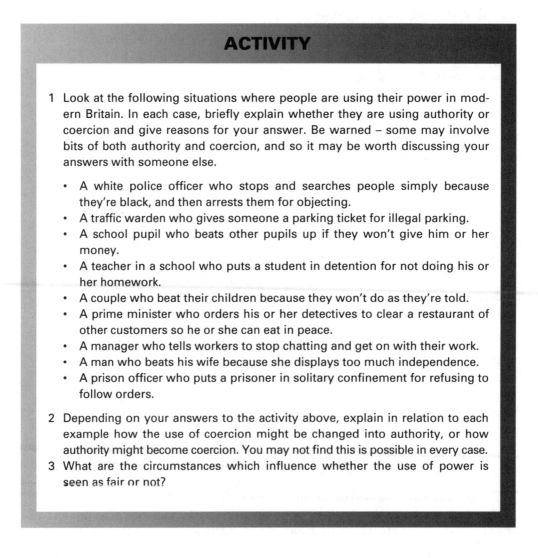

ACTIVITY

1 Look at the following situations where people are using their power in modern Britain. In each case, briefly explain whether they are using authority or coercion and give reasons for your answer. Be warned – some may involve bits of both authority and coercion, and so it may be worth discussing your answers with someone else.

- A white police officer who stops and searches people simply because they're black, and then arrests them for objecting.
- A traffic warden who gives someone a parking ticket for illegal parking.
- A school pupil who beats other pupils up if they won't give him or her money.
- A teacher in a school who puts a student in detention for not doing his or her homework.
- A couple who beat their children because they won't do as they're told.
- A prime minister who orders his or her detectives to clear a restaurant of other customers so he or she can eat in peace.
- A manager who tells workers to stop chatting and get on with their work.
- A man who beats his wife because she displays too much independence.
- A prison officer who puts a prisoner in solitary confinement for refusing to follow orders.

2 Depending on your answers to the activity above, explain in relation to each example how the use of coercion might be changed into authority, or how authority might become coercion. You may not find this is possible in every case.

3 What are the circumstances which influence whether the use of power is seen as fair or not?

TYPES OF POLITICAL SYSTEM

There are differences between societies in the amounts of power ordinary people have to influence government decisions, and these differences are shown in two opposing political systems: democracy and totalitarianism. While these two are presented as opposing systems, most political systems will fall somewhere between the two. It will be seen later, for example, that even in Britain, often seen as the 'home' of democracy, aspects of totalitarianism remain.

Democracy

Democracy is a system of government which basically involves 'government of the people, by the people, for the people', where ordinary people have some control over government decision-making. It is impractical for everyone in society to be permanently and directly involved in political decision-making, so often representatives are elected to represent people's opinions – such as MPs (members of parliament) and local councillors in Britain. This is known as representative or parliamentary democracy, and is found in Britain, France, Germany, the other countries of the European Union, and the USA. Electing representatives is an important part of a democracy. However, a democratic society usually includes many other features to ensure that representatives can be replaced if they follow unpopular policies and that people can freely express their opinions. Figure 8.1 illustrates the main features of a democracy.

DISCUSSION

In the light of figure 8.1 on the next page, do you think Britain is a democratic society? Do you think all individuals and groups have the same amount of power in society?

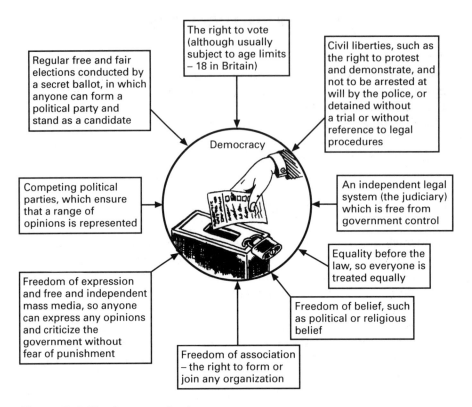

Figure 8.1 The features of a democracy

Totalitarianism

Totalitarianism is a system of government where society is controlled by a small powerful group – an elite – and ordinary people lack any control over government decision-making. There are no free elections and no civil liberties, and most of the features found in a democracy do not exist. The government rules by coercion rather than consent. People are forced to obey the government because of its control of the police, the courts, and the army. All the major social institutions, like the economy, the education system, religion, the legal system, the police, and the mass media, are strictly controlled by the government. Ideas opposed to those of the government are censored, and any opposition organizations crushed by force. Examples of totalitarian societies include Hitler's Germany and the People's Republic of China ('Communist' China).

A **dictatorship** is a form of totalitarianism where power tends to be concentrated in the hands of one person, such as Hitler.

POLITICAL PARTIES IN BRITAIN

A **political party** is a group of people organized with the aim of forming the government in a society. In a democracy, the existence of a range of political parties is essential if voters are to have a choice of candidates and policies to choose from. The discussion below covers the major parties in Britain which put up candidates for election to local councils, the British Parliament at Westminster, or the European Parliament in Strasbourg.

The Labour Party

The Labour Party was founded in 1906, and is today one of the two main political parties in Britain. Traditionally the Labour Party placed great emphasis on state ownership and workers' control of key sectors of the economy, such as the banks, insurance companies, and all the major industrial companies.

Some policies of the Labour Party (based on the 1997 election manifesto)

- Reducing hospital waiting lists, and more spending on the NHS.
- Raising standards in schools, and cutting class sizes to thirty or under for 5–7-year-olds in schools.
- More police officers on the beat.
- Reducing unemployment.
- A national minimum wage to tackle low pay.
- Defence of the welfare state, including state education and the NHS.
- Reducing VAT on domestic fuel.
- A referendum on reform of the voting system for Parliament.
- Ending the right of hereditary peers to sit and vote in the House of Lords.
- No increases in income tax rates for five years.
- Halving the time from arrest to sentencing for persistent young offenders.
- New laws to tackle racial harassment and racial violence.

In the early 1990s, many of the Labour Party's traditional policies were reviewed and changed, with the party adopting policies which it was thought would have more appeal to voters. These new policies resulted in the Labour Party becoming known as 'New Labour', with some policies more similar to those of the Conservative Party. The change from 'old' Labour to 'New Labour' is illustrated by the change in wording on the Labour membership cards shown here.

These new policies clearly succeeded with the voters. The Labour Party took power for the first time in eighteen years after winning the 1997 general election with a landslide victory, with the largest number of MPs of any party since 1945 and the largest number in the party's history.

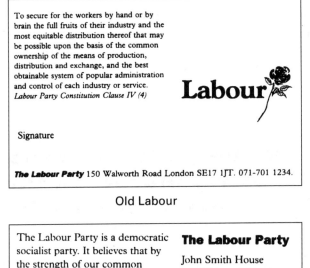

To secure for the workers by hand or by brain the full fruits of their industry and the most equitable distribution thereof that may be possible upon the basis of the common ownership of the means of production, distribution and exchange, and the best obtainable system of popular administration and control of each industry or service.
Labour Party Constitution Clause IV (4)

Signature

The Labour Party 150 Walworth Road London SE17 1JT. 071-701 1234.

Old Labour

The Labour Party is a democratic socialist party. It believes that by the strength of our common endeavour we achieve more than we achieve alone, so as to create for each of us the means to realise our true potential and for all of us a community in which power, wealth and opportunity are in the hands of the many not the few, where the rights we enjoy reflect the duties we owe, and where we live together, freely, in a spirit of solidarity, tolerance and respect.

The Labour Party

John Smith House
150 Walworth Road
London SE17 1JT

Telephone 0171-701 1234

New Labour

The 'Centre' Parties

The 'centre' parties have policies which fall between those of Labour and the Conservatives. They generally share a belief in freedom of the individual, some state assistance to the poor, and some state ownership of the economy, but largely support private industry.

- The *Liberal Democrats* were founded in 1988, and they are today the main 'third party' in British politics, though they do not have much prospect in the foreseeable future of ever forming a government. This means they can adopt policies knowing they will never have to take responsibility for implementing them.
- The *Green Party* mainly campaigns around environmental issues, and draws support from a wide range of people who are more concerned about this than any other political issue. There is also some evidence it attracts support from those who wish to register a 'protest vote' against the other parties.

The Conservative (Tory) Party

The Conservative Party is a very long-established political party, and is today one of the two main parties in British politics. The Conservative Party is opposed to any form of state ownership of the economy. It gets

Some policies of the Conservative Party (based on policies between 1979 and 1997 and the 1997 election manifesto)

- Private ownership of the economy, opposition to nationalization (state ownership), and putting already nationalized industries back into private ownership. Between 1979 and 1997, British Gas, British Steel, British Airways, British Telecom, British Rail, and the water and electricity industries were all sold off to private ownership.
- Free enterprise: limiting the interference of the state in the affairs of private business and the economy generally, and bringing 'market forces' into state services (like the NHS and education).
- Self-help, by making the individual rely less on support from the state.
- Cutting income tax and increasing indirect taxes (such as VAT).
- Law and order, with minimum sentences for repeat burglars and drug dealers; curfew orders and electronic tagging; and making parents legally responsible for the behaviour of their children.
- Limiting the power of trade unions.
- Private (rather than state) pensions.
- Higher standards in schools, more grant-maintained and grammar schools.
- Expansion of Assisted Places Scheme (allowing poorer children to go to private schools).

the bulk of its funds from big business, and draws much of its traditional support from the upper and middle classes and private business. After its crushing defeat in the 1997 general election, the Conservative Party began to review its policies, to try to present a more caring and compassionate image.

ACTIVITY

1 In addition to the policies outlined above, try to find out what other policies the political parties have in areas that interest you.
2 On the basis of the policies of the parties, why do you think many working-class people have traditionally voted Labour, while many middle-class people have traditionally voted Conservative?

INFLUENCING DECISION-MAKING IN A DEMOCRACY

There are a number of ways individuals can influence the decision-making process in a democracy. Joining a political party is an obvious way, which enables them to take part in formulating the policies of that party, which may eventually become government policy if the party wins a general election.

The existence of competing political parties, combined with free elections and freedom of speech, means that parties must represent a range of interests if they are to be elected or to stay in power: the need to attract voters means parties have to respond to the wishes of the electorate. Voting is the most obvious way ordinary people can influence political decisions.

A further method is by writing to their local MP or councillor to try to have their concerns taken up, or by writing to the press and using public opinion to pressurize elected politicians. However, individuals on their own have limited power, and the most effective way of influencing decision-making is to join together with others concerned about the same issue, by forming or joining a pressure group.

Pressure Groups

Pressure groups are organizations which try to put pressure on governments, councillors, and others with power to implement policies which

Pressure groups and political parties

Pressure groups differ from political parties in three main ways:

- They do not try to take power themselves by having their members elected to Parliament and forming a government.
- They do not claim to represent the interests of everyone, but only the particular concerns of some sections of the population.
- They are generally concerned with only one issue or a group of related issues rather than the wide range of issues on which political parties have to form policies.

they favour. Pressure groups, which are sometimes called interest groups, are important in a democracy as channels for the representation of interests and opinions which might otherwise be forgotten or ignored by those with power. They therefore help to keep political parties and governments in touch with public opinion.

Pressure groups in action: a 1990 poster for display, by the Midlands Campaign Against the Poll Tax

Pressure groups in action: a 1991 demonstration against the poll tax
Source: Denis Thorpe, *Guardian*

Pressure groups in action: a 1991 newspaper advertisement against the Gulf War
Source: Leamington Spa Courier

Pressure groups in action: a 1994 protest against a proposed school closure in Warwickshire
Source: Leamington Spa Courier

There are two main types of pressure group.

- *Protective or defensive groups* are concerned with defending the shared interests of their membership. Examples of these groups include the AA (the Automobile Association), Help the Aged, the NSPCC, trade unions and professional associations, and employers' organizations like the CBI (the Confederation of British Industry).
- *Promotional groups* are concerned with promoting a particular cause rather than protecting the interests of a particular group. Examples include ASH (Action on Smoking and Health), the Child Poverty Action Group (concerned with raising welfare benefits), environmental action groups like Greenpeace and Friends of the Earth, and animal rights groups like the Animal Liberation Front.

Table 8.1 gives examples of some pressure groups in Britain and indicates what the aims of each group are.

Table 8.1 Examples of pressure groups in Britain

Organization	Aim
Protective or defensive groups:	
Automobile Association (AA)	To protect the interest of motorists
Age Concern	To campaign on matters of concern to the elderly and to promote dignity and quality of life for the retired
Lord's Day Observance Society	To preserve Sunday as the Christian Sabbath
National Society for the Prevention of Cruelty to Children (NSPCC)	To protect children who are deprived, neglected or at risk of abuse
Confederation of British Industry (CBI)	To protect and promote the interests of British business and the private enterprise system
British Medical Association (BMA)	To protect and promote the interests of doctors
Law Society	To protect and promote the interests of lawyers
Trades Union Congress (TUC)	To protect and promote the interests of affiliated trade unions and the economic and social conditions and rights of workers
National Union of Teachers (NUT)	To protect and promote the interests of teachers and children in schools
Promotional groups:	
Action on Smoking and Health (ASH)	To promote opposition to tobacco smoking
Child Poverty Action Group (CPAG)	To promote action for the relief of poverty among children and families with children and to campaign for higher welfare benefits
Electoral Reform Society	To secure the use of the single transferable voting system in all elections and to establish proportional representation
Greenpeace	To protect the environment and the ecological balance of the earth

Shelter	To provide assistance to the homeless and promote changes in housing policy to eliminate homelessness and poor housing
Campaign Against Pornography (CAP)	To build a mass campaign against pornography and the violence against women it produces

Methods Used by Pressure Groups

There is a range of methods used by pressure groups to influence public opinion, political parties and governments.

- Contributions to the funds of political parties; for example, trade union support to the Labour Party or contributions to the Conservative Party by industry. The large contribution of the big brewers to Conservative Party funds encouraged the Conservative government in 1989 to abandon proposals aimed at eliminating the monopoly of the large breweries on pubs. Donations by the Formula One motor racing industry to the Labour Party in 1997 encouraged the Labour government to weaken proposals to ban tobacco advertising and sponsorship in motor racing. These are clear examples of powerful pressure groups in action.
- Lobbying MPs and government ministers. This means going to the entrance hall or lobby of the House of Commons or local MPs' 'surgeries' to put the group's case.
- Sponsorship of MPs: paying their election and other expenses in exchange for their support in the House of Commons. Trade unions and the Police Federation both do this.
- Advertising in the mass media.
- Leafleting.
- Organizing petitions or opinion polls to show how much support they have.
- Holding public meetings.
- Letter-writing campaigns to newspapers, local councillors, and MPs.
- Demonstrations.
- Organizing mass campaigns, such as those against new road building, or the campaign against the poll tax in 1989–91, which helped to bring about the abolition of this massively unpopular tax.
- Civil disobedience – breaking the law to bring attention to their cause. This kind of tactic is used by the Animal Liberation Front when it breaks into laboratories and releases animals used for experiments in scientific research. In the late 1990s, tunnelling under new airport and road sites to stop development became a popular tactic for a time.

- Strikes, to bring economic pressure on the government to change its policies.
- The provision of expertise. Pressure groups often have specialized knowledge gathered through research which they can lay at the disposal of the government, giving them a direct influence on government policy. For example, the Child Poverty Action Group, Shelter, and the CBI are all providers of expert knowledge to governments.

ACTIVITY

Imagine *either* that the council is planning to close a local school *or* that there are plans to open a dump for nuclear waste in your area. Plan out how you might organize a campaign to keep the school open or to stop the nuclear waste dump being opened. Think carefully of how you might get people together and all the activities you might engage in to influence those with power. What obstacles, including money, might you find in carrying out a successful campaign?

Are All Pressure Groups Equally Effective?

Pressure groups are important in a democracy as a means of representing a wide range of interests and influencing those with power. However, there are a number of criticisms of pressure groups and their effectiveness in influencing power-holders.

- Not all interests are represented through pressure groups. Not all groups in the population are equally capable of forming pressure groups. Disadvantaged groups like the poor, the unemployed, ethnic minorities, the handicapped, the mentally ill, and the old often lack the resources or education to make their voices heard. Substantial wealth and education mean some groups can run more effective campaigns to make their demands heard, such as employers' organizations like the CBI.
- Not everyone has the same chance of meeting top decision-makers. Getting to see decision-makers is far easier if you are from the same social class background. 'Friends in high places' and the 'old boys' network', which is considered in the discussion of public schools in chapter 13, mean that the interests of the upper and middle classes are generally more effectively represented than those of the working class.
- Some groups holding key positions in the economy are able to bring

pressure to bear on the government through strike action. For example, railway or power workers can cause widespread disruption by strike action, and so are more likely to get action on their grievances than, say, old age pensioners or students.

These factors are of some concern in a democracy, as not all pressure groups have the same amount of influence. Some interests get represented more effectively than others and some interests may not be represented at all.

INFLUENCES ON VOTING BEHAVIOUR

You would expect people to vote in elections purely on the issues, and on the policies held by the different parties. Some argue that 'issue-voting' has become more important in recent years, but research suggests that the

Like 'an asteroid hitting the planet': the 1997 General Election

The influences on voting behaviour which are covered in the main text are those which have been listed traditionally. However, the 1997 general election was such a landslide for the Labour Party (like 'an asteroid hitting the planet', as one political analyst put it) that many traditional influences were over-ridden. For example, the Conservatives got their lowest share of the vote since 1832 and all social groups showed a marked turn to Labour. Many Tory candidates in long-standing 'safe' Conservative seats were defeated, with the Conservatives losing every seat outside of England. Many Labour candidates were elected where there had never been a Labour MP before. This may have been partly because the Conservative Party had been in power for eighteen years and the voters were getting tired of one-party rule which was out of touch with the voters. However, in 1997 the Conservatives were also a badly divided party. There was much fighting within its ranks, and it was also surrounded by a series of scandals relating to 'sleaze' – immoral behaviour by Conservative MPs. A number of Conservatives later explained their election defeat using terms such as 'inhumane', 'greedy', 'disloyal', 'selfish', 'arrogant', 'out of touch', 'sleaze-ridden', and 'divided' to describe the way people saw their party. This situation swung many voters towards the reformed and less personally threatening 'New Labour'. The Conservative Party began reviewing its policies late in 1997, and the next election (due in 2002) will test how far the traditional explanations for voting behaviour have really changed.

political party for which people decide to vote is the result of a range of factors. Party policies are, surprisingly, a relatively minor factor among them.

The Family

As in other areas of life, the family plays an important role in political socialization or the formation of an individual's political beliefs. Many people tend to share the general political beliefs and attitudes of their parents, and continue to support the political party their parents did.

Geographical Area

Voting patterns seem to be associated with the geographical area in which people live. Those in the north of England, Scotland, Wales, and inner-city areas are more likely to support the Labour Party. Those in the southern parts of England and rural areas have traditionally been more likely to support the Conservative Party. This could be because of social class differences between these areas, with higher numbers of traditional working-class people, more unemployment, and social deprivation in areas supporting Labour.

Ethnic Origin

The ethnic group to which people belong appears to have an influence on their voting habits. Black and Asian people have traditionally been more inclined to support the Labour Party than other parties. This is because Labour has more sympathetic policies on immigration and race relations, and is more concerned with reducing the racial discrimination, social deprivation, and unemployment which ethnic minorities are more likely to encounter.

Religion

Religion is not a particularly important influence on voting in most of the United Kingdom, although members of the Church of England have traditionally been more likely to support the Conservative Party. However, in Northern Ireland voting coincides almost exactly with the divisions between Protestants and Catholics, with Protestants supporting parties which support union with Britain, and Catholics supporting parties sympathetic to a united Ireland.

Party Images

Most people have general impressions or images of what the political parties stand for, and evidence suggests the way most people vote is influenced by this 'party image', rather than by knowledge of what the actual

Party images in the 1997 general election
Photos: Ted Fussey

policies of the political parties are. For example, working-class people might vote Labour because it presents a more 'caring' image, supporting the NHS and education, and appears more sympathetic to the needs of the poor and disadvantaged than the 'uncaring' Conservatives, who seem to support big business and the well-off, and promote self-interest over the needs of the wider community.

This is perhaps why political parties, during election campaigns, often concentrate more in their advertising and television broadcasts on presenting particular images or impressions of themselves and their leaders (such as 'caring', 'efficient', and 'friendly') rather than on explaining what their actual policies are.

The Mass Media

The mass media are major agencies of socialization, and have important influences on people's general beliefs and opinions. Chapter 9 shows how many of the mass media tend to present a very conservative view of society – generally supporting the 'establishment' and the way things are currently organized in society. This may help to establish a long-term climate of opinion which benefits the Conservative Party at the expense of Labour and other parties. As table 8.2 shows for the 1987 and 1992 general

Table 8.2 Political parties supported by national daily newspapers in general elections: 1987, 1992, and 1997

Newspaper	Party support[a] and market share[b]		
	1987	1992	1997
Sun	Conservative (28%)	Conservative (28%)	Labour (29%)
Daily Express	Conservative (12%)	Conservative (12%)	Conservative (9%)
Daily Mail	Conservative (12%)	Conservative (13%)	Conservative (16%)
Daily Star	Conservative (9%)	Conservative (6%)	Labour (5%)
Daily Telegraph	Conservative (8%)	Conservative (8%)	Conservative (9%)
The Times	Conservative (3%)	Conservative (3%)	None (6%)
Financial Times	Conservative (2%)	Labour (2%)	Labour (2%)
Daily Mirror	Labour (22%)	Labour (22%)	Labour (18%)
Guardian	Labour (4%)	Labour (3%)	Labour (3%)
Independent	No party support (N/A)	No party support (3%)	Labour (2%)
Total circulation	14 761 000	13 189 000	13 112 000

[a] The party support of each newspaper is based on its broad voting recommendations and/or editorial tone on election day.
[b] Approximate, and figures are rounded to nearest per cent.
Source: Audit Bureau of Circulation; *Willings Press Guide 1992*; *The 1997 Guardian Media Guide*

ACTIVITY

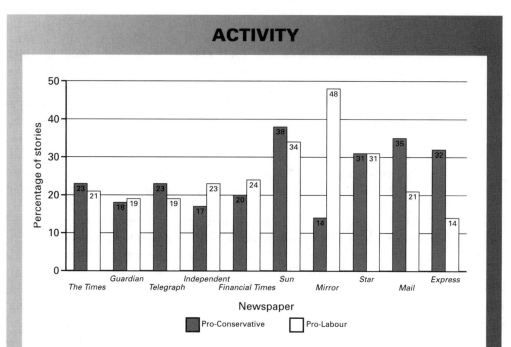

Figure 8.2 A Conservative bias? Percentage of stories favourable to one of the two main parties throughout the general election campaign: United Kingdom, 1997
Source: Adapted from the *Guardian*, based on research by Loughborough University's Communication Research Centre

Refer to table 8.2, then answer these three questions:

1 Which national daily newspapers that had previously supported the Conservatives supported Labour in 1997?
2 What market share was held by Conservative-supporting papers in (a) 1987 and (b) 1992?
3 What market share was held by Labour-supporting papers in 1997?

Now refer to figure 8.2, as well as table 8.2, and answer the following questions:

4 Which Labour-supporting paper in 1997 had a higher proportion of stories favourable to the Conservatives during the 1997 general election campaign?
5 Which newspaper gave exactly equally favourable treatment to both the two main parties during the 1997 general election campaign?
6 Which newspaper had the highest proportion of stories favourable to Labour during the 1997 general election campaign?
7 How might the evidence in table 8.2 and figure 8.2 be used to support or oppose the view that the majority of national daily newspapers are more likely to favour the Conservatives? Refer to some of the statistics to support your answer.

elections, nearly all the major national daily newspapers supported the Conservative Party, with the exception of the Labour-supporting *Daily Mirror* and the *Guardian*, and (in 1992) the *Financial Times*. In 1997, more of the press swung formally towards supporting Labour. However, as figure 8.2 shows, the bulk of the content of the major newspapers showed more positive stories for the Conservatives in their coverage of the 1997 election.

This illustrates clearly the conservative bias which tends to mark many of the mass media, and would appear to justify complaints that the mass media represent mainly the interests of the privileged upper- and upper-middle class, at the expense of working-class and minority group interests.

Because newspapers tend to put forward a particular political opinion, many people see them as unreliable sources of evidence, and turn to the television instead. There is little evidence to suggest that party political broadcasts on television have much influence in changing people's voting habits, except in cases when people find it difficult to make up their minds which way to vote. **Floating voters** are those with no fixed political opinions, who therefore regularly switch votes between parties from one election to the next. It is these voters who are most likely to be influenced by the media, and it is at these floating voters that many TV party election broadcasts are aimed.

The mass media and voting: key findings

- Where people already have established political views, the mass media are more likely to reinforce those views than to change them.
- People tend to be selective in their choice of programmes and newspapers, and they only see and hear what they want to. They will either choose those that present information which confirms their existing opinions and avoid those that conflict with them, or reject those aspects which do not conform with their existing ideas. For example, there are committed Labour voters and *Sun* readers who ridicule Conservative election broadcasts and ignore the Tory politics of the *Sun*.
- While in general the media are unlikely to change people's voting behaviour in the short term (such as in the run-up to a general election), they might be effective in changing attitudes over a longer period of time. For example, they might gradually change people's perception of a particular party or political leader. The *Sun* claimed in 1992 that 'It's the Sun wot won it' (for the Conservatives), by savage attacks on Labour leader Neil Kinnock. In 1997, the *Sun* claimed that 'It was the Sun wot swung it' (for Labour) by rallying behind Labour leader Tony Blair. However, a NOP/BBC poll in 1997 showed that over half of voters had decided how they would vote even before the election

Britain's Tory press: all these newspapers supported the Conservatives in the four general elections from 1979 to 1992. Their combined circulation accounted for around 75 per cent of all national daily newspapers sold in Britain

campaign had begun. This suggests that claims like those of the *Sun* are only likely to be of marginal importance in changing voters' minds, though this could be significant if election results are very close.

- The mass media are most likely to be influential on issues and parties which are new to people and about which people have little knowledge or experience.
- Floating voters are those most likely to be influenced by the media, particularly by party political broadcasts on television.
- Most of the media have, in the long run, supported the Conservative Party. This can create a long-term climate of opinion where more people are favourable to the Conservatives, and where opposition parties stand at a disadvantage.

The 'spin doctors'

'Spin doctors' really came into prominence in the 1990s in Britain, particularly in the 1997 general election. Spin doctors are people who, in general, work for political parties. Their job is to manipulate the media by providing a favourable slant to a potentially unpopular or controversial news item. The term comes from the idea of 'spinning' a ball in sport to make it go in the direction you want it to. The aim of spin doctors is to grab favourable headlines (or ones damaging to other parties) in newspapers, or sound bites on TV and radio. By getting across their version of policy, controversy, and events, in stories fed to ever more demanding journalists, they hope to make the media put across a good party image to voters.

Social Class

Social class has traditionally been the single most important factor influencing the way people vote, though this has been of declining importance since the 1970s. In Britain, the Labour Party has traditionally been seen as the party with policies representing the interests of the working class, and many working-class people have tended to vote Labour. In contrast, the Conservatives have been associated with the interests of the middle and upper classes.

However, not all working-class people vote Labour, and not all middle-class people vote Conservative. Traditionally about one-third of manual workers have voted Conservative, and about one-fifth of the middle class have voted Labour. In the elections between 1979 and 1992, even more manual workers than this voted Conservative, with more skilled manual workers voting Conservative than Labour in the 1983, 1987, and 1992 elections. The link between class and voting is illustrated in table 8.3. Working-class people who vote Conservative, and middle-class Labour voters, have traditionally been called **deviant voters**, because they seem to be voting against the party representing the interests of their class. Why do they do this?

Working-class Conservative voters

Deference voters

Working-class deference voters are those who see members of the upper and middle class as superior in 'breeding', coming from 'better families', who make better 'natural leaders' than those from their own class. The Conservative Party contains these sorts of people, and therefore it is supported. Such voters tend to be older, be female, and have lower incomes.

ACTIVITY

Table 8.3 How the social classes voted for the three main parties: 1979–97

Class[a]	1979			1987			1992			1997		
	Con. %	Lab. %	Lib. Dem.[b] %	Con. %	Lab. %	Lib. Dem. %	Con. %	Lab. %	Lib. Dem. %	Con. %	Lab. %	Lib. Dem. %
AB	64	21	16	56	13	31	55	23	22	40	33	22
C1	54	30	16	48	25	27	50	29	21	25	49	20
C2	41	44	15	43	36	21	41	40	19	24	56	14
DE	34	53	13	32	47	21	31	55	14	19	62	14

[a] See chapter 2 on 'Defining class by occupation' for details.
[b] The Liberal Democrats were in alliance with the Social Democratic Party (SDP) between 1979 and 1987. The SDP was dissolved in 1990 and no longer exists.
Source: Calculated from Ivor Crewe, 'Why Did Labour Lose (Yet Again)?', *Politics Review* (September 1992); 1997 data from BBC/NOP exit polls, *Sunday Times* (4 May 1997)

Refer to table 8.3 and answer the questions that follow.

1 Which two social classes were least likely to support the Labour Party in 1979 and 1997?
2 Which social classes in the table make up the working class? (Refer to chapter 2 if you're not sure.)
3 In which social class did support for the Labour Party decline the most between 1979 and 1992?
4 Which party increased its support in all social classes between 1979 and 1997?
5 The table shows that working-class support for Labour declined between 1979 and 1987. Which party gained most from this? Give evidence from the table to back up your answer.
6 In which social class did support for the Conservative Party decline the most between 1979 and 1997?
7 What evidence does the table show that the Conservative Party has traditionally been more likely to be supported by the middle class, and the Labour Party by the working class?
8 What evidence is there in the table that in the 1997 election the Labour Party succeeded in attracting more middle-class voters than at any time since 1979? Give evidence from the table to back up your answer.

They are found in manual occupations where individuals are isolated from other workers, work close to their bosses, and 'know their place'. Such groups might include farmworkers, domestic servants, and those working in very small businesses.

Pragmatic voters

Pragmatic (or practical) voters are those working-class people who have an instrumental attitude to voting, and will support whichever party offers them the greatest personal gain, such as more money, lower taxes and mortgage rates, and a higher standard of living. They are therefore motivated by pragmatic or practical reasons. Such voters will support the Conservative Party only so long as they feel it has more practical benefits to offer them than those of other parties.

This pragmatic, instrumental attitude means such voters have no particular party loyalty. They are more volatile, which means they are more likely to switch votes if another party offers them better personal benefits. Such workers tend to be those found in the 'new' working class, which was discussed in chapter 3.

Since the 1970s, the numbers of the traditional working class which provided the secure base of Labour support have declined, and the new 'pragmatic', instrumental, part has expanded to become the largest section of the working class. This has meant that while the bulk of support for the Labour Party still comes from the working class, fewer working-class people are committed to supporting Labour. In 1987 and 1992, only around 40–45 per cent of manual workers voted Labour, and as table 8.3 shows, only between 47 and 55 per cent of semi-skilled and unskilled manual workers voted for the Labour Party. Even in the 'landslide' victory of 1997, working-class support for the Labour Party was just 56 per cent among skilled manual and 62 per cent among semi- and unskilled workers.

No longer can the Labour Party automatically rely on support from the majority of the working class, because most of them are now part of the volatile and pragmatic 'new' working class. From 1979 until Labour's victory in 1997, the Conservatives proved successful in persuading this expanding group that they had more benefits to offer than the Labour Party, and the new working class provided much of the working-class support for the Conservative Party in the general elections of 1979, 1983, 1987, and 1992. However, the Conservatives lost this support in the 1997 election.

The new 'pragmatism' among working-class voters suggests that social class is becoming of much less importance in affecting the way people vote than it has traditionally been, particularly where the Labour Party is concerned.

Middle-class Labour voters

About one-fifth of the middle class have traditionally voted Labour against what would appear to be their middle-class interests. These voters are most likely to be found in three main occupational groups:

- Those in the 'caring' welfare professions, like teachers and social workers. These people tend to vote Labour because their daily work brings them into contact with the disadvantaged and their problems, and they feel the Labour Party is more likely to tackle such issues.
- Those who have experienced upward social mobility from working-class backgrounds may vote Labour out of a sense of loyalty to their working-class origins.
- Routine clerical workers who are facing proletarianization may support Labour because they see their living and working conditions getting worse, and their social status declining.

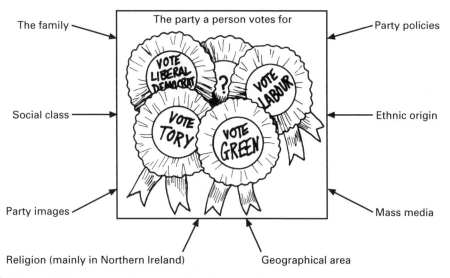

Figure 8.3 Factors influencing the way people vote

Volatility, Dealignment, and the Expansion of the Middle Class

The pattern of voting in Britain since the 1970s suggests three major related changes have occurred:

- The electorate has become more volatile – voters of all social classes are less committed to any one political party, and are more willing to change the party they vote for if another party offers them better personal benefits. People are voting more for their own self-interest rather than out of party loyalty, and on the basis of a party's policies and how well they perform, or might perform, in government. Voters have less loyalty to any one party, and the support of voters swings to and fro between different political parties.

- There is no longer a clear alignment (a matching up) of particular social classes with one of the two main parties – in particular, the working class is no longer clearly aligned with the Labour Party, but neither is the middle class with the Conservatives. Most voters no longer show loyalty to a party according to their social class. **Dealignment** (a mismatch) between class and voting has occurred.

- The middle classes have grown in size, now making up around 45–50 per cent of the population. This means any party that wishes to win power and form a government has to get support from both the working class and the middle class. This need to appeal to middle-class voters was one of the reasons for the Labour Party dropping many of its traditional policies in the early 1990s, and remodelling itself as 'New Labour'.

ACTIVITY

1 If there were a general election tomorrow, which political party would you vote for? Give reasons for your answer, explaining carefully what influenced you in making your decision.
2 Figure 8.3 on page 169 summarizes the key influences that sociologists have identified on voting behaviour. In the light of the exercise above, how far do you think the findings of sociologists confirm or deny your view? Which influences do you think are the most important?

WHY DO PEOPLE ABSTAIN IN ELECTIONS?

About 25 per cent of the electorate in general elections, and as many as 60 per cent or more in local elections, abstain – they fail to vote. Disadvantaged groups, such as the least educated and the poor, and younger and old people are the most likely groups to abstain from voting. In marginal seats, where the difference between the votes of the parties is very small – sometimes as little as one or two votes – abstention can actually swing the election result.

Aside from factors such as apathy, forgetfulness, bad weather, being away on holiday, or being kept in by illness, people may make a positive decision to abstain for several reasons. In safe seats, where there has traditionally been a large majority for one party, voters may not feel it is worth voting since the outcome of the election is so predictable. It may be there is no candidate standing from the party people would normally vote for, or they may not support or understand the policies of any of the different parties. In 1997, an estimated two million former Conservative voters abstained, withdrawing their support from the Conservative Party, but unable to bring themselves to vote for any other party.

Some voters might simply think elections are a waste of time, since the policies of all the parties are too similar and 'elections don't change anything anyway'. In such circumstances they may not bother to vote at all.

OPINION POLLS AND ELECTIONS

Opinion polls are social surveys which try to find out people's attitudes on many issues, and they are widely used to discover how people intend to vote in elections. They most commonly involve face-to-face interviews in the street, but telephone polls are becoming more popular in Britain.

The results of opinion polls provide the basis for reports about the 'state of the parties' which are regularly published in the newspapers, and in election periods polls are conducted daily. For example, during the six weeks of the 1997 general election campaign, forty-one opinion polls were carried out.

Why Opinion Polls are Sometimes Inaccurate

Opinion polls use sophisticated sampling techniques to obtain representative samples of the voting population. Often they can predict the outcome of elections accurately from asking no more than about 1000–1500 people. This is because the group they have questioned are a good representative cross-section of the entire population in terms of factors such as age, sex, social class, and geographical spread around the country. However, sometimes the opinion polls fail to predict the results of elections accurately (see the box on the polling disaster of 1992).

The reasons for this are quite varied, and many possible explanations are discussed in chapter 18 on the general problems of sampling and survey methods. Some possible problems with opinion polls are outlined below.

The opinion polls disaster of 1992

They got it badly wrong in 1992 . . .

Political party	Predicted result %	Actual result %
Labour	39	35
Conservative	38	43
Liberal Democrat	19	18
Others	3	4

The 1992 general election has gone down in history as the one that the opinion polls got wrong – never before had the polls been so far adrift from the actual election result. The polls predicted a small Labour victory of about 1 per cent, but the final result was a Conservative victory of about 8 per cent. An inquiry by the Market Research Society found three main reasons for this disastrous failure by the opinion polls:

1 There was a last-minute swing to the Conservatives which the opinion polls didn't pick up.
2 Those who refused to state their voting intention or to say 'don't know' were more likely to be Conservative voters – the so-called 'silent and shy' Conservatives.
3 There were errors in the way the samples were selected (see chapter 18 for a discussion of sampling techniques). Samples were biased towards the lower social classes, who are more likely to be Labour voters.

The pollsters did a variety of things to overcome these errors in 1997, including:

- Moving away from face-to-face interviews to telephone interviews. These help to overcome interviewer bias, and there is some evidence people are more honest over the telephone.
- Changing their sampling techniques (from quota to random sampling – see chapter 18).
- Marking 'don't knows' on the basis of the party they voted for in 1992, who they said would make the best prime minister, which party they thought would run the economy best, and so on.

... but they got it right in 1997

Political party	Predicted result %	Actual result %
Labour	47	45
Conservative	31	31
Liberal Democrat	16	17
Others	7	7

- They may not contain a representative sample of voters, which may lead to inaccurate results. This happened in 1992 (see box).
- Interviewer bias may mean people give inaccurate answers. People in face-to-face interviews may give the answer that they think is socially acceptable rather than what they really believe. For example, they may say they are prepared to pay higher taxes for better education and health care, but privately prefer (and vote for!) tax cuts. The 1992 general election showed a sharp contrast between what people said to pollsters and what they actually did when it came to voting. If a party is unpopular at the time, its supporters may be reluctant to admit to interviewers they support it – as happened with the 'silent and shy' Conservatives in 1992.
- The format and wording of questions may affect the results of the poll.

For example, respondents prefer to agree rather than disagree with statements which are put to them.

- People may change their minds during the course of the election campaign, after the poll is conducted, when they have heard more arguments and have had more time to make up their minds. Because of this, opinion polls are likely to become more accurate the closer they are to the day of the election.

- Some of those interviewed may decide not to vote, or not to be registered to vote because they are not on the electoral register, when it comes to the actual election, and this will distort the opinion poll's predictions. This is thought to have happened in 1992, when many voters (some of whom may have been interviewed by pollsters) didn't register to vote to try to avoid paying the community charge. (The community charge or poll tax was a local tax which, because it was based on payment by all those over 18 as listed on the electoral roll, led to some people refusing to register to vote. The tax was abolished after some of the largest protests ever seen in Britain.)

- Opinion polls might themselves change the way people decide to vote and therefore the results of the election. This was thought to have happened in 1992, when the polls were predicting either a small Labour victory or possibly a 'hung' parliament (where no party has overall control). This prediction may have persuaded some people to vote Conservative at the last moment.

How Opinion Polls Might Influence the Results of Elections

There is some evidence that opinion polls might not simply reflect voters' opinions, but actually help to form and change them, and therefore affect the eventual election results. For example, if the polls predict a large win for one party, its supporters may not bother to vote, thinking that it is a safe seat and the result a foregone conclusion. This could possibly result in that party actually losing the election if too many of its supporters did this. In the 1970 general election campaign, for example, four out of five polls predicted that Labour would win by a small majority. In fact, the Conservatives won with a majority of thirty parliamentary seats. The Labour Party thought that its lead in the opinion polls might have made the party workers and supporters assume they would win the election regardless of how they conducted their campaign. It was thought this complacency, created by the opinion polls, may have cost Labour the election.

If the polls predict that a certain party is going to win by a large margin, then supporters of another party which has no chance of winning might decide to vote for a third party in the hope of defeating the predicted winning party. This is known as **tactical voting**. An example might be committed Labour voters in a safe Tory seat, where Labour stands no chance of winning. If the opinion polls show that a Liberal Democrat is in second place, then Labour voters may decide to vote for the Liberal Democrat in the hope of defeating the Tory.

A final influence of opinion polls might be the *bandwagon effect*. This is where if the polls show one party to be in the lead, people may want to 'jump on the bandwagon' and be on the side of what they think will be the winning party.

Because opinion polls can affect the results of elections, some people have actually suggested that they are banned immediately before elections, as in France and Germany, where polls are not allowed in the last seven days of election campaigns.

IS BRITAIN A DEMOCRACY?

Earlier in this chapter you may have discussed whether Britain is a democracy or not. Much of this chapter has emphasized the democratic features of modern Britain, and if you look back to figure 8.1, then you may agree that many of the features listed there are indeed to be found in modern Britain. However, there are a number of weaknesses in British democracy.

Non-Elected Rulers

Democracy is meant to involve governments reflecting the interests of the people through elected representatives. However, the House of Lords and the monarchy are not elected, but both have considerable power in controlling which laws are passed. Unelected and unaccountable **quangos** (quasi-autonomous non-government organizations) took over many public services between 1979 and 1997, in areas such as health, training, and further education. These were spending over £50 billion a year of public money in 1997, nearly half of which had been removed from local government.

The Voting System

Voting in the UK is by the first-past-the-post system, under which the party that gets most votes in any constituency (voting area) wins that constituency. In general elections, the representative of the winning party becomes the constituency's MP, and the party getting the most MPs forms

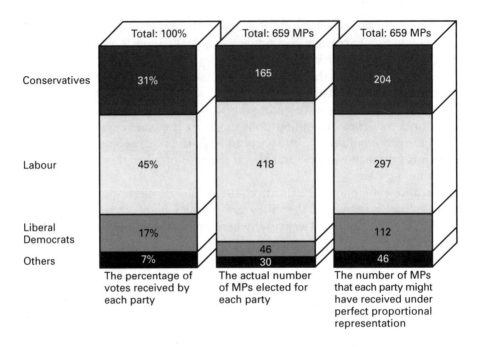

Figure 8.4 General election results: United Kingdom, 1997

the government. This means governments are often elected which represent only a minority of voters in the country as a whole. In fact, every government in Britain since 1945 has been elected with the support of less than half of the voting population. Figure 8.4 shows that in the 1997 general election, the number of MPs elected for each party in no way represented the parties' share of the votes in the country as a whole. Such circumstances mean that, while minority parties might collect a lot of votes in the country as a whole, they get few MPs, or none at all, in Parliament and therefore no representation. **Proportional representation** – which means the number of MPs elected for each party reflects the share of the vote received – would ensure that minority parties and interests were more adequately represented. Figure 8.4 also shows the number of MPs that might have been elected for each party in 1997 if perfect proportional representation had been adopted.

Elite Rule

As seen in chapter 4, wealth remains highly concentrated in the hands of a small upper class, which therefore has major influence in economic decision-making. For example, this class can decide where factories should be located and whether they should be opened or closed down, and it can control the workforce through hiring and firing. Democratically elected governments cannot afford to ignore this power, as they might face rising unemployment and other social problems if the upper class decided not to invest its money.

Most of those in the top elite jobs which wield power and influence in this country come from public school and upper- and upper-middle-class backgrounds (see chapter 13 on this). Even among Labour MPs, less than a quarter come from working-class backgrounds. This raises questions about the extent to which working-class interests are adequately represented.

Unequal Pressure Groups

As seen earlier in this chapter, not all interests are represented through pressure groups, and some pressure groups have a lot more wealth and power than others. It is the voices of the disadvantaged and the poor which are least likely to be heard.

Deciding the Issues

The political parties – not the population as a whole – often decide what the important issues are and which ones they are going to fight elections around. The mass media are mainly privately owned and controlled by a rich and powerful minority and have a conservative bias. They have an important role in forming 'public opinion' and, like political leaders, can decide the issues around which elections are fought.

The points raised above suggest that perhaps Britain is not quite as democratic as many people might believe, and that not everyone gets an equal chance to express her or his opinions and influence decision-making. This is likely to be true particularly of those holding radical opinions who want to change the way society is presently organized. While democracy in Britain has many strengths and freedoms which must be defended, it also has its limitations. The interests of democracy are perhaps best served by removing the limitations and reinforcing the strengths.

CHAPTER SUMMARY

After studying this chapter, you should be able to:

- Explain briefly what is meant by the terms 'power', 'authority', 'coercion', and 'politics'.
- Describe and explain the main features of a democracy, and how democracy differs from totalitarianism and dictatorship.
- Identify the main political parties in Britain which put up candidates in elections, and briefly describe some of their main policies.
- Explain what pressure groups are and how they differ from political parties.
- Describe, with examples, two types of pressure group.
- Describe the methods pressure groups use to influence those with power.
- Explain why some interests are better represented by pressure groups than others.
- Discuss the range of factors influencing voting behaviour.
- Discuss how the mass media might influence political attitudes.
- Explain what is meant by 'deviant voting' and explain both working-class and middle-class deviant voting.
- Explain why social class is becoming of less importance in influencing voting.
- Suggest reasons why people abstain in elections.
- Explain why opinion polls might sometimes fail to predict accurately the outcome of elections.
- Explain how opinion polls might themselves affect election results.
- Discuss the extent to which Britain might be regarded as a democracy.

KEY TERMS

authority	political party
coercion	politics
dealignment	power
democracy	proportional representation
deviant voter	quango
dictatorship	tactical voting
floating voter	totalitarianism

PROJECT SUGGESTIONS

1 Study the aims and activities of a local or national pressure group, interviewing members of the group and studying its literature and reports in newspapers. What methods does the group use to influence public opinion and how effective/successful is the group?

2 Carry out an opinion poll on the attitudes of students, workmates, or members of the public to the different political parties, their policies, and their leaders.

3 Carry out a survey among a sample of people of different ages and/or sexes and/or social classes, asking about their attitudes to some current political issue of major importance. Are there any differences between different groups?

4 Ask a sample of people what factors they think have the most influence on the way they vote, or the way they would vote if they are under voting age.

5 Carry out an opinion poll in your school, college, or workplace including the question, 'If there were a general election tomorrow, for which party would you vote?' Compare your findings with those of a current national opinion poll.

9 THE MASS MEDIA

THE POWER OF THE MEDIA: KEY QUESTIONS

The term 'mass media' refers to forms of communication which are directed at large mass audiences without any personal contact. The main media of mass communication include television, radio, newspapers and magazines, books, cinema, videos, advertising, CDs, video games, and the Internet – the worldwide network of interlinked computers.

In Britain, 97 per cent of the population watch television, with those over 16 spending nearly half of all free time watching it. Around fourteen million newspapers are sold every day. The media have become important sources of information, entertainment, and leisure activity for large numbers of people, and they have become key agencies of secondary socialization and informal education. Most people will base their opinions and attitudes, not on personal experience, but on evidence and knowledge provided by newspapers and television.

ACTIVITY

1 Work out approximately how many hours in a typical week you spend watching television or videos, listening to the radio or music, reading newspapers and magazines, or at the cinema.
2 Working out approximately how many hours a week you spend sleeping.
3 There are 168 hours in a week. Take away the number of hours you spend sleeping from this total. Now work out what percentage of your waking life you spend under the direct influence of the mass media (you can do this by dividing the number of hours spent watching TV, etc., by the number of waking hours and multiplying by 100).
4 List all the ways you think the mass media influence you in your life, such as your knowledge about current affairs, opinions, tastes in music and fashion, roles of men and women, etc.

You may have found from the previous activity that you spend a great deal of time under the direct influence of the mass media. You may also have found that the mass media provide the source of many of your ideas and opinions about the world.

If most of our opinions are based on knowledge obtained second-hand through the mass media, then this raises the important issue of the power of the mass media to influence our lives. Most people think and act in particular ways because of the opinions they hold and the knowledge they have, and many would agree that an 'informed' opinion – based on evidence – is the best opinion. However, do the mass media inform us about everything, and do they stress certain things in more favourable ways than others? Do they give false impressions of what is happening in society? The main mass media are privately owned and controlled, and run to make a profit. What effects does this pattern of ownership and control have on the content of the media? Does it create bias in them? What are the implications of this in a democracy? These are the sorts of questions which have interested sociologists and which will be explored in this chapter.

FORMAL CONTROLS ON THE MEDIA

Although the mass media in Britain are formally free to report whatever they like, and the government has no power in normal times to stop the spreading of any opinions through censorship, there are some formal limits to this freedom.

The Law

The law restricts the media's freedom to report anything they choose in any way they like. The principal legal limits to the media's freedom are shown in the box below.

Legal limits to the media's freedom

- *The laws of libel* forbid the publication of an untrue statement about a person which might bring him or her into contempt, ridicule, dislike, or hostility in society.
- *The Official Secrets Acts* make it a criminal offence to report without authorization any official government activity which the government defines as an official secret. These are extremely wide-ranging Acts, which are meant to protect the 'public interest'. However, many people argue they are often used to protect the political interests of governments.
- *Defence or 'D' notices* are issued by the government as requests to journalists not to report certain news items which the government believes to be 'against the national interest'. These usually concern military secrets and other information which might be useful to an 'enemy'.
- *The Race Relations Act* forbids the expression of opinions which will encourage hatred or discrimination against people because of their race.
- *The Obscene Publications Act* forbids the printing of anything that the high court considers to be obscene and indecent, and likely to 'deprave and corrupt' the public.
- *Contempt of Court* provision forbids the reporting and expression of opinions about cases which are in the process of being dealt with in a court of law. This is to prevent the jury forming opinions about a case from what they see or hear in the mass media, before they have heard the evidence for themselves.

The Government and the State

The government and the state have a number of direct and indirect controls over the mass media, particularly television and radio.

The BBC

The BBC is largely a state-owned body, which is controlled by a board of governors whose members are appointed by the home secretary. The BBC is financed by the state through the television licence fee, plus income from a series of private spin-off companies (like BBC Resources), which top up the licence fee income with substantial profits. The state can therefore have some control over the BBC by refusing to raise the licence fee. Although the BBC is not a private business run solely to make a profit like the independent commercial broadcasting services (independent TV and radio), and is not dependent on advertising for its income, it still has to compete with commercial broadcasting by attracting audiences large enough to justify the licence fee.

Independent broadcasting

Independent broadcasting includes all the non-BBC television and radio stations. These are controlled by a series of regulatory bodies whose members are appointed by the home secretary. These bodies include the Independent Television Commission, the Radio Authority, and the Broadcasting Standards Commission. These organizations are concerned with licensing the companies which can operate in the private sector, and between them they are responsible for the amount, quality, and standard of advertising and programmes on independent television and radio, and deal with any complaints.

The Press Complaints Commission

The Press Complaints Commission is a voluntary body appointed by the newspaper industry itself to maintain certain standards of newspaper journalism. It deals with public complaints against newspapers, but it has no real power to enforce effective sanctions as a result of these complaints.

OWNERSHIP OF THE MASS MEDIA

The mass media are very big business. The ownership of the main mass media in modern Britain is concentrated in the hands of a few large companies, which are interested in making profits. This concentration of ownership is shown in table 9.1.

Of the total circulation of national daily and Sunday newspapers, 87 per cent is controlled by just four companies, and over 60 per cent by two companies (News International and the Mirror Group). One individual, Rupert Murdoch of News International, owns the *Sun* and *The Times*, newspapers which make up about 35 per cent of all national daily news-

Table 9.1 Who owns what: national newspaper group ownership and interests in publishing, television, and radio, 1997

Company	British national daily newspaper sales % (1997)	National newspapers	Also owns	Share of British national voice[a] % (1996)
News International	35	*Sun, The Times, News of the World, Sunday Times*	40% of BSkyB; *HarperCollins* book publishers	10.6
Mirror Group	18	*Daily Mirror, Sunday Mirror, Daily Record, People*	43% of the *Independent* and *Independent on Sunday*; Live Television; Wire Television; 40% of Scottish Television	7.6
United News and Media	14	*Daily Express, Sunday Express, Daily Star*	Over 80 local newspapers; Miller Freeman Magazines; holdings in Channel 5 TV	6.9
Daily Mail and General Trust	16	*Daily Mail, Mail on Sunday*	Second-largest regional newspaper owners; holdings in Teletext, local radio and Reuters; 20% of ITN; 20% of West Country TV	7.8
The Telegraph	9	*Daily Telegraph, Sunday Telegraph*		1.9
Guardian Media Group	3	*Guardian, Observer*	Over 50 local papers; 15% of GMTV	2.0
Pearson	2	*Financial Times*	Longman book publishers; Future Publishing magazines; Thames Television; 25% of Channel 5 TV	0.6
Seven companies	97			37.4

[a] Combines audience and readership statistics for national and local press (except magazines), TV, and radio.
Source: Data from Audit Bureau of Circulation; *The 1997 Media Guide* (Guardian News Service ar d Steve Peak)

Rupert Murdoch of News Corporation is now the world's most powerful media owner, with substantial interests in TV, satellite broadcasting, film, and newspaper, magazine, and book publishing across the world

paper sales in Britain. Rupert Murdoch alone accounted for about 37 per cent of the total daily and Sunday newspaper sales in 1997. As table 9.1 shows, this concentration extends also to TV, radio, and book and magazine publishing. The details of who owns what are continually changing, but in 1997 Rupert Murdoch, for example, also owned 40 per cent of BSkyB and all of HarperCollins, the world's largest English-language book publishers. The same few companies therefore control a wide range of different media, and therefore a large proportion of what we see and hear in the media. This concentration of ownership gives a lot of power to business people who are neither elected nor accountable to the public.

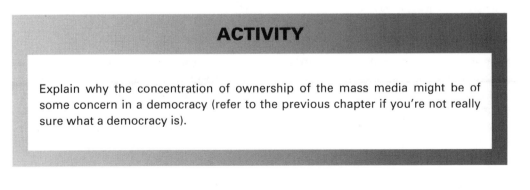

ACTIVITY

Explain why the concentration of ownership of the mass media might be of some concern in a democracy (refer to the previous chapter if you're not really sure what a democracy is).

Newspaper readership and social class

There are noticeable social class differences in newspaper readership, as shown in table 9.2.

Table 9.2 Reading of national daily and Sunday newspapers by social class: January to December 1996

Percentage of adults in each social class reading each paper in 1996

	A	B	C1	C2	D	E
Daily newspapers:						
Sun	6	9	18	30	34	26
Daily Mirror	3	7	12	19	20	13
Daily Mail	16	15	15	9	7	5
Daily Express	8	7	8	6	4	3
Daily Telegraph	21	13	6	2	2	1
Daily Star	1	2	3	7	8	4
The Times	18	10	4	1	1	1
Guardian	7	7	3	1	1	1
Independent	6	4	2	1	1	*
Financial Times	8	4	1	*	*	*
Sunday newspapers:						
News of the World	8	12	22	34	37	30
Sunday Mirror	4	8	14	21	22	14
Mail on Sunday	21	19	18	11	8	5
People	3	5	11	15	16	12
Sunday Times	30	19	9	4	3	2
Express on Sunday	11	9	9	7	4	3
Sunday Telegraph	17	9	5	2	2	1
Observer	6	7	3	1	1	1
Independent on Sunday	7	5	2	1	1	1

* Less than 1 per cent
Source: National Readership Surveys Ltd

Newspapers can be separated into three main groups: the 'quality' newspapers, the 'middle-brow' newspapers, and the mass-circulation 'popular' newspapers, also called the tabloid press. The middle class are far more likely to read the 'quality' newspapers and the manual working class make up the main readership of the 'popular' newspapers, particularly the *Sun, Daily Mirror,* and *Daily Star.* The *Daily Express* and *Daily Mail* are aimed primarily at the 'middle-brow' middle class, but have readers drawn from the whole social spectrum.

'Quality' newspapers

The 'quality' newspapers are large in size and serious in tone and content. They are concerned with news and features about politics, economic and financial problems, sport, literature, and the arts, and give in-depth, analytical coverage in longer articles and news stories. The main 'quality' national daily newspapers in Britain are *The Times*, the *Guardian*, the *Daily Telegraph*, the *Independent*, and the *Financial Times*.

'Middle-brow' newspapers

These fall between the 'quality' and the 'popular' newspapers, and include features of each. While they tend to have a more serious tone and content than the 'popular' press, they also cover a range of the more colourful issues found in the 'popular' papers and are also of the tabloid type (small in page size). The *Daily Mail* and the *Daily Express* are the main 'middle-brow' papers.

Daily Express

Daily Mail

'Popular' newspapers

In contrast to the 'quality' newspapers, 'popular' newspapers are of the tabloid type, and are generally referred to as the tabloid press. Although they carry 'news', they are much more likely to concentrate on the sensational aspects of the news, 'human interest' stories, such as scandals and celebrities, entertainment, sport, and other 'light' topics, written in very simple language combined with large headlines and many colour photographs. The 'popular' national daily newspapers in Britain are the *Daily Mirror*, the *Sun*, and the *Daily Star*.

ACTIVITY

Study table 9.2 on p. 186 and answer the following questions:

1 What percentage of social class C2 read the *Sun* in 1996?
2 Which daily newspaper was most widely read by those in class A?
3 Which two daily newspapers were most widely read by the working class?
4 What was the difference in the percentages of those in social classes A and E who read the *Guardian*?
5 Which Sunday newspaper was most widely read by those in social class E?
6 Which Sunday newspaper was the least read by nearly all social classes?
7 Compare one 'quality' and one 'popular' newspaper for the same day. Study the kinds of stories, advertisements, photographs and cartoons, and the language they use. List all the differences between them. In the light of your findings, suggest explanations for the different social classes of their readerships.

ACTIVITY

Study table 9.3 and answer the following questions:

1 Which of the mass media did newspaper readers use as their main source of news?
2 What percentage of newspaper readers used newspapers as their main source of news?
3 What percentage of newspaper readers saw television as the most believable source of news?
4 What percentage of newspaper readers saw newspapers as a more believable source of news than television?
5 Which medium did newspaper readers see as providing (a) the most truthful account of events and (b) the least truthful account of events?
6 Suggest reasons why most newspaper readers don't use newspapers as their main source of news and see them as less believable than television.
7 Do a small survey in your group based on the areas covered in table 9.3, and discuss the reasons why people see some of the media as more truthful than others.

Table 9.3 Newspaper readers' sources of news, and how far they believe
them

Main source of news	
Television	59%
Newspapers	30%
Radio	15%

Most believable source of news	
Television	57%
Newspapers	15%
Radio	15%

'The reporting is exactly or approximately in line with what really happened'	
Television	85%
Newspapers	48%
Radio	79%

'The reporting is undoubtedly different from what happened or bears no relation to the event'	
Television	13%
Newspapers	44%
Radio	12%

Sources: Adapted from *British Social Attitudes Survey* and *Sofres* for Télérama/La Croix

THE MASS MEDIA, PUBLIC OPINION, AND SOCIAL CONTROL

The mass media play a key role in providing the ideas and images which people use to interpret and understand much of their everyday experience, and they actively shape people's ideas, attitudes, and actions. The mass media therefore have an important role in forming public opinion. The pressure of public opinion can be a significant source of social control, in so far as most people prefer to have their behaviour approved of by others rather than feel isolated and condemned by them.

The survey results in table 9.3 show that most people do use and believe the mass media, particularly television, as their main source of news. However, their reliance on such sources may be misguided. This is because the mass media don't simply show 'the facts' on which people can then form opinions. They select facts and put an interpretation on them, frequently stressing the more conservative values of society. The mass media can then be said to act as an agency of social control. They carry this out in two main ways: agenda-setting and gate-keeping, and norm-setting.

Agenda-Setting and Gate-Keeping

Agenda-setting is the idea that the media have an important influence over the issues that people think about because the agenda, or list of subjects, for public discussion is laid down by the mass media.

Obviously, people can only discuss and form opinions about things they have been informed about, and it is the mass media which provide this information in most cases. This gives those who own, control, and work in the mass media a great deal of power in society, for what they choose to include in or leave out of their newspapers and television programmes will influence the main topics of public discussion and public concern. This may mean that some subjects are never discussed by the public because they are not informed about them.

The media's refusal to cover some issues is called **gate-keeping**. Such issues are frequently those potentially most damaging to the values and interests of the upper class. For example, strikes are widely reported (nearly always unfavourably), while industrial injuries and diseases, which lead to a much greater loss of working hours (and life), hardly ever get reported. This means that there is more public concern with tightening up trade union laws to stop strikes than there is with improving health

ACTIVITY

1 Study the main newspaper headlines or major television or radio news stories for a week. Draw up a list of the key stories, perhaps under the headings of 'popular newspapers', 'quality newspapers', 'BBC TV news', 'ITN news', and 'radio news' (this is easiest to do if a group of people divide up the work).

2 Compare your lists, and see if there is any evidence of agreement on the 'agenda' of news items for that week. If there are differences between the lists (check particularly the newspapers), suggest explanations for them.

and safety laws. Similarly, crime committed by black people gets widely covered in the media, but little attention is paid to attacks on black people by white racists. This tends to reinforce people's racial prejudices. A final example is the way welfare benefit 'fiddles' are widely reported, but not tax evasion, with the result that there are calls for tightening up benefit claim procedures, rather than strengthening agencies concerned with chasing tax evaders.

Norm-Setting

Norm-setting means the mass media emphasize and reinforce conformity to social norms, and seek to isolate those who do not conform by making them the victims of unfavourable public opinion. This is achieved in two main ways:

- Encouraging conformist behaviour, such as not going on strike, obeying the law, being brave, helping people, and so on. Advertising, for example, reinforces the gender role stereotypes of men and women.
- Discouraging non-conformist behaviour. The mass media often give extensive and sensational treatment to stories about murder and other crimes of violence, riots, social security 'fiddles', football 'hooliganism', homosexuality, and so on. Such stories, by emphasizing the serious consequences which follow for those who break social norms, are giving 'lessons' in how people are expected *not* to behave. For example, the early treatment of AIDS in the mass media nearly always suggested it was a disease that only gay men could catch. This was presented as a warning to those who strayed from the paths of monogamy and heterosexuality – both core values of British society.

Stan Cohen illustrates this idea of norm-setting very well in the following passage:

A large amount of space in newspapers, magazines and television and a large amount of time in daily conversation are devoted to reporting and discussing behaviour which sociologists call deviant: behaviour which somehow departs from what a group expects to be done or what it considers the desirable way of doing things. We read of murders and drug-taking, vicars eloping with members of their congregation and film stars announcing the birth of their illegitimate children, football trains being wrecked and children being stolen from their prams, drunken drivers being breathalysed and account- ants fiddling the books. Sometimes the stories are tragic and arouse anger, disgust or horror; sometimes they are merely absurd. What- ever the emotions, the stories are always to be found, and, indeed, so much space in the mass media is given to deviance that some sociologists have argued that this interest functions to reassure society that the boundary lines between conformist and deviant, good and bad, healthy and sick, are still valid ones. The value of the boundary line must continually be reasserted: we can only know what it is to be saintly by being told just what the shape of the devil is. The rogues, feckless fools and villains are presented to us as if they were playing parts in some gigantic morality play. (Stanley Cohen, ed., *Images of Deviance* (Penguin 1982), introduction)

ACTIVITY

1 How is deviance defined in the passage above by Stanley Cohen?
2 What does the passage suggest is one of the functions of the mass media's interest in deviance?
3 Give examples from the passage of (a) two types of deviant behaviour which are not regarded as criminal in modern Britain, and (b) two types of deviant behaviour which are regarded as criminal in modern Britain.
4 Think of one example of deviance which is currently receiving a lot of attention in the mass media and is of major public concern. Explain how this might be reasserting the value of the 'boundary line' between conformist and deviant behaviour.
5 Look at a range of newspapers and try to find examples of norm-setting headlines and stories. Explain in each case what types of behaviour are being encouraged or discouraged.

WHAT AFFECTS THE CONTENT OF THE MEDIA?

The mass media obviously cannot report all events and issues happening in the world. Of all the happenings that occur in the world every day, how is 'news' selected? Who decides which of these events is 'newsworthy'? The 'news', like any other product for sale, is a manufactured product. What factors affect the production and 'packaging' of this product? What decides the content of the mass media?

The Owners

Sometimes the private owners of the mass media will impose their own views on their editors. However, even when the owners don't directly impose their own views, it is unlikely that those who work for them will produce stories which actively oppose their owners' prejudices and interests, if they want to keep their jobs! The political leanings of the owners and editors are overwhelmingly conservative.

Making a Profit

The mass media are predominantly run by large business corporations with the aim of making money, and the source of much of this profit is advertising, particularly in newspapers and commercial television. It is this dependence on advertising which explains why so much concern is expressed about 'ratings' for television programmes, the circulation figures of newspapers, and the social class of their readers. Advertisers will usually advertise only if they know that there is a large audience for their advertisements, or, if the audience is small, that it is well off and likely to buy their products or services.

That newspapers are very concerned about selling advertising is shown by their commissioning of readership surveys. Such statistics as those shown in Figure 9.1 are important to newspapers because they help them to sell highly profitable advertising aimed at well-off business and professional people.

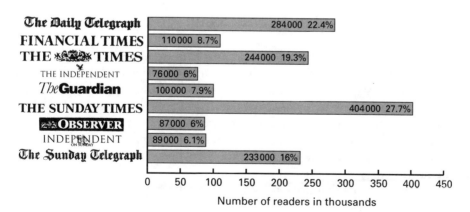

Figure 9.1 Quality newspapers read by business and professional people. The percentages in the bars are the percentage share of all newspapers (national daily, or Sunday, as appropriate) read by social class A

193

Advertising and media content

The importance of advertising affects the content of the media in the following ways:

- Audiences or readers must be attracted. If they are not, then circulation figures or TV ratings will fall, advertisers will not advertise, and the particular channel or newspaper may go out of business. The *Sunday Correspondent*, *Today*, *News on Sunday*, and the *London Daily News* are all newspapers which have collapsed in recent years for this reason. This means that what becomes 'news' is partly a result of commercial pressures to attract audiences by selecting and presenting the more colourful and 'interesting' events in society.
- In order to attract the widest possible audience or readership, it becomes important to appeal to everyone and offend no one. This leads to a conservatism in the media, which tries to avoid too much criticism of the way society is organized in case it offends the readers or advertisers. This may mean that minority or unpopular points of view go unrepresented in the mass media.
- It may lead to a distortion of the 'news' by concentrating on sensational stories, conflict, gossip, and scandal, which are more likely to attract a mass audience than more serious issues are. Alternatively, for those media which aim at a 'select' readership from the upper- and upper-middle classes, it is important that the news stories chosen should generally be treated in a conservative way, so as not to offend an audience which has little to gain (and everything to lose!) by changes in the existing arrangements in society.

News Values and 'Newsworthiness'

Journalists obviously play an important role in deciding the content of the mass media, as it is journalists who basically select what 'the news' is and decide on its style of presentation. News doesn't just happen, but is made by journalists. Research has shown that journalists operate with values and assumptions about which events are 'newsworthy' – these assumptions are called **news values**. These guide journalists in deciding what to report and what to leave out, and how what they choose to report should be presented.

Issues or events that are newsworthy include:

- Issues that are easily understood.
- Events that occur quickly or unexpectedly, such as disasters.
- Events that involve drama, conflict, excitement, and action.

- Events that are in some way out of the ordinary.
- Events that have some human drama or interest to them, such as the activities of famous personalities, scandal, or armed sieges.
- Events that are considered important – events in Britain are generally considered more important than those happening in the rest of the world, and national events are generally considered more important than local ones.
- Stories which it is assumed will be of interest to the newspaper's readership or TV audience – giving the readers what they want! This is of great importance if the audience or readership is to continue to be attracted and viewing figures kept up or papers sold.

Photo: Ted Fussey

The sudden death in a car accident of Diana, Princess of Wales, on 31 August 1997 was perhaps the most newsworthy story ever. For many days, Princess Diana's death dominated national and international newspaper and TV headlines. The mass media, including the Internet, plunged into an unprecedented competitive frenzy of Diana stories, covering every conceivable aspect of her life and the circumstances of her death. Newspaper sales increased by up to 50 per cent, and the funeral, six days later, broke all television viewing records. More than 31 million watched the funeral on television in Britain – three-quarters of the adult population – and an estimated one billion around the world, making it the biggest single televised event in history.

The idea of news values means that journalists tend to play up those elements of a story which make it more newsworthy, and the stories that are most likely to be reported are those which include many newsworthy aspects.

These features affecting the content of the media suggest that the mass media present, at best, only a partial view of the world.

ACTIVITY

1 Why do you think the story in the cartoon opposite might be 'newsworthy'?
2 Take any current major news story which is receiving wide coverage in the mass media. List the features of this story which make it 'newsworthy'.
3 Study one 'quality' and one 'popular' newspaper of the same day and compare their coverage of this story. For example, do they sensationalize it and present new 'angles'? What evidence is there, if any, that the news values of the 'popular' press differ from those of the 'quality' press? Give examples to back up your answer.
4 Imagine you wanted to run a campaign to prevent a new road being built in your neighbourhood (or choose any issue that interests you). In the light of your expert knowledge about news values, suggest activities you might undertake to achieve media coverage of your campaign, and explain why they might be considered newsworthy.

STEREOTYPING, SCAPEGOATING, AND THE MEDIA

Stereotyping of different social groups is a common feature of media coverage of events. Chapter 5 on gender role socialization considered the way that gender stereotypes are formed and reinforced throughout the whole range of the mass media. Two other groups which are frequently victims of media stereotyping are young people and black people. These two groups are also often used as **scapegoats** for many of society's problems. Scapegoats are simply groups or individuals blamed for something which is not their fault.

News values

Stereotyping and Scapegoating of the Young

The mass media often create a stereotype of all young people as trouble-makers, layabouts, and vandals, by exaggerating the occasional deviant behaviour of a few young people, such as 'lager louts', out of proportion to its real significance in society. The mass media provide for many people the only source of information about events, and therefore distort people's attitudes and give a misleading impression of young people as a whole. Old people, who tend to be more home-based, are particularly vulnerable to such stereotypes, as their impressions are formed very strongly by the media.

Folk devils and moral panics

In his book on the mods and rockers of the 1960s, *Folk Devils and Moral Panics*, Stan Cohen suggests that mass media stereotypes of young people, particularly where unusual or exceptional behaviour is involved, provide exciting stories and sensational headlines, and help to sell newspapers. He argues that young people have been used as a scapegoat to create a sense of unity in society, by uniting the public against a common 'enemy'. Young people are relatively powerless, and an easily identifiable group to blame for all of society's ills. Some young people who get involved in relatively trivial deviant or delinquent actions or groups, such as hooliganism,

197

'A pit bull terrier? No, they've cornered a social worker!'

Folk devils of 1991
Source: Reproduced by permission of *Punch*

vandalism, or soft drug abuse, are labelled in the media as **folk devils** or groups posing a threat to society. (**Labelling** is defining a person or group in a certain way – as a particular 'type' of person.) This causes a **moral panic** in society – an over-reaction suggesting that society itself is under threat. Editors, politicians, churchpeople, police, magistrates, and social workers then 'pull together' to overcome this imagined threat to society. The folk devils become visible reminders of what we should not be. In this view, young people play much the same role as witches in the past – an easy scapegoat to blame for all of society's problems. As a result of these moral panics, all young people may then get labelled and stereotyped as potentially troublesome or as a 'problem group'.

Stereotyping and Scapegoating of Black People

Black people are another social group which the mass media tend both to stereotype and to use as scapegoats. Black and Asian people make up only about 5 per cent of the population of Britain, yet frequently this small minority are presented in quite negative ways in the media, as if they were major causes of conflict and 'social problems' that otherwise wouldn't exist. These ethnic minorities often only appear in the media in the context of crime, drugs, and inner-city riots, as scapegoats on which to blame these problems. This creates, confirms, and reinforces public prejudices about black people among whites.

Degrading stereotypes of black people are still frequently found in books, films, and comics. Little is heard about their successes and achievements, their history and culture, or about the discrimination and deprivation they often face in housing, employment, and education. Attacks on black people by white racists rarely receive media coverage. Although these things are beginning to change, with more positive media coverage and television programmes aimed at black people, the media can still be said to produce negative stereotypes of black people and thereby reinforce the racism which is deeply entrenched in British society.

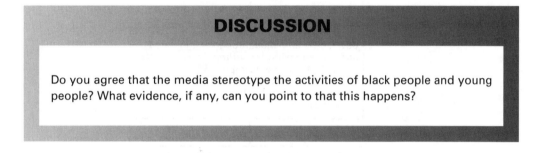

DISCUSSION

Do you agree that the media stereotype the activities of black people and young people? What evidence, if any, can you point to that this happens?

CRIME AND THE MEDIA

The mass media provide knowledge about crime and deviance for most people in society, including politicians, the police, social workers, and the public at large. The mass media tend to be very selective in their coverage of crime, exploiting the possibilities for a 'good story' by dramatizing, exaggerating, and sensationalizing some crimes out of all proportion to their actual extent in society. For example, attacks on old people and other crimes of violence – which are quite rare – are massively over-reported, giving a false and misleading impression of the real pattern and extent of such crimes. This process can create many unnecessary fears among people by suggesting that violence is a normal and common feature of everyday life. This is particularly likely in the case of the housebound elderly. A Home Office report in 1989 confirmed this view, arguing that TV programmes which stage reconstructions of unsolved crimes, such as the BBC's *Crimewatch UK*, exaggerate the level of dangerous crime and unnecessarily frighten viewers.

THE MEDIA, LABELLING, AND DEVIANCY AMPLIFICATION

As seen earlier in this chapter, the media's pursuit of 'good stories' means they often distort, exaggerate, and sensationalize the activities of some

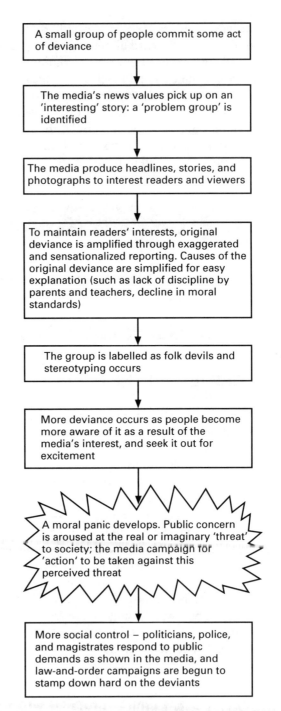

Figure 9.2 Deviancy amplification, moral panics, and the media

ACTIVITY

Study figure 9.2 and try to fill in each of the stages of any current moral panic in society.

groups. The media have the power to label and stereotype certain groups and activities as deviant, and present them as folk devils causing some imagined threat to society. Even if much of what is reported is untrue, this may be enough to whip up a moral panic – growing public anxiety and concern about the alleged deviance.

This can raise demands for action by the agencies of social control to stop it. Often these agencies, such as schools, social services, the police, and magistrates, will respond to the exaggerated threat presented in the media by taking harsher measures against the apparent 'trouble-makers'. Such action, particularly by the police, can often make what was a minor issue much worse, for example by causing more arrests, and amplify (or make worse) the original deviance. This is known as **deviancy amplification**. Groups which have fitted this pattern include mods and rockers in the 1960s and other youth sub-cultures, glue-sniffers, football 'hooligans', travellers on their way to Glastonbury or Stonehenge, and organizers of raves. Figure 9.2 illustrates the way the media can amplify deviance and generate a moral panic. Figure 9.3 shows a range of moral panics which have arisen in Britain since the 1950s.

BIAS IN THE MEDIA

Bias in the media is concerned with whether the media favour one point of view at the expense of others. Figure 9.4 summarizes a range of influences which can cause bias in the media. Many of these have been discussed elsewhere in this chapter.

Selection

The processes of agenda-setting, gate-keeping, and norm-setting mean some events are simply not reported and brought to public attention. Some of those that are reported may be singled out for particularly unfavourable treatment. In these ways, the mass media can decide what

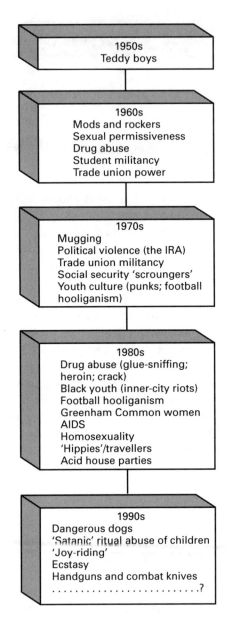

Figure 9.3 Folk devils and moral panics: Great Britain, 1950s–90s

the important issues are, what 'news' is, what the public should and should not be concerned about, and what should or should not be regarded as 'normal' behaviour in society.

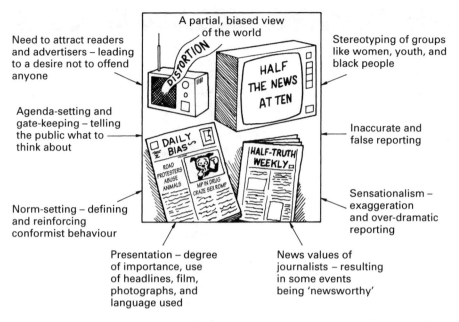

Figure 9.4 Sources of bias in the media

The Presentation of News

The way news items are presented may be important in influencing the way people are encouraged to view stories. For example, the physical position of a news story in a newspaper (front page or small inside column), the order of importance given to stories in TV news bulletins, the choice of headlines, and whether there is accompanying film or

Source: Socialist Worker

Mad Dogs and Englishmen

We have
Army, navy and air force
Reporting guidelines
Press briefings

We
Take out
Suppress
Eliminate
Neutralize
Decapitate
Dig in

We launch
First strikes
Pre-emptively

Our men are . . .
Boys
Lads

Our boys are . . .
Professional
Lion-hearts
Cautious
Confident
Heroes
Dare-devils
Young knights of the skies
Loyal
Desert rats
Resolute
Brave

Our boys are motivated by
An old-fashioned sense of duty

Our boys
Fly into the jaws of hell

Our ships are . . .
An armada

Israeli non-retaliation is
An act of great statesmanship

The Belgians are . . .
Yellow

Our missiles are . . .
Like Luke Skywalker zapping Darth Vader

Our missiles cause . . .
Collateral damage

We . . .
Precision bomb

Our PoWs are . . .
Gallant boys

George Bush is . . .
At peace with himself
Resolute
Statesmanlike
Assured

Our planes . . .
Suffer a high rate of attrition
Fail to return from missions

They have
A war machine
Censorship
Propaganda

They
Destroy
Destroy
Kill
Kill
Kill
Cower in their foxholes

They launch
Sneak missile attacks
Without provocation

Their men are . . .
Troops
Hordes

Theirs are . . .
Brainwashed
Paper tigers
Cowardly
Desperate
Cornered
Cannon fodder
Bastards of Baghdad
Blindly obedient
Mad dogs
Ruthless
Fanatical

Their boys are motivated by
Fear of Saddam

Their boys
Cower in concrete bunkers

Iraqi ships are . . .
A navy

Iraqi non-retaliation is
Blundering/Cowardly

The Belgians are also . . .
Two-faced

Their missiles are . . .
Ageing duds (*rhymes with Scuds*)

Their missiles cause . . .
Civilian casualties

They . . .
Fire wildly at anything in the sky

Their PoWs are . . .
Overgrown schoolchildren

Saddam Hussein is . . .
Demented
Defiant
An evil tyrant
A crackpot monster

Their planes . . .
Are shot out of the sky
Are zapped

Figure 9.5 Mad dogs and Englishmen
Source: Guardian (23 January 1991)

photographs will all influence the attention given to particular items. A story may be treated sensationally, and it may even be considered of such importance as to justify a TV or radio 'newsflash'. Where film is used, the pictures shown are always selected from the total footage shot, and may not accurately reflect the event. The actual images used in news films may themselves have a hidden bias. For example, in the reporting of industrial disputes, employers are often filmed in the peace and quiet of their offices, while workers are seen shouting on the picket lines or trying to be interviewed against a background of traffic noise. This gives the impression that employers are more calm and reasonable people and have a better case than the workers.

The media can also create false or biased impressions by the sort of language used in news reporting. This bias in the use of language in newspaper reporting is shown in figure 9.5. This shows a number of expressions that were used by the British press during the first week of the Gulf War against Iraq in January 1991.

ACTIVITY

In figure 9.5, 'we' refers to the American, British, and other allied forces; 'they' refers to the Iraqis with whom 'we' were at war.

1 Explain with particular examples how the language used to describe Iraq differs from the language used to describe the allied forces. What general impression is given of the Iraqis?
2 Try to think of examples of other sorts of language used in newspaper stories and headlines which might give a distorted or biased impression – for example, football fans being described as 'animals'.

Inaccurate and False Reporting

Other sources of bias lie in inaccurate reporting, because important details of a story may be incorrect. Politicians are always complaining that they have been inaccurately quoted in the press. False reporting, through either completely making up stories or inventing a few details, and the media's tendency to dramatize events out of all proportion to their actual significance in society, typical of much reporting of the royal family, are devices used to make a story 'more interesting' and sell newspapers – this is particularly common in the mass circulation tabloid press. Such methods mean the media can be accused of manipulating their audiences.

THE MASS MEDIA AND DEMOCRACY

Much of this chapter has suggested that the mass media act as a conservative influence in society, and give only a biased view of the world. However, some argue that the wealth of information provided by the mass media encourages and promotes a variety of opinions, and this enables the population to be informed on a wide range of issues, which is essential in a democratic society. It is perhaps useful to examine briefly some of the competing views on this aspect of the role of the mass media in modern Britain.

The media promote democracy

- Because the media in Britain are not controlled by the state, the risk of censorship by governments is reduced, and free speech is protected. Journalists are free to report and comment – within legal limits.

- The wide variety of privately owned media means a range of opinions are considered and public debates take place. By criticizing the actions of governments, the mass media can play an important 'watch-dog' role, and keep governments in touch with public opinion.

- The media give an unbiased account of news. TV news has to be impartial.

- The media accurately reflect public opinions that already exist in society rather than creating new ones. People wouldn't

The media restrict democracy

- The media (particularly newspapers) reflect the conservative views of their wealthy owners. While journalists are often critical and expose wrongdoing, they will frequently avoid issues which might cost them their jobs by upsetting newspaper owners.

- The variety of opinion presented is limited. Working-class political views, for example of strikes, are rarely reported. The ideas and actions of the least powerful groups are the most likely to be excluded. Those who in some way present a challenge or threat to the status quo – the existing way society is organized – are presented as irresponsible or unreasonable extremists.

- News values, agenda-setting, norm-setting, and other sources of bias mean only some issues are covered, and these are not presented in neutral ways. The media choose what to report and how to report it, and therefore provide a biased view of the world.

- The media do not simply reflect public opinion, but actively form and manipulate it. People can only form opinions on the basis

The media promote democracy

read newspapers or watch TV unless they were providing what their audiences wanted.

- Anyone can put his or her views across, by setting up a newspaper, distributing leaflets, and other means of communicating ideas.

The media restrict democracy

of the knowledge they have, and the media are primarily responsible for providing this knowledge. The owners of the mass media hold overwhelmingly conservative views, and their ownership gives them the power to defend their position by forming favourable public opinion.

- Only the rich have the resources necessary to publish and distribute a newspaper on a large scale, or to set up a television or radio station. The concentration of ownership of the mass media is a threat to democracy, as a small powerful group of media owners can control access to ideas, information, and knowledge. Those who wish to put forward alternative views to that presented in the mass media may not be allowed access to the media by their owners, and will therefore be denied any real opportunity to persuade public opinion of their ideas.

DISCUSSION

'That the mass media in Britain are owned by a small group of individuals who control the spread of ideas and information, and who are not elected or answerable to the public, means people's opinions are manipulated by a small minority. Far from promoting democracy, the mass media in Britain are a major threat to it.' Discuss this statement with others in your group.

INTO THE FUTURE

This chapter has examined only a very limited range of the mass media, but there is a dramatic communications explosion occurring as we enter the new millennium. Digital broadcasting will potentially lead to hundreds of cable and satellite television channels. In 1997, British Digital Broadcasting was licensed to launch more than fifteen new terrestrial (land-based) TV channels, and BSkyB was then planning to launch over two hundred digital satellite channels in 1998. Viewers may be able to receive thirty more digital terrestrial channels by the year 2000.

Already, the media have become a gigantic international business, with instant news from every part of the globe. International marketing of TV programmes and films to international audiences is backed by huge investments. The Internet has millions more people going 'on line' every year. TV and radio cards and modems for personal computers mean that computers are quite likely to replace televisions in our homes, with instant access to colossal amounts of information and entertainment from the entire globe. In 1997, technology was developing which will enable the Internet to be delivered to homes using the electricity mains. This will enable electricity companies to offer cheap Internet services to their customers at speeds thirty times greater than those presently available through modems attached to telephone lines. Newspaper sales have been steadily declining, and may well continue to do so, as more and more news services (and newspapers) appear in electronic form on the Internet.

The speed of technological change is now so great that the world is said to be rapidly becoming a 'global village'. This means that the whole world has become like one small village, with everyone (at least those who are affluent enough!) exposed to the same information and messages through mass media which cut across all national frontiers. It remains to be seen how the media will develop in the twenty-first century, but it seems likely there will be an enormous increase in the power of the already-powerful media companies.

DISCUSSION

How do you think the mass media will develop over the next century? Do you welcome or worry about the changes that might lie ahead, such as a huge increase in the number of TV channels? How do you think these changes might affect our daily lives?

CHAPTER SUMMARY

After studying this chapter, you should be able to:

- Explain what is meant by the term 'mass media'.
- Describe briefly the ways the law and the government might exercise control over the mass media.
- Describe the concentration of ownership of the mass media and explain why this might be of some concern in a democracy.
- Describe the differences between the 'quality' and the 'popular' newspapers, and their relationship to different social classes.
- Explain a variety of ways in which the mass media might form public opinion and exercise social control.
- Explain the terms 'agenda-setting', 'gate-keeping', and 'norm-setting'.
- Explain a range of factors influencing the content of the mass media.
- Explain, with examples, what is meant by 'news values'.
- Discuss, with examples, the role of the mass media in stereotyping and scapegoating.
- Explain how the mass media might give false impressions of crime.
- Explain how the mass media might amplify deviance.
- Explain a variety of ways in which bias may occur in the media.
- Explain the competing views of the role of the mass media in a democracy.

KEY TERMS

agenda-setting	moral panic
deviancy amplification	news values
folk devils	norm-setting
gate-keeping	scapegoats
labelling	

PROJECT SUGGESTIONS

1 Video BBC and ITV news bulletins for a week, or study 'popular' and 'quality' newspapers for a week, and compare their coverage of different events. What evidence is there of agenda-setting?
2 Study some of the 'popular' and 'quality' newspapers for a week and discuss the differences between them, for example by measuring the column inches given to different categories of news, advertising, TV, and photographs.

3 Carry out a study of newspapers, advertisements, or children's comics, looking at the presentation of ethnic minorities or women.

4 Carry out a survey to find out which of the mass media people see as most reliable in presenting the news. The questionnaire in chapter 18 could be used as a starting point. You could compare your results with those given in table 9.3 earlier in this chapter.

5 Compare two 'quality' and two 'popular' national Sunday or daily newspapers for the same days. Carefully analyse the headlines, types of story, photographs, and cartoons they contain. On the basis of this evidence, draw up a list of the news values you think each newspaper uses to decide which stories to include and which to exclude.

6 Interview the editor and other journalists on a local newspaper to find out how they decide what to print and what not to, what makes a story 'newsworthy', how far they think they exaggerate stories, and so on.

SOCIAL CONTROL, DEVIANCE, AND CRIME

10

In order for people to know how to behave in society, to be able to predict how others will behave, and therefore to live together in some orderly way, some shared values and norms are necessary. Without some measure of agreement on the basic ground rules, social life would soon fall into confusion and disorder. For example, imagine the chaos on the British roads if drivers stopped following the rules about driving on the left-hand side of the road, or stopping at red traffic lights.

Norms and values are learnt through socialization, but knowing what the norms are does not necessarily mean people will follow them. Social control is concerned with the various methods used to make sure people continue to obey those social values and norms which have been learnt through socialization. This is achieved by various positive and negative sanctions – rewards and punishments.

Together, socialization and social control help to maintain social conformity – conforming to social values and norms. Deviance is the term given to behaviour which is in some way socially unacceptable or not approved of – non-conformist behaviour.

ACTIVITY

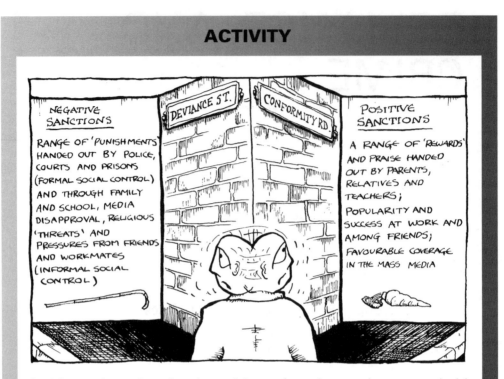

Social control: people make rules and then enforce them on the carrot-and-stick principle

Look at the cartoon above.

1 Explain in your own words the point the cartoon is illustrating.
2 List six possible consequences that might face a person who followed a deviant path as an adult.
3 Suggest four reasons why a person might fail to conform to social norms.
4 Identify and explain two ways in which not conforming to social norms might lead to success in society.
5 Much deviance is disapproved of to some extent, but can you think of forms of deviance in any society which might be welcomed by the majority of the public as opening the way for society to change and improve?

AGENCIES OF SOCIAL CONTROL

Social control is carried out through a series of agencies of social control, many of which are discussed in fuller detail in other parts of this book, but it is useful to summarize them here.

Formal social control
Photo: Ted Fussey

Formal Social Control

Formal social control is that which is carried out by an agency specifically set up to ensure that people conform to a particular set of norms, particularly the law. The police, courts, prisons, and sometimes the army, as in Northern Ireland, force people to obey the law through formal sanctions such as arresting, fining, or imprisoning those who break society's laws.

Informal Social Control

The following agencies carry out social control in an informal way. This means their primary purpose is not social control, but they play an important role in it none the less.

The family

This is where primary socialization takes place and children first learn about the basic values and norms of society. For example, children learn the difference between right and wrong, 'good' and 'bad' behaviour, norms governing gender roles, and acceptance of parental authority.

Children may become embarrassed or develop a guilty conscience if they break these rules. The approval or disapproval of parents can itself be an important element in encouraging children to conform, along with other sanctions such as praise and rewards, threats, teasing, and physical violence.

The school

This socializes pupils and sets standards of 'correct' behaviour, the forms of dress and so on which are expected by society. This is achieved by sanctions such as detentions, suspensions, expulsions, merit points, and other aspects of the hidden curriculum (see chapter 12 for a discussion of this). Through the actions of teachers and the way the school is organized, for example through streaming and examinations, pupils are encouraged to accept norms like the competitiveness, the gender roles, the ranking of people with unequal pay and status, and the inequalities in power and authority to which they are expected to conform in the wider society. In this way, the school helps to maintain the way society as a whole is presently organized, such as the inequalities between men and women and between managers and workers.

The peer group

The peer group is a very important group in providing an individual's view of herself or himself, and the desire for approval and acceptance by peers is itself an important source of social control. The fear of rejection and ridicule by peers may exert an enormous influence on an individual's behaviour. Such pressure may promote conformity to the wider norms of society, such as acceptance of traditional gender roles. However, conformity to the peer group may also promote deviance. This is particularly likely among young people, where peer pressure may encourage them to adopt forms of deviant behaviour, such as playing truant from school or under-age drinking.

The workplace

At work, there are frequently strong pressures from fellow workers to conform to work-related norms, and an individual who is labelled as a trouble-maker or uncooperative may find herself or himself denied promotion opportunities, allocated unpleasant jobs, or even dismissed. Fellow workers may use such negative sanctions as refusing to talk to or mix with workmates, ridiculing them, or playing practical jokes on those who fail to conform to their norms.

ACTIVITY

1 Give examples of six norms in each case to which you are generally expected to conform in *two* of the following: (a) at your school or college, (b) in your peer group, (c) at work.
2 Explain in each case how these norms are enforced, and outline the sanctions applied if you fail to conform to them.

The mass media

These are a major source of information and ideas, and can have powerful influences on people's attitudes, opinions, and behaviour. As discussed in chapter 9, the mass media carry out social control through the processes of norm-setting and agenda-setting. These generally encourage conformist behaviour, such as conformity to gender roles, promoted through advertising, or monogamy, through the AIDS campaign. This is achieved through such devices as the selection and presentation of news items, advertising, sensationalism, stereotyping, and scapegoating. By reporting the serious consequences which follow for those who break society's norms, and telling people what they should be thinking about, norm-setting and agenda-setting are effectively carrying out social control.

Religion

Religion is a belief system which may influence people's ideas about 'right' and 'wrong' behaviour, and this in turn may affect their behaviour. For example, the Christian religion promises rewards (heaven) to those who conform to its teachings, and punishments (an eternity in hell) to those who do not. Religious beliefs and teachings often support and re-inforce the values and norms of society by giving them a 'sacred' quality. The Ten Commandments in Christianity – 'thou shalt not kill . . . steal . . . commit adultery', etc. – reinforce values such as respect for human life, private property, and monogamous marriage. Feelings of guilt (a guilty conscience) may result if religious rules are broken by believers – a sort of inner police officer controlling behaviour.

CRIME AND DEVIANCE

The difference between crime and deviance

Deviance is any non-conformist behaviour which is disapproved of by society or a social group, whether it is illegal or not. It is norm-breaking behaviour, and can range from being eccentric to criminal activity.

Crime is the term used to describe behaviour which is against the law – law-breaking.

Juvenile delinquency is crime committed by those between the ages of 10 and 17, though the term 'delinquency' is often used to describe any anti-social behaviour by young people, even if it isn't criminal.

The Difficulty of Defining Deviance

Crime is easy to define, as the law states what a criminal act is. However, while deviance appears to be easy to define as any non-conformist behaviour, it is, in fact, quite difficult to pin down what members of any society or group actually regard as deviant behaviour. Deviance covers a very wide range of behaviour, and what is regarded as deviant will depend on the norms of a group or society. These norms differ between societies and between groups within the same society, and they change over time. Whether or not an act is defined as deviant will therefore depend on the time, the place, the society, and the attitudes of those who view the act. The following examples illustrate how definitions of deviance can vary according to a range of circumstances.

Non-deviant crime?

Most people commit deviant and even illegal acts at some stage in their lives, and there are many illegal acts which most people don't regard as particularly deviant. For example, parking and speeding offences, under-age drinking, pinching office stationery, or making unauthorized personal calls on the office phone are all illegal but extremely common, so it is difficult to see them as deviant. Some offences, like under-age drinking, are often seen as expected behaviour, and those who don't commit the offence may even be seen as deviant by those around them.

Attitudes to smoking have changed

The time

Deviance can only be defined in relation to particular norms, and norms change over time. For example, cigarette smoking used to be a very popular and socially acceptable activity, but is increasingly becoming branded as deviant, and smokers are now unwelcome in many places. Attitudes to abortion and homosexuality have also changed dramatically. Homosexuality is no longer seen as being as deviant as it once was, and it is becoming far more accepted by many people, including members of parliament. Fashion, of course, is an obvious example of changing norms – people today would generally be regarded as deviant were they to wear the fashions of seventeenth-century England, or even those of a few years ago.

The society

Norms, and therefore definitions of deviance, differ between societies. For example, consumption of alcohol is often seen as deviant and illegal in many Islamic countries, but is seen as normal in Britain. Topless bathing on a Mediterranean beach is quite acceptable, but not so in a local park in England. Smoking cannabis is generally regarded as deviant by most people in modern Britain (but see the next paragraph), but is normal behaviour in many countries of the Middle East.

The social group

Norms can vary between social groups in the same society, and so what may be acceptable in a particular group may be regarded as deviant in the wider society. For example, smoking cannabis is perfectly acceptable behaviour among Rastafarians in Britain, and among many young people who are not Rastafarians, although it is generally regarded as deviant by many adults, and it is illegal.

The place

The place where an act takes place may influence whether it is regarded as deviant or not. For example, it is seen as deviant if people have sex in the street, but not if it takes place between couples in a bedroom; fighting in the street is seen as deviant, but not if it takes place in a boxing ring. Similarly, killing may be seen as 'heroic' on a battlefield in wartime, but as murder in peacetime.

ACTIVITY

Apart from the examples given above:

1 Identify and explain two examples of acts which are against the law but are not usually regarded as deviant by most people.
2 Give three examples of deviant acts which are not against the law.
3 Identify and explain two examples of acts which are generally accepted by the majority of people in Britain, but which might be regarded as deviant in some social groups in Britain, for example ethnic minority or religious groups.
4 Explain the circumstances in which the following acts might not be regarded as deviant or illegal:
Two men having sex together.
Killing ten people.
Driving through red traffic lights.
Deliberately breaking someone's arm.
Punching someone in the face.
Breaking into someone's house and removing her or his possessions.
Taking children away from their parents by force.

Why are Some Deviant Acts Defined as Criminal while Others are Not?

Cannabis use in some countries of the Middle East is an extremely common practice, with few laws controlling its use, and yet alcohol consumption is strictly banned by laws which are vigorously enforced. In Britain, the opposite is more or less the case, despite the massive social cost caused by alcoholism in terms of family breakdown, days off work, acts of violence, and costs to the NHS, and little evidence that cannabis has any addictive properties. Why are there such differences in the way some acts are defined as criminal while other, similar acts are not? There are two broad competing views on this.

The consensus view

This view suggests that social rules are made and enforced for the benefit of everyone. The law and the definition of crime represent a consensus – a widespread agreement among most people – that some deviant acts are so serious that they require legal punishments to prevent them occurring. This may seem fairly clear in cases such as murder, rape, and armed robbery, but it is not so clear on other issues, like those of alcohol and soft drug abuse. From the consensus view, this would be explained by the varying norms found in different societies, which mean alcohol and drugs are viewed differently.

Inequalities in power

This view suggests that the law reflects the interests of the richest and most powerful groups in society, who have managed to impose their ideas and way of thinking on the rest of the population through the agencies of social control. Those in positions of influence in society, such as newspaper editors, politicians, owners of industry, powerful pressure groups, judges, and the police, are much better placed to make their definition of a crime stick than the ordinary person in the street. They also have the power to define some acts as criminal through newspaper campaigns, by passing laws in Parliament, or by treating some offences more seriously than others.

In this way the powerful are able to maintain their own position of power and influence by defining those activities which are against their interests as deviant or criminal. The issue of alcohol raised above could well be explained by the power of the wealthy large brewers and distillers. A further example is the way laws against picketing by trade unionists are much stronger and more rigidly enforced than those imposing health and safety standards on employers. Middle-class crimes such as tax evasion are often neither prosecuted, nor pursued as vigorously, nor punished as severely as a working-class offence such as social security fraud, which is much more likely to result in prosecution and a prison sentence.

DISCUSSION

Which view explaining why some deviant acts are defined as criminal while others are not do you find most convincing? Do you think the law is biased in deciding both which acts are defined as criminal, and which ones get pursued by the police and the courts?

THE PATTERN OF CRIME

Information on the pattern of crime is obtained from the official crime statistics. These are published each year by the Home Office from the records of local police forces.

Figure 10.1 shows a breakdown of the types of offence recorded by the police in 1996–7. It is notable that, despite wide media coverage of dramatic incidents such as attacks on the elderly, violence against the person made up only about 5 per cent of all offences in 1996–7. Most recorded assaults and crimes of violence do not result in any serious physical injury. Only a small proportion of such cases need professional medical attention, and in only a few of such cases is the victim admitted to hospital. In fact, as figure 10.1 shows, most crime is fairly small-scale property crime.

Criminal statistics are notoriously unreliable, so the pattern of crime shown in them must be treated with considerable caution. The problem of the crime statistics will be discussed shortly, but for the moment our concern will be with explaining the pattern shown in the official statistics.

The official crime statistics show that most crime is committed:
- In urban areas.
- Against property.
- By:
  - young
  - working-class
  - males.

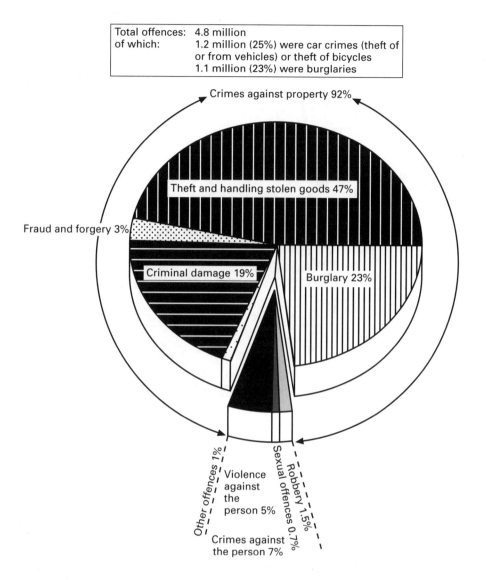

Total offences: 4.8 million
of which: 1.2 million (25%) were car crimes (theft of or from vehicles) or theft of bicycles
1.1 million (23%) were burglaries

Crimes against property 92%

Theft and handling stolen goods 47%

Fraud and forgery 3%

Criminal damage 19%

Burglary 23%

Other offences 1%

Violence against the person 5%

Robbery 1.5%

Sexual offences 0.7%

Crimes against the person 7%

Figure 10.1 Notifiable offences[a] recorded by the police: England and Wales, July 1996 to June 1997
[a] Notifiable offences are the more serious types of offence, either indictable offences, for which any suspect would have to be tried by jury at a crown court, or triable-either-way offences, which may be tried at either a magistrates' court or a crown court.
Source: Home Office

Why is the Crime Rate Higher in Urban Areas?

The official crime rate is significantly higher in urban areas than in rural areas. There are four main reasons for this.

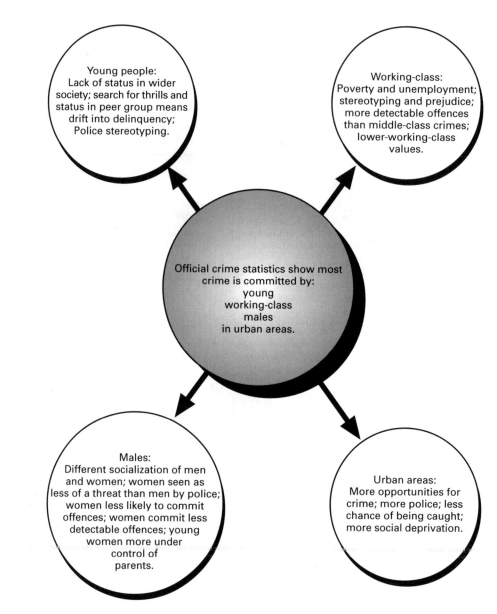

Figure 10.2 Explanations for the pattern of crime shown in the official crime statistics

More opportunity for crime

Large urban areas provide greater opportunities for crime: more and larger shops, warehouses and business premises, cars, houses, and other typical targets of crime.

Policing

There is a greater police presence in urban areas, so more crime is likely to be detected. Different policing methods also mean the police are more likely to take formal action (arrest and prosecution) in urban areas. In rural areas they are less likely to arrest offenders, preferring merely to issue more informal warnings, or in the case of young people perhaps visiting the offender's parents or her or his school.

Less chance of being caught

In the large cities, life is more impersonal and people do not know each other so well. Strangers are more likely to go unrecognized, and are therefore more able to get away with offences. Potential criminals are less likely to steal within a small rural community where everyone knows almost everybody else and suspicious 'strangers' in the community are likely to be noticed. Any local offenders are quite likely to be known in the community.

Social deprivation

Social deprivation and social problems, such as poor housing, unemployment, and poverty, are at their worst in the inner cities. These have been linked to crime, as people try to resolve their desperate situations through illegal means.

Why are Most Convicted Criminals Young?

Official statistics show that roughly half of all those convicted are aged 21 or under. Young people are caught in the transition between child and adult status: they are no longer expected to behave as children, but are denied the full rights and responsibilities of adults. They therefore often feel deprived of status in society and suffer from **status frustration**. This simply means they are frustrated at their lack of an independent status in society. The peer group provides some support for an identity and status independent of school or family, and therefore takes on a greater importance among young people than at any other age. Many young people lack the responsibilities involved in having children, in paying rent or mortgage repayments, and often in keeping down a job.

This lack of responsibilities and status, and the search for excitement and peer group status, mean many young people drift into minor acts of delinquency and clashes with the law. Peer group pressure may also give young people the confidence and encouragement to involve themselves in minor acts of delinquency which they would not engage in on their own. The idea of status frustration helps to explain why many young people give up crime as they grow older. Adulthood, marriage, parenthood, their own home, and employment give them a more clearly defined, independent status in society, and the peer group becomes less important for achieving status.

While most young people will break the law at some time, the kinds of offence they commit are usually fairly trivial and peer group related. For example, under-age drinking, vandalism, and shoplifting are the most common offences by young people. The reasons most often given for their law-breaking are to impress others, and boredom. Research conducted at the Centre of Criminology at Edinburgh University in 1990 found that about half the offences committed by 11–15-year-olds involved rowdiness and fighting in the street, with the rest consisting mainly of shoplifting (usually sweets) and vandalism (usually graffiti).

The police are likely to see young people as the source of problems, and this stereotype means the police spend more time observing and checking youths. As a result, more get caught, get defined as offenders, and appear in the statistics. In fact, the Edinburgh research found that young people are far more likely to be the victims of crime than to commit crimes, and these crimes are often committed by adults. The young complained of being followed by 'weirdos', bothered by 'flashers', alcoholics, and junkies, and in fear of rape and other sexual assaults. How-

Source: Guardian (2 November 1990), reproduced by permission of David Haldane

ever, the research found that the police often didn't take the complaints of the young seriously, seeing them primarily as trouble-makers. More than half had been moved on, told off, stopped and questioned, or stopped and searched during the previous nine months. This situation discourages young people from reporting offences against them, and reinforces the impression of young people as delinquents rather than the victims of crime.

DISCUSSION

Do you think the police stereotype young people, and unfairly make them out to be trouble-makers? What evidence do you have to back up your opinions?

Why are Most Convicted Criminals Male?

Males outnumber females by about 7 : 1 in the official statistics, and only about 4 per cent of the prison population are women. Why is this?

Owing to gender role socialization, men are more likely than women to carry out crimes of violence and other serious offences. Some suggest that more paternalism or sexism on the part of the police and courts means they regard female offenders as a less serious 'threat' than men, particularly for minor offences. They therefore adopt more informal approaches to their offences, such as unrecorded cautions or simply letting them off. The police are more likely to press charges in the case of men.

Women who commit crimes may benefit from the police stereotype that they are less likely than men to be criminals, and so are less likely to have their behaviour watched and get caught. Teenage girls are also likely to be more closely supervised by their parents, reducing the chances of their getting into trouble in the first place. Adult females may be less likely to get involved in crime owing to the constraints placed upon them by the demands of the housewife/mother role – caring for husbands, children, and dependent elderly relatives.

Women's offences are more likely to be less detectable offences, such as sexual offences, like prostitution, or petty theft, like shoplifting. The tough and dominant behaviour expected of men is more likely to lead to more serious and detectable criminal behaviour, and the police expect men to be the more probable criminals.

According to the Home Office, women are consistently treated more leniently by the law, with women first offenders about half as likely to be given a sentence of immediate imprisonment as their male counterparts.

However, others disagree with this view of the leniency of the law with regard to female offenders.

While women are far less likely to commit serious offences than men, those who do are likely to face more severe punishment than men, as it violates socially acceptable patterns of feminine behaviour. Women offenders are more likely to be remanded in custody (put in prison) than men while awaiting trial for serious offences, but in three-quarters of cases, women do not actually receive a prison sentence when they come to trial. Women are about twice as likely as men to be denied bail when charged with drug offences, and three times as likely for offences involving dishonesty. Many women in prison appear to have been sentenced more severely than men in similar circumstances – for example, by being imprisoned rather than given community service. Many women prisoners are there for not paying fines, or for committing theft trying to feed themselves or their children. Women are over twice as likely as men to be imprisoned for theft, and, in effect, many women are sent to jail for being poor.

Women are less likely than men to commit violent crime, but those who do often face more serious punishment than men committing similar offences. For example, Sara Thornton was given a life prison sentence in 1991 for killing her violent husband, while a man tried for killing his 'nagging' wife in the same year walked free after receiving a suspended sentence. Sara Thornton was only freed from prison in 1996 after a long campaign against her unjust treatment.

In general, then, women might commit less crime than men, but appear to suffer more serious consequences when they do. This may well be because in our society women are expected to be good and punished if they're not, but men are expected to go off the rails and so are punished less severely when they do.

ACTIVITY

1 Read carefully the previous section on why most convicted criminals are male. Try to think of any other reasons that you can. Make a list in order of importance of the reasons why women are less likely to be criminals than men.
2 How do you think police attitudes to women and crime could affect the number of female offenders recorded in the official crime statistics? Explain your answer carefully, with examples of particular crimes.
3 Women are more likely to be victims of some crimes than men. Suggest, with reasons, examples of some of these crimes.

Why are Most Convicted Criminals Working Class?

According to the official statistics, working-class people are more likely to be arrested and charged with crimes than those of other social classes. There are a number of possible explanations for this.

Poverty and unemployment

A Home Office research paper in August 1990 found a link between the level of crime and the state of the economy. Property crime in particular seems to rise when people are hard up, when poverty is on the increase and people need to provide for their families. Such hardship provides an obvious explanation for the most common offences of property crime, and would account for the high proportion of working-class criminals. In a society where there are wide inequalities in wealth and income, some level of crime is to be expected from those who live a more deprived life than others.

Stereotyping and prejudice

Working-class youth fit more closely the police stereotype of the 'typical criminal', and there is therefore a greater police presence in working-class areas than in middle-class areas. This means there is a greater likelihood of offenders being seen and arrested by the police when committing an offence than in middle-class areas. Crime rates will therefore be higher in working-class areas simply because there are more police to notice or respond quickly to criminal acts.

The activities of working-class youth are more likely to be defined by the police as criminal than the same behaviour in the middle class. For example, a case of university students getting drunk and wrecking a restaurant might result in their having to pay for the damage and be dismissed by the police as 'high jinks', but the same behaviour by working-class football supporters would be more likely to be seen as 'hooliganism', with resulting prosecutions for criminal damage.

Working-class youth are also more likely to be prosecuted if they are caught than the middle class. This is perhaps because they are less likely to benefit from informal processes of social control. For petty offences, middle-class youth are more likely to be dealt with by parents and teachers than by the law, with the police perhaps visiting the parents to give them a warning.

The prejudices of middle-class judges and magistrates may mean that, when working-class people appear in court, they are more likely to be seen as 'typical criminals' and found guilty. The middle class are more

ACTIVITY

Most judges and magistrates come from white, upper-middle-class or middle-class backgrounds.

1 Suggest ways this might influence judges and magistrates to give more favourable and sympathetic treatment to some groups and less favourable and unsympathetic treatment to others. Give examples of particular groups.
2 Imagine you are to appear in court on a shoplifting charge. You desperately want to get off lightly. Identify and explain four ways you might try to give a good impression to the judge or magistrate.
3 What might this activity suggest about the real pattern of crime in society?

likely to be found not guilty. Their offences may be seen more as a temporary lapse in otherwise good behaviour, and so are punished less severely than those of the working class.

Lower-working-class values

Some have suggested that the values of the lower working class often carry with them risks of brushes with the law. These values are discussed later in this chapter.

White-collar and corporate crime

White-collar crimes are offences committed by people in the course of their middle-class jobs.

Corporate crimes are offences committed by large companies which directly profit the company rather than individuals.

White-collar crimes are offences committed by people in the course of their middle-class jobs. These include offences such as bribery and corruption in government and business, fiddling expenses, professional misconduct, fraud, and embezzlement. Examples might include the case of Ernest Saunders, former chairman of Guinness, who in 1990 was convicted of theft of £8 million, false accounting, and conspiracy. Robert Maxwell, the media tycoon, embezzled millions of pounds from the Mirror Group's pension funds before his death in 1991. Nick Leeson bankrupted Barings Bank in 1995 after losing the bank £830 million.

Corporate crimes are offences committed by large companies which directly profit the company rather than individuals. These include offences like misrepresentation of products, industrial espionage, breaches of health and safety regulations, and hacking into rival companies' computers to obtain confidential information. British Airways did this in the early 1990s, to obtain confidential information about its rival Virgin Airlines.

White-collar and corporate crimes are substantially under-represented in official statistics, giving the impression that the middle class commit fewer offences. However, there may be many companies and white-collar criminals who simply don't get caught or even have their crimes detected. The impression gained from the official statistics that most crime is committed by the working class may therefore be quite misleading.

There are several reasons why white-collar and corporate crime are under-represented in the official statistics.

- Such crime is often 'without victims' and may benefit both the parties concerned. For example, in cases of bribery and corruption both parties stand to gain something. It is therefore hard to detect.
- There is often a lack of awareness that a crime has been committed and therefore it is not reported. For example, members of the public may lack the expertise to know if they are being misled or defrauded.
- Even if these crimes are detected, they are often not prosecuted. For example, violations of health and safety legislation often lead only to a reprimand. Crimes such as professional misconduct, medical negligence, industrial espionage, and computer fraud are rarely reported, to protect the interests or reputation of the profession or institution, and avoid the loss of public confidence which the surrounding scandal might cause. A typical example of this occurred in 1990, when it was reported that at least five British banks were being blackmailed by a group of computer hackers who had broken into their central computer systems. This was not reported to the police, but instead was investigated by a private security firm. This was so that the public would not find out about it, with the resulting damaging publicity to the banks' reputation and the loss of public confidence.

In general, the higher up you are in the social class hierarchy:

- The less likely you are to be arrested.
- The less likely you are, if arrested, to be prosecuted.
- The less likely you are, if prosecuted, to be found guilty.
- The less likely you are, if found guilty, to be given a prison sentence.

WHAT'S WRONG WITH THE OFFICIAL CRIME STATISTICS?

The previous section outlined some explanations of the pattern of crime as revealed in the official crime statistics. However, these are not as factual as they might appear, and there is a large percentage of crimes which are not discovered or reported: the 'dark number' of undiscovered crimes. Figure 10.3 from the 1996 British Crime Survey shows a large gap for many offences between the amount of crime committed and that finally recorded by the police.

This survey estimated that overall about four times as many offences are committed as the number recorded by the police, though for some categories of crime, such as vandalism, theft from the person, and theft from motor vehicles, the number is much higher. Many burglaries, rapes, crimes of domestic violence, wounding, and common assaults go unreported.

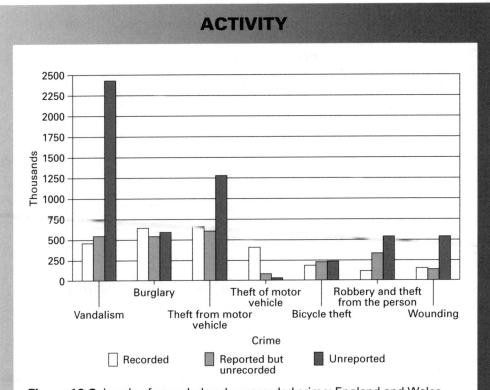

ACTIVITY

Figure 10.3 Levels of recorded and unrecorded crime: England and Wales, 1996
Source: Data from British Crime Survey, 1996. Home Office

Study figure 10.3 and answer the following questions:

1 Approximately how many crimes of vandalism were recorded in 1996?
2 Approximately how many thefts from motor vehicles were recorded in 1996?
3 Which type of crime, from all the crimes of that type, was the most likely to be recorded in 1996?
4 Which type of crime, from all crimes of that type, was most likely to be reported?
5 How many thefts from motor vehicles were there in total in 1996?
6 Approximately how many bike thefts were reported but unrecorded in 1996?
7 According to the statistics in figure 10.3, a high percentage of crimes of vandalism, thefts from motor vehicles, wounding, robbery, and theft from the person went unreported. Suggest reasons for this for each offence.
8 Suggest, with examples, reasons why the police may decide not to record a crime (a) which has been reported to them, and (b) which the police themselves have detected.
9 Explain how the information given in figure 10.3 might be used to show that the official crime statistics give a misleading impression of the extent of crime in society. Is there any evidence for the opposite view for particular types of crime? Be sure to give statistical evidence from figure 10.3.

Research from self-report studies and victim surveys suggests that the high proportion of young, urban, working-class males in the criminal statistics gives a misleading impression of the criminal population as a whole. In reality the ratio of working-class to middle-class crime and the ratio of male to female is much more equal than official statistics suggest. Therefore, the extent of crime and the type of people committing it are very different from those which the official statistics suggest. Why are the official crime statistics so inaccurate?

Self-report studies and victim surveys

Sociologists know that the number of crimes is far higher than the official statistics suggest, because of the use of self-report studies and victim surveys.

Self-report studies are anonymous questionnaires where people own up to committing crimes, whether they have been discovered or not. (Table 10.1 shows an example of a self-report study.)

Victim surveys involve people admitting to being the victim of a crime, whether or not they reported it. An example of a victim survey is the British Crime Survey, carried out by the Home Office. This tries to discover how much crime goes unreported by victims and unrecorded by the police. In this way, it is able to estimate how much crime there really is in society.

Table 10.1 Example of a self-report study

Acts of delinquency	Acts of delinquency
1 I have ridden a bicycle without lights after dark	19 I have taken things from big stores or supermarkets when the shop was open.
2 I have driven a car or motor bike/scooter under 16.	20 I have taken things from little shops when the shop was open.
3 I have been with a group who go round together making a row and sometimes getting into fights and causing disturbance.	21 I have dropped things in the street like litter or broken bottles.
4 I have played truant from school.	22 I have bought something cheap or accepted as a present something I knew was stolen.
5 I have travelled on a train or bus without a ticket or deliberately paid the wrong fare.	23 I have planned well in advance to get into a house to take things.
6 I have let off fireworks in the street.	24 I have got into a house and taken things even though I didn't plan it in advance.
7 I have taken money from home without returning it.	25 I have taken a bicycle belonging to someone else and kept it.
8 I have taken someone else's car or motor bike for a joy ride then taken it back afterwards.	26 I have struggled or fought to get away from a police officer.
9 I have broken or smashed things in public places like on the streets, cinemas, discos, trains or buses.	27 I have struggled or fought with a police officer who was trying to arrest someone.
10 I have insulted people on the street or got them angry and fought with them.	28 I have stolen school property worth more than about 5p.
11 I have broken into a big store or garage or warehouse.	29 I have stolen goods from someone I worked for worth more than about 5p.
12 I have broken into a little shop even though I may not have taken anything.	30 (Females only) I have had sex with a boy when I was under 16.
13 I have taken something out of a car.	31 (Males only) I have had sex with a girl when I was under 16 or with a boy when I was under 18.
14 I have taken a weapon (like a knife) out with me in case I needed it in a fight.	32 I have trespassed somewhere I was not supposed to go, like empty houses, railway lines or private gardens.
15 I have fought with someone in a public place like in the street or a dance.	33 I have been to an '18' film under age.
16 I have broken the window of an empty house.	34 I have spent money on gambling under 16.
17 I have used a weapon in a fight, like a knife or a razor or a broken bottle.	35 I have smoked cigarettes under 15.
18 I have drunk alcoholic drinks in a pub under 16.	36 I have had sex with someone for money.
	37 I have taken money from slot machines or telephones.

Acts of delinquency	Acts of delinquency
38 I have taken money from someone's clothes hanging up somewhere.	hanging up somewhere.
39 I have got money from someone by pretending to be someone else or lying about why I needed it.	41 I have smoked dope or taken pills (LSD, ecstasy, speed).
40 I have taken someone's clothes	42 I have got money/drink/cigarettes by saying I would have sex with someone even though I didn't.
	43 I have run away from home.

Source: Adapted from A. Campbell, *Girl Delinquents* (Blackwell 1981)

ACTIVITY

1 Work through the self-report study in table 10.1. List any offences you and/or your friends have committed but have not been caught for (no matter how trivial or whether they're on the list or not). What conclusions might you draw from your findings about the levels of undiscovered crime in society?

2 List five crimes which a victim might choose not to report to the police, and explain why in each case.

3 Have you or any of your friends ever been a victim (or suspected you might have been a victim) of a crime that you didn't report to the police? Explain the reasons why you didn't report it. What does this tell you about the real extent of crime in society?

The Failure to Report Crimes to the Police

As table 10.2 and figure 10.4 suggest, a large number of people who are victims of crime don't bother to report it to the police. There are a number of reasons for this, which you can compare with your own findings in the previous activity.

- The victims may think that the incident is too trivial to report; for example, where the incident involved no loss or damage, or the loss was too small, such as losing a small amount of money, garden tools, or bottles of milk.

Table 10.2 Reasons for not reporting incidents: by type of offence

Reason for not reporting %	Vandalism	Burglary	Vehicle thefts[a]	Bicycle theft	Assault	Robbery	Theft from person	Other thefts[b]	All offences
Too trivial/no loss	45	45	45	30	22	28	50	46	40
Police could do nothing	35	32	41	38	16	30	33	24	29
Police would not be interested	22	21	26	24	12	23	15	21	20
Dealt with matter themselves	11	16	9	12	47	21	12	11	19
Reported to other authorities	2	3	1	1	8	6	5	9	5
Inconvenient to report	3	2	6	6	2	2	6	4	4
Fear reprisals	2	2	Less than 1	–	11	11	Less than 1	1	4
Fear/dislike police	Less than 1	1	Less than 1	–	1	–	1	Less than 1	Less than 1
Other	4	7	3	6	9	11	4	6	5

[a] Thefts from vehicles and attempted thefts of and from them.
[b] Other household thefts and thefts of personal property.

Source: 'The 1996 British Crime Survey', *Home Office Statistical Bulletin* (September 1996)

- The victims may think there is little point in reporting the incident as they feel the police could not do anything about it, by either recovering their property or catching the offenders; for example, cases of shoplifting or being pickpocketed.
- The victims may fear embarrassment or humiliation at the hands of the police or in court. Groups working with rape victims such as the Rape Crisis Line estimate two out of three rape victims do not report the crime because of embarrassment, because they think the police won't take them seriously, or because they are made to feel it is their own fault they got raped. Recent rises in the number of reported rapes and

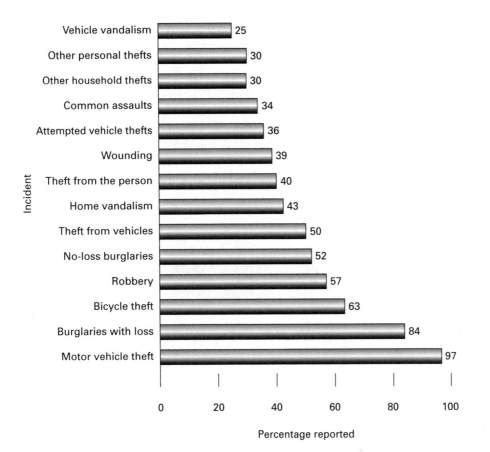

Figure 10.4 Percentage of incidents reported to the police: 1996
Source: Data from British Crime Survey, 1996. Home Office

crimes of domestic violence are often explained by changing police practice, and their growing willingness to treat such offences in a more serious way and to be more sympathetic to the victim.

- People may not report offences because they will themselves be in trouble. Some crimes benefit both parties, and there is no obvious victim. The consequence of reporting such offences will harm all concerned. For example, offences such as the illegal supplying of drugs, under-age sex, or giving and accepting bribes involve an agreement between both parties, and both will lose out if the police find out. Similarly, the illegal drug user who gets ripped off is more likely to be charged with an offence than shown sympathy by the police, and is therefore extremely unlikely to report the incident.

- The victim may fear reprisals if the crime is reported, for example the blackmail victim afraid of the consequences of reporting the black-mailer.
- Victims may feel it is a private matter they would rather deal with themselves. Examples might include offences such as theft or assault between friends.
- Victims may not be aware an offence has been committed. 'Lost' property may have been stolen, and while the media often report cases of hoax gas-meter readers and so on, there may be many people who never actually realize they have been the victims of such a hoax.

ACTIVITY

1 Refer to figure 10.4 on page 235. Which offence was (a) most likely to be reported to the police and (b) least likely to be reported to the police? Suggest reasons for this in each case.

Refer to table 10.2 on page 234.

2 Which offence was not reported in 50 per cent of cases because it was too trivial or involved no loss?
3 Which offence was most likely not to be reported because people dealt with the matter themselves?
4 Which offence was most likely not to be reported because it was thought the police could do nothing?
5 What were the three most common reasons given for not reporting offences?
6 How do you think the evidence in figure 10.4 and table 10.2 might be used to challenge the view in the official crime statistics that most criminals are young, male, and working-class?

The Failure of the Police to Record a Crime

The police may decide not to record an offence because they may regard the matter as too trivial to waste their time on, such as the theft of a very small sum of money, or the vandalism of a car window. They may not record an incident because it has already been satisfactorily resolved, or because the victim does not wish to proceed with the complaint.

They may regard the person complaining as too unreliable to take his or her account of the incident seriously, as in the case of complaints made by a tramp, a drug addict, or a drunk. The police may think that a report of an incident is mistaken, or that there is simply insufficient evidence to show that a crime has been committed.

In some cases, the police may regard an incident as nothing to do with them, even though an offence has been committed. This has traditionally been true in cases of domestic violence, such as wife-battering and rape within marriage, with such incidents being dismissed as a relatively unimportant 'domestic', and no offence being recorded or charges preferred.

ACTIVITY

The police often have a great deal of work to do, and every arrest they make involves considerable paper work. The police also have discretion over whether to arrest and charge someone for some offences. For example, pub closing time may involve lots of trouble, but the police can choose to move people along rather than arrest them.

1 Suggest six examples of crimes which the police might turn a blind eye to. Give reasons for your answer.
2 Suggest six crimes the police would be forced to record and investigate. Give reasons for your answer.
3 Sometimes the police seem to take some offences more seriously than at other times, and this results in increasing numbers of arrests and prosecutions for these offences, for example drink-driving at Christmas. List, with examples, all the factors you can think of which might make the police occasionally increase their levels of activity against some offences.

IS THE CRIME RATE INCREASING?

Much of what was said in the previous section suggests that the official crime statistics provide no real guide to the type or extent of crime, and must therefore be used with great care. Such care must also be applied to statistics which show increases in the amounts of recorded crime. Much public concern has been expressed at the huge increase in recorded crime, such as that between 1981 and 1995 as shown in figure 10.5.

Increases in the amount of recorded crime need not necessarily mean

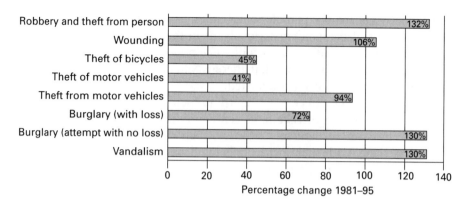

Figure 10.5 Changes in crimes recorded by the police: England and Wales, 1981–95
Source: Data from British Crime Survey, 1996. Home Office

there are more crimes being committed, or that people are at greater risk of being victims of crime. The increases could be explained by a wide range of factors, which suggest more offences are being discovered and reported but not necessarily that more offences are actually being committed.

- More sophisticated police training, communications, and equipment, such as the use of computers, forensic science, and DNA testing, and higher policing levels all lead to increasing detection rates. Neighbourhood Watch schemes may also lead to more crimes being detected.
- A stronger desire by the police to prosecute certain offenders due to changing police attitudes and policies towards some offences, such as a crack-down on prostitution, drug-dealing, or drink-driving. This may give the impression of an increase in crimes of that type, when it is simply that the police are making extra efforts and allocating more officers to prosecute such crimes, and therefore catching more offenders.
- Changes in the law make more things illegal, such as rape in marriage.
- Easier communications make reporting of crime easier, such as mobile phones.
- Changing social norms – for example, changing attitudes to rape among the police and the public may have resulted in more rapes being reported, even though no more have been committed. The same might apply to crimes like domestic violence and child abuse, which are also statistically on the increase.
- People have more to lose today and more have insurance cover. Insurance claims for theft need a police report, so more crime is reported. For example, nearly all car thefts are reported today so people can claim the insurance money, and rising numbers of recorded burglaries

may simply reflect more people with household contents insurance policies.

- People may be bringing to the attention of the police less serious incidents. This may be because they have become less tolerant of lawbreaking, or because they see the police as more likely to be able to help them, or simply because they want the police to take more action.

It is an irony of the official statistics that attempts to defeat crime by increased levels of policing, more police pay and resources, and a determination to crack down on offences, can actually increase the levels of recorded crime. The more you search for crime, the more you find; and the official crime rate rises.

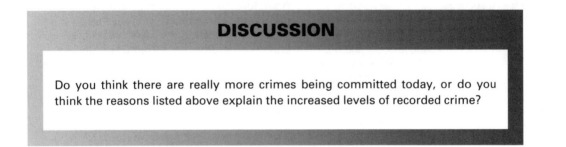

DISCUSSION

Do you think there are really more crimes being committed today, or do you think the reasons listed above explain the increased levels of recorded crime?

EXPLAINING CRIME AND DEVIANCE

Deviance covers very wide and varied forms of behaviour, and definitions of deviance and crime vary widely between societies and change over time. It is impossible to be born a criminal or a deviant, because crime and deviance involve legal and social rules, and what counts as deviant or criminal will depend on how society defines these rules. No single explanation can possibly provide an adequate account of all forms of deviance. The following sections briefly cover some of the major theoretical explanations which have been offered by sociologists for deviance, particularly criminal deviance.

Anomie

An American sociologist, Robert Merton, suggests that all societies set goals which people are encouraged to achieve, such as making money and career success. Norms or social rules define the socially approved ways of achieving these goals, such as hard work and educational qualifications.

Merton's rule-breakers

INNOVATORS	RITUALISTS	RETREATISTS	REBELS
Try to achieve success by illegitimate means, such as theft	Continue to work within the system but give up trying for success, for example office workers stuck in a dead-end job and simply 'going through the motions' with no ambition	Abandon both the goals and the means of achieving them, and become drop-outs, turning to drink, drugs, or some other deviant behaviour	Reject society's goals and the accepted means of achieving them, and replace them with their own, for example revolutionaries

Most people are what Merton calls conformists – they try to achieve society's goals in approved ways.

Merton argues deviance arises when the approved ways of achieving society's goals don't correspond with the actual situation individuals are in. In these circumstances, anomie results. This is a situation where people face confusion and uncertainty over what the social norms are, as these no longer help them to cope with the conditions they find themselves in. For example, many disadvantaged groups such as the poor and the lower working class have little chance of achieving society's goals by acceptable means, because they face disadvantages in education or are stuck in dead-end jobs with no promotion prospects. A strain is therefore placed on these individuals – they want to achieve the goals but lack the opportunities for doing so by conventional means. Merton suggests people may respond to these difficulties in achieving society's goals by breaking the rules, for example turning to crime or other deviant behaviour. He identifies four different types of rule-breaking: innovation, ritualism, retreatism, and rebellion. Innovators, for example, break the accepted rules for achieving success and turn to illegal means of achieving society's goals, such as theft. The cartoon above illustrates these four types of deviance.

DISCUSSION

Look at the cartoon on 'Merton's rule-breakers'.

1 Which one of the four types of rule-breaker would those who fiddled their income tax normally be considered as?
2 Explain in what way each of Merton's rule-breakers is deviant, and how each would have to change to become conformist.
3 Classify each of the following acts/groups according to Merton's ideas:
   Someone cheating in exams.
   A teacher who has lost interest in the job, but carries on teaching.
   A heroin addict.
   The IRA.
   A tramp.
   A lazy student who only pretends to do any work.
4 Suggest two examples of your own for each type of rule-breaking (or deviance), and explain how your examples show each type of deviance.

Sub-Cultural Explanations

A **sub-culture** is a smaller culture held by a group of people within the main culture of a society, in some ways different from the dominant culture, but with many aspects in common. Figure 10.6 illustrates, with examples, this idea of a sub-culture. Sub-cultural explanations of crime and deviance suggest that those who commit crime share some values which are to some extent different from the main values of society as a whole.

Status frustration and the deviant sub-culture

While most lower-working-class young people accept the main goals of society, like wealth and educational success, they have little chance of attaining them. This is because they live in deprived areas, with poor schools and the worst chances in the job market. They therefore develop status frustration. This simply means they lack status in society, and feel frustration at being unable to achieve such status by accepted means.

Their response to this sense of status frustration is to develop a set of alternative, deviant values which provides them with alternative ways of gaining status – a deviant sub-culture. Delinquent acts are based on a

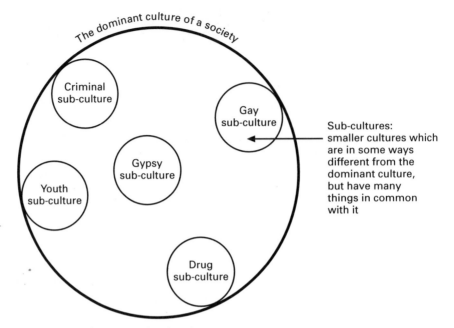

Figure 10.6 Culture and sub-cultures

deliberate reversal of accepted norms. At school, playing truant, messing about in class, and destroying school property may replace the values of studying and exam success. Stealing becomes a means of getting money, replacing career success, and vandalism replaces respect for property. Such acts of delinquency enable some lower-working-class youths to gain a status in their peer group which the wider society has denied them. Delinquency also gives them a way of getting their revenge on the system which has condemned them to failure.

The lower-working-class sub-culture

Some suggest that the values of lower-working-class male sub-culture can often lead to crime among young people. This sub-culture encourages men to demonstrate their toughness, their masculinity, and their 'smartness', and to pursue excitement and thrills. These features of working-class life can lead to clashes with the law. For example, the concern with 'toughness' might lead to offences like assault.

These values may become exaggerated in the lives of young males who want to achieve status in their peer group by engaging in delinquent acts to show how tough and smart they are. A 'good night out' might consist of a few drinks, a fight outside the pub, a rampage round the streets with mates, and a run-in with the police, with everyone competing to show they are more 'macho' than the rest.

Labelling Theory

Labelling theory is concerned with two main features:

- The process whereby some people committing some actions come to be defined or labelled as deviant, while others do not.
- The consequences which follow once a deviant label has been applied, and how this may create more deviance or crime.

The first of these issues was discussed earlier in this chapter, so here the emphasis will be on the consequences which follow once a deviant label has been applied.

The deviant 'master status'

Labelling theorists point out that most people commit crimes and other deviant acts at some time in their lives, but not everyone becomes defined as a deviant or a criminal. For labelling theorists, what is important in explaining crime is the consequences of being caught and labelled.

Once someone is caught and labelled as a criminal or deviant, the label attached may become the dominant label or **master status** which overrides all other characteristics of that person – she or he becomes, not someone's wife/husband, mother/father, friend, or business associate, but an 'ex-con' or a 'hooligan'.

Once a person is labelled as 'mad' (mentally ill), as a football hooligan, as a thief, or as a failure at school, the label may have quite serious consequences for his or her life, as people are treated differently according to the label. Each label carries with it a range of prejudices and images – the football hooligan, for example, is often seen as irresponsible, violent, a drunkard, a racist, and a serious threat to society. A person with a conviction for theft may be seen as fundamentally untrustworthy and never to be left alone with valuables, and if things go missing this may automatically reinforce suspicions that they have been stolen by the labelled thief. The bottom-stream pupil in school may be seen as a 'waster', and thoroughly untrustworthy and unreliable. Once labelled, a person's behaviour might be interpreted differently from that of a person not labelled as deviant. For example, teachers may treat some questions from bottom-stream 'delinquents' as red herrings, but regard the same questions from top-stream conformists as intelligent and worthy of discussion. Much the same could apply when different pupils offer excuses for not doing homework, missing games, and so on. Someone with a history of mental illness may have signs of eccentricity interpreted as evidence of his or her mental illness, but the same behaviour might pass unnoticed in a person not labelled as mentally ill.

Deviant careers

Labelling may lead to a **deviant career**. This simply means people start acting the way they have been labelled. For example, a man caught in an isolated act of stealing may be prosecuted, imprisoned, and labelled as a 'criminal' and later as an 'ex-con' – friends desert him, employers refuse to offer him jobs, and the man may then begin to see himself primarily as a criminal. Since alternative opportunities are closed off to him, and everyone treats him as a criminal anyway, he may then turn to crime as a way of life and follow a deviant career of crime.

In this way, labelling theory suggests that the attachment of a label can actually generate more deviance. For example, prisons and borstals play a key role in making the label of 'criminal' and, later, 'ex-con' stick. They immerse offenders in a criminal sub-culture, increase the opportunities to learn about crime, and make it extremely hard for them to go back to living a 'normal' life when they are released. More crime may therefore result as alternative opportunities are limited.

CONCLUSION

This chapter has shown that the definition and explanation of deviance and crime are no simple matters. This is hardly surprising given the very wide range of behaviour that the term 'deviance' covers.

ACTIVITY

In each of the cases listed below:

1 Identify a possible label which may be attached to the person concerned as a result of her or his deviant behaviour.
2 Outline how a 'deviant career' might develop by describing the possible consequences of the labelling for the person's future life and relationships.
3 Suggest ways that a person might avoid being labelled even after she or he has committed the deviant act.

A young woman caught shoplifting.
A male teacher who publicly declares himself to be gay (homosexual).
A person who is temporarily admitted to a mental hospital as a result of a nervous breakdown.
An 18-year-old man who gets arrested during a fight at a football match.

We must recognize that deviance, and even crime, are not by any means always harmful to society. Much crime remains fairly trivial, and the wide range of non-conformist behaviour, its quirks and oddities, add a richness of colour and variety to what might otherwise be a drab existence.

Without deviance, even without crime, there would be no possibility of innovation and change. The rebels and the reformers, the heretics and the inventors, and campaigners for peace and justice have all been labelled as deviants or criminals at one time or another. Yet it is these non-conformists who have contributed to changes which many would regard as of benefit to all. Deviance should be treated with an open mind, for what is regarded as deviant today is often the accepted behaviour of tomorrow.

CHAPTER SUMMARY

After studying this chapter, you should be able to:

- Define social control and explain how it is carried out formally and informally through agencies of social control.
- Explain the difference between crime and deviance.
- Explain how and why definitions of deviance vary.
- Explain the link between deviance and power.
- Describe and explain the pattern of crime shown in the official crime statistics.
- Explain why white-collar and corporate crime often go undetected or unrecorded.
- Explain a range of reasons why the official crime statistics provide no accurate record of the full extent of crime in society.
- Explain why an increase in the official crime rate might not necessarily mean that there has been an increase in the real amount of crime.
- Provide a range of sociological explanations of crime, delinquency, and deviance.
- Describe and explain the ideas of labelling and deviant careers.

KEY TERMS

anomie
deviant career
master status

status frustration
sub-culture

PROJECT SUGGESTIONS

1 Using secondary sources (see chapter 18), give an account of the pattern of crime in your own area, and compare it with the national crime statistics. Perhaps interview the local police for information.

2 Do a survey about attitudes to some deviant or illegal act, such as under-age drinking or drug abuse.

3 Carry out a case study of a Neighbourhood Watch scheme.

4 Carry out a self-report study (you might use the self-report study included in this chapter as a starting point) or a victim survey (perhaps using the British Crime Survey to help you devise your questions) among a small sample in your school, college, or workplace, and try to discover how much undiscovered and/or unreported crime there is. Compare your results with those in the British Crime Survey.

THE FAMILY AND MARRIAGE

11

Most people are raised in families, and so we might think we know all about them. We may make assumptions that people will fall in love with someone of the opposite sex and get married, start having children, and form their own family. We may have the impression that the typical family unit in Britain consists of parents and a couple of children, with Dad out working and Mum staying at home looking after the kids, but with both partners sharing a lot of jobs around the home. We may believe the family is the only place where children can be properly brought up, and that it is a source of unconditional affection – a place to retreat to whenever things get too much or go wrong in the outside world.

On the other hand, you may believe that the family is in decline, pointing to rising rates of divorce, extra-marital sex, and abortion, with rising numbers of lone-parent families. You might point to rising levels of child abuse, violence against women, vandalism and crime, and drug abuse. You would not be alone in holding such a belief – the mass media, politicians, the police, social workers, teachers, and religious leaders have all at some time or another tried to 'blame the family' and lack of parental control for a wide range of problems in society.

There is, whatever way you look at it, a controversy over the family. This chapter will attempt to throw some light on some of these issues, and the variety of forms of marriage and the family.

WHAT IS THE FAMILY?

A family is a group of people who are related by **kinship** ties: relations of blood, marriage, or adoption. The family unit is one of the most important social institutions, which is found in some form in nearly all known societies. It is a basic unit of social organization, and plays a key role in socializing children into the culture of their society.

DIFFERENT FORMS OF THE FAMILY AND MARRIAGE

Even though the family is found in nearly every society, it can take many different forms. Marriage and family life in earlier times in Britain, and today in many other societies, can be organized in quite different ways from family life in modern Britain. Sociologists use a number of different terms to describe the wide varieties of marriage and the family. Table 11.1 summarizes these varieties.

The Nuclear Family

The **nuclear family** means just the parents and children, living together in one household. It is sometimes called the two-generation family, because it contains only the two generations of parents and children. In Britain in 1996, 40 per cent of people lived in this type of family.

The Extended Family

The **extended family** is a grouping consisting of all kin. There are two main types of extended family: the classic extended and the modified extended family.

The classic extended family

The **classic extended family** is made up of several nuclear families joined by kinship relations. The term is mainly used to describe a situation where many related nuclear families or family members live in the same house, street, or area and the members of these related nuclear families see one another regularly. It may be horizontally extended, where it contains just two generations, with aunts, uncles, cousins, etc., or vertically

Table 11.1 Forms of marriage and the family

Forms of:	Description
Marriage	
Monogamy	One husband and one wife
	Found in Europe, the USA, and most Christian cultures
Serial monogamy	A series of monogamous marriages
	Found in Europe and the USA, where there are high rates of divorce and remarriage
Arranged marriage	Marriages arranged by parents
	Found in the Indian sub-continent and Asian community in Britain
Polygamy	Marriage to more than one partner at the same time
	Includes polygyny and polyandry
Polygyny	One husband and two or more wives
	Found in Islamic countries like Egypt and Saudi Arabia.
Polyandry	One wife and two or more husbands
	Found in Tibet, among the Todas of southern India, and among the Marquesan Islanders
Family structure	
Nuclear family	Two generations: parents and children living in the same household
Extended family	All kin including and beyond the nuclear family
Classic extended family	An extended family sharing the same household or living close by
Modified extended family	An extended family living far apart but keeping in close touch by phone, letters, and frequent visits
Inheritance	
Patrilineal descent	Property and title passes through the male side of the family
Matrilineal descent	Property and title passes through the female side of the family
Residence	
Patrilocal	Married couple live with or near the husband's family
Matrilocal	Married couple live with or near the wife's family
Neo-local	Married couple set up home apart from either the husband's or wife's family
Authority	
Patriarchal family	Authority held by males
Matriarchal family	Authority held by females
Symmetrical family	Authority shared between male and female partners
Results of marriage breakdown	
Reconstituted family	One or both partners previously married, with children of previous marriages
Lone-parent family	Lone parent, most commonly after divorce or separation (though may also arise from death of a partner or unwillingness to marry)

extended, where it contains more than two generations, such as grand-parents and grandchildren as well as parents and their own children.

The modified extended family

The **modified extended family** is one where related nuclear families, although they may be living far apart geographically, nevertheless maintain regular contact and mutual support through visiting, the phone, and letters: continuing close relations made possible by modern communications. This is probably the most common type of family arrangement in Britain today.

ACTIVITY

1 Do a brief survey among your friends or workmates and find out how many live in nuclear families, how many live in classic extended families, and how many have modified extended families. You will have to think of suitable ways of measuring the features of these families, such as how near relatives live, how often they see one another, what other relatives live in the house-hold apart from parents and children, and so on.
2 Ask them what it is like living in these different types of family. On the basis of your findings and using also your own experience of family life, make a list of the advantages and disadvantages of living in each type of family.

The Lone-Parent Family

The lone-parent or single-parent family is increasingly common in Western societies. In 1996, 11 per cent of people in Britain lived in this type of family. Although lone-parent families can also arise from the death of a partner, they are today largely a result of the rise in the divorce rate. In 1996 almost 23 per cent of all families with dependent children were lone-parent families, and nine out of ten of these lone parents were women. Increasingly, lone-parent families are arising from a simple lack of desire to get married – in 1996 nearly 40 per cent of lone mothers fell into this category. About three-quarters of lone-parent families receive income support.

The Reconstituted Family

The **reconstituted family** is a family where one or both partners have been married previously, and they bring with them children of a previous marriage. This 'reconstitutes' the family with various combinations of step-mother, step-father, and step-children. Such families are increasingly common in Western societies, as a result of rising divorce rates and remarriages. In Britain, about 40 per cent of all marriages involve remarriage for one or both partners, and at least one in ten children today live in step-families, with parents of one or more previous marriages.

The Symmetrical Family

The **symmetrical family** is one where the roles of husband and wife or of cohabiting partners have become more alike (symmetrical) and equal. There are more shared tasks within relationships rather than a clear division between the jobs of male and female partners. Both partners are likely to be wage earners. It remains a popular impression that most families in modern Britain are symmetrical, but evidence which will be discussed later in this chapter suggests this is not the case.

Monogamy

In modern Britain and the rest of Europe, the USA, and most Christian cultures, **monogamy** is the only legal form of marriage. Monogamy is a form of marriage in which a person can have only one husband or wife at the same time. Monogamy has not traditionally been the most common form of marriage in the world, though it is rapidly becoming so as Western ideas of marriage spread through the world, as societies modernize. In a society where monogamy is the only form of legal marriage, a person who marries while still legally married to someone else is guilty of the crime of **bigamy** – a serious offence punishable by imprisonment.

Serial monogamy

In modern Britain, most of Western Europe, and the USA there are high rates of divorce and remarriage. Some people keep marrying and divorcing a series of different partners, but each marriage is monogamous. The term **serial monogamy** is sometimes used to describe these marriage patterns. This form of marriage has been described as 'one at a time, one after the other and they don't last long'!

Arranged Marriages

Arranged marriages are those where the marriages of children are organized by their parents, who try to match their children with partners of a similar background and status. The arranged marriage is more a union between two families than between two people, and romantic love is not necessarily present between the marriage partners. They are typically found among Muslims, Sikhs, and Hindus. The arranged marriage is still common in the Asian community in Britain, where the custom is often more strictly enforced than in the Indian sub-continent. This is because the present generation of parents here often still stick to the customs which existed when they left India for Britain many years ago.

DISCUSSION

What are the advantages and disadvantages of arranged marriages? How do you think arranged marriages might be changing in Britain, and what pressures do you think there might be on the survival of the custom in Britain?

Polygamy

While marrying a second partner without divorcing the first is a crime in Britain, in many societies it is perfectly acceptable to have more than one marriage partner at the same time. **Polygamy** is a general term referring to marriage between a member of one sex and two or more members of the opposite sex at the same time. There are two different types of polygamy: polygyny and polyandry.

Monogamy   Polygyny   Polyandry

Polygamy

Polygyny

Polygyny is the marriage of one man to two or more women at the same time. It is widely practised in Islamic countries such as Egypt and Saudi Arabia. It is also practised (illegally) among some Mormons in the state of Utah in the USA. The possession of several wives is often seen as a sign of wealth and success and generally only those men who can afford to support several wives practise polygyny. Because of this, even where polygyny is allowed, only a small number of men actually practise it. In any case, the numbers of men and women in most societies are usually fairly evenly balanced, and there are not enough women for all men to have more than one wife.

Polyandry

Polyandry is the marriage of one woman to two or more men at the same time. This is rare and is found in only about 1 per cent of all societies. Polyandry appears to arise where living standards are so low that a man can only afford to support a wife and child by sharing the responsibility with other men. It is found among the Todas of southern India and the Marquesan Islanders, and has been reported as occurring in parts of Tibet.

Patterns of Family Inheritance

As well as the variety of marriage relations, there are also differences in the patterns of inheritance in the family. **Patrilineal descent** is the system where the inheritance of title, property, and position as family head is passed down through the male side of the family, from father to son. An example of this is the way the succession to the British throne is passed through the male side of the royal family. **Matrilineal descent** is the system where inheritance is through the female side of the family.

Patterns of Residence

Different societies have different traditions about where the newly married should live. **Patrilocal residence** is the system where a married couple lives by tradition with or near the husband's family. **Matrilocal residence** is the system where the couple lives with or near the wife's family. In modern Britain, families tend to be **neo-local**, in that couples are not expected to move near either the husband's or the wife's family.

Patterns of Authority

Patriarchy is a term used to describe the dominance of men over women. A patriarchal family is one where the father, husband, or eldest male is usually the chief authority and decision-maker. An example of this was the family in Victorian Britain, but many writers would argue the modern British family remains patriarchal. **Matriarchy** describes the dominance of women over men. Matriarchal families are where power and authority is held by the most senior woman. These are rare, but there is some evidence of them in rural Japan.

CHANGES IN THE FAMILY IN BRITAIN

The family in Britain has gone through a number of changes since the beginnings of industrialization, and it continues to change today. The extent of some of these changes thought to have occurred in the family has often been exaggerated, and misleading conclusions drawn. Each of these changes will be examined in turn. The key changes which have commonly been thought to have occurred are summarized in the box below, and then discussed.

Major changes in the family in Britain

1 The changing role of the family in society, with the removal of some tasks once performed by the family to other social institutions, including the state.
2 The change from the classic extended family to the privatized nuclear family as the most common form of the family.
3 The emergence of the symmetrical family.
4 A move to more child-centred families.
5 A decline in average family size.
6 A rising divorce rate and higher rates of remarriage.
7 The emergence of the lone-parent family.

Change 1: The Changing Role of the Family in Society

The family in Britain and most other societies has traditionally had a number of responsibilities placed upon it (its functions), primarily connected with its role in the preparation of children to fit into adult society. These tasks of the family, and how they've changed during the course of this century in Britain, are described below.

Traditional responsibilities

- *Reproduction of the population* – the reproduction and nurturing of children. Having children was often seen as the main reason for marriage, as a means of passing on family property and providing a future workforce.

How they have changed

- In Britain since the 1970s, there has been a steady increase in the reproduction of children and sexual relations before and outside of marriage. In 1996, for example, nearly 36 per cent of children were born outside marriage. These changes might be explained as follows:
  - The availability of modern methods of contraception and of safe and legal abortion reduces the risks of unwanted pregnancy.
  - The decline of extended family life has meant less social pressure from relatives to maintain 'moral standards' and keep sexual relations within marriage.
  - Growing **secularization** – the decline in importance of religious beliefs, practice, and institutions – means people are less concerned with conforming to religious moral beliefs as guides to their sexual behaviour. (There is more on this in chapter 14.)
  - The welfare state and increasing job opportunities have made it easier for a woman to support a child financially without a husband or help from relatives.

Traditional responsibilities

- The family and kinship network traditionally played a major role in *maintaining and caring for dependent children* – housing, clothing, and feeding those children who were still unable to look after themselves. Before this century in Britain, most children were often poorly looked after because of poverty.

- The family provided most of the *help and care for the young, the old, the sick, and the poor* during periods of illness, unemployment, and other crises. Poverty often meant poor health and poor health care.

- The *primary socialization and social control of children*. The family is where society's new recruits first learn the basic values and norms of the culture of the society they will grow up in. For example, it is in the family that children first learn the difference between what is seen as 'right' and 'wrong', 'good' and 'bad' behaviour, the norms governing gender roles, and the acceptance of parental and other adult authority. These rules are reinforced by sanctions, such as praise and rewards.

- The family used to be one of the only sources of *education* for young people in Britain, and it still is in many less developed societies. Before compulsory schooling was provided by the state in Britain from 1880, many children from working-class families were very poorly educated by today's standards, and illiteracy rates were extremely high.

How they have changed

- Although the maintenance of children is still very important, the modern nuclear family is less dependent on relatives for this help and assistance, and relies more on the state. Welfare benefits like social security and child benefit, and the social services, including social workers working with families, all help parents to maintain their children.

- This has become shared with the state through the NHS and the social services. Homes for the elderly, hospitals, welfare clinics, GPs, old age pensions, unemployment benefit, and income support reduce the dependence on kin for money and support.

- The family still retains the major responsibility for the socialization of very young children, but the increase in the number of nurseries and playgroups has meant this is no longer restricted to the family. The state educational system now helps the family with the socialization of school-age children, and the mass media also play an important role.

- The education of children has been mainly taken over by the state, and is now primarily the responsibility of professional teachers rather than parents. All children between the ages of 5 and 16 now have to attend school by law. However, the family continues to play an important socializing and supporting role in preparing a

Traditional responsibilities

How they have changed

- Before industrialization and the growth of factory production in Britain, the family was a *unit of production*. This means that the family home was also the work-place, and the family produced most of the goods necessary for its own survival. Children would learn the skills needed for working life from their parents. An example of this was the domestic industry producing wool in eighteenth-century Britain. The whole family, including children, would work at home (hence the 'domestic system'), preparing, spinning, and weaving wool.

child for school, and encouraging and supporting her or him while at school. The family still has a major effect on a child's level of educational achievement.
- Since the early nineteenth century in Britain, work has been mainly based in factories and offices, not in the home. Families do not generally produce the goods they need any more; they go out and buy them. The skills required for adult working life are therefore no longer learnt in the family, but at the place of work, at colleges or on government-supported job training schemes.

Change 2: The Emergence of the Privatized Nuclear Family

A traditional view in sociology was that the main form of the family in Britain changed from the classic extended family before industrialization to the privatized nuclear family in the late twentieth century. However, research has shown that both nuclear and extended families were common in pre-industrial Britain, with the nuclear family perhaps being the most common. The family in Britain can be said to have developed through three basic stages.

ACTIVITY

1 Go carefully through the section on page 255 on the traditional responsibilities of functions of the family and how they have changed. Make a list summarizing these changes under two main headings: (a) the tasks traditionally performed by the family, and (b) who performs these functions today: family, or government and state, or shared between them.
2 Identify two ways that the family provides for the well-being of its members.
3 Do you think the changes that have occurred in the family's functions have made it more or less important in society today? Back up your viewpoint with evidence.
4 Imagine all families were banned by law tomorrow. What tasks currently carried out in your own family would someone else have to perform? Who would do these tasks, do you think?
5 Consider all the ways you can think of that the family a child is born into might affect the chances she or he gets in life, such as in health, education, and job opportunities. Be sure you explain the connection between family background and the life chances you identify.

The pre-industrial family

At this stage, the family was a unit of production which produced most of society's goods in small family workshops based in houses and farms (the domestic system), where family members would live and work together. The nuclear family was the most common form.

The early industrial classic extended family

With industrialization in nineteenth-century England, factory production replaced the domestic system, and the family ceased to be a unit of production. People began to go outside the home to work in factories, offices, and mines. Early industrialization strengthened the extended family, especially in the working class. This was because in the new industrial towns wages were low, unemployment was high, housing conditions and health were very poor, and working-class poverty was widespread. Relatives often provided the only sources of help and support against the insecurity and hardship of poverty and unemployment, so most working-class people strengthened links with kin through the formation of extended families.

The late twentieth-century privatized nuclear family

Over about the last one hundred years, a traditional view has been that the extended family has largely disappeared in modern Britain, with the typical family form in Britain becoming the **privatized nuclear family**. This means the nuclear family is separated and isolated from its extended kin, and has become a self-contained, self-reliant, home-centred unit. Life for the modern privatized nuclear family is largely centred on the home – free time is spent doing jobs around the house and leisure is mainly home- and family-centred. DIY, gardening, watching television, or going out as a family to pleasure parks like Alton Towers are typical family activities. The modern nuclear family has thus become a very private institution, isolated from wider kin and often from neighbours and local community life as well.

The following explanations have been offered for this decline of extended family life and the process of privatization.

- Industrial societies require a geographically mobile labour force, with people able and willing to move to other areas of the country to find work, improve their education, or gain promotion. This often involves leaving relatives behind, thus weakening and breaking up traditional extended family life. The small size of the modern isolated nuclear family and its lack of permanent roots in an area (such as wider kin) means that it is geographically mobile, which some sociologists argue makes it ideally suited for life in an industrial society.
- Industrial societies have become more meritocratic – occupational status is mainly achieved on the basis of talent, skill, and educational qualifications, rather than whom you know. Extended kin therefore have less to offer family members, such as job opportunities, reducing reliance on kin.
- Educational success and promotion often involve upward social mobility and this leads to differences in income, status, lifestyle, and attitudes and values between kin. Kin have less in common, and this contributes to the weakening of extended family ties.
- With the development of higher standards of living and the provision of welfare services by the state for security against ill-health, unemployment, and poverty, people have become less dependent on kin for help in times of distress. This further weakens the extended family.

The modified extended family

While there is evidence that nuclear families have become the most common form of the family in industrial society, geographical separation does not necessarily mean all links with kin are severed. Often, in the age of mass communications and easy transportation, the closeness and mutual support between kin, typical of classic extended family life, are retained by letter writing, telephone, and visiting. It has therefore been suggested that the typical family today in Britain is not simply the isolated nuclear family, but this modified form of the extended family.

The continued existence of the classic extended family

While the most common type of family found in modern Britain is the nuclear family or the modified extended family, there is evidence that the classic extended family still survives today in modern Britain in two types of community:

- Traditional working-class communities. These are long-established communities dominated by one industry, like fishing and mining, in the traditional working-class industrial centres of the north of England, and in inner-city working-class areas. In such communities, there is little geographical or social mobility, and children usually remain in the same area when they get married. People stay in the same community for several generations, and this creates a close-knit community life – it is the type of community shown in TV 'soaps' such as *Coronation Street* or *EastEnders*. Members of the extended family live close together and meet frequently, and there is a constant exchange of services between extended family members, such as washing, shopping, and baby-sitting between female kin, and shared work and leisure activities between male relatives. Such extended family life declined in the 1990s, as traditional industries closed down and people were forced to move away in search of new employment.
- The Asian community. There is evidence that the extended family is still very common among those who came to Britain in the 1960s and 1970s from India, Pakistan, and Bangladesh. The extended family usually centres on the male side of the family, with grandfathers, sons, grandsons and their wives, and unmarried daughters. Such a family life continues to be an important source of strength and support in such communities.

The return of the extended family?

Britain's ageing population (which is discussed in chapter 16) means that a growing number of people are reaching old age, and often living well into their eighties. This means that there is an increase in the number of extended three- and four-generation families, with more children growing up in extended families alongside several of their grandparents and even great-grandparents. This return of the extended family can only be expected to increase with the growing numbers of the elderly.

The myth of 'cereal packet' families

The popular image of the family in Britain in the late twentieth century has been described as the 'cereal packet family'. This is the image often promoted in advertising, with 'family size' breakfast cereals, toothpaste,

The 'cereal packet' family, with a working father married to a home-based mother caring for two small children, makes up only about 5 per cent of all households

and a wide range of other consumer goods. This popular 'happy family' image often gives the impression that most people live in a 'typical family' with the following features:

- It contains two parents and about two dependent children.
- These parents are married to one another, and neither of them has been married before.
- The husband is the breadwinner, with the wife staying at home and primarily concerned with housework and childcare.

This 'cereal packet' image of the 'typical family' is very mistaken, and there is a wide range of family types and household arrangements in modern Britain.

Households and families

Figure 11.1 shows the different types of household in Britain in 1996, and the types of household people were living in (a household is simply either one person living alone or a group of people living together at the same address). In 1996, only 24 per cent of households contained a married/cohabiting couple with dependent children, and only 40 per cent of people lived in such a family. This alone shows that the 'cereal packet' image of the nuclear family does not represent the arrangement in which most people in Britain live.

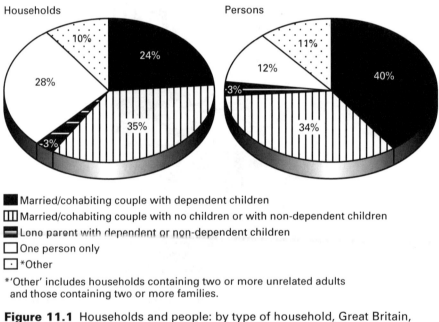

Households   Persons

■ Married/cohabiting couple with dependent children
Ⅲ Married/cohabiting couple with no children or with non-dependent children
▬ Lone parent with dependent or non-dependent children
☐ One person only
⊡ *Other

*'Other' includes households containing two or more unrelated adults and those containing two or more families.

Figure 11.1 Households and people: by type of household, Great Britain, 1996
Source: Data from General Household Survey

Families with dependent children

Figure 11.2 examines families with dependent children. This shows that in 1996, 23 per cent of such families were lone-parent families, nearly nine out of ten of them headed by women. Although 77 per cent of families with dependent children were headed by a married or cohabiting

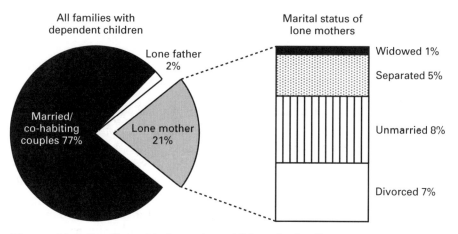

Figure 11.2 Families with dependent children: by family type and, for lone mothers, by marital status, Great Britain, 1996
Source: Data from Labour Force Survey, 1996

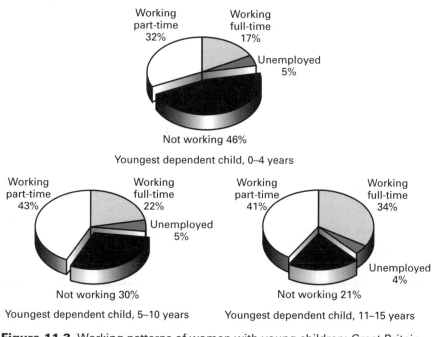

Figure 11.3 Working patterns of women with young children: Great Britain, 1996
Source: Data from Labour Force Survey, 1996

couple, this doesn't mean that most of these families conformed to the 'cereal packet' image.

- A number of these families were reconstituted families, in which one or both partners were previously married. About 10 per cent of children under age 16 lived in such a family in 1991.
- Most of these families were dual-worker families, where both parents were working. In 1996 well over half of married couples with children had partners who were both working. As figure 11.3 shows, large numbers of mothers with dependent children work in paid employment, with the numbers increasing as children get older. In 1996, 60 per cent of all women with dependent children were working.
- The 'cereal packet' 'happy family' stereotype, of a working father married to a home-based mother caring for two small children, in 1996 made up less than 5 per cent of all households.

ACTIVITY

Refer to figure 11.1 on page 262:

1 What percentage of households in 1996 consisted of one person only?
2 What percentage of people in 1996 were living in households consisting of a married or cohabiting couple with no children or with non-dependent children?

Refer to figure 11.2 on page 263:

3 In 1996, what percentage of all families with dependent children were lone-parent families?
4 What percentage of families with dependent children were headed by a lone mother who was widowed?
5 What was the main cause of lone motherhood?

Refer to figure 11.3 on page 263:

6 What percentage of mothers whose youngest child was aged 0–4 years were not working in 1996?

7 Identify two trends which occur as the youngest dependent child gets older.

8 What does figure 11.3 suggest might be the main restriction on mothers with young children going out to work? Suggest ways this restriction might be overcome.

9 Suggest reasons why so many people seem to believe that the 'cereal packet' family is the most common type of family.

Conclusion

This section has suggested that it is very misleading to assume that the 'cereal packet' image of the family represents the reality of family life in Britain. Only a small minority of families are of this type. It is much more realistic to recognize that there is a wide variety of family types in modern Britain, and future trends would suggest growing numbers of extended, dual-worker, reconstituted, and lone-parent families.

Change 3: The Emergence of the 'Symmetrical' Family?

There is a common belief that the relations between male and female partners in the family in Britain have become more equal in the second half of the twentieth century. The assumption has been that there has been a change from segregated to integrated conjugal roles, and the emergence of a more 'symmetrical' or equally balanced family, with male partners taking more responsibility for housework and childcare. **Conjugal roles** are simply the roles played by male and female partners in marriage or in a cohabiting couple. There are said to be two main types:

- **Segregated conjugal roles**, where male and female partners play very different roles in the family, with a clear division and separation between the male's role and the female's role.
- **Integrated** (or joint) **conjugal roles**, where there are few divisions between male and female partner's roles.

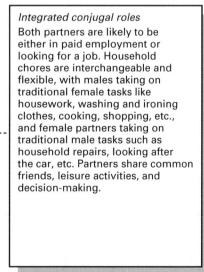

Segregated conjugal roles
Husband and wife or partners in cohabiting couples have clearly separated roles.
Male role: responsibility for bringing in income and the heavier jobs around the home (repairing household equipment and house repairs). He will have separate (male) friends and different leisure activities from his female partner, and be responsible for major decisions affecting the family.
Female role: housewife, with responsibility for housework, shopping, cooking, childcare, etc. She is unlikely to have paid employment.

Integrated conjugal roles
Both partners are likely to be either in paid employment or looking for a job. Household chores are interchangeable and flexible, with males taking on traditional female tasks like housework, washing and ironing clothes, cooking, shopping, etc., and female partners taking on traditional male tasks such as household repairs, looking after the car, etc. Partners share common friends, leisure activities, and decision-making.

Figure 11.4 Segregated and integrated conjugal roles

The change from segregated to integrated roles

This supposed change is thought to have occurred for a number of reasons.

- The improved status and rights of women have forced men to accept women more as equals and not simply as housewives and mothers.
- The increase in the number of working women has increased women's independence and authority in the family – where the female partner has her own income, she is less dependent on her male partner, and she has more power and authority. Decision-making is therefore more likely to be shared.
- The importance of female partners' earnings in maintaining the family's standard of living may have encouraged men to help more with housework – a recognition that the women cannot be expected to do two jobs at once.
- Improved living standards in the home, such as central heating, TV, videos and stereos, and 'all mod cons', have encouraged men to spend more time at home, and share home-centred leisure with their female partners.
- The decline of the close-knit extended family and greater geographical mobility in industrial society have meant there is less pressure from kin on newly married or cohabiting couples to retain traditional roles – it is therefore easier to adopt new roles in a relationship. There are often no longer the separate male and female networks (of friends and especially kin) for male and female partners to mix with. This increases their dependence upon each other, and may mean men and women who adopt new roles avoid being teased by friends who knew them before they got married or began cohabiting.

The myth of integrated roles

A 1997 study by the Office for National Statistics showed that rising numbers of men were choosing to become 'house-husbands', and raise children rather than work, leaving their partner to become the family breadwinner. This reversal of traditional roles reflects the growing earning power of women at work, and provides some evidence of changing attitudes among some men towards childcare and housework. However, this trend appears to be mainly happening only in those relatively few families where the woman earns more than the man, and it is financially practical to swop roles.

Evidence from a number of surveys suggests that women still perform the majority of domestic tasks around the home, even when they have paid jobs themselves. This is true even among full-time working women,

Have conjugal roles really changed?

where one would expect to find the greatest degree of equality. Cooking the evening meal, household cleaning, washing and ironing, and caring for sick children are still mainly performed by women (see figure 11.5). Data published in 1997 by the Office for National Statistics showed that women spent on average nearly twice as long as men each day (five hours) cooking, cleaning, shopping, washing and looking after the children. A *World in Action* TV documentary in June 1991 found that housework was the second largest cause of domestic rows, after money.

There does seem to be evidence of some role integration in leisure activities and decision-making, but housework and childcare remain predominantly 'women's work'. While men are perhaps more involved in childcare than they used to be, this would appear to be in the more enjoyable activities like playing with the children and taking them out. The more routine jobs such as bathing and feeding and taking children to the doctor are still done predominantly by women, and it is still mostly women who get the blame if the house is untidy or children are dirty or badly dressed.

While there is some evidence of husbands doing marginally more around the home in recent years, this change would appear to have been massively exaggerated. In a majority of marriages the traditional roles of women and men remain.

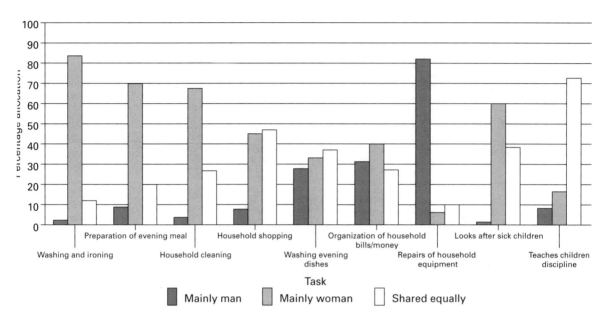

Figure 11.5 Household division of labour among married or cohabiting couples: Great Britain
Source: Based on data from British Social Attitudes Survey, 1992

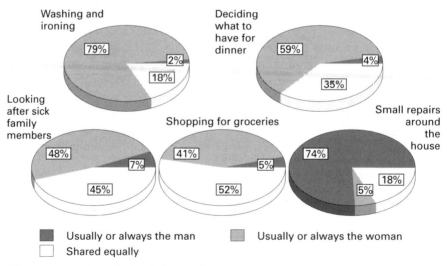

Figure 11.6 Household division of labour among married or cohabiting couples, Great Britain
Source: Based on data from British Social Attitudes Survey, 1994

ACTIVITY

Refer to figures 11.5 and 11.6. These show the results of surveys which were conducted in 1992 and 1994. Then answer the following questions:

1 Overall, which three household tasks were the most likely to be performed mainly by women?
2 Overall, which two household tasks were the most likely to be performed mainly by men?
3 Who is most likely to look after sick children or other sick family members?
4 Which household task is the least likely to be performed mainly by men?
5 Overall, which three household tasks are most likely to be shared equally?
6 Who is most likely to decide what to have for dinner, to prepare the evening meal, and either to be solely responsible for washing up or to share it with their partners?
7 Outline all the evidence in figures 11.5 and 11.6 which suggests that it is largely a myth that the family is a 'partnership of equals' today.

How far is there equality between partners in a household you know well? It could be your own home, or any household where there are children. Put the following questions to the male partner of the household.

1 Have you ever ironed your partner's blouse?
2 What foods do your children refuse to eat?
3 What do the following cost: a loaf, a jar of instant coffee, a packet of tea, a packet of butter, a tin of baked beans, a packet of soap-powder, and a packet of toilet rolls?
4 How does the washing machine work?
5 What would you use to clean the kitchen floor?
6 How do you empty the vacuum cleaner bag?
7 What days are the bins emptied?
8 What brand of washing powder do you use?
9 When did you last do the family shopping alone?
10 When did you last draw up the shopping list alone?
11 When did you last clean the loo?
12 What is the children's favourite meal?
13 How many hours a week do you spend on housework?
14 When did you last clean the bathroom or kitchen taps?
15 When did you last clean the bath or shower, or the kitchen/bathroom sinks?

Source: World in Action, June 1991

Compare your findings with others in your group. What conclusions do your findings suggest about the apparent change towards growing equality between men and women in the family?

Change 4: The Changing Position of Children in the Family

Children and the family in the nineteenth century

In the nineteenth century, the father and husband was the head of the family, and often had a great deal of authority over other family members. He would often have little involvement in the care of his children. In upper- and middle-class families, children might see relatively little of their parents, often being sent off to private boarding schools or being looked after by a nanny or governess. In working-class families, children in the early nineteenth century were seen as workers and an economic asset to the family, as they were able to work in the factories and mines and bring money into the house. Generally, children had low status in the family, and were expected 'to be seen and not heard'.

Children and the family in the twentieth century

During the course of the twentieth century, families have become more child-centred, with family activities and outings often focused on the interests of the children. The amount of time parents spend with their children has more than doubled since the 1960s, and parents are more involved with their children, taking an interest in their activities, discussing decisions with them, and treating them more as equals. Often, the children's welfare is seen as the major family priority, frequently involving the parents in considerable financial sacrifice and cost.

The causes of child-centredness

- Families have got smaller this century, and this means more individual care and attention can be devoted to each child.
- In the nineteenth century, the typical working week was between 70 and 80 hours for many working-class people. Today, it is more like 44 hours and is tending to get shorter. This means parents have more time to spend with their children.
- Increasing affluence, with higher wages and a higher standard of living, has benefited children, as more money can be spent on them and their activities.
- The social security system provides a wide range of benefits designed to help parents care for their children. The welfare state has increased demands on parents to look after their children properly: social workers, for example, have a wide range of powers to intervene in families on behalf of children, and have the ultimate power to remove children from families if parents fail to look after them properly.
- Paediatrics, or the science of childhood, has developed this century, with a wide range of research and popular books suggesting how parents should bring up their children to encourage their full development. For example, Dr Spock's childcare books have been sold to millions of parents. 'Parenting skills' have now been recognized as a very important aspect of children's educational and social development.
- Compulsory education and more time spent in further education and training have meant young people are dependent on their parents for longer periods of time. 'Childhood' has itself become extended.
- Children's lives have become more complex, with more educational, medical, and leisure services for them. This frequently involves parents in ferrying children to schools, cinemas, friends, and so on.
- Growing traffic dangers and parental fears (largely unjustified) of assaults against their children have meant that children now travel more with parents rather than being left to roam about on their own as much as they used to.

Change 5: The Decline in Average Family Size

Over the last century, the birth rate has been declining in Britain. This has meant that average family size has been dropping, from around 6 children per family in the 1870s to an average of around 1.8 children per family in 1996. The reasons for this change are discussed in chapter 16 on population.

Change 6: The Rising Divorce Rate

One of the most startling changes in the family in Britain this century has been the general and dramatic increase in the number of marriages to end in divorce, as shown in figure 11.7. The number of divorces rose from 29 000 in 1951 to 155 000 in 1995, with the number of divorces doubling during the 1970s. Britain has one of the highest **divorce rates** (numbers divorcing per thousand married people) in the European Union, and

ACTIVITY

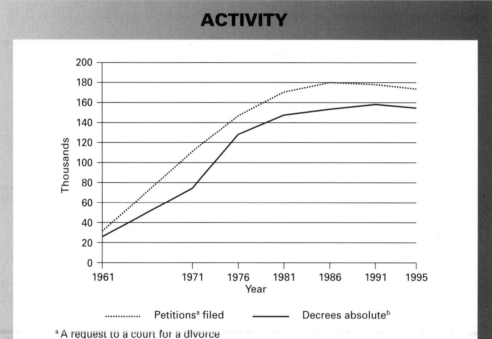

··········· Petitions[a] filed   ——— Decrees absolute[b]

[a] A request to a court for a divorce
[b] The final divorce

Figure 11.7 Divorce: England and Wales, 1961–95
Source: Data from *Social Trends 12* and *21; Annual Abstract of Statistics 1997*

Study figure 11.7 and answer the following questions:

1 Approximately how many divorce petitions were filed in 1976?
2 How many decrees absolute were there in 1986?
3 In what year was there the highest number of decrees absolute?
4 About how many more decrees absolute were there in 1981 than in 1961?
5 Figure 11.7 shows there is a large difference between the number of divorce petitions (requests to a court to grant a divorce) and the number of decrees absolute (the final divorce) granted. Suggest explanations for this.

Divorce and 'broken homes'

Divorce is the legal termination of a marriage, but this is not the only way that marriages and homes can be 'broken'. Homes and marriages may be broken in 'empty shell' marriages, where the marital relationship has broken down, but no divorce has taken place. Separation – through either choice or necessity (like working abroad or imprisonment) – may also cause a broken home, as may the death of a partner. So homes may be broken for reasons other than divorce, and divorce itself is often only the end result of a marriage which broke down long before.

estimates have suggested more than 40 per cent of marriages in the 1990s were likely to end in divorce.

Who gets divorced?

While divorce affects all groups in the population, there are some groups where divorce rates are higher than the average. Teenage marriages are twice as likely to end in divorce as those of couples overall, and there is a high incidence of divorce in the first five years of marriage and after about twelve to fourteen years (when the children are older or have left home). The working class, particularly semi- and unskilled, has a higher rate of divorce than the middle class. Childless couples and partners from different social class or religious backgrounds also face a higher risk of divorce.

ACTIVITY

Go through the groups above, and suggest explanations why each of them is more at risk of divorce than most of the rest of the population. Can you think of other groups who might have a higher risk of divorce than most people?

Explanations for the rising divorce rate

Rising divorce rates must be treated with considerable caution, and assessed against changing legal, financial, and social circumstances, if misleading conclusions about the declining importance of marriage and the

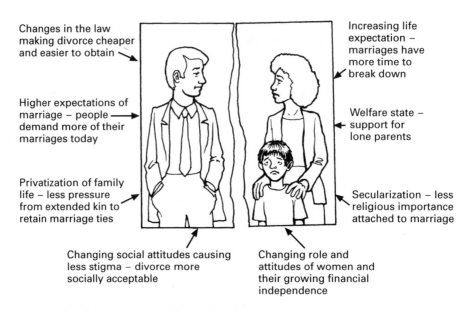

Changes in the law making divorce cheaper and easier to obtain

Higher expectations of marriage – people demand more of their marriages today

Privatization of family life – less pressure from extended kin to retain marriage ties

Increasing life expectation – marriages have more time to break down

Welfare state – support for lone parents

Secularization – less religious importance attached to marriage

Changing social attitudes causing less stigma – divorce more socially acceptable

Changing role and attitudes of women and their growing financial independence

Figure 11.8 The causes of the rising divorce rate

family are to be avoided. The increase may simply reflect easier and cheaper divorce procedures enabling the legal termination of already unhappy 'empty shell' marriages rather than a real increase in marriage breakdowns. It could be that people who in previous years could only separate are now divorcing as legal and financial obstacles are removed.

There are two broad groups of reasons for the increase in the divorce rate. First, there have been changes in the law which have gradually made divorce easier and cheaper to get. Each change in the divorce law has increased the divorce rate. However, legal changes alone do not explain the increasing divorce rate – legal changes often reflect changing social attitudes and norms. The second group of explanations is therefore made up of those changes in society which have made divorce a more practical and socially acceptable way of terminating a broken marriage.

Changes in the law

Before 1857, divorce could only be obtained by the rich, since each divorce needed a private Act of Parliament. As a result, there were very few divorces. Since that time, changes in the law have made it easier to get a divorce, particularly during the twentieth century.

THE MATRIMONIAL CAUSES ACT OF 1857

This made divorce procedure easier and cheaper, but still beyond the financial means of the lower middle class and the working class. Men had more rights in divorce than women, and divorce was only possible if it could be proved in court that a 'matrimonial offence' such as adultery, cruelty, or desertion had been committed. Even by 1911, there were only about 600 divorces a year.

THE MATRIMONIAL CAUSES ACT OF 1923

This gave women equal rights with men in divorce for the first time, and therefore gave more women the opportunity to terminate unhappy marriages.

THE LEGAL AID AND ADVICE ACT OF 1949

This gave financial assistance with the costs of solicitors' and court fees, which made it far more possible for working-class people to cope with the costs of a divorce action.

THE DIVORCE LAW REFORM ACT OF 1969

This came into effect in 1971, and was a major change. Before the 1969 Act, a person wanting a divorce had to prove before a court that his or her spouse had committed a 'matrimonial offence', as mentioned above. This frequently led to major public scandals, as all the details of unhappy marriages were aired in a public law court. This may have deterred many people whose marriage had broken down from seeking a divorce. Also, marriages may have broken down – become 'empty shell' marriages – without any matrimonial offence being committed.

The 1969 Act changed all this, and made 'irretrievable breakdown' of a marriage the only grounds for divorce. It is now no longer necessary to prove one partner 'guilty' of a matrimonial offence, but simply to demonstrate that a marriage has broken down beyond repair. After 1971, one way of demonstrating 'irretrievable breakdown' of a marriage was by two years of separation. This change in the law led to a massive increase in the number of divorces after 1971.

THE MATRIMONIAL AND FAMILY PROCEEDINGS ACT OF 1984

This allowed couples to petition for divorce after only one year of marriage, whereas previously couples could normally divorce only after three years of marriage. This led to a record increase in the number of divorces in 1984 and 1985.

THE FAMILY LAW ACT OF 1996

This came into effect in 1998, and increased the amount of time before a divorce can be granted to eighteen months. This was an attempt to stem the rising number of divorces by increasing the time for 'cooling off'.

Changes in society

THE CHANGING ROLE OF WOMEN

This is a very important explanation for the rising divorce rate. Around three-quarters of divorce petitions (requests to a court for a divorce) are presented by women, and three out of four of all divorces were granted to women in 1996. This suggests more women than men are unhappy with the state of their marriages, and are more likely to take the first steps in ending a marriage. This may well be because women's expectations of life and marriage have risen during the course of the twentieth century, and they are less willing to accept a traditional housewife/mother role, with the sacrifices of their own lives, independence, and careers this involves.

The employment of married women has increased this century. For example, in 1931, only 10 per cent of married women were employed, but this had gradually risen to about 70 per cent in 1996. This has increased their financial independence, and reduced the extent of dependence on their husbands. This makes it easier for women to escape from unhappy marriages, and in the event of marriage breakdown, there are a range of welfare state benefits to help divorced women, particularly those with children.

HIGHER EXPECTATIONS OF MARRIAGE

People's expectations of what marriage should be like have risen this century, and couples (especially women) expect and demand far more from married life today than their parents might have settled for. The mass media (especially television) often emphasize the romantic aspects of marriage, and they also provide us with images of and insights into other people's relationships which earlier generations didn't have. People therefore have come to expect more companionship, understanding, and sexual compatibility in their marriage, rather than the financial security which seemed more important in the past. Consequently couples are more likely to end a relationship which earlier generations might have tolerated.

CHANGING SOCIAL ATTITUDES

Divorce has become more socially acceptable, and there is less social disapproval and condemnation (stigmatizing) of divorcees. Divorce no longer hinders careers through a public sense of scandal and outrage. As a result, people are less afraid of the consequences of divorce, and are more likely to seek a legal end to an unhappy marriage rather than simply separating or carrying on in an 'empty shell' marriage.

GROWING SECULARIZATION

Secularization – the decline in religious belief – has meant that divorce is not seen so much today as breaking solemn vows or morally wrong, and many people today probably do not attach much religious significance to their marriage.

INCREASING LIFE EXPECTATION

People live to a greater age than they did in the early years of the twentieth century, and this means the potential number of years a couple may be together, before the death of a partner occurs, has increased. This gives more time for marriages to 'go wrong' and for divorces to occur. It has been suggested that the divorce courts have taken on the role in finishing unhappy marriages that the undertaker once did!

THE GROWTH OF THE PRIVATIZED NUCLEAR FAMILY

This has meant that, during marital crises, it is no longer so easy for marriage partners to seek advice from or temporary refuge with relatives, and there is also less social control from extended kin pressuring couples to retain marriage ties.

ACTIVITY

1 Go through all the reasons suggested above for the rising divorce rate, putting them in what you think is their order of importance.

2 Study television advertisements or television 'soaps' for a few days. What kind of overall impressions are given of married life today? Refer to particular advertisements or 'soaps' as evidence for your findings. Do you agree or disagree with the view that these create higher expectations of marriage today? Explain the reasons for your answer.

3 Of couples married in 1987, 58 per cent of men and 53 per cent of women said that they had lived with their partners beforehand, and living together before marriage was seen as one of the major social changes of the 1980s and 1990s. However, many of these people eventually marry. What social pressures are there that push people towards conforming to the norm of marriage? Write down all the reasons you can think of why so many people continue to marry eventually, despite the high divorce rate and previous experience of living together outside marriage. Discuss your reasons with others in your class.

Change 7: The Emergence of the Lone-Parent Family

One of the biggest changes in the family has been the growth of the lone-parent family (also known as the single-parent or one-parent family). Britain now has one of the highest proportions of lone-parent families in Europe, and the percentage of such families has tripled since 1971. About 23 per cent of all families with dependent children were lone-parent families in 1997 – nine out of ten of them headed by women. More than one in five (21 per cent) dependent children now live in such families, compared to just 7 per cent in 1971.

Nearly one in four families with dependent children are lone-parent families, 90 per cent of them headed by women
Photo: Ted Fussey

Why are there more lone-parent families?

The rapid growth in the number of lone-parent families can be explained by a number of factors, some of which have already been discussed earlier in explaining the rising divorce rate and in the chapter on women. These include:

- *The greater economic independence of women.* Women have greater economic independence today, both through more job opportunities and through support from the welfare state. This means marriage, and support by a husband, is less of an economic necessity today compared to the past.
- *Improved contraception, changing male attitudes, and fewer 'shotgun weddings'.* With the wider availability and approval of safe and effective contraception, and easier access to safe and legal abortion, men may feel less responsibility to marry women should they become preg-

nant, and women may feel under less pressure to marry the future father. There are therefore fewer 'shotgun weddings'.

- *Changing social attitudes.* There is less social stigma (or social disapproval and condemnation) attached to lone parenthood today. Women are therefore less afraid of the social consequences of becoming lone parents.
- *Unemployment and poverty.* Rising levels of poverty, including unemployment, during the 1980s and 1990s put increasing strains on family life. This led to more married or cohabiting partners ending their relationships, with one partner being left with the sole or main responsibility for any children. In most cases, this was more likely to be the woman.

The growth in lone parenthood has been seen by some as one of the major signs of the 'decline' of conventional family life and marriage. Lone-parent families – and particularly lone never-married mothers – have been portrayed by some of the media and conservative politicians as promiscuous parasites blamed for everything from rising juvenile crime to housing shortages, rising drug abuse, educational failure of children, and the general breakdown of society. However, the never-married lone mother only accounts for one-third of all lone parents, with most lone parenthood arising from divorce, separation, or widowhood. Even among the never-married lone mothers, the vast majority cohabited with the father and have registered his name on the birth certificate.

Nailing the myths

A Home Office report in 1985 found no difference in the crime rates between youngsters from lone- and two-parent families. Even if there were such a link, it would probably be caused by poverty rather than lone parenthood, as lack of childcare facilities means many lone parents have to depend on inadequate state benefits to live. This is likely to explain other factors linked in the popular imagination to lone parenthood, such as lower educational achievement. A misleading myth is that of single teenage mothers getting pregnant to jump the queue for social (council and housing association) housing. There is very little evidence for this. Research in 1996 by the Economic and Social Research Council found that only 10 per cent of the small minority of women who became mothers prior to any partnership with the father were living alone with their child in social housing six months after the birth. Many live with their parents, and many single, never-married parents have been in cohabiting relationships which break down. In effect, this is no different from marriages that break down.

Fortunately, many people do not share the horror images of lone parenthood which the media sometimes portray. In a 1993 national survey,

DISCUSSION

Do you believe that a lone parent can bring up her child as well as a married (or cohabiting) couple? Do you believe that people who want children ought to get married? Do you believe that to grow up happily, children need a home with both their mother and father? Is it better for a child to grow up with one loving, caring parent, or with two who don't get on very well? Do you believe young single mothers deserve help and support from society, or should they be condemned for being irresponsible?

48 per cent of people agreed that 'a single mother can bring up her child as well as a married couple', and only 52 per cent agreed with the suggestion that 'people who want children ought to get married'. A third of people disagreed with the suggestion that 'to grow up happily, children need a home with both their mother and father'.

CRITICAL VIEWS OF THE FAMILY

The 'cereal packet' image of the 'typical family' has already been questioned earlier in this chapter, but the view of the warm and supportive 'happy family' which is often presented in the mass media has been questioned on a more fundamental level by many writers.

The 'Darker Side' of Family Life

While the family is often a warm and supportive unit for its members, it can also be a hostile and dangerous place. The growing privatization of family life can lead to emotional stress in the family. Family members are thrown together, isolated from and lacking the support of extended kin, neighbours, and the wider community. Tempers become easily frayed,

Today the domestic household is isolated. The family looks inward upon itself; there is an intensification of emotional stress between husband and wife, and parents and children. The strain is greater than most of us can bear. Far from being the basis of the good society, the family, with its narrow privacy and tawdry secrets, is the source of all our discontents. (Edmund Leach)

emotional temperatures and stress levels rise, and – as in a pressure cooker without a safety valve – explosions occur, and family conflict is the result. This may lead to violence, divorce, psychological damage to children, perhaps even mental illness and crime.

The breakdown of marriages which leads to divorce is often the end result of long-running and bitter disputes between partners. The intense emotions involved in family life often mean that incidents that would appear trivial in other situations take on the proportion of major confrontations inside the family. The extent of violence in the family is coming increasingly to public attention, with rising reports of the physical and sexual abuse of children, the rape of wives by their husbands, and wife- and baby-battering. One in four murders takes place in the family. This is the darker side of family life.

Because of the private nature of the family, accurate evidence on the extent of violence and abuse inside the family is difficult to obtain, and fear or shame means that it is almost certain that most of such incidents are covered up.

The abuse of children

There are several different types of abuse of children. *Sexual abuse* refers to adults using their power to perform sex acts with children below the age of consent (16 for heterosexual and lesbian acts and 18 for male homosexual acts). *Physical abuse* refers to non-sexual violence. *Emotional abuse* refers to persistent or severe emotional ill-treatment or rejection of children, which has severe effects on their emotional development and behaviour. *Neglect* refers to the failure to protect children from exposure to danger, including cold and starvation, and failing to care for them properly so that their health or development is affected.

In 1997, Department of Health statistics showed there were 32 369 children and young people under the age of 18 on child protection registers in England for various forms of abuse. There were 13 729 children registered for physical injury or sexual abuse alone, 8511 for neglect, and a further 5072 for emotional abuse alone (see figure 11.10). These figures were for England alone, and only for abuse which was brought to the attention of social services departments. It is very likely that much abuse goes on that is undiscovered.

Some indication of this is shown by statistics from Childline, the free confidential counselling service for children, established in 1986. In the ten years to 1996, out of the 152 000 children helped, 41 000 (27 per cent) called about sexual and physical abuse.

ACTIVITY

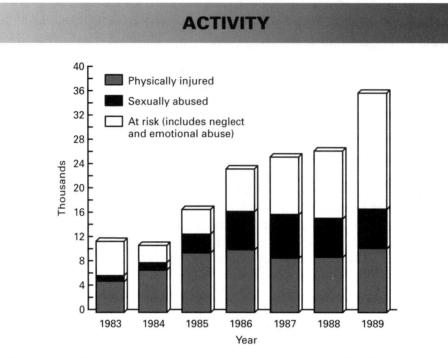

Figure 11.9 Physical and sexual abuse: estimated number of children aged 0–16, England and Wales, 1983–9
Source: 'Child Abuse in 1989', NSPCC Research Briefing no. 11 (NSPCC 1990)

Study figure 11.9 and answer the following questions:

1 About how many children in total under 16 were physically or sexually abused or at risk in 1985?
2 About how many children were sexually abused in 1989?
3 About how many more children under 16 were physically injured in 1989 compared to 1984?

Refer to figure 11.10:

4 In the year ending 31 March 1997, for which two categories of abuse were children and young people most commonly put on child protection registers?
5 What percentage of children and young people were registered for sexual abuse alone?
6 Suggest reasons why the number of child abuse cases recorded in the NSPCC report on 1989 and in the Department of Health statistics in 1997 might not give a true picture of the extent of child abuse. Do you think the increase in the number of reported cases of child abuse means the problem is growing? What other explanations might there be for the increasing reporting of child abuse?

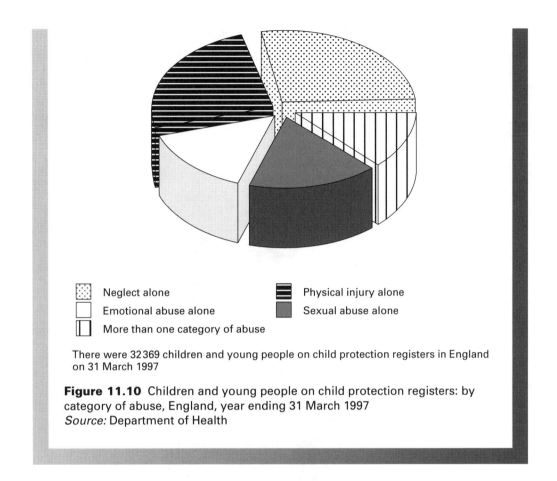

Neglect alone

Emotional abuse alone

More than one category of abuse

Physical injury alone

Sexual abuse alone

There were 32 369 children and young people on child protection registers in England on 31 March 1997

Figure 11.10 Children and young people on child protection registers: by category of abuse, England, year ending 31 March 1997
Source: Department of Health

Violence against women

There is widespread evidence of violence by men against their female partners – battered wives. Such violence is often not taken very seriously by the police or courts, being dismissed as a 'domestic dispute' – which seems to suggest violence against women is seen in some quarters as an acceptable and normal part of a relationship! Certainly the type of physical violence battered women are subject to by their male partners would quite probably result in prosecution and imprisonment if it was carried out against a stranger outside the family. The largest survey ever conducted on domestic violence in Britain, in 1993, found that one in ten women had been victims of violence from their partners in the past twelve months, with 28 per cent of women suffering physical injury. Only 22 per cent of the attacks were reported to the police. A 1996 survey in Surrey discovered an even worse picture, with 31 per cent of women having experienced violence from a known man, 24 per cent having been beaten up, 16 per cent living in constant fear of domestic violence, and 13 per cent feeling suicidal or suffering depression. Two-thirds of victims of domestic violence had not sought help because they were afraid, ashamed, or saw it as a private matter.

Statistics such as these, and the widespread growth of refuges for battered women since the 1970s, reflect the extent and seriousness of the problem of violence against women in the home, much of which goes unreported and undiscovered.

'Can I have a black eye, too, Ma?' asks the little girl.
'Wait till you're old enough to get married, pet,' says her mother.

This cartoon from 1896 shows domestic violence was the norm then, but are things really much better today?

Rape in marriage

Rape is when someone is forced to have sex against her or his will, often accompanied by the actual or threatened use of violence. A representative survey carried out in 1989 for Granada Television's *World in Action* programme reported that over one in four (28 per cent) of women had been raped, with most rapes being committed by husbands on their wives.

- One in seven women (14 per cent) in the survey had been raped by their husbands, compared with 12 per cent by acquaintances and boyfriends, and 2 per cent by strangers.
- Four out of five of the raped wives reported that rape by their husbands was a frequent occurrence.
- Nearly half (44 per cent) of the rapes within marriage were accompanied by the actual or threatened use of violence.
- One in five wives suffered physical injury.

Such sexual violence in the family, then, would appear to be disturbingly common, but only as recently as 1991 was rape within marriage confirmed as a criminal offence by the Court of Appeal.

Feminist Criticisms of the Family

Feminist writers – those concerned with establishing equal rights for women – have been responsible for highlighting much of the violence against women in the family. However, they also have a range of other criticisms of the family, arguing that it is an institution that serves men's needs better than women's, and that it particularly oppresses and exploits women. Many of these criticisms are covered in other chapters, and the following is simply a brief summary of them.

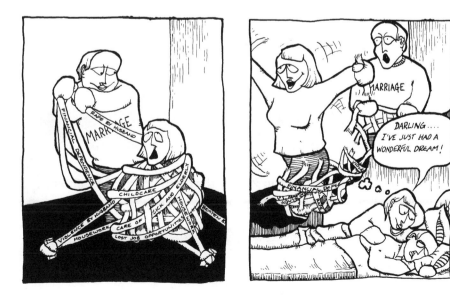

- Far from the popular impression of growing equality between male and female partners in the family being correct, inequalities continue. As seen earlier in this chapter, women still have most of the responsibility for housework, even when they are in full-time employment. Most women work both outside the home in paid employment, and inside the home as housewives and mothers. They have two jobs to the man's one.

- Feminists emphasize that housework is, in fact, unpaid labour. The government's New Earnings Survey put the value of work done by women in the home at £313 a week. The value of the housework performed free by many women is illustrated by the Mercantile and General insurance company's 'Housewife's sickness income benefit', introduced in 1991. This paid benefits up to £10 000 per year or £192 per week to cover the costs of hiring help should a housewife no longer be able to perform domestic tasks such as food preparation, shopping, cleaning, and other household tasks.

- It is still mainly women who give up paid work (or suffer from lost/restricted job opportunities) to look after children, the old, the sick, and male partners. Women still take most of the responsibility for childcare and child rearing, and are most likely to get the blame from society if these tasks are not performed 'properly'.

- As seen in chapter 6, women's position in the family remains a primary source of discrimination and disadvantage in the labour market. Employers are often unwilling to employ or promote married women, particularly in jobs with high levels of pay and responsibility. Marriage poses no such problem for men.

- The family is a major source of gender role socialization, which causes women to underachieve (do less well than they are able) in a wide range of areas, and which keeps women in a secondary position to men in many areas of social life.

Looked at from these points of view, women have much to lose from the present organization of the family.

DISCUSSION

Discuss the view that men have much to gain, and women much to lose, from marriage and the family.

ALTERNATIVES TO THE FAMILY

Communes

Communes are self-contained and self-supporting communities. They developed in Western Europe, Britain, and the USA in the 1960s, among groups of people wanting to develop alternative lifestyles to conventional society because of the political or religious beliefs they held.

Communes often try to develop an alternative style of living and a kind of alternative household, with the emphasis on collective living rather than individual family units. A number of adults and children all aim to live and work together, with children being seen as the responsibility of the group as a whole rather than of natural parents. Many communes tended to be very short-lived, and only a few remain in Britain today.

The Kibbutz

The Israeli **kibbutz** is a form of commune, and is one of the most famous and successful attempts to establish an alternative to the family. Here, the emphasis is on collective child rearing, with the community as a whole taking over the tasks of the family. In the early kibbutzim, child rearing was separated as much as possible from the marriage relationship, with children kept apart from their natural parents for much of the time and brought up in the Children's House by metapelets. These were a kind of 'professional parent' combining the roles of nurse, housemother, and educator. The role of the natural parents was extremely limited, and they were only allowed to see their children for short periods each day. The children were seen as the 'children of the kibbutz' – they were the responsibility of the community as a whole, which met all of their needs. Children would move through a series of children's homes with others of the same age group until they reached adulthood.

In recent years, the more traditional family unit has re-emerged in the kibbutzim, with natural parents and children sharing the same accommodation, but the kibbutz remains one of the most important attempts to find an alternative to conventional family structures.

ARE MARRIAGE AND THE FAMILY DECLINING SOCIAL INSTITUTIONS?

The Case for Decline

In the 1990s, it was estimated that more than 40 per cent of marriages would end in divorce, and that almost one in four children (24 per cent) would experience a parental divorce by their sixteenth birthday. In Britain today, nearly a quarter of families with dependent children have just one parent. In 1996, over 36 per cent of births were outside of marriage. There are well over a million cohabiting couples who have refused to tie the marriage knot – one in twelve of all couples. This is expected to rise to 1.7 million by 2020, making up around one in seven of all 'couple' households. Twenty-three per cent of all non-married women began cohabiting between 1991 and 1994. Research by the Office for National Statistics in 1997 (published in *Population Trends 89*) found six in every ten couples married in 1994 gave identical addresses. This provides strong evidence that these couples were cohabiting before marriage (and this 'living in sin' includes 41 per cent of those getting married in a religious ceremony). Living together before or outside of marriage has been one of the major social changes of the late twentieth century. The Policy Studies Institute has calculated that, if these trends continue, by the year 2010 the majority of couples will cohabit before marriage, the majority of marriages will end in divorce followed by remarriage, and nearly all births will be outside marriage.

It is statistics like these which have made the state of the family a major battleground for politicians, with the suggestion that the very existence of the family is threatened by rising rates of divorce, cohabitation, lone parenthood, and reconstituted families. This picture of the family in decline has been blamed for a wide range of social ills, such as declining moral standards, social disorder, drug abuse, rising crime rates, vandalism, football hooliganism, and increasing levels of violence in society. However, this view of the family in decline has to be treated with considerable caution: the causes of those social ills all too often blamed on the family are many and complex, and those who blame the family are often searching for simple solutions to complex problems.

The Case against Decline

Although the divorce rate has gone up, the evidence suggests that it is easier divorce laws, reduced social stigma, and more sympathetic public attitudes which have caused this, rather than more marriage breakdowns. In the past, many couples may have been condemned, by legal and financial obstacles and social intolerance, to suffer unhappy 'empty shell' marriages or to separate without divorcing. If the law were changed to make divorce harder to get, couples would continue to separate without divorcing.

Marriages today are more likely to be based on love and companionship rather than the custom and financial necessity of the past. Of all divorced people, 75 per cent remarry, a third of them within a year of getting divorced. This shows that what they are rejecting is not the institution of marriage itself, but a particular marriage partner – they divorce hoping to turn an unhappy marriage into a new, happier one. The marriages that exist today are therefore probably much stronger and happier than ever, since unhappy relationships are easily ended by divorce.

Many of those who cohabit eventually marry – about 60 per cent of first-time cohabitations turn into marriages – and about 75 per cent of the population are married by the age of 50. It would appear that marriage remains an important social institution, even in the light of the high divorce rate and previous experience of living together outside marriage.

Despite the record numbers of children being born outside of marriage, nearly 80 per cent of those births in 1996 were registered jointly by the parents, and the same address was given by both parents in three out of four of these cases. This suggests that most children are still being born into a stable relationship, and live in families with concerned parents who are simply reluctant to tie the legal marriage knot. Most dependent children still live in families headed by a married or cohabiting couple.

What really seems to be happening is not so much that the family and marriage are in decline but that they are changing. There are more lone-parent families, more reconstituted families, more gay and lesbian families, more experiments in living together before marriage, and fewer people prepared to marry simply to bring up children. Nevertheless, marriage remains an important social norm, and strong pressures from parents, peer groups, and the responsibilities brought about by the birth of children continue to propel most people into marriage.

But perhaps it doesn't really matter whether or not couples are married or have been married before, or whether there is one parent or two. Though the form of the family will keep on changing, the importance of the family lies in its role as a stable and supportive unit for one or two adults and their dependent children. In that sense, the ideal of the family perhaps still remains intact.

DISCUSSION

Is the family of less importance in society today than it used to be? Do you think the family is in decline?

CHAPTER SUMMARY

After studying this chapter, you should be able to:

- Describe the different forms of marriage and the family.
- Describe how the role of the family in society has changed.
- Explain the change from the classic extended family to the privatized nuclear family (or modified extended family) and provide evidence for the continued existence of the extended family.
- Explain the link between the nuclear family and industrial society.
- Explain why the 'cereal packet' image of the family is an inaccurate view of the family in modern Britain.
- Explain the apparent change from segregated to integrated conjugal roles, and criticize the view that marriages have become partnerships of equals.
- Explain why families have become more child-centred.
- Explain the reasons for the rising divorce rate and identify the groups most at risk of divorce.
- Explain why there has been a large increase in the number of lone-parent families.
- Criticize, with evidence, the view that the family is a 'happy' institution.
- Describe alternatives to the family.
- Explain the arguments and evidence for and against the view that the family and marriage are of declining social importance.

KEY TERMS

arranged marriage
bigamy
classic extended family
communes
conjugal roles
divorce rate
extended family
feminist
integrated conjugal roles
kibbutz
kinship
matriarchy
matrilineal descent
matrilocal residence
modified extended family

monogamy
neo-local residence
nuclear family
patrilineal descent
patrilocal residence
polyandry
polygamy
polygyny
privatized nuclear family
reconstituted family
secularization
segregated conjugal roles
serial monogamy
symmetrical family

PROJECT SUGGESTIONS

1 Investigate how far conjugal roles have really become more integrated, by carrying out a series of interviews with five or six families in the community to discover how work is divided between men and women in the home. Use equal numbers of middle-class and working-class families and/or different age groups and/or different ethnic groups to discover whether there are any social class, age, or ethnic differences. You might use the questions earlier in this chapter, and figures 11.5 and 11.6, on equality of partners in the home as a basis for your research.

2 Using secondary sources (see chapter 18), carry out a study of the variety of family types in Britain today. Alternatively, carry out a survey in your school, college, or workplace about the types of family people live in and how family life differs between nuclear and extended families. Take into account different class, ethnic, or religious backgrounds.

3 Carry out a survey of attitudes towards arranged marriages among different age groups or males and females in the Asian community.

4 Carry out a study among lone-parent families, finding out the major problems they encounter.

5 Carry out a survey on attitudes to divorce among a small sample of people from different religious, ethnic, or age groups.

12 SCHOOLING IN BRITAIN

```
┌─────────────────────────────────────────────────┐
        KEY ISSUES IN THIS CHAPTER
└─────────────────────────────────────────────────┘
```

- Education in Britain before 1944.
- Secondary education for all: the tripartite system.
- Comprehensive schools.
- Streaming, labelling, and the self-fulfilling prophecy.
- More recent developments in education.
- The purposes of education.

Education is a major social institution, and schools in Britain command a captive audience of virtually all children between the ages of 5 and 16. During this period of compulsory schooling, children spend about half of the time they are awake at school – about 15 000 hours of their lives.

The sociology of education covers a vast area, and it is impossible in this book to cover all aspects. This chapter therefore takes as its focus the school system, rather than further and higher education, and concentrates on two main aspects of this: the main changes which have occurred in the school system since 1944, and what the purposes of education are.

EDUCATION IN BRITAIN BEFORE 1944

The pattern of free and compulsory state education we know today is a relatively recent phenomenon in Britain. It was only in 1870 that the state first began to provide free education, and this was only made compulsory in 1880. One of the major pressures for this came from the need for a numerate and literate population, who could learn the increasingly complex skills they required for adult working life in an industrial society.

The Forster Education Act of 1870 established free elementary schools, which provided a very limited and narrow education in the 'three Rs' of

Photo: Michael Dyer LRPS

reading, writing, and arithmetic, with often a fourth 'R' of religion added as well. However, secondary education (which taught a much wider range of subjects, equipping people for middle-class jobs) remained restricted mainly to middle-class children because the schools were fee-paying.

Until 1944, most children attended only free and compulsory elementary schools to the age of 14, with their limited educational opportunities and narrow curriculum (a curriculum is a course of study). The education system was therefore divided along social class lines, with a fee-paying secondary education for middle-class children leading to middle-class jobs as adults, and a free and compulsory elementary education for the

Photo: Michael Dyer LRPS

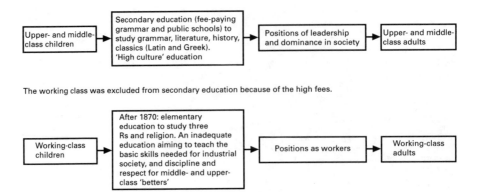

Figure 12.1 The education system before 1944

working class leading only to working-class jobs. Figure 12.1 illustrates this class-divided system of schooling.

The limited education of the majority of the population was shown when, in the Second World War (1939–45), many army recruits were found to be illiterate. Many had ability, but had not been able to receive a secondary education because their parents could not afford the fees. This wastage of human resources and talent made many people fear that Britain's industrial position would be threatened by such a poorly educated labour force.

It was against this background of the need for educational reform that the Butler Education Act of 1944 made secondary education free and compulsory for all to the age of 15.

SECONDARY EDUCATION FOR ALL:
THE TRIPARTITE SYSTEM

The 1944 Education Act introduced three stages of free state education: primary (age 5–11), secondary (age 11–15), and further education. All children were to go through the primary and secondary stages, with the secondary stage divided into three types of school. These three types of secondary school became known as the **tripartite system**. The 1944 Act was based on the principle of equality of educational opportunity.

The principle of **equality of educational opportunity** is that every child, regardless of social class background, ability to pay school fees, ethnic background, or sex, should have an equal chance of doing as well as his or her ability will allow.

The 1944 Education Act tried to ensure equality of educational opportunity in three main ways:

- Secondary education was made free and compulsory for all.
- Three kinds of secondary school were set up to cater for children with three different types of ability, so all children would have a chance to develop to the full whatever abilities they had.
- These three types of school were all meant to be of equal status, so no one would have better or worse chances in life depending on the sort of school she or he went to. This idea of 'equal but different' was known as **parity of esteem**.

The 11+ Exam and the Three Types of Secondary School

The 1944 Education Act assumed children could be divided up into three categories, with three different types of ability and aptitude, that could best develop their potential in three different types of secondary school. It was thought these three different sorts of ability were fixed by the age of 11, were unlikely to change, and could be reliably and accurately measured at age 11 by a special intelligence quotient test (IQ test). This became known as the 11+ exam. According to how well they did in this exam, children went to one of three different types of secondary school, which were thought to provide the most suitable environment for pupils to develop to the full the different types of talent they had.

- The top 15–20 per cent of children passing the 11+ exam went to *grammar schools*, where they followed an academic curriculum preparing them for GCE O- and A-levels at ages 16 and 18.
- The 'less academic' pupils who showed more practical ability were sent to *technical schools*, aimed at occupations like technicians, engineers, and skilled manual work. Not many of these schools were developed.
- The large majority (about 60–70 per cent) who failed their 11+ were sent to *secondary modern schools*, which were thought to be more suited to lower-ability pupils.

This tripartite system, with three types of secondary school catering for children of three different types of ability, was based on the idea that it was possible to predict at the age of 11 the type of occupation children would be suited to as adults, and therefore select them for an appropriate form of education. Figure 12.2 illustrates the tripartite system, and the social class into which most pupils went from each type of school.

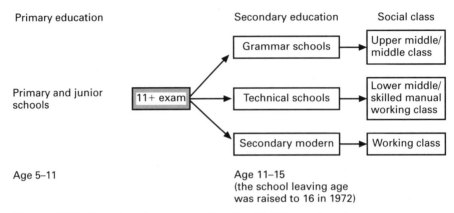

Figure 12.2 The tripartite system after the 1944 Education Act

Criticisms of the Tripartite System

There were a number of criticisms of the tripartite system, which made many people question the fairness of the selection process and led them to doubt the claim that the system was offering real equality of educational opportunity.

Criticism

- The 11+ exam was an unfair, unreliable, and inaccurate selection test.

- There was no parity of esteem between the three types of school. Grammar schools offered better life chances to their pupils.

Explanation

- The 11+ IQ test proved to be very unreliable as an indicator of ability and future potential. Some very bright pupils failed the 11+, and the exam did not allow for late developers (children whose ability develops as they get older). A report as early as 1957 estimated at least 12 per cent of children were sent to the 'wrong' schools. It became clear that intelligence wasn't fixed at the age of 11 and could be improved with good teaching and encouragement.

- The grammar schools always had higher status than the technical or secondary modern schools, and were seen by parents, employers, and pupils themselves as better schools. They had better teachers and facilities, and only they provided the educational qualifications necessary for better-paid middle-class jobs. Not many technical schools were set up, and secondary modern schools were generally seen as inferior schools, with less qualified staff, poorer facilities, and limited educational and job opportunities for their pupils. More than 75 per cent of all pupils were leaving school without any academic qualifications, and so often only had access to lower-status and poorer-paid, working-class occupations.

- The system reinforced social class divisions.

- More middle-class children passed the 11+ exam and went to grammar school than working-class children, who were more likely to go to low-status secondary modern schools. The education system was therefore continuing to divide people along social class lines as it had done before the 1944 Education Act.

- The self-fulfilling prophecy (discussed later in this chapter) meant that many pupils in secondary modern schools were almost guaranteed to fail in education.

- Teachers in secondary modern schools often had low expectations of pupils labelled as 'not very bright' after failing the 11+ exam. Such pupils often lowered their aspirations and, because of the self-fulfilling prophecy, were almost guaranteed to fail.

- There were geographical differences in the availability of grammar school places.

- There were many more grammar school places available in some parts of the country than others. This meant children in some areas had a better chance of getting a grammar school place, so that where a child lived, rather than her or his ability, could affect whether she or he got a grammar school place or not.

Research in the 1950s and early 1960s suggested that the talent, ability, and potential of many children in the secondary modern schools were being wasted. It was felt that this wasted talent could be better developed in comprehensive schools, as these would enable more people to obtain qualifications and train for the skilled occupations which the economy desperately needed. As a result, in the 1960s the tripartite system began to be replaced in most of the country by comprehensive education.

DISCUSSION

Do you think that the intelligence you are born with is fixed for all time? How do you think teachers and schools might improve the ability of people to think, develop their skills, and improve their intelligence?

COMPREHENSIVE SCHOOLS

A comprehensive school is one which accepts pupils of all abilities. Comprehensive reorganization of secondary education was a further attempt to achieve equality of educational opportunity, and to overcome the basic unfairness and inequalities of the tripartite system.

Comprehensive education abolished both selection at age 11 by the 11+ exam and the three types of secondary school. Children in most areas now, regardless of their ability, generally transfer to the same type of school at the age of 11, with no selection by examination.

The Advantages of Comprehensive Schools

- The possibility of educational success and obtaining qualifications remains open throughout a child's school career, since moving between streams and classes within one school is easier and more likely to happen than moving between different types of school in the tripartite system.
- Late developers, whose intelligence and ability improve later in life, can be catered for better in the comprehensive system.
- Talent is less likely to be wasted, particularly among working-class children, and there is more opportunity for all children to reach their full potential and gain some educational qualifications.

- The large size of many comprehensive schools means there are more teachers teaching a wider range of subjects to meet the needs of pupils of all abilities, with a wide variety of equipment and facilities. This benefits all pupils and gives them greater equality of opportunity to develop whatever talents they may have.
- Fewer children leave school without any qualifications in the comprehensive system, and more obtain higher standards than under the tripartite system.
- If all children attend the same type of school, then children of different social classes are more likely to mix together, thus avoiding the social class divisions between grammar schools and secondary modern schools found in the tripartite system. This helps to promote better understanding between people from different social class backgrounds.

Criticisms of Comprehensive Schools

Comprehensive schools are not without their critics.

- Setting up comprehensive schools often involves merging several schools on different sites, and a lot of time may be wasted in moving between different buildings.
- The schools' large size may make it impossible for staff to know all pupils personally. This may create discipline problems and the talents of individuals may not be noticed and developed.
- Where comprehensives draw their pupils from a certain neighbourhood, the social class pattern of that neighbourhood will be reflected in the school. For example, a school in a working-class neighbourhood will have mainly working-class pupils, so the aim of social mixing between children of different social classes is defeated.
- One of the major criticisms is that because these schools contain pupils of all abilities, brighter children are held back by the slower pace of learning of the less able. Critics argue this wouldn't have happened in the grammar schools, which catered for 'high-flyers'.

ACTIVITY

Drawing on the material above and below and your own experiences at school, whether a comprehensive or grammar school, list the advantages and disadvantages of grammar schools versus comprehensive schools.

- Where selective (grammar) schools continue to exist, they 'cream off' the most able pupils, so the comprehensives are little different from the secondary moderns of the tripartite system.
- Streamed comprehensives (see below) can be much like the tripartite system within a single school (as figure 12.4 illustrates).

STREAMING, LABELLING, AND THE SELF-FULFILLING PROPHECY

Much research has suggested that predicting whether a child will be a 'success' or 'failure' through testing or teachers' judgements, and labelling him or her as 'bright' or 'slow', can actually make that child a success or failure. Such predictions and labelling can affect an individual's view of him- or herself – his or her self-esteem – and the individual may act in accordance with the prediction made and the label attached. This process of predicting that something will happen, and of pupils acting in the way teachers expect them to act in accordance with the label they have been given, is known as the **self-fulfilling prophecy**. Figure 12.3 illustrates this process.

One of the problems which is still found in schools (including comprehensives) is that of streaming. Streaming or banding is a system used in schools to separate pupils into different groups according to their predicted ability. Many comprehensives continue to stream pupils, and this has been shown to be unfair and harmful to the self-esteem and educational performance of bottom-stream pupils, particularly those from working-class and ethnic minority (especially Afro-Caribbean) backgrounds.

Evidence suggests that teachers' judgements of pupils' ability are influenced by factors other than ability alone. For example, teachers seem to take into account things like standards of behaviour, dress, and speech. They also seem to be influenced by the social class background of pupils, with the assumption that pupils from middle-class backgrounds are 'brighter' and 'more cooperative' than those from working-class homes. Streaming therefore seems to reflect the class divisions in society, with many children from lower working-class homes placed in lower streams.

Once placed in bottom streams, pupils may become victims of the self-fulfilling prophecy – those pupils labelled as 'bottom-stream material' may take on the characteristics expected of them by teachers. Because more working-class children tend to be put into bottom streams by teachers, and middle-class children continue to dominate the higher streams, streamed comprehensives continue to divide pupils along social class lines in much the same way as the tripartite system did, but this time within a single school. Figure 12.4 illustrates this process.

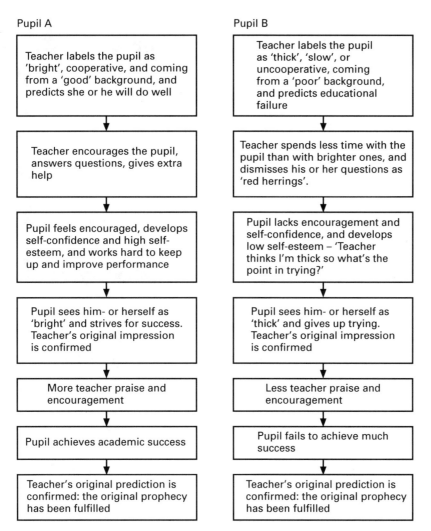

Figure 12.3 The self-fulfilling prophecy: two examples

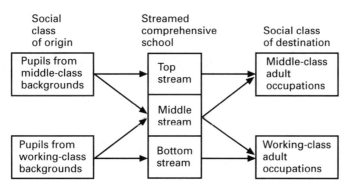

Figure 12.4 Social class divisions and streaming

ACTIVITY/DISCUSSION

1 In a streamed school, the best and most qualified teachers are often kept for the upper-stream classes. Why do you think this is the case? How might it affect the progress of those facing the greatest difficulties in the lower streams?

2 List all the reasons you can think of to explain why pupils from lower working-class homes are more likely to be placed in lower streams than those from middle-class homes.

3 Have you had any experience of the self-fulfilling prophecy in your own schooling? How do you know whether teachers think you are 'bright' or not, and how do you think this has affected your progress?

Table 12.1 The effects of streaming on children's recorded ability between the ages of 8 and 11 years

Measured ability at 8 years of age – test scores	Children in an *upper* stream	Children in a *lower* stream
	Average change in test scores between 8 and 11 years	Average change in test scores between 8 and 11 years
41–45	+5.67	−0.95
46–48	+3.70	−0.62
49–51	+4.44	−1.60
52–54	+0.71	−1.46
55–57	+2.23	−1.94
58–60	+0.86	−6.34

+ indicates improvements in score, − indicates deterioration in score.
Source: Adapted from J.W.B. Douglas, *The Home and the School* (Panther/Grafton Books 1967)

ACTIVITY

Study table 12.1 and answer the following questions:

1 What average change occurred in the test scores of children in a lower stream whose test score at 8 years of age was 55–7?

2 What average change occurred in the test scores of children in an upper stream whose test score at 8 years of age was 46–8?

3 Which ability group in which stream showed (a) the greatest deterioration in test scores, and (b) the greatest improvement in test scores?

4 What does table 12.1 suggest about the effects of streaming on children's educational performance? List all the factors you can think of which might explain this, drawing on your own experiences at school.

The anti-school sub-culture

The anti-school sub-culture

Most schools generally place a high value on things such as hard work, good behaviour, and exam success. One of the effects of streaming and labelling is to divide pupils into those in the top streams who more or less conform to these aims and therefore achieve high status, and those in the bottom streams who are labelled as 'failures' by the school and are therefore deprived of status. In response to this, bottom-stream pupils often rebel against the school and develop an alternative set of values, attitudes, and behaviour in opposition to the aims of the school. This is called an **anti-school sub-culture**, and provides a means for bottom-stream pupils to achieve some success and status in their peer group. Among such pupils, truancy, playing up teachers, messing about, breaking the school rules, and generally disrupting the smooth running of the school become a way of getting back at the system and resisting a schooling which has labelled them as 'failures' and denied them status.

Mixed-Ability Teaching

Many comprehensives use mixed-ability teaching to overcome the problems of streaming. This is where all pupils of the same age, regardless of their ability, are taught in the same classroom. Some see this as a disadvantage of comprehensive schools, since it is argued that 'more intelligent' pupils are held back by the 'less able'. Others, however, argue that in mixed-ability groups the more intelligent pupils can have a stimulating influence on the less able, and that the problems created by the self-fulfilling prophecy are easier to avoid. Mixed-ability teaching also helps to avoid creating divisions between pupils on the basis of home and social class background. Recent research has shown that mixed-ability teaching in fact has no negative effect on the 'high-flyers', improves the performance of the 'less able', and makes no difference to a school's overall examination performance.

ACTIVITY/DISCUSSION

1 Make a brief summary chart in two columns comparing the advantages and disadvantages of comprehensive schools.
2 Suggest measures that could be taken to make comprehensive schools better for all pupils.
3 Do you think streaming and setting or mixed-ability teaching is better for pupils' progress? Give some evidence to back up your view from your own experiences at school.

MORE RECENT DEVELOPMENTS IN EDUCATION

While the comprehensive system has succeeded in improving overall educational standards compared to the tripartite system, the education system came under increasing criticism in the 1980s and 1990s for not reaching high enough standards and for not meeting the needs of employers and industry closely enough. As a result, attempts have been made to raise standards and to tie all parts of the education system more closely to the needs of industry.

DISCUSSION

1 Do you think standards are falling in schools today? Make sure you are able to refer to evidence to back up your point of view.
2 What should the aims of schooling be? Should schools be concerned mainly with meeting the needs of industry and fitting people into the job market? Or should they be concerned with the development of individuals, allowing them to pursue and develop their interests?

Making Schools More Aware of Industry

Attempts here include:

- Sending teachers from schools (and further education) into industry to develop their understanding, which they can then apply in their teaching.
- Work experience programmes for year 10 and 11 pupils in schools to ease the transition from school to work.
- New educational courses which are more closely related to the world of work and concerned more with learning work-related skills. For example, work-based NVQs (National Vocational Qualifications), and school/college-based GNVQs (General National Vocational Qualifications) were developed to provide nationally approved and recognized qualifications for vocational courses. Advanced GNVQs were intended as a vocational alternative to A-levels.

Raising Standards

Activity-based learning

Teaching has become more student-centred and activity-based, with the aim of developing students' skills and understanding. GCSE, A-level and AS-level, and GNVQ have become more activity- and skills-based exams, and involve students doing more coursework. This has led to much better exam results among 16–18-year-olds. Modular exams (which students can take in parts) aim to ensure that all students can obtain some qualifications by allowing them to resit parts of a course, and AS-levels aim to encourage 16–18-year-olds to study a broader range of subjects, and make them more flexible and less specialized.

The National Curriculum and national testing

To improve standards across the country, the 1988 Education Reform Act set up the National Curriculum, a range of subjects that must be studied by all pupils. All students now have to study a Core Curriculum including English, mathematics, and science, and a series of Foundation subjects including history, geography, design and technology, information technology, a modern foreign language, art, music, physical education, and religious education. There are set 'programmes of study' and 'attainment targets' (goals which all teachers are expected to enable students to reach), with testing (the 'SATs') at ages 7, 11, 14, and 16 to ensure these targets are met and standards maintained. National testing in English and maths for 9-year-olds was brought in in 1998.

National 'league tables'

Schools and colleges are now required to publish tables of testing (SATs) and exam (GCSE/A-level and GNVQ) results. These are designed to give parents and students an idea of how well schools and colleges are doing. By encouraging competition for students between schools and colleges, these 'league tables' aim to raise overall standards. However, there is much concern that league tables of results don't really reveal how well a school is doing. This is because, as the following chapter shows, the social class background of students can affect how well they perform in education. League tables could conceal underperforming schools in advantaged middle-class areas and successful schools in more deprived working-class areas. In 1997, the government was making moves to change the league tables so that they would compare students' test and exam results with earlier test results, to show how much progress students had made. This 'value-added' approach promised to give a much fairer and more accurate picture of how well a school or college was doing.

Local management of schools

Local management of schools (LMS) gives schools (rather than the local education authority) much greater control of their budgets, and a wide range of other aspects of the school. This is designed to make schools more responsive to local needs and the wishes of parents.

Formula funding

Schools are funded by a formula which is largely based on the number of pupils they attract. It was thought this would drive up standards by rewarding 'successful' schools that attracted pupils (and hence money), giving less successful schools the incentive to improve.

Open enrolment and parental preference

Parents are now allowed to express a preference for the school of their choice, and a school cannot refuse a pupil a place if it has vacancies. This was designed to raise the quality of teaching and exam results by encouraging competition between schools. Unpopular schools run the risk of losing pupils and therefore money. In many cases, parents don't really have much choice of school, as places are usually filled up by those living in the school's 'priority area' (the area from which children are admitted first).

Opting out

A few schools in the 1990s chose to 'opt out' of local education authority control and run their own affairs, with funding direct from the government. These were known as grant-maintained schools. Again, it was thought that making schools fully responsible for all their affairs would help to drive up standards. The Labour government was proposing in 1997 to abolish grant-maintained status, and replace it with a new category of 'foundation school'.

City technology colleges

City technology colleges (CTCs) are schools which are independent of local education authorities, are sponsored by private industry, and specialize in science and technology. It was thought that by specializing these schools would raise standards in these subjects, and produce the skills that were needed by industry.

The Office for Standards in Education

The Office for Standards in Education (OFSTED) was established to conduct regular four-yearly (now six-yearly) inspections of all state schools. This aimed to ensure schools were doing a good job, by publishing their inspection reports and requiring schools to take action on any weaknesses identified. OFSTED was also given responsibility for inspecting local education authorities in 1997.

Education Action Zones

The Labour government was proposing in 1997 to set these up as a way of targeting resources on deprived areas, where there were the greatest educational problems in terms of children not doing as well as they should. These zones are considered a little more in the following chapter.

The 1980s and 1990s were a period of frenzied change in education, all aimed at improving standards. The Labour government which was elected in 1997 promised to make education its top priority. In 1997, it created a Standards Task Force and a Standards and Effectiveness Unit, and published far-reaching proposals to raise levels of literacy and numeracy, and to drive up standards in schools. How effective and successful the changes of the 1980s and 1990s prove to be will only be discovered in the years ahead. For example, it will be 2003 before the first child leaves school who has studied and been tested on the entire National Curriculum. However, there will undoubtedly be more changes to come in the schooling system as Britain enters the twenty-first century.

The Parent's Charter

In 1994, the government published the (updated) 'Parent's Charter' as part of its proposals to raise the standards in education. Schools now have to:

- Provide a written report on each child's progress at least once a year.
- Be inspected regularly by government-approved inspectors who identify the strengths and weaknesses of a school, and take action to overcome any weaknesses.
- Publish tables of exam results, National Curriculum test results, and truancy rates, and report on what pupils do when they leave school.
- Publish a school prospectus or brochure, giving details of the aims of the school, the subjects and other activities offered, and their exam results compared with local and national results.
- Hold an annual meeting between parents and school governors.
- Produce a governors' report and send it to all parents, including the standards achieved, examination and National Curriculum test results, the school budget, the amount of truancy, and what school leavers do after they leave school.

The 'Parent's Charter' is supposed to help parents to choose the 'best' schools and encourage schools to improve their performance.

ACTIVITY/DISCUSSION

1 Do you think the recent changes in education will succeed in raising standards? Go through each of the changes, and explain in each case why it might or might not improve standards.
2 Do you think schools alone can be held responsible for exam results and truancy rates? What other factors might influence how good a school's exam results are, and whether pupils play truant or not?

THE PURPOSES OF EDUCATION

The provision of education is an incredibly expensive business, eating up about £38 billion a year – more than 12 per cent of general government spending in 1996 – and a twentieth of the total wealth of Britain. Why is such importance attached to the provision of education in modern industrial society? What does education contribute to society? Why are schools necessary in industrial societies and why is education to the age of 16 compulsory? The answer to these questions lies in the *functions* that education performs in society.

ACTIVITY

1 List all the reasons you go/went to school. What benefits (if any!) do you think going to school has brought you?
2 How do you think your life would differ if you didn't have/hadn't had to go to school?
3 Now read the following sections (to the end of the chapter) on the role that education plays in society, and compare them with your own reasons for going to school. Which do you think are the more important, from your point of view?
4 What problems might there be for individuals and society if compulsory education were to be abolished tomorrow?

Education and the Economy

In a complex industrial society, the education system plays an important role in preparation for working life in two respects:

- *Producing a labour force with the skills needed for working life.* A literate and numerate workforce is more or less essential in an industrial society, and there is the need for specific skills related to particular jobs, such as computing, engineering, technical drawing, car maintenance, typing, and science. The things learnt at school will generally affect the kind of job and training opportunities open to people after school.
- *Selecting people for different occupations.* Modern industrial societies are generally meritocratic, with most social positions being achieved on the basis of experience and exam qualifications. In schools, people are graded and receive different qualifications, which are used by employers and other educational institutions to select suitable people for work and further courses.

Through exams, schools sort pupils out, and decide the kinds of occupation they will eventually get – for example, who will become middle-class professionals or skilled or unskilled workers. Education will therefore influence the individual's eventual social class position as an adult. In a few cases, education can be a means of upward social mobility into the middle class for children from a working-class family. Figure 12.5 illustrates this link between education and the class structure.

Socialization

The school is an important agency of secondary socialization, continuing the process of socialization which begins in the family. Schools transmit from one generation to the next the culture of a society. For example, the school curriculum hands on knowledge about history, geography, science, English language and literature, and so on. Children also learn how to develop relationships with others and to adopt many of the norms of the society to which they belong. These are aspects of the hidden curriculum, which is discussed below. Society is therefore reproduced and each new generation integrated into society.

Social Control

Schools act as important agencies of social control, which encourage children to learn and conform to the values and norms expected by society. This is mainly carried out through what is known as the hidden curricu-

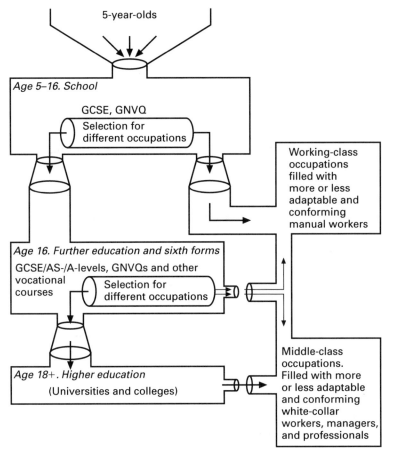

Figure 12.5 Education and the class structure

lum – 'hidden' because there are no obvious, organized courses in 'obedience and conformity' as there are in mathematics or English. Nevertheless, this hidden curriculum is present throughout schooling, and those who conform to it are likely to be rewarded, while those who don't are likely to be branded as non-conformists by the school and may find themselves getting into trouble. Some features of this hidden curriculum, and what is being taught, are listed below.

The hidden curriculum

Features of the hidden curriculum	What is being taught
Privileges and responsibilities given to older pupils	Respect for elders
School rules, detentions and suspensions, rewards like merit badges, prizes, good marks, etc.	Conformity to society's rules and laws, whether you agree with them or not
School assemblies	Respect for religious beliefs
Males and females often playing different sports, having different dress rules, and being counselled into different subjects, further education courses, and careers; many teachers having different expectations of boys and girls	Males and females being expected to conform to gender stereotypes, with males as the main workers and 'breadwinners', and women working in the home and in a narrow range of 'female occupations' which are often extensions of their domestic role
Competitive sports and competition against each other in class rather than cooperating together; students being tested individually – being encouraged to rely on themselves rather than others	Workers having to compete for jobs and wages, and individuals having to stand on their own two feet – not joining with other workers
Respecting authority of teachers regardless of what they say or do; pupils always having to justify where they're going and why, and do as they're told	Respect for those in authority, such as bosses at work and the police
Punctuality/being on time – time belonging to the school, not the pupil	Good time-keeping at work – the employer pays for the worker's time, so it belongs to the firm, not the worker
Concentrating on schoolwork, whether or not it's boring and whether or not you want to do it	Workers having to accept boring, menial, repetitive jobs

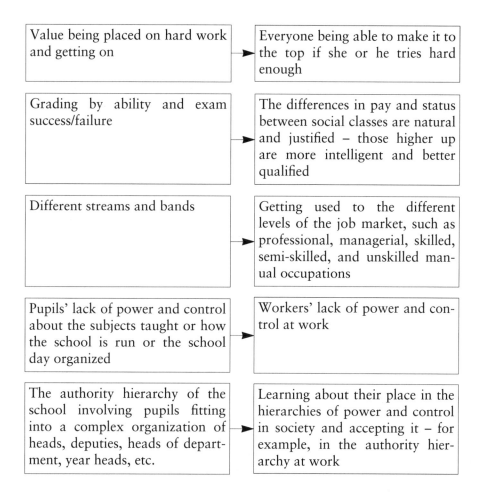

Value being placed on hard work and getting on	Everyone being able to make it to the top if she or he tries hard enough
Grading by ability and exam success/failure	The differences in pay and status between social classes are natural and justified – those higher up are more intelligent and better qualified
Different streams and bands	Getting used to the different levels of the job market, such as professional, managerial, skilled, semi-skilled, and unskilled manual occupations
Pupils' lack of power and control about the subjects taught or how the school is run or the school day organized	Workers' lack of power and control at work
The authority hierarchy of the school involving pupils fitting into a complex organization of heads, deputies, heads of department, year heads, etc.	Learning about their place in the hierarchies of power and control in society and accepting it – for example, in the authority hierarchy at work

ACTIVITY

1. Describe in detail five features of the hidden curriculum found in your school, or the one you once attended, which reflect the values of society outside school.
2. Drawing on your own experiences at school, what features of your education do you think prepared you/will prepare you most for life after school? Think of particular subjects studied and activities undertaken, and the features of the hidden curriculum discussed above which were/are found in your school.

Implementing Government Policy

Schools have often been used as a means of carrying out government policies. For example, comprehensive schools were originally established by a Labour government in an attempt to create both more equal opportunities in society and greater social equality. Some schools in areas where there is widespread poverty have been given extra teachers and more resources than other schools in an attempt to relieve the disadvantages faced by the poor in education. Multicultural courses are also organized in many schools in an attempt to stop the spread of racist ideas, and encourage respect for people from different cultural backgrounds. Equal opportunities policies have been adopted to reduce the effects of gender stereotyping by encouraging girls to go into subjects like science and computing, which have been traditionally dominated by boys.

Preparing for Social Change

As well as encouraging people to accept traditional ideas which will lead to order and stability in society, schools also prepare pupils for a rapidly changing industrial society. Since the 1970s there has been a massive increase in the use of computers in schools and the development of computer courses, in an attempt to prepare pupils for a world after school in which computer technology plays a central role. Information technology is now a National Curriculum Foundation subject. The importance attached to computing in schools was shown in 1997, when the government was planning to connect every state school in the country to the Internet through a 'National Grid for Learning'. Attempts in the late twentieth century to make pupils more adaptable and aware of the world of work, and to make schools more closely related to the needs of the economy, are partly due to the demands of a rapidly changing industrial economy.

This chapter has shown that one of the most important consequences of education is the influence it has on people's life chances, and for most people it affects in a very direct way their occupational opportunities – and social class position – as adults. This important result of education has been reflected in the attempts to establish equality of opportunity in education, first in the tripartite system and then with comprehensive schooling, so that all children can have the best educational opportunities in life. However, despite these attempts, inequality in education remains. This continuing inequality is the theme of the following chapter.

CHAPTER SUMMARY

After studying this chapter, you should be able to:

- Outline briefly the education system before 1944.
- Explain what is meant by equality of educational opportunity.
- Describe the tripartite system, explain how it tried to achieve equality of educational opportunity, and criticize its weaknesses.
- Describe and explain the changes brought about by the comprehensive system, and explain how it tried to overcome the weaknesses of the tripartite system.
- Discuss the arguments for and against comprehensive schools.
- Explain what is meant by streaming, labelling, the self-fulfilling prophecy, and mixed-ability teaching, and the problems associated with each of them.
- Explain how the government has tried in recent years to improve standards in schools and make them more aware of the needs of industry.
- Outline some recent changes in the education system.
- Describe and explain the role of education in society.
- Explain what is meant by the 'hidden curriculum', and how it reflects the values of society outside schools.

KEY TERMS

anti-school sub-culture
equality of educational opportunity
parity of esteem

self-fulfilling prophecy
tripartite system

PROJECT SUGGESTIONS

1 Do interviews with a sample of people from three different age groups (such as 16–25, 35–50, and over 60) asking them about their views and experience of schools today compared to the past, and whether they think standards have fallen or not.
2 Do a study of work experience schemes in a local school, perhaps interviewing pupils and teachers about the aims and usefulness of such schemes.
3 Find a school that still has streaming, and interview a group of bottom-stream pupils to discover whether there is any evidence of the self-fulfilling prophecy at work. For example, find out whether they feel as valued and encouraged by teachers as those in higher streams. Is there any evidence of the emergence of an anti-school sub-culture?

4 Do a survey asking a range of people (parents, school-leavers, people in jobs, current students, etc.) about what they think the purposes of schooling should be, such as getting qualifications, getting a job, being able to think for themselves, etc. Compare the results from the different groups you ask.

INEQUALITY IN EDUCATION

13

The 1944 Education Act, the tripartite system, and the comprehensive system which replaced it all aimed to secure equality of educational opportunity for all children, regardless of their social class, ethnic background, or sex. However, despite these efforts, sociological evidence has made it clear that not all children of the same ability achieve the same success in education, and inequalities in educational opportunity remain. The failure of pupils to do as well in education as they should, given their ability, is called **underachievement**. The evidence suggests that social class origins (the social class of a child's parents), ethnicity, and gender continue to have an influence on how well people do in education, even when they are of the same ability, and these factors appear to be more important than innate (inborn) ability in affecting the level of educational achievement or success. This chapter will look at the patterns of inequality remaining in education, and some of the explanations for them.

ETHNICITY AND UNDERACHIEVEMENT

The Facts

Many children from ethnic minority backgrounds tend to do as well as and often better than many white children. For example, Indian Asians are more likely to get better GCSE and A-level results, to stay in education post-16, and to enter university than white students. However, those of Pakistani and Bangladeshi origin, and particularly males from Afro-Caribbean homes, tend to do less well than they should given their ability. There is some evidence that Afro-Caribbean males may actually be falling further behind, and they are at the bottom of the heap by the time they reach GCSE. Most of what follows focuses mainly on the Afro-Caribbean group, though some of the points also apply to the Pakistani and Bangladeshi ethnic minorities as well.

- They appear to have below average reading ability.
- The tend to get fewer and poorer GCSE results than children of white or Indian origin.
- Male Afro-Caribbeans are over-represented (that is, there are more than there should be given their numbers in the population as a whole) in special schools for those with learning difficulties and in special units for children with emotional and behavioural difficulties.
- Afro-Caribbean pupils are between three and six times more likely to be permanently excluded from schools than whites of the same sex.
- They are over-represented in lower streams. Evidence suggests they are put in lower streams even when they get better results than pupils placed in higher streams.
- They are more likely than other groups to leave school without any qualifications.
- They are less likely to stay on in education post-16, and when they do, they are more likely to follow vocational courses rather than the higher-status academic courses.
- Relatively fewer obtain A-levels and go on to higher education at universities (though Afro-Caribbean females do better than both Afro-Caribbean and white males).
- In the population as a whole, they are generally less qualified than those of white or Indian origin.

Explaining the Underachievement of Some Ethnic Minorities

The pattern of underachievement of Pakistani, Bangladeshi and Afro-Caribbean children has a number of explanations.

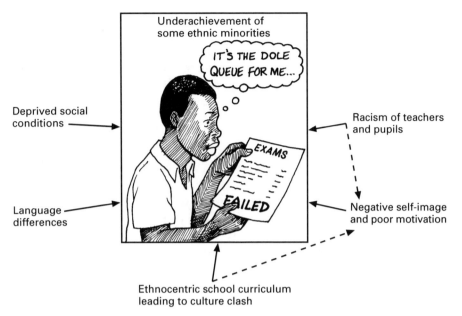

Figure 13.1 Ethnicity and educational underachievement

Social conditions

Such children often face a series of disadvantages in social conditions, such as poor-quality housing, overcrowding, and higher rates of unemployment in their homes, which contribute to difficulties in coping with school work. Many of the factors discussed below explaining working-class underachievement also affect these ethnic minorities, as they tend to be mainly working class.

Racism

Research in primary and secondary schools has found an unusually high degree of conflict between white teachers and Afro-Caribbean pupils. Teachers often hold stereotypes, with more positive expectations of Asians (as relatively quiet, well-behaved, and highly motivated) than of Afro-Caribbeans, whom they often expect to be trouble-makers. This may mean teachers label Afro-Caribbeans and take swift action against them. Research in 1990 found that Afro-Caribbean children, unlike whites and Asians, are often punished not for any particular offence but because they have the 'wrong attitude'.

Racism is as widespread among teachers and pupils as it is in the rest of society. Afro-Caribbean male pupils, in particular, are more likely to fight racism and form anti-school peer groups, reinforcing their labelling by teachers as trouble-makers. This might explain the high level of black exclusions from school, since most permanent exclusions are for disobedience of various kinds, such as refusing to comply with school rules, verbal abuse, or insolence to teachers.

An ethnocentric curriculum

Because of racism in both the school and the wider society, many Afro-Caribbean children in Britain may grow up with a negative self-image – a lack of self-respect and confidence because they feel they are in some ways rejected. The school curriculum tends to be ethnocentric, which may contribute to this low self-esteem. **Ethnocentrism** means that school subjects concentrate on a particular society and culture – in this case white British society and culture – rather than recognizing and taking into account the cultures of different ethnic communities. This may cause a culture clash between home and school for Afro-Caribbean pupils. Textbooks still frequently carry degrading stereotypes of people from non-white races. This may lead to low motivation in school and poor educational achievement.

ACTIVITY/DISCUSSION

1 What evidence can you think of from your own experiences at school which suggests that the cultures of ethnic minorities are either ignored or treated in a degrading way? Think about the subjects you studied, the textbooks you used, and the kinds of activity you undertook.

2 Many schools today are trying to include the cultures of the ethnic minorities in school subjects and activities. What evidence is there of this happening in your experience? Give examples.

3 Discuss the following statements: (a) 'Cultural differences between people of different ethnic groups are very important and should be recognized and welcomed in schools', and (b) 'anti-racism should only be discussed in schools which have a mix of different ethnic groups.'

Language

Some Afro-Caribbean children speak a different dialect of English, Creole or 'Caribbean English', and children from other ethnic groups may have a language other than English used in their homes. This language difference may cause difficulties in doing some school work and communicating with the teacher, and may cause disadvantages at school. Teachers may mistake language difficulties for lack of ability (leading to the self-fulfilling prophecy), and because Caribbean English is non-standard English, it may be unconsciously penalized in the classroom, because most teachers are white and middle-class. The same may apply to Bangladeshi pupils, who may be seen as 'low ability' because they may speak English as a second or additional language rather than as their first. Such cultural difficulties may present obstacles to motivation and progress at school.

ACTIVITY

1 Go through the explanations above for the underachievement of some ethnic minorities, putting them in what you think is their order of importance. Give reasons why you have put them in that order.
2 For each of the explanations, suggest changes that could be made in both school and society which might help to improve the educational performance of these ethnic minorities.

GENDER DIFFERENCES IN EDUCATION: THE UNDERACHIEVEMENT OF BOYS

There are marked differences between the sexes in education. Until the late 1980s, the major concern was with the underachievement of girls. This was because, while girls used to perform better than boys in the early years of their education (up to GCSE), after this they tended to fall behind, being less likely than boys to get the three A-levels required for university entry and less likely to go into higher education. However, in the early 1990s girls began to outperform boys in all areas and at all levels of the education system. The main problem today is with the underachievement of boys, although there are still concerns about the different subjects studied by boys and girls.

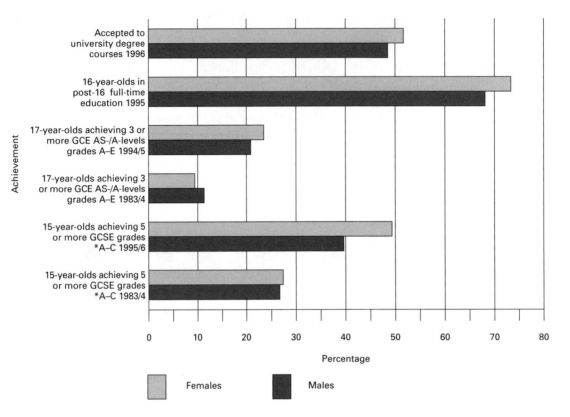

Figure 13.2 Some male and female differences in educational achievement
Source: Adapted from *Separate Tables* (Department for Education and Employment 1997); *UCAS Annual Report 1996*

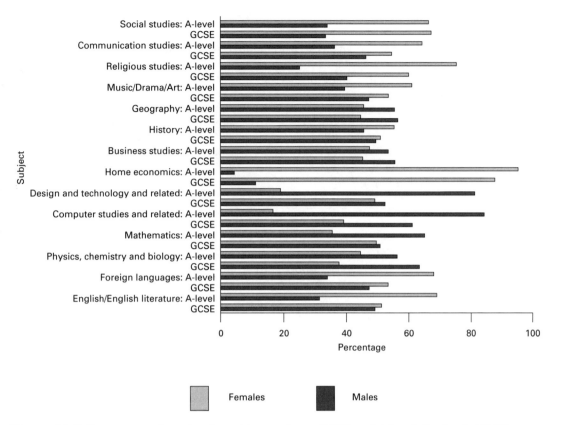

Figure 13.3 Percentage of entries: by subject and sex, GCSE and A-level, England, 1994/5
Source: Adapted from *Separate Tables* (Department for Education and Employment 1997)

Table 13.1a GCSE achievements of 15-year-old males and females: by subject group, entries, and pass rate (percentage achieving grades *A–C), England, by end 1994/5

Subject group	Male entries	Pass rate %	Female entries	Pass rate %
Sciences[a]	824 112	44.9	799 817	47.3
Social sciences[b]	380 515	46.1	335 439	53.1
Arts[c]	897 733	48.3	981 576	63.6
Total students entering any subject	274 893	68.5	267 414	79.2

Table 13.1b GCE A-level achievments of male and female candidates by subject group, entries, and pass rate (percentage achieving grades A–E), England, by end 1994/5

Subject group	Male entries	Pass rate %	Female entries	Pass rate %
Sciences[a]	122 173	81.5	80 376	81.9
Social sciences[b]	101 283	77.2	114 047	76.2
Arts[c]	65 096	86.2	129 206	88.5
General studies	28 520	85.1	28 230	78.8
Total entries for all subjects	317 072	81.4	351 859	82.2

[a] Includes subjects like biology, physics, chemistry, single/double science, mathematics, computer studies, craft, design and technology, and home economics.
[b] Includes subjects like business studies, geography, history, area studies, economics, humanities, social studies, physical education, and vocational studies.
[c] Includes subjects like art and design, English, English literature, drama, communication studies, foreign languages, classical studies, music, creative arts, and religious studies.
Source: Adapted from *Separate Tables* (Department for Education and Employment 1997)

The Facts

- Girls do better than boys at every stage in National Curriculum SAT (Standard Assessment Test) results in English, maths, and science.
- Girls are now more successful than boys at every level in GCSE, and in every major subject (including traditional boys' subjects like design, technology, maths, and chemistry) except physics. In 1995–6, 49.3 per cent of girls got five GCSEs (grades *A–C) compared to 39.8 per cent of boys (see figure 13.2). In English at GCSE, the gender gap is huge, with nearly two-thirds of girls getting a grade *A–C, compared to less than half of boys.

ACTIVITY

Refer to tables 13.1a and 13.1b

1 Which subject group at GCSE had a higher number of female entries than male entries?
2 Which subject group had the highest number of male entries at GCSE but a higher female pass rate?
3 For all the students entering any GCSE subject, by how many percentage points did the pass rate for females exceed that of males?
4 At A-level, which subject group showed the greatest difference between the number of male and female entries?
5 Comparing GCSE and A-level entries, which subject group showed more male entries than female at GCSE, but more female entries than male at A-level?
6 In which subject groups did females get better pass rates than males at both GCSE and A-level?

Refer to figure 13.2 on page 322:

7 What difference was there between the percentage of female and male students obtaining five or more GCSE grades *A–C in 1995/6?
8 Identify two trends in the percentage of 17-year-olds achieving three or more GCE AS/A-levels between 1983/4 and 1994/5.

Refer to figure 13.3 on page 323:

9 In which GCSE subjects were there more female than male entries in 1994/5?
10 In which three GCSE subjects was the gap between the percentage of male and female entries the greatest?
11 In which A-level subjects were there more male than female entries in 1994/5?
12 In which three A-level subjects was the gap between the percentage of male and female entries the greatest?
13 Which subject showed the greatest gap between the percentage of male and female entries at both GCSE and A-level?
14 Suggest explanations for the difference in subjects males and females choose to study at GCSE and A-level.

- A higher proportion of females stay on in post-16 sixth-form and further education, and post-18 higher education.
- Female school leavers are now more likely than males to get three or more A-level passes (see figure 13.2).
- More females than males now get accepted for full-time university degree courses.

But problems still remain for females:

- Females and males still tend to do different subjects, which influence future career choices. Broadly, arts subjects are 'female', science and technology subjects 'male'. This is so at GCSE, and becomes even more pronounced at A-level and above. Girls are therefore less likely to participate after 16 in subjects leading to careers in science, engineering, and technology.
- Girls achieve fewer high-grade A-levels than boys with the same GCSE results.
- There is little evidence that girls' better results at 16 and above lead to improved post-school opportunities in terms of training and employment. As discussed in chapter 6, women are still less likely than men with similar qualifications to achieve similar levels of success in paid employment.
- In the 16–59 age group in the population as a whole who are in employment or unemployed, men tend to be better qualified than women. However, this gap has decreased among younger age groups, and can be expected to disappear if females keep on outperforming males in education.

Explaining Gender Differences in Education

The change to girls outperforming boys is still a fairly recent development, and research to explain it is still at an early stage. What follows are some suggested explanations for:

- The huge improvement in the performance of girls.
- The underperformance of boys.
- The subject choices that continue to separate males and females.

Why do females now do better than males?

- *Equal opportunities*. The work of sociologists in highlighting the educational underperformance of girls in the past led to a greater emphasis in schools on equal opportunities. This was to enable girls to fulfil their potential more easily. These policies included things like monitoring teaching and teaching materials for sex bias to help schooling to meet the needs of girls better. Teachers are now much more sensitive about avoiding gender stereotyping in the classroom, and this may have overcome many of the former problems which girls faced in schools.

- *More employment opportunities and changing female attitudes*. The number of 'male' jobs has been declining in recent years, while there are growing employment opportunities for women. This may have made girls more ambitious and less likely to see having a home and family as their main role in life. Many girls growing up today have mothers working in paid employment, and this provides more positive role models for them. Many girls now recognize that the future involves paid employment, often combined with family responsibilities. Sue Sharpe found in *Just like a Girl* in 1976 that girls' priorities were 'love, marriage, husbands, children, jobs, and careers, more or less in that order'. When she repeated her research in 1994, she found these priorities had changed to 'job, career and being able to support themselves'. These factors may all have provided more incentives for girls to gain qualifications.

- *The women's movement*. The women's movement (discussed in chapter 6) has achieved considerable success in challenging the traditional stereotype of women's roles as housewives and mothers. This means many women now look beyond the housewife/mother role as their main role in life.

- *Girls work harder*. There is mounting evidence that girls work harder and are better motivated than boys:
  — They put more effort into their work.
  — They spend more time on doing their homework properly.
  — They take more care with the way their work is presented.
  — They concentrate more in class (research shows the typical 14-year-old girl can concentrate for about three or four times as long as her fellow male students).
  — They are generally better organized – for example, in bringing the right equipment to school and meeting deadlines for handing in work.

  It has been suggested that the above factors may have helped girls to take more advantage of the increasing use of coursework in GCSE, A-level, and GNVQ. Such work often requires good organization and sustained application, and girls appear better in these respects.

- *Girls mature earlier than boys*. By the age of 16, girls are estimated to be more mature than boys by up to two years. Put simply, this means

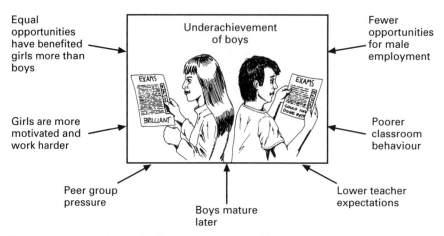

Figure 13.4 Gender and educational underachievement

girls are more likely to view exams in a far more responsible way, and recognize their seriousness.

Why do boys underachieve?

Many of the reasons given above also suggest why boys may be underachieving. However, there are some possible additional explanations.

- *Teacher expectations.* There is some evidence that staff are not as strict with boys as with girls. They are more likely to extend deadlines for work, have lower expectations of boys, are more tolerant of disruptive, unruly behaviour from boys in the classroom, and accept more poorly presented work.
- *Poorer behaviour.* Boys are generally more disruptive in classrooms than girls. They may lose more classroom time learning things because they are sent out of the room or sent home. Four out of every five permanent exclusions from schools are of boys – most of these are for disobedience of various kinds, and usually come at the end of a series of incidents.
- *Peer pressure.* Boys appear to gain 'street cred' and peer group status by not working. This may explain why they are less conscientious and lack the persistence and application required for exam success, particularly in new coursework styles of assessment.
- *The decline in male employment.* The decline in traditional male jobs may be a factor in explaining why many boys are underperforming in education. They may lack motivation because they may feel that getting qualifications won't get them anywhere anyway, so what's the point in bothering?

ACTIVITY/DISCUSSION

1 Go through the reasons suggested above for why girls outperform boys in education. List the explanations in what you think is their order of importance and, drawing on your own experiences at school or college, try to think of any other explanations for the underachievement of boys.

2 Discuss the steps that might be taken in schools to improve the performance of boys.

Why do males and females still tend to do different subjects?

As you will have discovered from the earlier activity on table 13.1a, 13.1b and figures 13.2 and 13.3, there is still a difference between the subjects that males and females do at GCSE and above. Females are still more likely to take arts and social science subjects, like English literature, history, foreign languages, and sociology, and males are more likely to take scientific and technological subjects, particularly at A-level and above (even though girls get better results when they do take them!). This is despite the National Curriculum, which makes maths, English, and science compulsory for all students.

These differences might be explained as follows:

- Gender socialization (discussed in chapter 5) may encourage boys to develop more interest in technical and scientific subjects.
- In giving subject and career advice, teachers may be counselling girls and boys into different subject options, according to their own gender stereotypes of 'suitable subjects'.
- Science and the science classroom are seen as 'masculine' because gender stereotyping is still found in textbooks, with the 'invisibility' of females particularly obvious in maths and science textbooks. This reinforces the view that these are 'male' subjects.
- Boys tend to dominate science classrooms, grabbing apparatus first, answering questions directed at girls, and so on. This all undermines girls' confidence and intimidates them into not taking up these subjects.

DISCUSSION

The following comments are from year 11 boys talking about doing English and science:

'I hate it! I don't want to read books.'

'Science is straightforward. You don't have to think about it. There are definite answers. There are no shades to it.'

'In science, everything is set out as a formula, and you have the facts. All you have to do is apply them to the situation.'

'When you read a book, it's like delving into people's lives. It's being nosey.'

'English is about understanding, interpreting ... you have to think more. There's no definite answer ... the answer depends on your view of things.'

'I don't like having discussions – I feel wrong ... I think that people will jump down my throat.'

'That's why girls do English, because they don't mind getting something wrong. They're more open about issues, they're more understanding ... they find it easier to comprehend other people's views and feelings.'

'You feel safe in science.'

Source: Adapted from Eirene Mitsos 'Boys and English: Classroom Voices', *English and Media Magazine*, no. 33, Autumn 1995

What points do you think are being made about English and science? Do you agree? Why do you think males and females tend to do different subjects? How do you think these choices might be linked to gender role socialization in society as a whole?

SOCIAL CLASS AND UNDERACHIEVEMENT

The Facts

Social class is one of the key factors that determine whether a child does well or badly at school. There are major differences between the levels of achievement of the working class and middle class and, in general, the higher the social class of the parents, the more successful a child will be in education. The degree of social class inequality in education begins in the primary school and becomes wider as children move through the education system, with the higher levels of the education system dominated by middle-class students.

ACTIVITY

Look at figure 13.5:

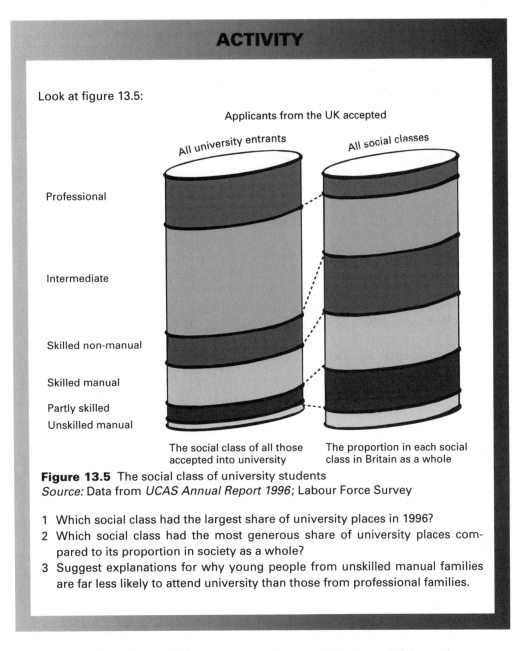

Applicants from the UK accepted

All university entrants

All social classes

Professional

Intermediate

Skilled non-manual

Skilled manual

Partly skilled

Unskilled manual

The social class of all those accepted into university

The proportion in each social class in Britain as a whole

Figure 13.5 The social class of university students
Source: Data from *UCAS Annual Report 1996*; Labour Force Survey

1 Which social class had the largest share of university places in 1996?
2 Which social class had the most generous share of university places compared to its proportion in society as a whole?
3 Suggest explanations for why young people from unskilled manual families are far less likely to attend university than those from professional families.

Lower-working-class children, compared to middle-class children of the same ability:

- In the tripartite system were far more likely to fail the 11+ exam and go to secondary modern schools.
- Are more likely to start school unable to read.
- Do less well in National Curriculum SATs (Standard Assessment Tests).

- Are more likely to be placed in lower streams.
- Generally get poorer exam results.
- Are more likely to leave school at the minimum leaving age of 16, many of them with no qualifications of any kind. Only about half of young people from unskilled manual families stay on in post-16 full-time education, compared to about 9 in every 10 from managerial and professional families.

In addition, a high proportion of A-level students and sixth-formers, and those entering further and higher education, are from the middle class: a much higher proportion than is justified by the proportion of the middle class in society as a whole. Even when the working class do enter further education, they are more likely to take lower-status courses than students from middle-class backgrounds, such as vocational courses rather than A-levels leading to higher education.

The working class is under-represented in higher education. As figure 13.5 shows, in 1996 74 per cent of university students came from middle-class backgrounds, even though only about 45–50 per cent of the population was middle class. Young people from the highest income groups have a 73 per cent chance of getting to university, compared to only a 7 per cent chance for those from manual families living in council homes in areas of high unemployment.

Explaining Working-Class Underachievement

Poverty and home circumstances

Poverty and low wages are concentrated among the semi-skilled and unskilled levels of the working class, and can have an important effect on school performance. Poor housing conditions such as overcrowding or poor heating can make study at home difficult, and a higher level of sickness in such homes may affect school attendance and mean falling behind with lessons. Low wages or unemployment may mean that educational books and toys are not bought, which may affect a child's educational development before and during her or his time at school. There may also be a lack of money for school trips, sports equipment, geometry sets, pocket dictionaries, calculators, and the other hidden costs of free state education. It may be financially difficult for lower-paid parents to support children in education after school leaving age, no matter how bright their prospects. This is a particular problem as there are few grants for further education students, and in higher education university grants have largely been replaced by student loans. In such circumstances, children may be encouraged to leave school as soon as possible and get a job or go onto a

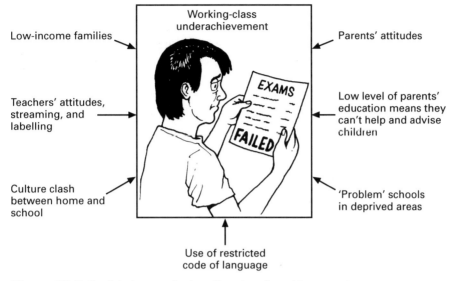

Figure 13.6 Social class and educational underachievement

training scheme, to support themselves and bring some money into the house.

Parents' attitudes to education

Middle-class parents on the whole seem to place a higher value on their children's education and take more interest in their progress at school than working-class parents. Evidence suggests middle-class parents visit the school more frequently to discuss how their children are getting on, and this interest grows as the children reach the more important stages of education as they get older, when exam options are selected and career choices loom. Middle-class parents are also more likely to encourage their children to stay at school beyond the minimum leaving age.

These differences between working-class and middle-class parents, however, do not necessarily indicate that working-class parents have a 'poor attitude' to education. Working-class parents are more likely to work longer hours, doing shiftwork and overtime, and are less likely than the middle class to get paid for time off work. This may mean it is more difficult for working-class parents to visit schools, rather than that they don't care about their children's progress. Middle-class parents also, of course, can more easily afford to continue to support their children in education after the age of 16. The interest shown by middle-class parents may be due to the importance of educational qualifications in obtaining their own middle-class occupations. By contrast, working-class parents may see education as of less importance because they may have found their own education had little relevance to their working-class jobs. This may lead to poor motivation of some working-class children in school and therefore lower levels of achievement, regardless of ability. Parental attitudes can also affect the child's learning by the lower value placed on books or educational toys in many lower-working-class homes.

Parents' level of education

Because they are generally themselves better educated, middle-class parents tend to understand the school system better than working-class parents. Lower-working-class parents may feel less confident in dealing with teachers at parents' evenings, and in dealing with subject options and exam choices. Middle-class parents know more about schools, the examination system, and careers and so are more able to advise and counsel their children on getting into the most appropriate subjects and courses. They can hold their own more in disagreements with teachers (who are also middle class) about the treatment and education of their child. They know what games and books to buy to stimulate their children's educational development both before and during schooling (and have the money to buy them) and can help their children with school work generally. As a consequence, even before they get to school, middle-class children may have learned more as a result of their socialization in the family. These advantages of a middle-class home may be reinforced throughout a child's career at school.

The catchment area

Catchment areas are the areas from which primary and secondary schools draw their pupils. Schools in deprived areas, where there may be a range of social problems such as high unemployment, poverty, juvenile delinquency, crime, and drug abuse, are more likely to have discipline problems owing to the accumulated effects of the environment on children's behaviour, and hence a higher turnover of teachers. This may mean that children from the most disadvantaged backgrounds have the 'worst' schools. In contrast, schools in middle-class neighbourhoods will probably have fewer discipline problems, and have a better learning environment. Additionally, schools in middle-class areas will have more active and wealthy parent teacher associations able to provide extra resources for the school. This has been confirmed by surveys by the National Confederation of Parent Teacher Associations. These have found that parents contribute more than a quarter of the money spent on books and equipment in primary schools. Parents in poorer areas may find it difficult to make such contributions to school funds, and therefore the schools in such areas may lack the resources found in schools in wealthier, middle-class areas.

Language use: the restricted and elaborated codes

Success at school depends very heavily on language – for reading, writing, speaking, and understanding. Bernstein has argued that there is a relationship between language use and social class, and that the language used by the middle class is a better instrument for success at school than the language used by the working class. He argued that the language used by the lower working class has a restricted code while the language used by the middle class has an elaborated code.

The restricted code

The **restricted code** of language is used by both middle-class and working-class people, but is more characteristic of working-class people. It is the sort of language which is used between friends or family members – colloquial, everyday language, with limited explanation, sometimes ungrammatical and limited in vocabulary. This form of language is quite adequate for everyday use with friends because they know what the speaker is referring to – the context is understood by both speakers and so detailed explanation is not required. Bernstein argues that lower-working-class people are mainly limited to this form of language use.

The elaborated code

The **elaborated code** of language is used mainly by middle-class people. It is the language of strangers and individuals in some formal context, where explanation and detail are required – like an interview for a job, writing a business letter, writing an essay or examination answer, or in a school lesson or textbook. It has a much wider vocabulary than the restricted code.

Bernstein argues that the language used in schools is the elaborated code of the middle class, and that it is the middle-class child's ability to use the elaborated code that gives her or him an advantage at school over working-class children. The elaborated code of the middle class is more suited to the demands of school work, since understanding textbooks and writing essays and examination questions require the detail and explanation which is found mainly in the formal language of the elaborated code. Middle-class children who are used to using the elaborated code at home will therefore find school work much easier and learn more in school than those working-class children whose language is limited only to the restricted code. In addition, the teacher may mistake the working-class child's restricted use of language for lack of ability, and therefore expect less from the child. The self-fulfilling prophecy may then come into effect.

The culture clash

Schools are mainly middle-class institutions, and they stress the value of many features of the middle-class way of life, such as the importance of hard work and study, making sacrifices now for future rewards, the 'right' form of dress, behaviour, manners, and language use, 'good' books, good TV programmes, 'quality' newspapers, and so on. This means that middle-class children may find that school greets them almost as an extension of their home life, and they may start school already familiar with and 'tuned in' to the atmosphere of the school, such as the subjects that will be explored there, seeking good marks, doing home-work, good behaviour, a cooperative attitude to teachers, and other features of middle-class culture. Consequently, they may appear to the teacher as fairly intelligent and sophisticated.

For the working-class child, the atmosphere and values of the school may be quite unfamiliar and different to those of his or her home. This is likely to result in a culture clash between her or his home and social class background and the middle-class culture of the school. This culture clash may partly explain working-class underachievement.

Teachers' attitudes, streaming, and labelling

Teachers are middle class, and children from middle-class homes who share the same standards and values as the teacher are often likely to be seen by teachers as 'more intelligent'. Teachers' judgements of children's ability are often influenced by the types of home children come from. Even if children really are of equal ability, teachers are more likely to think working-class children are less intelligent because of the assumptions they hold about their home backgrounds. This may explain why working-class children tend to be found more in the lower streams of streamed comprehensive schools. As shown in the previous chapter, the evidence suggests that teachers expect less from children in lower streams and give them less encouragement than those in higher streams. Teachers may label lower-stream pupils as 'low achievers', and such pupils are then almost guaranteed to fail – victims of the self-fulfilling prophecy.

Because of all the factors discussed above causing the underachievement

The double test for working-class children

Taken together, the factors in the home, social class background, and the school discussed in this chapter help to explain why working-class children do less well at school than middle-class children of the same ability. Schools test all pupils when doing subjects like mathematics, English, or science. However, for the working-class child there is a double test. At the same time as coping with the academic difficulties of school work which all children face, working-class children must also cope with a wide range of other disadvantages and difficulties.

These problems on top of the demands of academic work explain working-class underachievement in schools. These disadvantages start in the primary school and become more and more emphasized as children grow older, as they fall further and further behind and become more disillusioned with school. In this context, it is perhaps not surprising that a large majority of those who leave school at age 16 every year, with few or no qualifications, come from lower-working-class backgrounds.

---

of working-class pupils in schools, bottom-stream pupils are very often working class and such pupils will often form the anti-school sub-culture which was discussed in the previous chapter. They then themselves reject the school which has already rejected them as 'failures' and 'thick'. They look forward to leaving school at the earliest possible opportunity, often before taking any GCSEs or other formal qualifications.

ACTIVITY

1 Put the following explanations for working-class underachievement in what you think is their order of importance: home circumstances; parents' attitudes to education; parents' level of education; the catchment area; language use; the culture clash; teachers' attitudes, streaming, and labelling.
2 In the light of your list, suggest ways that schools and teachers might improve the performance of pupils who face social class disadvantages in education.
3 Do you think schools can make up for problems that begin outside of school, such as in the home and the neighbourhood? Give reasons for your answer.

COMPENSATORY EDUCATION

Because of the disadvantages in education arising from social class background, **positive discrimination** has been attempted as a solution to working-class underachievement. This means that schools in deprived areas, where home and social class background are seen as obstacles to success in education, are singled out for more favourable treatment. They are given more resources than schools in other areas, in terms of better-paid teachers and more money to spend on buildings and equipment. This is an attempt to compensate for the problems of disadvantage faced by the poorer sections of the working class in schooling (hence the term **compensatory education**).

The idea of positive discrimination is based on the idea of equality of opportunity, since it is argued children from disadvantaged backgrounds and poor homes can only get an equal opportunity in education to those who come from non-disadvantaged backgrounds if they get unequal and more generous treatment to compensate.

The policy of positive discrimination and compensatory education was put into practice by the government setting up **Educational Priority Areas** in the 1970s. These were areas where unemployment was high and there were poverty, overcrowding, many children whose home language was not English, and large concentrations of unskilled and semi-skilled working-class people. Schools in these areas were given extra money and teachers. Compensatory education didn't really succeed, and Educational Priority Areas were abandoned in the early 1980s. However, the Labour government in 1997 re-established a very similar approach with its Education Action Zones. These are aimed at targeting money and other resources at areas where educational performance is poor, in an attempt

ACTIVITY

1 Explain how you think each of the features of a 'good' school which Rutter et al. describe opposite might help pupils of all backgrounds and abilities to make more progress.
2 Are there any other features that you would expect to find in a 'good' school?
3 List at least six characteristics, based on your own opinions, of a 'good' teacher'. How important do you think the role of the teacher is in the educational progress of pupils compared to the home, the neighbourhood, and the pressures of friends?

Do schools make a difference?

Michael Rutter, Barbara Maughan, Peter Mortimore, and Janet Ouston, in their book *Fifteen Thousand Hours: Secondary Schools and their Effects on Children* (Open Books 1979), reported research they had carried out in twelve schools. This study attempts to show, in the face of much previous research suggesting the opposite, that 'good' schools can make a difference to the life chances of all pupils. Rutter et al. suggest that it is features of the school's organization which make this difference. These features are summarized below.

- Teachers are well prepared for lessons.
- Teachers have high expectations of pupils' academic performance, and set and mark classwork and homework regularly.
- Teachers set examples of behaviour; for example, they are on time and they use only officially approved forms of discipline.
- Teachers place more emphasis on praise and reward than on blame and punishment.
- Teachers treat pupils as responsible people, for example by giving them positions of responsibility looking after school books and property.
- Teachers show an interest in the pupils and encourage them to do well.
- There is an atmosphere or ethos in the school which reflects the above points, with all teachers sharing a commitment to the aims and values of the school.
- There is a mixture of abilities in the school, as the presence of high-ability pupils benefits the academic performance and behaviour of pupils of all abilities.

---

to improve standards. Schools have not so far been able to overcome or compensate for the disadvantages arising from home and social class background and it remains to be seen how successful the new Education Action Zones will be.

PRIVATE EDUCATION: THE INDEPENDENT SCHOOLS

A final problem for the principle of equality of educational opportunity in Britain is the continued existence of a fee-paying private sector of education – the independent schools. Pupils at these schools are largely the children of wealthier upper-middle- and upper-class parents who have decided to opt out of the free, state-run comprehensive system and can afford to pay for a private education.

Founded in 1495, Loughborough Grammar School is one of the oldest schools in the independent sector

There are many poor-quality schools in the private sector of education, but the public schools are a small group of independent schools belonging to what is called the 'Headmasters' Conference'. These are long-established private schools, many dating back hundreds of years, which charge fees often running into thousands of pounds a year. The two most famous boys' public schools are probably Eton (boarding fee £13 400 a year in 1997) and Harrow, and many of the 'top people' in this country have attended these or other public schools. A public school education means parents can almost guarantee their children will have well-paid future careers bringing them power and status in society.

The Case for Independent Schools

The defenders of private education point to the smaller class sizes and better facilities of the public schools than those found in the state system, which means children have a better chance of educational success. Many teachers are paid more, examination results are often better, and pupils have a much higher chance of getting into university. Many defend private education on the grounds that parents should have the right to spend their money as they wish, and improving their children's life chances is a sensible way of doing so.

The Case against Independent Schools

Many remain opposed to private education, arguing that most people do not have the money to purchase a private education for their children, and it is wrong that the children of the well-off should be given more advantages in education than the poor. Many of these schools have charitable status, which entitles them to receive various tax benefits on gifts of money and reduced rates. Until 1997, they also received a state subsidy in the form of the Assisted Places Scheme, which paid for poorer children with ability to attend private schools. This means public schools were and are effectively subsidized by the taxpayers, the vast majority of whom can't afford to attend them. The taxpayer also pays the cost of training the teachers in these schools, since they attend state-run universities and colleges. The existence of private schools undermines the principle of equality of educational opportunity, because social class background rather than simply ability becomes the key to success in education. Not all children of the same ability have the same chance of paying for this route to educational success.

The quality of teaching in independent schools is often no better than in state-run comprehensives. However, their pupils may obtain better results because classes tend to be smaller than in comprehensives, allowing more individual attention, and the schools often have better resources and facilities. For example, Eton College in 1997 had assets of £131 million – slightly less than Body Shop, but with the added advantage of charitable status! The opponents of private education argue more money should be spent on improving the state system so everyone has an equal chance in education.

Research has shown that even when children who go to private schools, especially the public schools, get worse examination results than children who go to comprehensive schools, they still get better jobs in the end. This suggests that the fact of attending a public school is itself enough to secure them good jobs, even if their qualifications are not quite as good as those of pupils from comprehensives.

Elite Education and Elite Jobs

A public school education remains an essential qualification for the elite jobs in society – that small number of jobs in the country which involve holding a great deal of power and privilege. Although only about 7 per cent of the population have attended independent schools (and public schools are only a proportion of these schools), many of the top positions

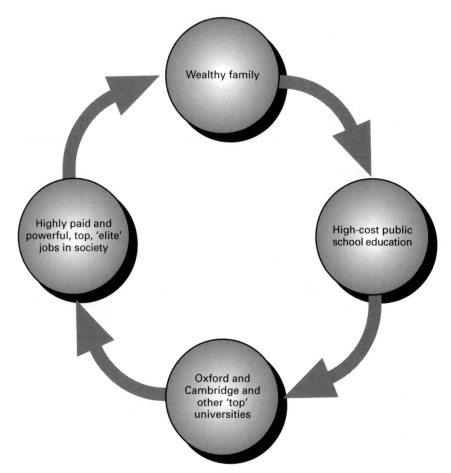

Figure 13.7 The old boys' network

in the Civil Service, the courts, the Church of England, industry, banking, and commerce are held by ex-public school pupils.

In many cases, even well-qualified candidates from comprehensive schools will stand a poor chance of getting such jobs if competing with public school pupils. The route into the elite jobs is basically through a

DISCUSSION

Should private education be abolished? It might be useful to think at the same time about whether private medicine should be abolished – there are many similarities.

public school and Oxford and Cambridge universities (where about 50 per cent of students come from public schools). This establishes the 'old boys' network', where those in positions of power recruit others who come from the same social class background and who have been to the same public schools and universities as themselves. This shows one aspect of the clear relationship which exists between wealth and power in modern Britain, and how being able to afford a public school education can lead to a position of power and influence in society.

IS EQUALITY OF EDUCATIONAL OPPORTUNITY POSSIBLE TO ACHIEVE?

Despite the efforts of first the tripartite system and now the comprehensive system to secure equality of educational opportunity, children of equal ability but from different ethnic backgrounds, of different sexes, and from different social classes are still not achieving the same success in education. Compensatory education has not overcome the disadvantages faced by many pupils in education.

We live in an unequal society, where different groups and classes do not start the educational race on equal terms. In such a society, the combined effects of socialization, home and social class background, teachers' attitudes, the white, middle-class language and culture of the school, and the continued existence of a privileged private sector of education will mean the realization of the ideal of equality of educational opportunity will remain an impossible dream.

DISCUSSION

It has been suggested that reforming schools is as worthwhile an exercise as rearranging the furniture on the *Titanic* – the luxury liner that sank on its first voyage. This is because in terms of improving life chances, schools often do not make much difference to social class, gender, or ethnic inequalities in society as a whole, so reforming schools is basically a pointless exercise. Do you agree?

CHAPTER SUMMARY

After studying this chapter, you should be able to:

- Explain what is meant by educational underachievement.
- Describe, and give a range of explanations for, the differences in achievement in relation to ethnicity, gender, and social class.
- Explain what is meant by positive discrimination and compensatory education.
- Discuss the arguments for and against the existence of the private sector of education.
- Explain the obstacles to the achievement of equality of educational opportunity.

KEY TERMS

compensatory education	positive discrimination
educational priority areas	restricted code
elaborated code	underachievement
ethnocentrism	

PROJECT SUGGESTIONS

1 Observe classroom activities and try to see if boys and girls behave differently in class and are treated differently by teachers. For example, do they sit separately? Are boys asked more questions? Are boys more troublesome? Does this vary in different subject classes and between male and female teachers? Draw conclusions about the hidden curriculum and gender socialization in schools.

2 Make a study of class, ethnic, or gender differences in educational achievement in a local school or college. For example, examine subject choices and exam results.

3 Interview a sample of school students from different class or ethnic groups, and/or of different sexes, asking them what the major influences are on their subject choices and on whether they stay at school after 16 or not.

RELIGION

14

KEY ISSUES IN THIS CHAPTER

- ■ A definition of religion.
- ■ The role of religion in society.
- ■ Religion, social conflict, and social change.
- ■ The secularization thesis.

Sociologists are not generally concerned with whether religious belief is 'true' or not. In many ways this does not matter, for the fact is that millions of people hold religious beliefs, and these beliefs have given rise to powerful movements and institutions. In modern Britain, there are millions of followers of the main religions of Christianity, Islam, Hinduism, and Sikhism. Religious belief is therefore certainly real enough in its consequences. Sociologists are mainly interested in these consequences, or the role and significance of religion in society.

A DEFINITION OF RELIGION

There is no single agreed definition of religion, but organized religions and religious beliefs are likely to include all or some of the following features:

- A belief in the supernatural (some sort of belief in God or gods) or in symbols which are in some way regarded as sacred, such as a cross or totem pole.
- A set of teachings and beliefs (theology), usually based on some holy book, such as the Bible or the Koran.
- A series of rituals or ceremonies to express these beliefs, either publicly or privately. For example, most religions contain rituals such as getting on your knees to pray, church services, singing, fasting, or lighting candles.
- Some form of organization of the worshippers/believers, such as priests, churches, mosques, and temples.
- A set of moral values which guide or influence the everyday behaviour of believers, such as the ten commandments in Christianity.

THE ROLE OF RELIGION IN SOCIETY

The role of religion in society can be broadly categorized under three headings: individual support, social integration, and social control.

Individual Support

Religion can play an important role for individuals in a number of ways.

- Religion can provide a source of comfort, explanation, and meaning for individuals when faced by strains and crises in their lives, such as war, death, accidents, and natural disasters. Funeral services, for example, act as a source of comfort for the bereaved – either with beliefs in life after death, or through the support gained in such moments of stress through the gathering of friends and relatives. Church attendances soar during wartime.
- Religious ceremonies can give believers a feeling of identity and security and a sense of belonging to a group that cares about them, and unite them around a shared moral code of behaviour.
- Religion can provide a source of explanation and understanding of questions such as the meaning of life and death, or an explanation or justification for an individual's social position. For example, in the

Indian caste system (see chapter 2), the Hindu religion provides an explanation for an individual's position in the social hierarchy.

- Religious groups still carry out some important welfare roles for individuals, even though many of these have been taken over by the welfare state. For example, the Salvation Army remains the largest provider of sleeping accommodation for homeless single men in the country, and its work with 'down and outs' is renowned.

Social Integration

Religion is part of the culture or way of life of a society, and it helps to maintain cultural traditions. Society can only survive if people share some common beliefs about right and wrong behaviour. Durkheim, writing in the nineteenth century, saw religion as a kind of social glue, binding society together and integrating individuals into it by encouraging them to accept basic social values. For example, he saw worshipping together as a means of reinforcing a sense of solidarity in a social group, and it is partly through religion that an individual is socialized into the values of a society. The dominant Christian culture of Britain maintains traditions like Christmas, baptism, and monogamous marriage, and tries to encourage conformity to society's norms. For example, monogamous marriage is seen as 'God-given', and the ten commandments, with their rules about stealing, murder, adultery, and so on, in many ways reinforce society's norms.

This set of moral beliefs and values may have been so deeply ingrained through socialization that it may have an effect on the everyday behaviour of believers and non-believers alike. For example, if the rules about killing, stealing, and adultery are broken, most individuals will experience a guilty conscience about doing something 'wrong', and this is a powerful socializing and controlling influence over the individual.

In ethnic minority communities in Britain, religious beliefs and customs are often a means for these groups to maintain their own cultural identity and traditions. Sikh and Hindu temples and Muslim mosques often play an important role in integrating such communities, acting as focal points of community life as well as religious life.

Social Control

Religion is the sigh of the oppressed creature, the heart of a heartless world, and the soul of soulless conditions. It is the *opium* of the people.

Karl Marx, 1844.

Karl Marx, writing in the nineteenth century, described religion as 'the opium of the people'. This is because he saw religious belief as an illusion – an hallucinatory drug – attempting to justify existing arrangements in society and encouraging people to accept them. He saw religion doing this in two ways.

First, religion justifies existing inequalities in income and power in society, by explaining the position of the rich and poor as 'the will of God'. For example, the Hindu religion provides a religious justification for the inequalities of the Indian caste system, and the Bible is riddled with quotations such as 'It is easier for a camel to pass through the eye of a needle, than for a rich man to enter the Kingdom of Heaven.' Poverty and resignation to it therefore become, in themselves, virtues. As a result, the poor are more likely to accept their position in society.

Religion: the opium of the people?

The rich man in his castle,
The poor man at his gate,
God made them, high or lowly,
And ordered their estate.

This is the third verse of the traditional Christian hymn 'All Things Bright and Beautiful' and illustrates well Marx's view of religion justifying social inequality.

Second, Marx believed religion provided comfort for the poor, and drew their attention away from their present misery and the inequalities and injustices of this world with promises of a future, golden life after death. In this way, the poor are encouraged to put off the pursuit of personal happiness and rewards in this life for some future reward in heaven. These two aspects of religion, Marx believed, could only benefit the privileged and powerful, since the poor are encouraged to find 'salvation' through religion rather than challenging the position of the rich and powerful.

ACTIVITY

1 Explain what point the cartoon opposite is making.
2 'Religion mainly encourages people to accept the way things are.' Suggest evidence both for and against this view.

RELIGION, SOCIAL CONFLICT, AND SOCIAL CHANGE

As well as acting as a stabilizing and integrating force in society, religion can also be a source of social change and conflict, causing divisions and instability in society. For example, in Northern Ireland, competing religious beliefs between Catholics and Protestants have been partly responsible for massive social unrest for centuries. The present round of 'the troubles' there has involved armed conflict with the British army since 1969. In the Indian sub-continent, warfare between Muslims and Hindus was in part responsible for the division of a once united India into two separate countries, India and Pakistan. In the 1980s and 1990s, these divisions were added to by conflicts between Hindus and Sikhs. In the 1990s, the former Yugoslavia disintegrated into warring factions of Serbs, Croats, and Bosnians, often aligned on religious lines.

Religion has been responsible for major social change. For example, in South America, Roman Catholic priests – followers of a doctrine mixing Communism and Catholicism called **liberation theology** – have played major roles in fighting against political dictatorships and poverty. In Iran, an Islamic revolution led to the overthrow of the monarchy (the shahdom) and the establishment of an Islamic republic in 1978–9. Islam has become a major international force for social change in the late twentieth century, and the spread of Islamic **fundamentalism** (a return to the literal words of holy texts) has attempted to forge social changes in much of the Islamic world based on literal interpretations of the Koran. This generally involves the removal of 'decadent' Western cultural influences, changes in the position of women (such as the wearing of veils, being banned from driving and going out in public unaccompanied, and being refused access to some education and occupations), and the establishment of legal punishments which to most Western eyes are barbaric, such as public flogging, beheading, or the amputation of the hands of persistent thieves.

THE SECULARIZATION THESIS

The word 'secular' means 'non-religious', and the secularization thesis is simply the suggestion that religion and religious beliefs are of declining importance both in society and for the individual.

Secularization is the process whereby religious thinking, practice, and institutions lose social significance.

Secularization can then be examined in terms of three aspects: religious thinking – the influence of religion on people's beliefs and values; religious practice – such as the levels of church membership and church attendance; and religious institutions – the extent to which churches and other religious institutions have maintained their social influence and wealth.

ACTIVITY

1 Take each of the three aspects of secularization – religious thinking, religious practice, and religious institutions – and in each case suggest four ways you might measure whether secularization is occurring (apart from those given above).
2 Using the measures you have drawn up, suggest how, in each case, the indicators may not necessarily provide reliable evidence of a decline of religion in society.

The Problem of Measuring Secularization

The previous activity may have shown you that the main difficulty with deciding whether secularization has taken place is how religion and religious belief are defined and measured. For example, is church attendance a good way of measuring how much religious belief there is in a society? Does going to church mean you really believe in God? Can you be religious without attending religious ceremonies?

Church membership figures are very unreliable as sources of evidence for secularization because different denominations have different ways of defining membership. For example, the Catholic Church decides membership on the basis of those who are baptized as Catholics, but this tells us nothing about their beliefs as adults. The Methodists decide on the basis of those attending a membership service, while the Church of England may use indicators such as baptisms, confirmations, or those attending key services such as Easter Communion.

Table 14.1 shows the results of a survey on people's religious beliefs in Great Britain. Sociologists would want to ask what the indicators used actually mean. For example, what do people mean by 'God', 'sin', the 'soul', and that 'God is important in my life' (in what ways?)? If people say they believe in God, does this mean it influences their everyday behaviour?

ACTIVITY/DISCUSSION

Refer to table 14.1 on the next page while you do this activity. This gives some indicators of religious belief. Some of these indicators refer mainly to the Christian religion. If you come from another religious background, replace the Christian indicators with others that apply to your religious group. For example, replace 'commandments' under 'Indicators of orthodox belief' with rules your own religion might expect you to obey, and substitute 'mosque', 'temple', 'synagogue', etc., for 'church' under 'Indicators of institutional attachment'.

1 List the ten most important indicators of religious commitment in table 14.1 which, in your opinion, show that Britain has become a secular society. Explain the reasons why you think these indicators are important.
2 Are you a religious person? How many of the forty-eight indicators in table 14.1 would you answer 'yes' to? How many would you answer 'no' to?
3 Study the 'Indicators of moral values'. Do you think these are necessarily good indicators of religious commitment? Do religious people have to support them? Does not supporting them mean a person is not religious? Discuss this with others if you are in a group.

Religion

Because of these problems of interpreting and measuring the extent of religious belief and practice, there is no clear agreement among sociologists over whether and to what extent secularization has occurred.

Table 14.1 Indicators of religious commitment: Great Britain

Indicators of religious disposition	% of sample	Indicators of orthodox belief	% of sample
Often think about meaning and purposes of life	34	Believe in personal God	31
		(Believe in spirit or life force)	39
Never think life meaningless	50	Believe in:	
Often think about death	15	God	76
Often regret doing wrong	8	Sin	69
Need moments of prayer, etc.	50	Soul	59
Define self as a religious person	58	Heaven	57
Draw comfort/strength from religion	46	Life after death	45
God is important in my life	50	The devil	30
Have had a spiritual experience	19	Hell	27
		Personally fully accept commandments demanding:	
		No other gods	48
		Reverence of God's name	43
		Holy Sabbath	25

Indicators of moral values		Indicators of institutional attachment	
Absolute guidelines exist about good and evil	28	Great confidence in church	19
Personally fully accept commandments prohibiting:		Church answers moral problems	30
		Church answers family problems	32
		Church answers spiritual needs	42
Killing	90	Attend church monthly	23
Adultery	78	Denomination:	
Stealing	87	Roman Catholic	11
False witness	78	Protestant (established)	68
Agree with unrestricted sex	23	Free church/Non-conformist	6
Terrorism may be justified	12	Believe religion will become:	
Following acts never justified:		More important in future	21
Claiming unentitled benefit	78	Less important in future	40
Accepting a bribe	79	Believe in one true religion	21
Taking marijuana	81	Religious faith an important value to develop in children	14
Homosexuality	47		
Euthanasia	30		
Political assassination	77		
Greater respect for authority: good	73		
Willing to sacrifice life	34		

Source: Adapted from M. Abrams, D. Gerard, and N. Timms (eds), *Values and Social Change in Britain* (Macmillan 1985)

Religious beliefs have been replaced by scientific explanations

ACTIVITY

1 Explain in your own words the point being made in the cartoon above.
2 Look at the following religiously based explanations. Suggest a scientific explanation for each event.
   (a) God made the walls of Jericho come tumbling down.
   (b) 'Mad' people are possessed by evil.
   (c) AIDS is God's vengeance for immorality.
   (d) Witches cure people by casting magic spells.
   (e) 'And the Lord sent a sign ... and all the land of Egypt was corrupted by a swarm of flies.'
   (f) 'And the Lord appointed a set time ... and all the cattle of Egypt died: but of the cattle of the children of Israel died not one.'
   (g) Lazarus was dead, and 'when Jesus came, he found that he had lain in the grave four days already ... it was a cave and a stone covered the entrance ... Jesus said "Take ye away the stone" ... and "Lazarus, come forth." And he that was dead came forth, bound hand and foot with grave-clothes.' Christ had made Lazarus rise from the dead.

Despite the problems in measuring secularization, there does seem to be a general decline in participation in organized religion in modern Britain. Table 14.1 suggests that while many people claim to continue to hold some orthodox beliefs and moral values based on Christianity, most people do not have much attachment to Christian institutions. In a supposedly Christian country, only about 12 per cent of the population are members of a Christian church, less than a half of marriages involve a Christian ceremony, and less than a quarter of all English babies are now being baptized, compared with two-thirds in 1950.

The reasons for growing secularization

The apparent growth of secularization would seem to be the result of the combination of a number of factors.

- Advances in science and technology now provide scientific explanations for questions traditionally answered by religion, such as the origin of the universe and the causes of famine and disease. The 'miracles' of yesterday have become today's scientific discoveries. The development of scientific knowledge and explanation tends to undermine religious belief.
- The growth of the welfare state has removed many of the tasks that used to be performed by religious institutions, such as the provision of education, and financial aid in times of distress. This reduces the significance of religion in people's lives.
- The development of the mass media, particularly television, has replaced the church as the main source of authority and knowledge for many people. People are now more likely to form their opinions on the basis of what they read in the newspapers or watch on TV rather than what religion or the church has to say.

Competing Evidence on Secularization

Much of the secularization debate has been focused on the Christian religion in Britain, and there would appear to be little evidence of secularization occurring in the ethnic minority religions. On the contrary, such

Some indicators of secularization

religious belief is perhaps growing in strength, particularly in the Muslim community. The following section, therefore, primarily concentrates on some of the competing arguments and evidence both for and against the view that secularization is occurring in the Christian religion in modern Britain.

Evidence for secularization

The decline of religious thinking

Religious beliefs have become less important to individuals in guiding their morals in everyday life. A MORI poll in 1996 found only 43 per cent of people believed there was a god. Various churches' traditional disapproval of divorce, contraception, abortion, sex outside of marriage, illegitimacy, and homosexuality appears to have little impact on people's behaviour. The rising number of divorces, lone-parent families, children born outside marriage, and couples living together without getting married, as well as the growing acceptance of homosexuality, extra-marital sex, and the widespread use of contraception among Catholics in direct opposition to Catholic teachings, and rising levels of drug abuse, pornography, and violent crime might all be used as evidence for the declining importance of religious morals and beliefs in people's lives.

The fragmentation of belief

The fragmentation of belief means that there is no longer one set of beliefs which most people share, but fragments of different types of belief. Many people continue to hold religious beliefs of some kind, but drawn from a wide area. Christianity now has to compete with tarot cards, paganism, American Indian religious beliefs, self-help therapies, and spiritual healing, New Age mysticism, palmistry and horoscopes, astrology, witchcraft, and beliefs in the paranormal (like extra-sensory perception). This is on top of the growing adoption by some outside of the ethnic minority communities of Hinduism, Buddhism, and Islam. Each person can now mix his or her own personal, do-it-yourself religious cocktail. Instead of everyone uniting around one religion, traditional religious thinking has been replaced by a kind of pick-and-mix religion chosen, after shopping around, from the wide range of beliefs available in the 'spiritual supermarket'.

DISCUSSION

Do you think Christian religious thinking is in decline in modern Britain? Do you think there is a fragmentation of religious belief? Try to think of evidence both for and against these views.

The decline of religious practice

There has been a decline in church membership and church and Sunday school attendance in all the major Christian denominations. Traditional churches have lost one member every six minutes since 1975.

Only around 2 per cent of the population go to Church of England services on most Sundays, compared to about 40 per cent in 1851. Only about 20 per cent go at least once a month and only about half of the population goes to any religious service at all each year. In 1995, the Church of England had the lowest attendance at Sunday services in twenty years, and there are declining attendances at Christmas and Easter. The Catholics, too, are losing support, with around 50 000 fewer people attending mass each year. This makes Britain one of the most irreligious countries in the Christian world. Many of those who attend may do so for reasons other than religious belief, such as family pressure or because friends or relatives are being buried or married. The picture may, therefore, be even worse for religious practice.

While many people do still make use of religious ceremonies for the 'rites of passage' marking significant stages in life – such as baptism, marriage, and funerals – these may only be used to give a sense of occasion, and for most people they may have little religious significance. Most people never attend a church apart from these occasions, and in any case the numbers of these ceremonies are declining. For example, more than half of all marriages are now civil marriages (non-religious ceremonies).

ACTIVITY

Answer the following questions yourself, and perhaps do a small survey, to see how much you and other people in modern Britain know about religion.

1 In how many days does the Bible say the earth was created?
2 What was the name of the garden where Adam and Eve were tempted?
3 Who killed Goliath?
4 Whom did God tell to build an ark?
5 Who was thrown into the lion's den?
6 Who was turned into a pillar of salt?
7 Who was the father of Cain and Abel?
8 What were the gifts the three wise men brought to the baby Jesus?
9 In what town did Jesus grow up?
10 What feast was prepared for the prodigal son?
11 Which disciple betrayed Jesus for thirty pieces of silver?
12 When Jesus was crucified, who was the Roman governor of Jerusalem?
13 Name the first book of the Bible.
14 Give five of the ten commandments.
15 Who gave the Sermon on the Mount?
16 Complete the following: 'Blessed are the meek, for . . . '.
17 Who turned water into wine?
18 How many days did Jesus spend in the wilderness?
19 In which religion is Bar Mitzvah a ceremony?
20 By what name are members of the 'Society of Friends' often known?
21 Which religion has the Koran as its sacred book?
22 Which is the holy book of the Sikh faith?
23 Who was the founder of Islam?
24 Which is Islam's holiest city?
25 Members of which religions in Britain normally worship in a temple?
26 Name three Hindu gods.
27 In which country was Buddha born?
28 Which religion has its laws set out in the Talmud?
29 Which is the oldest, and which the newest, of these faiths: Buddhism, Hinduism, Islam, Christianity, Sikhism?
30 Which religion celebrates Divali?

(Answers are at the end of the chapter.)

The decline of religious institutions

The power and influence of the church in society have declined. The status of the clergy is steadily declining, they are hard to recruit, and they often have lower pay than unskilled manual workers. Church buildings are closing and crumbling today, with over 1250 churches being closed since 1970. In the much poorer society of the past they were built, expensively decorated, well maintained, and repaired. There is likely to be a greater social protest at the closure of a branch of McDonalds than there is at the closure of a Christian church.

The church used to have great influence in the state and society, in terms of law-making (such as on divorce and abortion), education, politics, and social welfare. Today, the welfare state has taken over many of these roles, with free state education, the social services, the NHS, state benefits, old people's homes, and so on to care for the sick, the poor, the unemployed, and other disadvantaged groups.

Religion is fighting a losing battle to survive, by uniting in the **ecumenical movement**. This seeks to achieve greater unity between different Christian churches, such as the Church of England, the Roman Catholic and the Methodist Churches. This could be seen as a classic example of religion – drowning in a sea of apathy, indifference, and empty churches – desperately clutching at straws trying to save itself. Ecumenism might

ACTIVITY

Study table 14.2 and answer the following questions:

1 How many people belonged to Anglican churches in 1985?
2 By how many did the membership of the Roman Catholic Church decline between 1975 and 1995?
3 What percentage of the population belonged to a Trinitarian church in 1995?
4 Identify two trends shown in the membership of non-Trinitarian Christian churches in table 14.2.
5 Which three churches or religions are estimated to increase membership most between 1995 and 2005?
6 How might the evidence in the table be used to show that religion is not necessarily declining in the United Kingdom?
7 There has been a decline in the number of religious marriages in Britain, and over half of all marriages today are civil ceremonies. Do you think this necessarily means there is a decline in religious belief? What other explanations might there be?

Table 14.2 Membership of churches and other religions: United Kingdom, 1975–2005

Church or religion	1975	1985	1995[a]	2005[b]
Trinitarian churches:[c] thousands				
Anglican	2298	2017	1760	1492
Roman Catholic	2605	2279	2003	1686
Presbyterian	1589	1322	1120	889
Methodist	577	474	421	356
Baptist	236	243	229	229
Pentecostal	102	137	183	232
Other Trinitarian	586	656	778	872
Total Trinitarian	7993	7128	6494	5756
% of adult population	18.0%	15.5%	13.9%	12.0%
Non-Trinitarian churches: thousands				
Mormons	100	134	171	220
Jehovah's Witnesses	80	97	131	160
Spiritualists	57	49	40	31
Church of Scientology	20	50	150	750
Other non-Trinitarian	82	68	63	60
Total non-Trinitarian	339	398	555	1221
% of adult population	0.7%	0.9%	1.2%	2.5%
Other religions: thousands				
Muslims	204	435	586	780
Sikhs	115	160	350	450
Hindus	100	130	145	155
Jews	114	105	96	87
Buddhists	13	23	45	70
Others	24	41	57	72
Total other religions	570	894	1279	1614
% of adult population	1.3%	1.9%	2.7%	3.4%
All religions: thousands	8902	8420	8328	8591
% of adult population	20.0%	18.0%	17.8%	17.9%

[a] Figures for Trinitarian churches are for 1994; figures for all other churches are estimates.
[b] Estimate.
[c] Trinitarian churches are Christian churches which believe God consists of three persons: father, son, and Holy Spirit.
Source: UK Christian Handbook

therefore be interpreted as a sign of the weakness of the churches, as they are no longer able to stand on their own feet.

The growing number of competing religions, churches, and sects means there is no longer one main church or body of shared religious belief around which people are united. Religion can no longer attract people without packaging itself in many different guises, to appeal to a whole variety of consumer tastes. It has become like washing powder on supermarket shelves, with all the rival manufacturers competing desperately to sell the same product to a declining market.

Religion itself is becoming secularized. It no longer provides a lead for people and seems to follow trends rather than set them. The only way religion can maintain any support is by repackaging itself and watering down or abandoning traditional beliefs and customs – by itself becoming 'less religious'. Take, for example, trendy 'happy-clappy' and 'rave-in-the-nave' services (mixing loud rock music, disco lights, and dancing), the acceptance of easier divorce laws and allowing divorced people to remarry in churches, the growing acceptance of abortion, the abolition of Latin in Catholic services, the ordination of women priests, and the growing acceptance of homosexuality by the church. These might all be seen as evidence of this collapse of traditional beliefs. In October 1997, the *Sunday Times* reported that a majority of the forty-four diocesan bishops of the Church of England no longer believed cohabiting couples, traditionally regarded as 'living in sin', were necessarily committing a sin. So it would appear that even the clergy are becoming secularized and abandoning their traditional beliefs.

Evidence against secularization

The continuing importance of religious thinking

Religious belief of various kinds remains very widespread. Surveys show that, although around 70 per cent of the population thinks religion is losing its influence, 76 per cent of people still claim to believe in God, 69 per cent in sin, and 57 per cent in heaven (see table 14.1 earlier in this chapter). There is still widespread belief in the supernatural; many remain superstitious and believe in horoscopes, ghosts, and so on. (See, for example, the range of religious activities discussed earlier under 'The fragmentation of belief'.)

Rising rates of crime, divorce, births outside marriage, and so on have a wide range of causes, and cannot be explained as simply arising from declining religious beliefs. Religious beliefs still play an important role in underpinning many social values and social welfare policies. Table 14.1 shows that many people in Britain still support religiously based moral values, such as attitudes to stealing, killing, and adultery.

The widespread acceptance of religiously based beliefs such as the importance of caring for the poor may have forced the state to take over many of the social welfare responsibilities formerly carried out by the church.

A controversial vicar is calling for dramatic changes in the way churches operate. For unless drastic steps are taken, he fears we could soon be witnessing the end of Christianity itself.

And vicar Dennis Randall believes that unless Holy men are prepared to move with the times, they will soon be left preaching to rows of empty pews.

PACKED

Christmas has traditionally meant big business for the churches, with standing room only in packed houses throughout the country. But all that is changing, and this year vicars are bracing themselves for record low attendances.

FALL

Over the last few years there has been a dramatic fall in the number of people going to church. And religious chiefs fear that unless action is taken to stop the rot, thousands of churches around Britain could soon go under.

STEEPLES

Rev. Randall believes several factors are responsible for the fall in attendances. 'There's been a lack of investment' he told us. 'Too much money has been spent on steeples, and not enough on the churches themselves. We're stuck with old, outdated buildings. Most of them lack even basic toilet facilities.'

FORMAL

'Hymns are also outdated. Some of them are literally hundreds of years old. And I'm sure many young people are put off by the formal dress code. For instance, a church is probably the only place in Britain where you aren't allowed to wear a hat.'

'That's what churches need' says controversial vicar

Could churches like this soon be closing their doors for the last time. (Inset) Rev. Randall yesterday.

SHORTCOMING

Failure to compete in an increasingly competitive Sunday morning environment has been another major shortcoming, according to Rev. Randall. 'DIY superstores and Garden Centres are pulling in the punters in their thousands', he told us.

'They offer shopping, refreshments, play areas for the kids and free car parking. And all we have to offer is a cold seat, a couple of hymns and a few stories about God you've probably heard a hundred times before. It's no wonder we're losing out.'

OUTSKIRTS

Among many suggestions he has put forward is the construction of new, out-of-town 'super-churches'. 'The whole idea of the little church on the corner is completely outdated. We should be building big, new churches on the outskirts of town, with late opening, seven nights a week, and free car parking.'

SPACE

Steps should also be taken to attract people to church. 'Prime land is wasted on cemeteries. We could use this space to have attractive garden displays, fun fairs for kids, and car washes. Everyone washes their car on a Sunday.'

FINAL

Rev. Randall believes a huge commercial opportunity exists in the form of Sunday lunches. 'If we served up good, basic, traditional nosh, at reasonable prices, we'd have the punters queuing up for it', he told us.

The Reverend also dreams of the day when churches will be granted drinks licenses. 'It's ridiculous', he told us. 'You can buy a drink in any pub in the country. But if you're in a church you can't. Britain must be the only country in the world that has such outdated licensing laws. God only knows what tourists make of it all.'

FRONTIER

Rev. Randall believes the key to future success will be attracting young people back to church. 'We must try to get families back. It's all well and good the old folks turning up – they're always welcome – but a lot of them are only interested in the free cup of tea afterwards. And they're not exactly the most generous people in the world when the collection plate comes round.'

BISHOP

So far Rev. Randall's suggestions have met with a cautious response from the Archbishop of Canterbury. 'He hasn't actually replied yet', Rev. Randall admitted, 'but he's been very busy lately.'

ROOK

Meanwhile, the Reverend tells us that he hopes to attract a bumper congregation to his church on Christmas Day, by lining up a troup of exotic dancers to top the bill. 'There's nothing in the Bible to say thou shalt not have strippers on', he joked yesterday. 'And besides, anything that puts arses on pews is good business in my book.' To overcome the drinks ban Rev. Randall will be inviting parishioners to bring along their own bottle of wine.

An article from *Viz*
Source: *Reproduced with permission of JBP/House of Viz*

ACTIVITY/DISCUSSION

Read the spoof article from *Viz* magazine. The article is intended to be amusing, but how far do you think it highlights the kinds of thing that are happening to religious institutions today?

1 Do you think religious institutions are becoming less religious in the face of competing demands from DIY superstores, garden centres, and the lure of television? What evidence can you think of to back up your view?
2 Do you think religious institutions should follow some of the suggestions (somewhat adapted!) of the 'Rev. Randall', and water down traditional beliefs and practices in order to get 'more arses on pews'?
3 Make a list of your own suggestions for ways religious institutions might attract more people.

The strength of religious practice

Believing in God does not necessarily mean going to church, and going to church does not necessarily mean believing in God. In the past many people may have attended church regularly only because church-going was seen as necessary to achieve respectability in the community. The decline in church attendance today therefore may not necessarily mean that there has been a decline in belief, only a decline in the social pressure to attend church.

The desire for religious belief and commitment is still very strong today. People are simply disillusioned with the traditional churches and are expressing their beliefs in different ways. For example, declining church attendance may simply mean that people prefer to practise their religion more in the privacy of their own homes, in 'house groups', or with services on TV and radio, rather than going to church.

As table 14.2 shows, there has actually been an increase in membership of other Christian groupings, such as the Mormons and the Jehovah's Witnesses, and of other religions.

Despite an overall decline in church attendance, the fact that many people continue to make use of religious ceremonies for the 'rites of passage' such as baptism, marriage, and death may show they still believe it is important for religion to 'bless' the important stages in their lives. About 90 per cent of funerals involve a religious ceremony.

The decline in the number of people marrying in churches and the increase in civil weddings could be because many involve second marriages for one or both partners, or because of the cost, not because of a lack of religious belief.

The continuing influence of religious institutions

Although the power and influence of religious institutions, particularly the Church of England, may have declined since the nineteenth century, they remain important in a number of ways.

- Church of England bishops have seats in the House of Lords (the 'Lords Spiritual').
- The monarch must be a member of the Church of England, is crowned by the Archbishop of Canterbury, and since the time of Henry VIII has been Head of the Church of England, and 'Defender of the Faith'.
- The Church of England remains the established (or 'official') church in England.
- The Church of England is extremely wealthy, with investment funds of an estimated £3 billion in 1991, and it is one of the largest landowners in the country.
- Since the 1944 Education Act, all schools have been legally obliged to hold a religious ceremony each day, and the 1988 Education Reform Act reaffirmed and strengthened the requirement to hold assemblies of a broadly Christian nature and teach Christian beliefs for at least 51 per cent of the time allocated to religion in schools.

Evangelical Christianity

The fastest growing Christian movement in Britain in the 1980s and 1990s was evangelical Christianity, part of a worldwide revival of Christianity. **Evangelicalism** is a broad collection of Christians sharing a fundamentalist belief in the Bible – accepting that the Bible is God's literal word and should be followed strictly. Many evangelicals believe in the second coming of Christ, faith healing, speaking in tongues, miracles, casting out of demons, and possession by evil. They campaign against witchcraft, satanism, black magic, any form of occult activity, smoking, drinking, sexual promiscuity, and homosexuality.

More than half of all new Anglican priests in 1990 were evangelical 'born-again' Christians, and nearly one-quarter of Anglican bishops, including the Archbishop of Canterbury, Dr George Carey, are evangelicals.

The year 1990 saw 200 000 people taking part in 'March for Jesus' rallies throughout Britain, and a decade of evangelism was launched in 1991. This was a ten-year campaign in Britain (with supporters from all the major churches) to win new recruits to Christianity. This new evangelicalism initially appeared to be reviving the religious passion and commitment lacking in the traditional churches, and looked set to halt and even reverse the decline in religious belief and church attendance which has been going on throughout much of the twentieth century. However, the latest church attendance statistics suggest the movement may not have achieved the success that was hoped for.

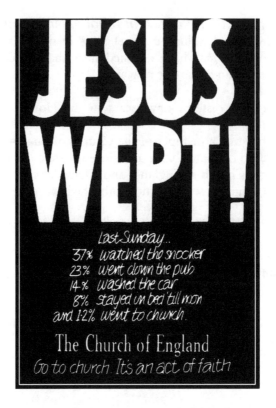

The Church fights back: a draft advertisement prepared for a Church of England media conference, to promote the church when religious advertising on TV became legal in 1993

- Religious institutions still provide many schools, such as Catholic and Church of England voluntary schools.
- There remains a religiously defined 'day of rest' on Sundays, and many people still regard this as their day off (albeit for shopping, leisure and pleasure – rather than religion – in many cases!).
- Churches can still wield a lot of political influence. The Church of England's 'Faith in the City' report in 1985 caused a huge row when it attacked the government over poverty and social deprivation. A similar row occurred in 1997 when a further report on unemployment and poverty – backed by bishops and leaders of all the twelve main Christian churches – attacked the Conservative government's record and, in effect, supported Labour party policies just before a general election.
- Religious groups can still act as powerful pressure groups influencing those in positions of power in society. For example, LIFE and SPUC (the Society for the Protection of the Unborn Child) are mainly Catholic organizations seeking to make abortion completely illegal, and have been very effective (though unsuccessful) in raising the issue of abortion in the House of Commons. In Northern Ireland, the Pres-

byterian Church (in its various forms) and the Catholic Church play major political roles.

- Religion remains very important in the ethnic minority communities. Mosques, temples, and synagogues are often a focus of social and cultural life as well as religious life.

It is unrealistic to expect religion not to change with the times. 'Rave services' and the like are simply trying to make the church more 'seeker-friendly' – accessible and attractive to people who before had no contact with the church. The wide variety of churches today simply represents different ways of expressing belief. Evangelical Christianity is the fastest growing form of Christianity in Britain, and the religious fundamentalism this involves cannot be regarded as 'watered-down' religion.

CONCLUSION

This chapter has shown that, while religion can play an important role for the individual and in society, there does seem to be evidence that religion is of declining significance in Britain. However, whether secularization is judged to have taken place or not will be influenced by the indicators of religious commitment which are used. While many people in Britain still claim to hold religious beliefs and to support religiously based moral values, there is little evidence of their showing much participation in religious activities. Nevertheless, evangelicalism may yet be a major force for Christian revival in the twenty-first century, and may reverse or at least halt the decline of the Christian churches which has been one of the most significant social trends of the twentieth century.

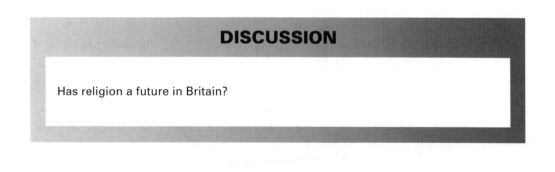

DISCUSSION

Has religion a future in Britain?

CHAPTER SUMMARY

After studying this chapter, you should be able to:

- Give a definition of religion.
- Explain, with examples, the role of religion for the individual and society.
- Explain how religion can act as an agency of social control.
- Explain with examples, how religion can influence social change and conflict.
- Explain what is meant by the term 'secularization'.
- Explain some of the problems with measuring religious belief, particularly the difficulties of using church membership and attendance statistics.
- Explain the reasons why society may have become more secular.
- Provide a range of arguments and evidence both for and against the secularization thesis.

KEY TERMS

ecumenical movement	fundamentalism
evangelicalism	liberation theology

PROJECT SUGGESTIONS

1 Carry out a study of church attendance figures over time in some local church(es) – are people becoming less religious as measured by church attendance? Try to discover some reasons for this.
2 Interview some local clergy from a variety of denominations and faiths – or members of the public – about whether and in what ways religion is or is not becoming less important.
3 Study the role of a church/mosque/temple in the local community, including interviews with religious leaders.
4 Ask a sample of people of different ages about what, if any, religious beliefs they hold. Table 14.1 or the questions on religious knowledge in this chapter may give you some ideas for a questionnaire. Relate your findings to the secularization debate.
5 Investigate a local evangelical group, exploring their beliefs, the commitment required, and the occupations (social class), sex, and ages of those involved.

The answers to the questions on p. 357 are as follows:
1 Six. 2 Eden. 3 David. 4 Noah. 5 Daniel. 6 Lot's wife.
7 Adam. 8 Gold, frankincense and myrrh. 9 Nazareth. 10 The fatted calf. 11 Judas Iscariot. 12 Pontius Pilate. 13 Genesis 14 *Not* to: have any other gods but me, make any graven image, worship any graven image, take the name of God in vain, kill, steal, commit adultery, bear false witness, covet neighbour's wife/house, etc., to keep the Sabbath holy. 15 Jesus. 16 'they shall inherit the earth'. 17 Jesus. 18 Forty.
19 Judaism. 20 Quakers. 21 Islam. 22 Guru Granth.
23 Mohammed. 24 Mecca. 25 Sikhism, Hinduism, and Buddhism.
26 Shiva, Vishnu, Krishna, Ganesh, etc. 27 India. 28 Judaism.
29 Hinduism is the oldest, Sikhism the newest. 30 Hinduism.

15 WORK AND LEISURE

Without work, it is difficult to see how society could survive in the form to which we have grown accustomed. The building of roads, houses, hospitals, schools, shops, and factories, the education of children, the production of food and consumer goods, the provision of services, health, welfare, and leisure activities all involve people working. Even when most of us relax from work by watching television, going to a sports centre or a cinema, going out for a meal or to the pub, someone else is working to provide these services.

When we meet someone for the first time, one of the first things we usually find out about them is what they do for a living. In fact, it is quite likely that most people we do meet as adults are a result of contacts made through work. The kinds of leisure pursuit we follow and the time and money available to enjoy them are all related to our work. For this reason, work is central to both society and the lives of the individuals who make it up.

In this chapter, the major issues covered are the importance of work, the factors which influence whether or not work may be an enjoyable experience, and the role of trade unions in the workplace. The changes that have occurred in employment patterns in modern Britain, the changing nature of technology and its consequences for the individual and society, and the patterns of leisure are other key themes.

Figure 15.1 The importance of work

THE IMPORTANCE OF WORK

Work is the production of goods or services that usually earns a wage or salary or provides other rewards, though some work, like housework, remains unpaid. Work is an important element in occupying, directing, and structuring the individual's time – the demands of working life involve a high degree of discipline if jobs are to be kept. It is, for most people, the single biggest commitment of time in any week, and it is perhaps one of the most important experiences affecting people's entire lives. Work influences:

- *Status and social class.* The work a person does is generally the most important single factor deciding status in modern societies – most people categorize themselves and others by the job they do. Work is therefore central to the individual's sense of identity and self-esteem. For most people, the work they do provides their sole or major source of income and a person's occupation is a major factor deciding her or his social class.
- *Life chances.* How money is earned, how much, in what working conditions, and how long it takes decide in many ways the kind of life a person will lead. For example, income from work – and future possibilities for promotion and therefore increasing income – will affect the kind of housing and mortgage a person can afford, and therefore the residential area he or she will live in. The hours worked and whether working conditions are good or bad can have major effects on health. Shiftwork, nightwork, long hours of overtime, and work carrying risks

Attitudes to work

The *extrinsic or instrumental attitude to work* is one in which the most important thing about a job is high wages. This attitude is usually found in uninteresting and repetitive jobs such as assembly line work, where high wages are a means of compensating for otherwise boring work, and of achieving satisfaction outside work in leisure time.

The *intrinsic attitude to work* is one in which the most important feature of a job is the amount of pleasure, fulfilment, and satisfaction it offers. High pay is not seen as the only, or most important, reason for doing the job. This attitude is found in professional jobs such as nursing and teaching, and among craft workers.

of industrial disease, accidents, and stress can have serious consequences for a person's health and life expectation.

- *Friendship and community life.* Work is a major place for meeting people and for making friends. The nature of the work situation can affect how much 'social mingling' there is at work and therefore how easily friendships can be made. In the case of traditional working-class communities which are dominated by one industry for generation after generation, such as traditional coal mining and fishing communities, relationships formed at work are likely to be the basis for community life, as workmates are often neighbours, kin, and childhood friends.

- *Values and attitudes.* Work is an important socializing experience that shapes the individual's values and attitudes. Attitudes to trade unions, for example, are likely to be formed by people's experiences at work and the solidarity which develops there. The extent to which people can adopt future planning will frequently depend on how secure their employment is, and whether they can look forward to promotion and increased pay.

- *Family life.* Work will affect the amount of money and time available for family life. Full-time working married or cohabiting women generally have less time for leisure, as they are often expected to do two jobs – their paid work and unpaid housework inside the home.

- *Leisure activities.* The number of hours spent at work and the income earned will obviously affect the time available for leisure activities and the money available to enjoy them. However, a person's occupation and her or his experiences at work can have a direct effect on how leisure time is spent. Parker saw the relationship between work and leisure falling into three main patterns, which he called the opposition, neutrality, and extension patterns (see table 15.1).

Table 15.1 Patterns of relationship between work and leisure

Work–leisure pattern	Nature of work	Typical occupations	Nature of leisure
Opposition	Physically hard and dangerous male-dominated occupations	Steelworkers, miners, deep-sea fishermen	Opposition to work: escape from hardships of work through drinking and gambling with workmates
Neutrality	Boring and routine work, leading to apathy and indifference	Routine clerical workers, shop assistants	Nothing much to do with work (neutral): leisure for relaxation with home and kin, like DIY and going out with the family
Extension	High levels of personal commitment, involvement, and job satisfaction	Professionals and managers – doctors, teachers, social workers, and business executives	Because work is so interesting or demanding, leisure is work-related – work extends into leisure time; for example, business executives playing golf or eating out with clients, teachers using their own time to run school trips/ holidays with pupils

UNEMPLOYMENT

Nothing shows the importance of work more than the loss of a job, or not being able to find one. Being made redundant is nearly always a shattering experience for the individual, particularly for older people who stand poorer chances of finding another job than those who are younger. Throughout the 1980s and 1990s, unemployment and the threat of unemployment, were major problems in Britain, and they show every indication of being a depressingly permanent feature of life for the foreseeable future.

The Causes of Unemployment

The causes of unemployment are varied.

- The development of new technology, with fully automated work processes using computers and microelectronics, requires fewer workers.

ACTIVITY

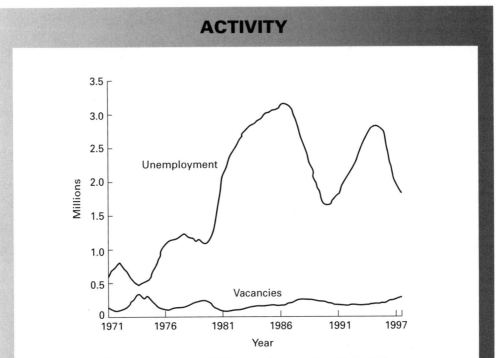

Figure 15.2 Unemployment and Jobcentre[a] vacancies: United Kingdom, 1971–97
[a]About one-third of all vacancies are notified to Jobcentres
Source: Data from *Labour Market Trends*

Study figure 15.2 and answer the following questions:

1 In approximately which years were there 2 million unemployed?
2 In which year was unemployment at its highest?
3 Approximately how many vacancies were there in 1986?
4 Identify two trends shown in figure 15.2.
5 How might the evidence in figure 15.2 be used to challenge the view that 'the jobs are there if people really want them'?
6 Suggest as many reasons as you can for the fact that, even during periods of high unemployment, job vacancies may remain unfilled.

- The increase in the working population, including more married women working and more people working to retirement age, reduces the number of unfilled job vacancies.
- Foreign competition from manufactured goods, such as Japanese cars and electrical goods, and the decline of older manufacturing industries have led to many factory closures.
- A depression in the economy, and the unwillingness of governments to invest in job creation schemes, such as road and house building programmes to create employment opportunities, have kept the number of jobs down.
- The skills workers possess may become redundant or obsolete, and they may lack the skills required for the jobs available. This may mean that, despite unemployment, those job vacancies that are available may remain unfilled. It is also possible job vacancies may not be in the same area of the country as the unemployed.

Attempts to Reduce Unemployment

Attempts to reduce unemployment have involved schemes such as job sharing, where two people working part-time share a full-time job. Trade unions have been pressing for a reduction in the working week and longer paid holidays, both of which would, they say, reduce unemployment. Other measures which might be taken include extending the period of compulsory full-time education by raising the school leaving age, reducing the retirement age, more state investment in job creation schemes, and more retraining opportunities for older workers with redundant skills.

One method which has been used to reduce the numbers of people appearing in the unemployment statistics has been the development of government job training schemes for the unemployed, and 'welfare to work' programmes such as those devised by the Labour government in 1997. These aimed to get young people off the dole and into employment. Those on such schemes are not counted as unemployed as far as the official unemployment statistics are concerned. However, while some of the unemployed find work after being on such schemes, often many are only temporarily removed from the unemployment figures and do not find full-time, permanent jobs.

Who is Most at Risk of Unemployment?

Neither all groups in the population nor those in different areas of the country face the same risks of unemployment. Some groups and areas are far more likely to face unemployment than others.

- Young people (18–24), because they need training and cannot compete with those already trained.
- Older people (over 55), as they have a limited working life. Employers are reluctant to retrain them if they have redundant skills, or to offer them jobs if unemployed.
- Non-white people more than white people – an effect of racism and educational underachievement (see chapters 7 and 13). In 1996, about 8 per cent of white people were unemployed, compared to 13 per cent of Indians, 21 per cent of Afro-Caribbeans, and 26 per cent of Pakistanis/Bangladeshis.
- Semi-skilled and unskilled manual workers more than skilled manual

Figure 15.3 Unemployment rate by region: percentage of workforce unemployed, April 1997
Source: Data from *Labour Market Trends*

and non-manual workers, since they are more disposable and more easily replaceable.

- Men more than women, because men are more likely than women to be in higher-paid, full-time employment in the manufacturing industries which are hardest hit by unemployment.

- The north, which tends generally to be hit harder when unemployment strikes than the more prosperous south. (This is sometimes referred to as the north–south divide.) As figure 15.3 shows, in April 1997 Northern Ireland and the north had the highest rates of unemployment in the United Kingdom, followed by Scotland. However, unemployment in the early 1990s hit the south quite badly, even though it still remained slightly higher in northern areas.

The Consequences of Unemployment

The importance of paid work for individuals and society is shown by the effects of its loss – unemployment.

Consequences for individuals

- The loss of the identity, status, and self-esteem which are obtained through work may undermine a person's self-confidence. The endless search for work and the stigma of dependence on welfare benefits and social services are likely to undermine self-esteem further and contribute to growing demoralization and despair.

- Poverty, mounting debts, and hardship arising from the loss of an adequate regular income may create stress and anxiety in coping with daily life. The loss of a home may result for home-owners or tenants if mortgages or rent cannot be paid.

- Social isolation, with the loss of friendships formed through work, particularly as there is little money to spend on leisure

Consequences for society

- More discipline at work, with declining influence and membership of trade unions and fewer strikes, as people worry about their jobs.

- An increase in political unrest. The high levels of unemployment in the 1980s in Britain were accompanied by periodic outbreaks of rioting in many of the inner cities.

- More racism and scapegoating, as people try to find easy answers to their unemployment and try to lay the blame on

375

Consequences for individuals

Consequences for society

activities, such as going to the pub with friends. More free time, but with little money to enjoy it, may result in boredom.
- More ill-health, brought on by a poorer diet and stress.

vulnerable groups such as black people and youth.

- More social problems such as poverty, homelessness, mental illness, and rising rates of crime, suicide, alcoholism, and drug abuse.

- Increasing stress in the family. There may be confusion over roles in the family, for example the 'role swapping' which may occur with working wives and unemployed husbands. 'Getting under one another's feet' may be a problem, particularly if both partners are unemployed.

- Rising levels of stress in the family may cause more family breakdowns, higher divorce rates, and more violence in the home, such as wife-battering and child abuse.

ACTIVITY

Imagine you were to lose your job, or left school or college and were unable to find work while your friends were working. List all the ways this would affect or change your life. What conclusions can you draw about the importance of work in the lives of individuals?

INDUSTRIALIZATION, MECHANIZATION, AND AUTOMATION

Craft Production

Before industrialization, work was mainly agricultural but with some small-scale **craft production** based in the home. In craft production, a worker has full control of the production process, and makes a complete product from start to finish using manual skills and hand tools. An example would be hand-making and finishing a pair of shoes.

| Craft production | Mechanization | Assembly line production | Automation |

The Division of Labour

In industrial society, work becomes factory-based, and the **division of labour** develops very rapidly. This is a term referring to the way work is divided up into a large number of specialized tasks, each of which is carried out by one worker or group of workers. In modern industrial society, the division of labour has been developed so highly that most jobs have been reduced to a few simple tasks requiring very little skill – they have been deskilled. Today, most workers make only one small part of a finished product. This often leads to little satisfaction and pride for the worker, compared to the craft worker who used to make an entire product, and many craft skills have been taken over by machinery today.

Industrial society

An industrial society is one which has the following features:
- The production of goods is mainly carried out by machines rather than using craft skills.
- The workforce is urban-based, in industrial towns and cities, rather than rural-based, in agriculture in the countryside.
- Work is based in factories and offices, rather than the home.
- The workforce is dependent for its livelihood on earnings gained through working for others, rather than self-produced goods and foodstuffs.

Mechanization

Mechanization involves the production of goods by machines, which take over the manual skills involved in craft production. *Assembly line production* is a further development of mechanization. Here, as products travel along a moving conveyor belt, each worker uses machines to carry out the

Car assembly line production
Source: Peugeot Talbot

same small task until the product is finished at the end of the line. Because the tasks required of each worker are so routine and simple and require little skill or training, such work is often boring, repetitive, and unsatisfying.

From the employer's point of view, assembly line production is fast, cheap, and efficient, because workers can be cheaply and quickly trained, as there are so few skills involved in the work, and they can easily be

Computers play a key role today in car design and engineering development
Source: Rover Group

replaced. Henry Ford, founder of the Ford Motor Company, was one of the first to use assembly lines for the mass production of cars at the beginning of the twentieth century. This soon became the model for the production of cars internationally, and the assembly line is widely used in many manufacturing industries today.

Automation

Automation is the process where machinery and computers not only make goods, but also control the speed of production, the input of raw materials, and the correction of any mistakes, with very little human supervision. Automation has become very widespread in the late twentieth century in many industries because of the development of the microchip and computer technology. It is most obvious in the production of cars today using robot technology. However, computer technology and software such as word-processors have also transformed many aspects of routine clerical work, such as record keeping, monitoring sales and orders, and mailshots to customers. Many aspects of routine management work have been largely automated as well, for example with the application of computer spreadsheets to accounting tasks.

ALIENATION AND JOB SATISFACTION

- *Job satisfaction* is concerned with how much enjoyment, involvement, and pleasure people get from their work. Sociologists have attempted to measure the degree of job satisfaction by looking at factors such as how much absenteeism there is at work, how much involvement there is in work-based social clubs and similar activities, and how many strikes there are.
- **Alienation** is the condition where workers have no job satisfaction or fulfilment from their work. Work becomes meaningless and workers have an extrinsic or instrumental attitude to their job.

Two Views of Alienation

The Marxist view

Karl Marx believed alienation came about because the workers lacked power and were exploited at work. The workers have little control over the work they do, and they own neither the products they produce nor the means of producing them, with all the products and the profits going to the factory owner – the capitalist. In many cases, the workers cannot even afford to buy the products they spend all day producing. Marx believed that only in a communist society, where industry was owned by all the people rather than private individuals, could work be really satisfying and fulfilling. (See chapter 3 for a fuller discussion of Marx's ideas.)

Blauner's view

Blauner described four main aspects of alienation.

- *Powerlessness.* The worker has no control over decisions that are made at work; for example, a lack of control over working conditions or management decisions.
- *Meaninglessness.* Work is seen as pointless and boring, as it often involves making only one small part of a finished product.
- *Isolation.* The worker feels isolated from fellow workers. Friendships are hard to form and the worker feels like a cog in a machine.
- *Self-estrangement.* The worker feels his or her full potential is not being fulfilled, with no personal creativity or self-expression in the work – a feeling that anyone could do the job.

The type of technology used and the way it is used can have an effect on how much alienation or job satisfaction workers derive from their work.

Working conditions – health and safety standards; 'perks' and facilities; the amount of noise, smell, speed, and pace of work; the amount of social contact possible with other workers

The attitude of employers, such as fairness in industrial relations and a willingness both to enter into agreements with trade unions and to stick to them

The amount of judgement, skill, and creativity involved in the work

The amount of independence and responsibility which workers are given at work

The challenge and variety of tasks performed at work

The level of wages and opportunities for promotion, with more responsibility, more interesting work, and increasing pay. 'Dead-end jobs' are likely to limit job satisfaction

The technology used in the work

Figure 15.4 Factors influencing job satisfaction and alienation

For example, craft production often involves a high level of job satisfaction. This is because the craft worker is responsible for the production of a complete product, and the work involves a high level of skill in using hand tools, and demands creativity and judgement. The skills of craft

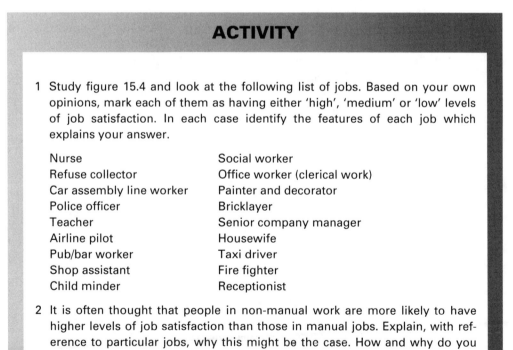

ACTIVITY

1 Study figure 15.4 and look at the following list of jobs. Based on your own opinions, mark each of them as having either 'high', 'medium' or 'low' levels of job satisfaction. In each case identify the features of each job which explains your answer.

Nurse	Social worker
Refuse collector	Office worker (clerical work)
Car assembly line worker	Painter and decorator
Police officer	Bricklayer
Teacher	Senior company manager
Airline pilot	Housewife
Pub/bar worker	Taxi driver
Shop assistant	Fire fighter
Child minder	Receptionist

2 It is often thought that people in non-manual work are more likely to have higher levels of job satisfaction than those in manual jobs. Explain, with reference to particular jobs, why this might be the case. How and why do you think this might be changing?

workers often give them independence, responsibility, and control in the work situation. By contrast, assembly line work often involves high levels of alienation. Here, the speed of the assembly line decides how fast the worker must work, and each worker makes only a small part of the finished product. Such work requires little skill and is very boring and repetitive. The worker lacks control over the speed of work, and the speed and noise of the assembly line often prevent the development of any real social contact with other workers.

Figure 15.4 illustrates the range of factors which can influence the amount of satisfaction found in work.

Responses to Alienation

Workers do not take alienating work lying down, and there is a wide range of methods used to resist it. Some typical responses of workers to alienating work include:

- Producing poor quality, faulty goods, or providing a poor service to customers.
- Taking unofficial breaks ('going to the toilet'), and extending official ones to get some relief.
- High levels of absenteeism and 'skiving off', with large numbers of workers 'off sick'.
- Leaving the job because it is so boring. A high turnover of workers is common in alienating work.
- Conflict with management, with workers using trade unions to 'get back' at management, through actions such as lack of cooperation, strikes, and working to rule.
- Attempts to achieve more creativity outside work in leisure time to compensate for the lack of meaning in work, such as DIY activities or gardening.
- Industrial sabotage. This concerns actions aimed at destroying the workplace, machinery, or goods produced – literally putting a spanner in the works – to get some temporary relief from alienating work. Laurie Taylor and Paul Walton describe this process graphically:

> They had to throw away half a mile of Blackpool rock last year, for, instead of the customary motif running through its length, it carried the terse injunction 'Fuck Off'. A worker dismissed by a sweet factory had effectively demonstrated his annoyance by sabotaging the product of his labour. In the Christmas rush in a Knightsbridge store, the machine which shuttled change backwards and forwards suddenly ground to a halt. A frustrated salesman had demobilized it by ramming a cream bun down its gullet. In our researches we have been told by Woolworth's sales girls how they clank half a dozen buttons on the till simultaneously to

win a few minutes rest from 'ringing up'. Railwaymen have described how they block lines with trucks to delay shunting operations for a few hours. Materials are hidden in factories, conveyor belts jammed with sticks, cogs stopped with wire and ropes, lorries 'accidentally' backed into ditches. Electricians labour to put in weak fuses, textile workers 'knife' through carpets and farmworkers cooperate to choke agricultural machinery with tree branches. (Laurie Taylor and Paul Walton, 'Industrial sabotage: motives and meanings' in Stanley Cohen (ed.), *Images of Deviance* (Penguin 1971).)

Attempts to Reduce Alienation

In the face of declining work satisfaction and the consequences of this for the efficient running of industry, a number of attempts have been made to overcome feelings of alienation among the workforce and increase their involvement in their work.

Teamwork, job rotation, and job enlargement involve a group of workers carrying out a complete operation, swapping around jobs to vary the skills used and the routine of work, and making each particular job cover a wider range of activities. These changes may make otherwise boring jobs more interesting, and lead to more responsibility and control at work, and more social contact among workmates. This method has been successfully used at the Volvo car factories in Sweden.

Attempts have been made to increase the workforce's sense of control at work through worker participation in management decision-making and 'worker directors'. With flexitime, workers have to work the normal total hours each week, but can work some long days and some short ones at their own discretion, as long as they are completed between certain hours each day, for example between 8 a.m. and 7 p.m. This gives the worker more independence and choice at work. This practice is more likely to be found in office work than factory work, as there are less pressures to keep machinery running.

To encourage workers to identify themselves as having a stake in the firm's success, profit-sharing schemes have been developed. These are an attempt to motivate the workers by a promise of a share in the firm's profits if they work harder.

Who Gets Job Satisfaction Today?

Industrialization, changing technology, and the division of labour have meant that most jobs today require little skill or creativity, and work for many people has become a boring, mind-numbing experience. There are probably only a minority of people today who really enjoy their work. Craftworkers, artists, and those in professional and managerial occupations are likely to find some intrinsic job satisfaction. Professional caring jobs such as those in medicine, nursing, social work, and teaching are often personally satisfying jobs because of the responsibility and commitment involved in caring for people. However, many workers lack the independence and responsibility found in such occupations, and it is likely that the majority of workers have an instrumental attitude to work. It is not something they enjoy or identify with. Work is primarily and simply a means of getting the money to enjoy 'real life' outside work, rather than an enjoyable and satisfying activity in its own right.

DISCUSSION

Do you agree that most work today is basically unsatisfying? What could be done to make work a more fulfilling experience for people?

THE EFFECTS OF CHANGING TECHNOLOGY ON SOCIETY

The development of technology has had important effects in deskilling work, and has generally had negative consequences on the way people experience their work. But there are wider effects.

- As technology changes, new skills are needed and old skills become redundant, and retraining of workers is becoming increasingly important. Educational institutions are more and more concerned with providing people with new qualifications to meet the demands of industry for changing expertise, and the emphasis now is on the adaptability of workers to adjust to rapidly changing technology.
- Many of the dirtier physical aspects of work have disappeared, as have some of the more repetitive tasks, as machines have taken over jobs formerly done by people. As a consequence, the numbers of unskilled and semi-skilled workers have been reduced.
- A long-term rise in underemployment and unemployment is a real possibility, especially among less qualified workers, as machines take over jobs. Even skilled manual jobs have been wiped out by new techno-

Does automation threaten all jobs?

logy, such as robot technology taking over the jobs of car workers, and computerized desk-top publishing and typesetting dramatically reducing the need for printers. In the High Street today, for example, cash dispensers outside every bank and computerized bar-code checkouts at supermarkets have led to thousands of redundancies among bank and shop staff.

- While new technology threatens existing jobs, it also creates new ones. More skilled manual and white-collar supervisory jobs are created, such as technicians, engineers, computer programmers, and administrators, which are necessary for maintaining and servicing the new technology, and administering and organizing production. However, it remains to be seen whether these will be enough to make up for the job losses.

- If enough new jobs are not created, and unless there is a substantial increase in spending by the welfare state, one consequence of technological change might be even more widespread poverty.

- New technology has generated more flexible work patterns, with more shiftwork, nightwork, six-day working, and overtime to keep complex automated processes running twenty-four hours a day. At the same time, automation can produce cheaper and better-quality products in a shorter space of time. As industry becomes more productive and efficient, there is the possibility of a shorter working week, earlier retirement, and more leisure time.

- The late twentieth century saw a massive expansion of DIY activities of various kinds, as people sought to fill expanding leisure time and find some satisfaction and creativity from exercising skills which were increasingly denied at work.

DISCUSSION

Do you think that technological change will have good or bad effects on society and the individual's experience of work?

THE CHANGING OCCUPATIONAL STRUCTURE

The themes which have been discussed in much of this chapter so far have contributed to quite dramatic changes in the pattern of employment in Britain over the past two centuries. The key changes, which are all related to each other, are summarized in the box below, and then discussed.

Major changes in the occupational structure

1 The growth of the service economy.
2 The decline of manual occupations and the increase in non-manual occupations.
3 The decline of semi- and unskilled manual work and the increase in skilled manual work.
4 The division of the workforce into core and periphery workers, and the casualization of employment.
5 The growing employment of women.

Change 1: The Growth of the Service Economy

The pattern of work has shifted from a predominantly agricultural economy before industrialization, when most people were working in agriculture (this is often referred to as the *primary sector* of the economy).

With the beginning of the Industrial Revolution about two hundred years ago, most people began to move into manufacturing industries (known as the *secondary sector*) in the nineteenth century, concerned with the production of goods. The second half of the twentieth century has seen a decline in manufacturing, with most people working in the service sector (or *tertiary sector*) of the economy. The service sector is concerned with administration, information, communication, catering, the leisure industry, sales, finance and insurance, transport and distribution, and the running of government services such as the health, welfare, and education services. This shift in employment patterns between the three sectors of the economy is often referred to as the change to a service economy. Table 15.2 on page 388 illustrates this change between 1971 and 1996.

This change has meant that the numbers of people employed in different industries has changed, as figure 15.5 shows.

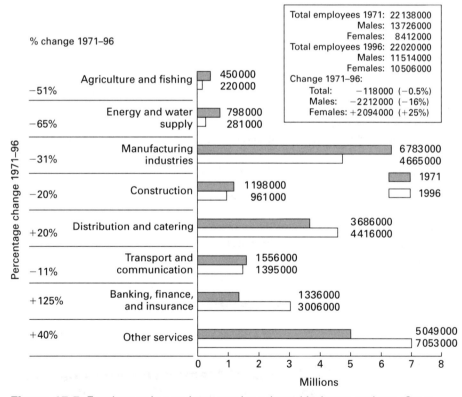

Figure 15.5 Employees in employment: by selected industry and sex, Great Britain, 1971–96
Source: Adapted from *Social Trends 21* (HMSO 1991); Labour Force Survey, 1996

Table 15.2 Employees in employment: by industry, 1971–96

Industry	1971	1996	% change
Agriculture and fishing	450 000	220 000	−51
Manufacturing	8 065 000	4 665 000	−42
Services	11 627 000	15 871 000	+37

Source: Derived from *Social Trends 21* (HMSO 1991); *Labour Market Trends*

ACTIVITY

Read the section on the growth of the service economy on pages 386–7, study figure 15.5 on page 387 and answer the following questions:

1 How many people were employed in manufacturing industries in 1971?
2 Which industry employed 1 336 000 workers in 1971?
3 Which industry employed the most workers in 1996?
4 How many more people were employed in banking, finance, and insurance in 1996 than in 1971?
5 Which industry employed the smallest number of workers in 1996?
6 Which two industries showed the greatest percentage decline between 1971 and 1996?
7 How many more women employees were there in 1996 than in 1971?
8 What percentage change was there between 1971 and 1996 in the number of male employees?
9 Classify each of the following jobs as either 'manufacturing' or 'services':

Bank clerk	Carpenter
Car assembly line worker	Teacher
Assistant in burger bar	Shipbuilder
Lorry driver	Shop assistant
Tool maker	Baker

Change 2: The Decline of Manual Occupations and the Increase in Non-Manual Occupations

The change towards a service economy has meant there has been a decline in the proportion of the labour force working in manual occupations, and

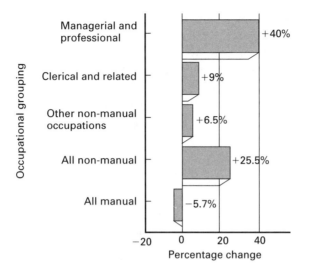

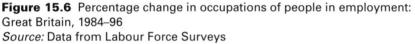

Figure 15.6 Percentage change in occupations of people in employment: Great Britain, 1984–96
Source: Data from Labour Force Surveys

a rapid increase in the percentage engaged in non-manual occupations, especially in routine clerical and sales work, and in managerial and professional work. This is illustrated in figure 15.6.

Change 3: The Decline of Semi- and Unskilled Manual Work and the Increase in Skilled Manual Work

Traditional industries such as shipbuilding, mining, and the iron and steel industries have declined. These employed many semi- and unskilled workers. This, combined with the speed of technological change, has meant that many semi- and unskilled manual jobs have disappeared, as machinery has taken over tasks that were previously carried out by labourers. New, skilled workers are required to operate new machinery and to maintain computerized industries.

Change 4: Core and Periphery Workers and the Casualization of Employment

One of the biggest changes in recent times has been the division of the workforce into core workers and periphery workers. *Core workers* are the well-paid and qualified people who make up the full-time, permanent workers in a workplace. *Periphery workers* are those who are often part-time, employed on a casual, temporary basis. They tend to be low-paid, and companies will often have little obligation to them. Increasingly, the numbers of core workers are reducing, and more firms are ceasing to employ staff directly themselves, and sub-contracting the work to self-employed individuals or other firms instead. For example, a company may no longer employ its own cleaning and catering staff, but contract the work out to another, cheaper specialist firm.

There is therefore much less security of employment, as companies try to increase their flexibility by cutting the number of core employees, and relying more on periphery workers. Full-time permanent jobs have been disappearing, to be replaced by part-time or temporary work. This means many workers today face job insecurity (the fear of losing their job), and increasingly people no longer find themselves with secure, full-time, permanent, long-term employment. In 1996, nearly one in four people in employment were working part-time, and there were over 1.6 million temporary workers in Britain. According to the 1996 Labour Force Survey, about 40 per cent of temporary employees were temporary because they could not find a permanent job, and about one in four men were working part-time because they could not find a full-time job.

This *casualization* of the workforce – that is, people being employed by companies only as and when required, on temporary or part-time contracts to do specific short-term tasks – was one of the main changes in the labour market in Britain during the 1980s and 1990s. This trend appears likely to continue, with growing numbers of people facing several changes of job in their lifetimes, a lack of job security, and increasing part-time, temporary work or no work at all.

Change 5: The Growing Employment of Women

There has been a large increase in the number of women in paid employment, contrasting with a decline in the numbers of men employed. There are several points worth noting about the employment patterns of women.

- A large proportion of the increase in the numbers of women working outside the home has been among married women. Far more women work part-time than men, as table 15.3 shows, and in 1996 about half of married or cohabiting women in employment were in part-time work, compared with about a third of non-married and non-cohabiting women.
- Women generally work in different types of jobs to men.
  — They are more likely than men to be in non-manual work, though this is usually in the more 'menial' non-manual occupations, such as routine clerical work and sales assistants. Even those women in the professions are most commonly found in the lower ones such as teaching, nursing, and social work.

— They are most likely to be employed in the service sector of the economy.

The position of women in paid employment was discussed extensively in chapter 6. You should refer to this for further detail on the employment patterns of women, and explanations for it.

Table 15.3 Employees in employment: by sex and full- or part-time status, Great Britain, 1971–96

	1971 (000s)	1984 (000s)	1991 (000s)	1996 (000s)
Women in employment[a]	8 412	8 938	10 280	10 506
Full-time	5 216 (62%)	5 006 (56%)	5 839 (57%)	5 817 (55%)
Part-time	3 197 (38%)	4 012 (44%)	4 441 (43%)	4 689 (45%)
Men in employment[b]	13 726	11 618	11 754	11 513
Full-time	13 589 (99%)	11 183 (96%)	11 123 (95%)	10 624 (92%)
Part-time	137 (1%)	435 (4%)	631 (5%)	889 (8%)

[a] Women aged 16–59
[b] Men aged 16–64
Source: Adapted from Labour Force Surveys

ACTIVITY

Study table 15.3 and answer the following questions:

1 How many women were in employment in 1991?
2 How many women were in part-time employment in 1971?
3 By how many did the number of part-time women workers increase between 1971 and 1996?
4 According to table 15.3, state whether each of the following statements is true or false:
  (a) There were more men in employment in 1971 than in 1996?
  (b) Between 1971 and 1996, the numbers of women working full-time increased more than the numbers of women working part-time.
  (c) The numbers of men working part-time increased by 642 500 between 1971 and 1996.
  (d) The numbers of women in full-time employment increased between 1981 and 1996.
  (e) The table might be misleading because the men included come from a wider age range than the women.
5 Suggest reasons why women are more likely to work part-time than men.

TRADE UNIONS

Trade unions are organizations of workers formed for the protection of their members' interests. A trade union is an example of a protective pressure group (these are discussed in chapter 8). Most larger workplaces today will have a shop steward or convener – a union representative elected by union members in a particular workplace – to advise and assist union members. The strength of trade unions lies in the fact that they represent the interests of large numbers of workers, who can act together as one force to negotiate with management. The unity of workers is the union's strength.

The trade union movement in Britain began in the nineteenth century, and today trade unions play an important part in the working life of the nation. About 31 per cent of the employed workforce belonged to a trade union in 1996. Growth in trade union membership has been greatest among white-collar workers in recent years, partly due to the expansion of these occupations. However, the process of proletarianization of white-collar workers, which was discussed in chapter 3, has certainly contributed to their turn to trade unionism.

What do Trade Unions Do?

Individuals have little power on their own to improve or change things in the workplace, and uniting together with other workers is the most effective way for workers to defend their interests. Individuals join unions to benefit from the wide range of activities which unions carry out. These activities include:

- Bargaining with employers for better wages, overtime rates, and bonuses.
- Improving the working hours and terms and conditions of employment of their members. These might include a shorter working week, longer paid holidays, maternity benefits, better pension and sick pay schemes, improved promotion prospects and training schemes, improved health and safety at work, and better canteen and sports facilities.
- Fighting against unfair dismissal and reducing the risks of redundancy, and protecting and promoting the rights of workers in areas such as health and safety at work and employment law.
- Providing legal and financial assistance to members, such as taking an employer to court for causing injury due to negligence in safety standards, and providing strike pay.

- Acting as pressure groups, putting pressure on those with political power in society to reform industrial and employment legislation, and campaigning on other general issues of interest to their members, such as unemployment or declining standards in the NHS.

The Methods Unions Use to Protect their Members' Interests

Negotiation with management is one of the most common everyday activities of unions. Elected representatives of the workforce, such as shop stewards or conveners, play an important role in discussing grievances and improvements in wages and working conditions with employers. Negotiation may go on at the level of the individual workplace or of the area, or at the national level with employers' organizations.

Legal action is sometimes taken against employers; for example, because the employer is to blame for an industrial accident or disease, or because the employer has broken the employment laws in some way.

Overtime bans, 'going slow', or working to rule are frequent forms of industrial action used by trade unions to put pressure on an employer during an industrial dispute. By banning overtime and by working strictly to the employer's rulebook and to agreements reached between a trade union and the employer, workers can slow down production and therefore bring pressure to bear on an employer by eating into his or her profits.

By refusing to work at all, by going on strike, workers can bring production to a standstill. The strike weapon is generally used by unions only as a last resort when all negotiations with employers have broken down. Official strikes are those approved by the union leadership; unofficial strikes are not.

The Declining Membership and Influence of Trade Unions

In recent years the power and influence of trade unions in both society and the workplace have declined. As shown in figures 15.7 and 15.8, both the number of trade union members and the percentage of the employed labour force belonging to trade unions have declined since their peaks in 1978.

There are three broad explanations behind the decline in the influence and membership of trade unions.

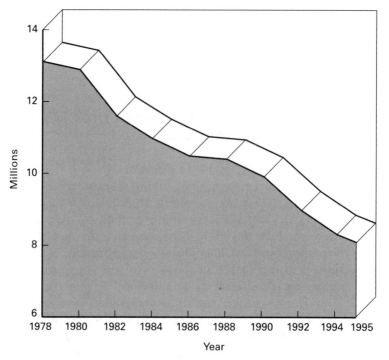

Figure 15.7 Trade unions in decline: membership figures, United Kingdom, 1978–95
Source: Data from *Labour Market Trends* (February 1997)

Changes in the law

A series of employment laws has been passed limiting the power of trade unions. These have reduced the power of unions in a number of ways.

- It is now necessary for a secret ballot of the membership to be held before industrial action such as strikes and overtime bans can be taken, with the threat of court action if the unions fail to comply. This can limit the speed with which a trade union can end a dispute, as well as allowing workers who are not familiar with the issues to vote.
- The right to picket has been limited (picketing is trying to persuade fellow workers not to work during a strike by meeting them outside the workplace). This restricts the ability of a trade union to bring pressure to bear on an employer by disrupting the everyday routine of the workplace, and to spread a strike to other areas.
- It is now a legal requirement to hold a secret ballot before union funds can be used to support political parties or campaigns.
- The closed shop has been made illegal. (In a closed shop, all the workers must belong to the trade union, and a refusal to join will result in dismissal.) This weakens the power of the union to represent all those in the workplace.

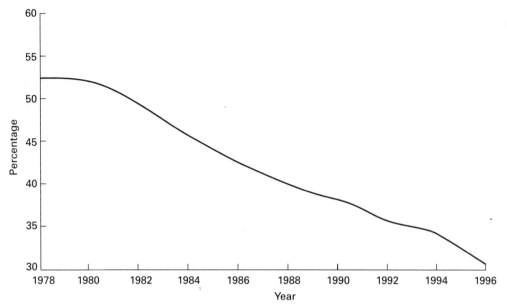

Figure 15.8 Trade union members as a percentage of the employed workforce: Great Britain, 1978–96
Source: Data from *Employment Gazette* (May 1990, June 1991); *Labour Market Trends* (June 1997)

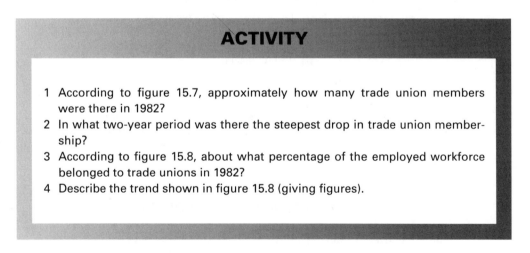

ACTIVITY

1 According to figure 15.7, approximately how many trade union members were there in 1982?
2 In what two-year period was there the steepest drop in trade union membership?
3 According to figure 15.8, about what percentage of the employed workforce belonged to trade unions in 1982?
4 Describe the trend shown in figure 15.8 (giving figures).

Higher levels of unemployment

Higher levels of unemployment, especially in older manufacturing industries where trade unions have traditionally been well represented, have reduced union membership and power, and made those in employment unwilling to take industrial action in case they lose their jobs. The decline in industrial stoppages (strikes) as unemployment rises is shown in figure 15.9.

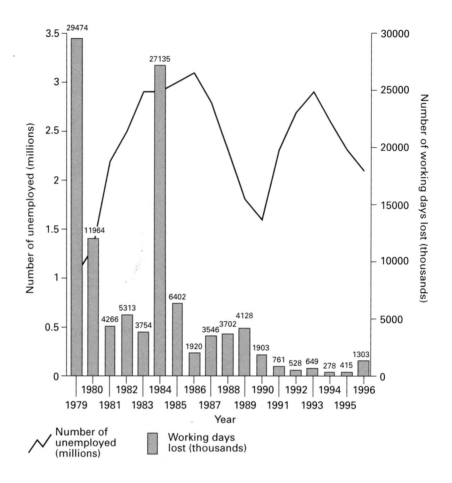

Figure 15.9 Industrial stoppages and unemployment: working days lost due to industrial disputes, 1979–96. The high level of strikes in 1979 was due to the 'winter of discontent' and that of 1984 was due to the year-long miners' strike.)
Source: Data from *Labour Market Trends; Annual Abstract of Statistics 1992* and *1997*

Changing patterns of employment

There has been a fall in traditional full-time employment and an increase in part-time and temporary workers, who are less likely to join unions. There has also been an increase in the proportion of the workforce employed in small companies, where it is often difficult for unions to organize.

The decline in the traditional working class

There has been a reduction in the numbers of the traditional working class once employed in the disappearing heavy industries formerly concentrated in the north of England, such as mining and shipbuilding, and dock-labour forces. Such workers were traditionally committed trade union supporters. The 'new' working class found in the newer, lighter industries mainly in the south of England are less likely to be union members. (See chapter 3 for a discussion of the 'traditional' and 'new' working classes.)

ACTIVITY/DISCUSSION

Do employers and workers have different interests?

1 What does the cartoon suggest might be some of the causes of strikes?
2 Suggest other issues at work which might provoke trade unions into taking strike action.
3 Discuss the following statement: 'Workers should have the right to join together in trade unions to protect their interests, and should be allowed to take any non-violent action they choose in order to do so, provided the majority of the members support it. Any attempts by the government to limit the power of trade unions undermines workers' rights and can only benefit the employer.'

LEISURE

What is Leisure?

Leisure time is not simply time not spent at work, because activities like travelling to work, personal care, housework, shopping, childcare, and sleeping are all essential commitments of time which most people would not regard as leisure. Leisure time and activity generally involve:

- Time free of practical commitments, such as work and study.
- Activities which are self-imposed and freely chosen.
- Activities which the individual considers to be personally enjoyable.

The distinction between 'work time', 'committed time', and 'leisure time' is sometimes difficult to make, and some activities are not easy to separate. For example, cooking for a family every day may be seen as a real work chore by a housewife, but it might be seen as an enjoyable leisure pastime by those who are not compelled to do it every day. The same activity may be work for one person and yet not work for another. The following examples illustrate this.

- Decorating your own home yourself is not generally seen as work, but would be for the painter you employed to do it for you. Similarly, some people may not see this as 'committed time' but as an enjoyable leisure activity.
- Watching a professional football match would be leisure for most people, but not for the newspaper reporter who has to write a report on the game, or for the players.
- People in professional and managerial work might use their leisure time to carry out work-related activities, such as business people entertaining clients at home or playing golf with them, or teachers going on school trips with pupils.
- Some jobs involved work-related responsibilities at all times, as in the case of doctors or the police.
- Some people may enjoy their work so much that they take it up as a leisure activity, such as professional musicians.

ACTIVITY

1 Keep a record for one week of the time you spend on all your various activities. Classify them under the headings 'work time', 'committed time', and 'leisure time'. (Count studying as 'work time' if you are in full-time education.) Keep a record of those activities which you find difficult to classify under any of these headings.
2 Present your findings in the form of a pie chart (there are 168 hours in a week), with a category 'other' for activities which don't really fit under the main headings.
3 Explain why you found the activities in 'other' difficult to classify.
4 What do your findings tell you about:
   (a) the amounts of real leisure time you have?
   (b) the restrictions on expanding your leisure time?
   (c) the difficulties of distinguishing between work and leisure?

The Changing Pattern of Leisure

In pre-industrial Britain, the division between work and leisure was more blurred than it is today. People worked in the family home, which was a unit of production, and people had greater control over when to work and when to enjoy their leisure. Work and leisure were also more closely linked. For example, people might mix business and pleasure, by going to a country fair not only to enjoy themselves but also to sell a few of their goods.

With industrialization, work moved outside the home to factories, and people lost control over their work and leisure time: people had to work for employers who decided the length of the working day and the length of holidays. Leisure therefore became clearly separated from work.

This century the basic working week has been shortened, reduced to an average of about 38 hours a week in 1996, as shown in figure 15.10. This means people have more time for leisure today, even though many people work much longer hours than the basic working week. Longer holidays and more part-time work have also increased leisure time. All this has meant that the leisure industry, including travel and tourism as well as lcisure and fitness centres and so on, has been one of the fastest growing industries of the late twentieth century.

Paid holidays have increased, and higher incomes have raised standards of living. This has enabled people to take advantage of increased leisure time to pursue more varied and ambitious activities. Widespread car

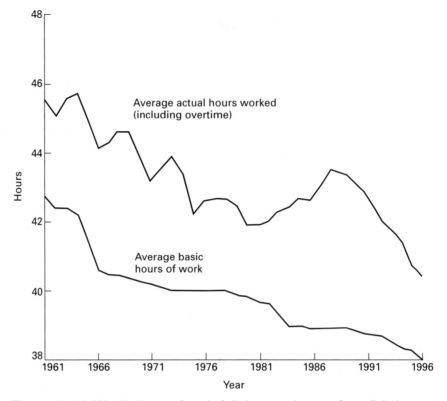

Figure 15.10 Weekly hours of work: full-time employees, Great Britain, 1961–96
Source: Data from *Social Trends 21* (HMSO 1991); *Labour Market Trends*

ownership, for example, has opened up a range of leisure activities, and more working-class people have access through package holidays to places like Greece and Spain that were once only available to the rich.

Rapid changes in technology have occurred this century, which have affected the nature of leisure activities. Increased alienation at work, with deskilling through new technology, has meant that many people are trying to achieve satisfaction and creativity outside work through creative leisure pursuits. The massive growth of the DIY industry and the prolific spread of garden centres illustrates this.

Leisure has itself become a highly organized and commercialized business. The mass production methods employed in manufacturing industry have been applied to leisure activities, such as the mass production of stereo systems and video recorders to cater for the products of the record and music industries. Mass entertainment such as spectator sports, television, the cinema and video, the package holiday industry, the DIY industry, and spectacular (and expensive) developments such as Alton Towers and Disneyland are very big business indeed. Fewer people make

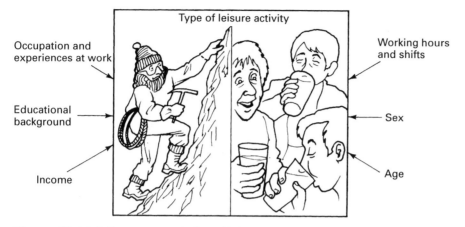

Figure 15.11 Influences on choice of leisure activity

their own entertainment today, and large businesses make huge profits organizing leisure activities for the 'masses'.

Factors Influencing the Choice of Leisure Activity

Social class

Social class differences in leisure have been exaggerated, but differences in income, car ownership, educational qualifications, and working hours mean that middle- and working-class people often follow different leisure activities. For example, they are likely to read different books, magazines, and newspapers, watch different TV programmes and films at the cinema, join different organizations, eat and drink in different pubs, wine bars, and restaurants, and travel to different holiday destinations. Some leisure activities are denied to the working class simply because of the high costs involved. For example, the high membership fees of private golf clubs, and the expense of activities such as flying and motor racing, effectively bar such activities to the working class, and much of the middle class.

Age

Age has an obvious influence on the choice of leisure activities. The leisure of young single people tends to be spent outside the home in the company of their peer group. They may gain some economic independence from either a wage packet or benefits obtained on training schemes, but lack the financial commitments and responsibilities of household bills, children, and the burden of paying rent or a mortgage. This means young people are more leisure-centred than perhaps any other age group except the retired. The most common leisure activities among the young are going to the cinema, pubs, and discos, as well as listening to music.

Young couples tend to be more home based, as they have little spare money for leisure, after buying or renting a home, buying furniture, and starting a family. DIY, home and car maintenance, and watching the TV or video are likely to be typical activities.

Middle-aged people tend to have the most money available for leisure. Children have grown up, the mortgage is nearly paid off and there is more disposable income to spend on leisure activities like holidays and eating out.

Older retired people are more likely to be home based than any other group, through either choice, ill-health, pressure of declining income, or poverty. Reading, gardening, television, and other inexpensive pursuits are likely to be typical activities.

Sex

A person's sex has an important influence on the choice of leisure activity. As a result of gender role socialization, men and women show different leisure interests and some leisure activities are more associated with one sex than another. For example, knitting, dancing, horse-riding, aerobics, and keep-fit are more likely to be pursued by women; car maintenance, DIY, watching or playing football, and weight-training by men. As table 15.4 shows, women in full-time employment generally have less time available for leisure activities than men.

Occupation and work experience

A person's occupation can have important effects on leisure activities. The hours worked, how much overtime has to be worked, and the amount of shiftwork and nightwork can all restrict leisure opportunities.

The experience of work is perhaps one of the most important factors influencing non-work behaviour and leisure, as discussed earlier in this chapter when Parker's research on the opposition, neutrality, and extension patterns was considered (see table 15.1 on page 371).

ACTIVITY

Table 15.4 Time use in a typical week: by employment status and sex, Great Britain, 1995

	Full-time employees	
	Males	Females
Weekly hours spent on:		
Employment, study, and travel to and from work	53	48
Essential activities[a]	24	30
Sleep	57	58
Free time	34	31
Free time per weekday (hours)	4	4
Free time per weekend day (hours)	8	6

[a] Housework and personal care including essential shopping, childcare, cooking, eating, washing, getting up and going to bed, household maintenance, and pet care
Source: Adapted from *Social Trends 26*

Study table 15.4 and answer the following questions:

1 How many hours a week did females in full-time employment spend on essential activities?
2 Who spent the most time each week on employment, study, and travel to and from work?
3 Which category of time use showed the greatest difference between males and females?
4 What evidence is there in the table to back up the view that women in paid employment have two jobs while men only have one?
5 List all the explanations you can think of for the differences between male and female full-time employees shown in the table.
6 What restrictions are there on the leisure activities of women which men don't usually face? Think about things like women going alone into pubs or discos, going home alone at night, and responsibilities for elderly relatives, husbands, and children.

CHAPTER SUMMARY

After studying this chapter, you should be able to:

- Describe and explain the importance of work, and the range of ways it can affect a person's life.
- Explain the difference between an instrumental and an intrinsic attitude to work.
- Describe and explain a range of causes and consequences of unemployment.
- Describe and explain the groups most at risk of unemployment.
- Suggest ways unemployment might be reduced.
- Describe the main features of an industrial society.
- Explain what is meant by craft production, mechanization, assembly line production, and automation.
- Explain what is meant by job satisfaction and alienation, and outline Marx's and Blauner's views of alienation.
- Describe and explain a range of factors which might influence the amount of job satisfaction a worker enjoys.
- Describe how workers respond to alienation.
- Describe attempts to increase job satisfaction.
- Describe and explain the possible effects of changing technology on society.
- Describe and explain how the occupational structure has changed in Britain in the twentieth century.
- Explain what trade unions are and why individuals join them.
- Describe the methods unions use to protect their members' interests.
- Explain why the influence of trade unions has declined in recent years.
- Explain what is meant by leisure, and why it is sometimes difficult to make the distinction between work and leisure activities.
- Describe how leisure has changed in the twentieth century.
- Outline a range of factors which influence the choice of leisure activity.

KEY TERMS

alienation	division of labour
automation	mechanization
craft production	work

PROJECT SUGGESTIONS

1 Interview a sample of people in different types of work, or in the same work, asking them about the kinds of thing they like or dislike about their job. Try to draw conclusions about the factors influencing job satisfaction and alienation.

2 Carry out a survey among some unemployed people, asking about how they spend their time, the problems they encounter, whom they feel is to blame for their unemployment, etc.

3 Using secondary sources (see chapter 18), carry out a study of the pattern of unemployment in your area, such as the age, sex, and ethnic background of the unemployed.

4 Carry out a study of the introduction of new technology into a workplace, its advantages and disadvantages and workers' attitudes towards it. You could study, for example, the introduction of bar-code checkouts in supermarkets, computers into district nursing, office work, or other workplaces.

5 Carry out a study of the structure and activities of a local trade union branch.

6 Carry out a survey of people involved in several different leisure activities to see if patterns emerge in terms of social class, age, gender, etc.

16 POPULATION

KEY ISSUES IN THIS CHAPTER

- The importance of information on population.
- Key terms used in the study of population.
- Population size.
- Population change in Britain.
- Urbanization.

The study of population is known as **demography**. Evidence about the size and composition of Britain's population is obtained mainly through the census. This is a survey which asks questions of the entire population of a country. Censuses have been carried out every ten years since 1801, with the exception of 1941, when the Second World War made it impractical to hold one. Censuses are carried out by the Office of Population Censuses and Surveys, which is directed by the Registrar-General.

The 1991 census was carried out at a cost of £135 million, and asked questions about age, sex, marital status, ethnic group, country of birth, relationships within the household, housing, change of address within the last year, employment, higher qualifications, having the use of a car, and long-term illness. Questions about ethnic group, long-term illness, and central heating were asked for the first time in 1991.

Other information on population is obtained through the compulsory registration of births, marriages, and deaths at local Registry Offices, and through the General Household Survey.

In this chapter, the main changes in the population of Britain this century will be considered, together with some of the social consequences of these changes.

THE IMPORTANCE OF INFORMATION ON POPULATION

In order for a government to plan its policies with regard to social policy, the allocation of scarce resources, land, housing, education, and finance, it is necessary to have accurate information and estimates of future trends in population size and distribution. It is important to know, for example, whether the population is increasing or decreasing, and what proportion of the population will be at school, working (or possibly unemployed), and retired in fifteen or twenty years' time. Such information will influence, for example, the number of schools, hospitals, and houses that will need to be built, the number of teachers, doctors, and nurses to be trained, the number of jobs that will be required, and the number of welfare benefits to be paid out. Details about employment help government and businesses to plan jobs and training, and transport information makes possible future planning on road building and public transport. Details on ethnic groups help to identify racial disadvantage, and allocate resources and plan programmes to meet the needs of minority groups. Health information enables health authorities to plan services and facilities for long-term sick and elderly people. These changes cannot be made overnight, and so governments need this information to plan for the future.

KEY TERMS USED IN THE STUDY OF POPULATION

- The **birth rate** is the number of live births per 1000 of the population per year.
- The **general fertility rate** is the number of live births per 1000 women of child-bearing age (15–44) per year.
- The **death rate** (or mortality rate) is the number of deaths per 1000 of the population per year.
- The **infant mortality rate** is the number of babies who die in their first year of life per 1000 live births per year.
- **Life expectation** is an estimate made about the number of years the average person can be expected to live. It is based on information about existing patterns of infant mortality and death. Estimates of life expectation can be based on any age, but the most common are life expectation at birth and at one year. Generally, the older you get, the more life expectation increases, as early childhood diseases and accidents of youth are overcome.
- **Migration** is the term used to describe the movement of people from one area to another. **Emigration** is movement out of a country or area on a permanent basis, and **immigration** is movement into a country or

area on a permanent basis. **Net migration** is the term used to describe the *difference* between immigration and emigration, and therefore whether the population of a country or area has gone up or gone down when both emigration and immigration are taken into account. Net migration is usually expressed in terms of a net gain (+) or a net loss (−) of population. For example, in 1995 in the UK there were about 246 000 immigrants and 191 000 emigrants. The net migration figure is obtained by subtracting the number of emigrants (191 000) from the number of immigrants (246 000), giving a net migration figure of +55 000 (a net gain or increase in population through migration).

- A *natural increase* (+) or *decrease* (−) in population is the term used to describe changes in the size of a population due to changes in the number of births and deaths, but it excludes migration. A *net natural change* is the term used to describe the difference in population size after both births and deaths are taken into account. As for net migration, a *net natural increase* should be preceded by a + sign, and a *net natural decrease* by a − sign. For example, in 1995 there were 732 000 births and 642 000 deaths. The net natural change in population size was therefore +90 000 (the difference between the 732 000 births and the 642 000 deaths).

ACTIVITY

In 1981 the population of the United Kingdom was approximately 56 352 000. There were 731 000 births and 658 000 deaths. The population gained 153 000 people from outside the United Kingdom, and lost 233 000 who left the United Kingdom.

By 1995, the population had risen to 58 806 000. In that year there were 732 000 births, 642 000 deaths, 246 000 immigrants, and 191 000 emigrants (based on data from *Population Trends*, no. 87 (Office for National Statistics 1997)).

Use the information above to complete the following table:

Year	Total population	Births	Deaths	Net natural change	Immigrants	Emigrants	Net migration	Total population change
1981								
1995								

- **Population projections** are attempts to predict future changes in population size. These involve complex calculations based on past and present trends in the fertility rate, the birth rate, the infant mortality rate, the death rate, average life expectation, and migration patterns. Accurate population projections are very difficult to make because of the wide range of economic, social, and political factors which might influence future developments in any of these areas.

- The **dependent population** is that section of the population which is not in work and is supported by others. This includes the under-16s (who are still at school); the over-60/65s (who have retired); housewives; many lone-parent families; the unemployed; the chronically sick and handicapped; prisoners; and students in full-time education.

- The **dependency ratio** is the proportion of those working compared to those who are dependent.

- *Age distribution* refers to the percentage of the population which falls into the various age groups.

- The **dependent age groups** are those under age 16 and over retirement age (60 for women and 65 for men). These have increased this century because of the raising of the school leaving age and more people reaching old age.

- *Sex distribution* refers to the proportion of males and females in the population. The **sex ratio** of a population is the proportion of males to females, expressed as the number of males per 1000 females in the population.

- *Regional distribution* is the percentage of the population which lives in different geographical areas (such as urban and rural areas).

- *Occupational distribution* is the percentage of the population working in different occupations.

POPULATION SIZE

There are three main factors which can affect the size of a population, and whether it increases or decreases. These factors are the birth rate, the death rate, and migration.

Population trends are often derived from natural changes in population size (changes in the number of births and deaths) as migration patterns are quite difficult to predict. The basic rules for interpreting figures and graphs showing natural changes in population size are:

- Whenever the birth rate *equals* the death rate, there will be no natural change in population size: for every baby born, someone dies.

- Whenever the birth rate is *higher* than the death rate, there will be a

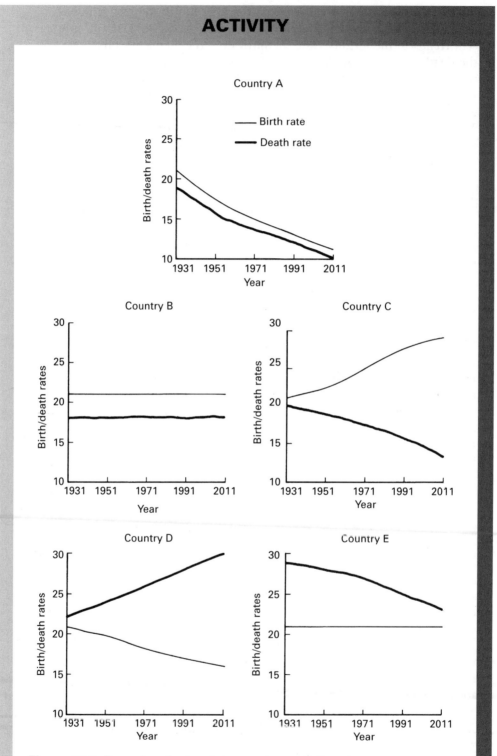

Figure 16.1 Examples of natural changes in population size

Study figure 16.1 on the opposite page and answer the following questions, assuming there is no migration:

1 What is happening to the population size of country A?
2 What is happening to the population size of country B?
3 In which countries is there a natural decrease in population size?
4 In which country is population size increasing the fastest? Explain your answer.
5 In which country is population size decreasing the fastest?
6 Suggest two possible reasons for both the rising death rate and the falling birth rate in country D.
7 Suggest three possible consequences for society of a falling birth rate.

natural increase in population size: more babies are being born than there are people dying. This means that even if there is a falling death rate and a falling birth rate, but the birth rate still remains higher than the death rate, the size of the population will continue to increase.

● When the birth rate is *lower* than the death rate, there will be a natural decrease in population size: the number of births is simply not enough to replace the numbers who die.

POPULATION CHANGE IN THE UNITED KINGDOM

The population of the United Kingdom rose from about 10.5 million in 1801 (the first census) to an estimated 58.8 million in 1996. This increase was not a gradual process. Between 1801 and 1851, for example, the population doubled from 10.5 million to 22.3 million, and nearly doubled again in the second half of the nineteenth century, to 38.3 million by 1901. The major reasons for this growth were the falling death and infant mortality rates, while the birth rate remained relatively unchanged. In the twentieth century, a continuing fall in the death rate as well as a falling birth rate slowed down population growth, and there has been greatly improved life expectancy.

Figure 16.2 illustrates the main changes in population in the twentieth century, with projected changes for the twenty-first century.

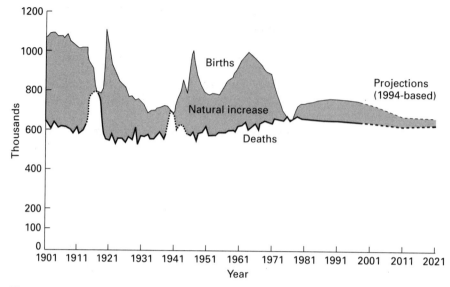

Figure 16.2 Population changes and projections: United Kingdom, 1901–2021
Source: Data from *Social Trends 16* and *20* (HMSO 1986 and 1990); *Annual Abstract of Statistics 1997*

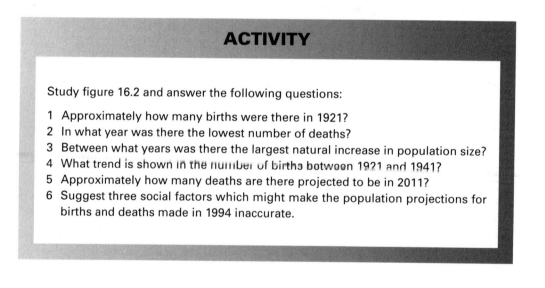

ACTIVITY

Study figure 16.2 and answer the following questions:

1 Approximately how many births were there in 1921?
2 In what year was there the lowest number of deaths?
3 Between what years was there the largest natural increase in population size?
4 What trend is shown in the number of births between 1921 and 1941?
5 Approximately how many deaths are there projected to be in 2011?
6 Suggest three social factors which might make the population projections for births and deaths made in 1994 inaccurate.

Changes in the Death Rate, Infant Mortality Rate, and Average Life Expectation

The overall increase in the population of the UK since 1870 has been caused by the gradual decline in the death rate. A century ago it was 22 per 1000; in 1902 it was 18 per 1000; and in 1996 it was around 11 per 1000. The infant mortality rate has also fallen, from around 142 per 1000 live births in 1902 to around 6 per 1000 in 1996. Average life expectation has consequently risen, as shown in figure 16.3.

Explanations for changes in the death rate, infant mortality rate, and life expectation

Improved hygiene, sanitation, and medicine

Public hygiene and sanitation have improved enormously since the early nineteenth century, with the construction of public sewer systems and the provision of clean running water. These changes, together with improved public awareness of hygiene and the causes of infection, have contributed to the elimination in Britain of the great epidemic killer diseases of the past, such as cholera, diphtheria, and typhoid, which were spread through infected water and food. These improvements in environmental conditions were more important than medical advances in wiping out the epidemic diseases. The importance of these changes is shown by the scale of death caused by epidemic diseases in the past. For example, between 1337 and 1351 the Black Death, a plague carried by black rats, is estimated to have wiped out about one-quarter of the British population, and in 1918 flu killed about 250 000 people.

Advances in medicine and science, such as vaccines and the development of penicillin, antibiotics, and other life-saving drugs, and advances in surgery and medical technology, such as transplant surgery, have further contributed to the decline in the death rate. More sophisticated medical care means that people now survive illnesses that would have killed them even in the recent past. Before the twentieth century, the highest mortality rates were among babies and young children, but today death rates rise the older you get. The major causes of death today in Britain are from the non-infectious degenerative diseases, such as cancer and heart disease.

Higher living standards

Rising standards of living have further assisted in reducing death rates. Higher wages, better food, more amenities and appliances in the home, and greatly improved housing conditions, with less damp, inside toilets,

413

ACTIVITY

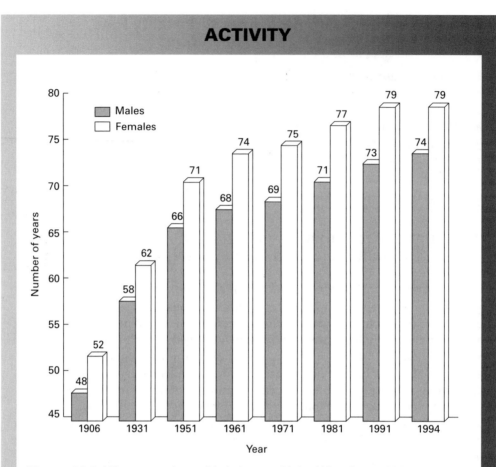

Figure 16.3 Life expectation at birth: by sex, United Kingdom, 1906–94
Source: Data from *Population Trends* (various years)

Study figure 16.3 and answer the following questions:

1 What was the life expectation of females in 1931?
2 What was the difference between the life expectation of males and females in 1961?
3 Identify three trends shown in figure 16.3 between 1906 and 1994, and suggest reasons for them.
4 Using the data given in figure 16.3, draw a line graph to show the same information.
5 Suggest three reasons why life expectation is greater for women than for men.
6 Suggest reasons why life expectation has increased more for women than for men in the period between 1906 and 1994.

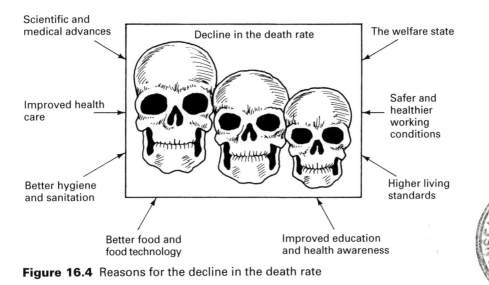

Scientific and medical advances

Improved health care

Better hygiene and sanitation

Decline in the death rate

The welfare state

Safer and healthier working conditions

Higher living standards

Better food and food technology

Improved education and health awareness

Figure 16.4 Reasons for the decline in the death rate

and running hot water, have all assisted in improving the health and life expectation of the population. Because of improved transportation and food technology, a wider range of more nutritious food is available, with improved storage techniques (such as freezing), making possible the import of a range of foodstuffs, including more affordable fresh fruit and vegetables all the year round.

Public health and welfare

There has been a steep rise of state intervention in public welfare, particularly since the establishment of the welfare state in 1945. The NHS has provided free and comprehensive health care, and there is much better ante-natal and post-natal care for mothers and babies. More women have children in hospitals today, and there are health visitors to check on young babies, which helps to explain the decrease in the infant mortality rate. The wide range of welfare benefits available helps to maintain standards of health in times of hardship, and old people in particular are cared for better today, with pensions and a range of services like home helps, social workers, and old people's homes.

Health education

Coupled with these changes has been a growing awareness of nutrition and its importance to health. Improved educational standards generally, and particularly in health education, have led to a much better informed public, who demand better hygiene and public health, and welfare legislation and social reforms to improve health. Bodies like the Health Education Authority seek to improve the health of the public by education, such as emphasizing the benefits of exercise, giving up smoking, and eating a balanced diet. The public outcries in the 1980s and 1990s over risks of food poisoning, such as salmonella in eggs, 'mad cow disease' in beef, listeria in cook-chill foods, and the *E. coli* food poisoning outbreak in 1996–7 (which killed 20 people), are all evidence of this growing health awareness, particularly in recent years.

Improved working conditions

Working conditions improved dramatically in the twentieth century. Technology has taken over some of the more arduous, health-damaging tasks, and factory machinery is often safer than it was last century. Higher standards of health and safety at work, shorter working hours, more leisure time, and earlier retirement ages have all made work physically less demanding and therefore have reduced risks to health.

Sex differences in life expectation

In chapter 3, major social class differences in health and life expectation were discussed, but such differences also exist between men and women. These issues are discussed in more depth in the next chapter.

In most younger age groups, the population is roughly evenly divided between the sexes, but in the older age groups there are far more women than men. In 1996, about two-thirds of people aged 75 or over, and about three-quarters aged 85 or over, were women. There are therefore slightly more women than men in the population as a whole. This is because there is a higher death rate among men and life expectation for women is longer: in 1994, average life expectation was 79 for women, but only 74 years for men. Figure 16.3 on page 414 shows these differences in life expectation between 1906 and 1994.

Changes in the Birth Rate

Over the twentieth century, the birth rate has been declining in the UK, from 28 per 1000 in 1902 to about 12.5 per 1000 in 1995. The only major exceptions to this trend were the post-war 'baby booms' of 1920 and 1947, as men and women started families delayed by separation during the war. There was a further baby boom in the late 1950s and 1960s, when increases in the standard of living and low unemployment meant

Why do women live longer than men?

- Evidence suggests that boys are the weaker sex at birth, with a higher infant mortality rate, and women seem to have a better genetic resistance to heart disease than men.
- The process of gender role socialization means men are more likely to be brought up to shrug off illnesses, drink and smoke more (with all the consequences for health), are more aggressive and take more risks, are less careful in what they eat, and are not socialized to show their emotions as much as women and so have less outlet for stress. Women are socialized to 'take care of themselves' more than men, and they are more likely to visit doctors, which may mean they receive better health care.
- Men generally live more hazardous lives than women. The more dangerous occupations are more likely to be done by men, such as construction work, and men are therefore more at risk of industrial accidents and diseases. In the home, men are more likely to do the dangerous and risky jobs, such as jobs using ladders and climbing on the roof. Men also make up the majority of car drivers and motor-cyclists, and are therefore more at risk of death through road accidents.
- Men are more likely to work full-time and to work longer and more unsociable hours, such as overtime working and shiftwork, which can be harmful to health.
- Jobs carrying high levels of responsibility are more commonly done by men, which may cause higher levels of health-damaging stress.
- Men retire later than women (age 65 compared to 60). Evidence suggests that the later retirement age of men could be an important factor in reducing their life expectation. (Note: women's retirement age is planned to increase to 65 in the period between 2010 and 2020.)

ACTIVITY/DISCUSSION

1 Which of the reasons given for women living longer than men do you think is most important? Give your reasons.
2 Do you think that men's 'macho' behaviour is an important factor in shortening their lives? Suggest evidence for this from your own experiences.
3 'The growing equality of women with men is a threat to women's health.' Explain this statement. Do you agree? How might this situation be avoided (apart from stopping women becoming more equal!)?

417

some parents felt they could afford more children, and improved welfare services and payments made having extra children less of a hardship. However, with increasing unemployment and hardship in the 1980s and early 1990s, birth rates declined once again. A decline in the birth rate has meant that the average family has been getting smaller, from about 6 children per family in the 1870s to about 1.8 in 1996. Despite the declining birth rate, the population has continued to grow slowly, because the birth rate has remained slightly higher than the death rate.

Explanations for the falling birth rate and smaller family size

Contraception

More effective and cheaper methods of contraception have been developed in the twentieth century, and society's attitudes to the use of contraception have changed from disapproval to acceptance. This is partly because of growing secularization, and the declining influence of the church and religion on people's behaviour. The availability of safe and legal abortion since 1967 has also helped in terminating unwanted pregnancies. Family planning is therefore easier.

The compulsory education of children

Since children were barred from employment, and education became compulsory in 1880, they have ceased to be an economic asset that can contribute to family income through working at an early age. They have therefore become an economic liability and a drain on the resources of parents, as children have to be supported for a prolonged period in compulsory education. Parents have therefore begun to limit the size of their families, to secure for themselves and their children a higher standard of living. The move to a more child-centred society has assisted in this restriction of family size, as smaller families mean parents can spend more money and time on and with each child.

ACTIVITY/DISCUSSION

1 What sort of pressures might influence governments either to promote or to restrict the use of contraceptive devices?
2 What are the social pressures which influence whether or not individuals choose to use contraception?

Figure 16.5 Reasons for the decline in the birth rate

The changing position of women

The changing position of women, particularly this century, has involved more equal status with men and greater employment opportunities. Women today have less desire to spend long years of their lives bearing and rearing children, and many wish to pursue a career of their own. While most women do eventually have children, there is a growing proportion who are choosing not to do so. For example, 20 per cent of 35-year-old women in 1989 were childless, compared to 12 per cent in 1979.

The declining infant mortality rate

In the nineteenth century, the absence of a welfare state meant many parents relied on their children to care for them in old age. However, many babies failed to survive infancy, and it was often uncertain whether children would outlive their parents. Parents therefore often had many children as a safeguard against some of them dying. The decline in the infant mortality rate and death rate has meant less children are dying before adulthood and old age, so parents need no longer have many children as security against only a few surviving. In addition, the range of agencies which exist to help the elderly today mean people are less reliant on care by their children when they reach old age.

A geographically mobile labour force

Industrial societies generally require a geographically mobile workforce, which means a workforce that can easily move to other areas for work or promotion. This may have been a factor in encouraging smaller families, as they can more easily pack up and move elsewhere.

Photo: Ted Fussey

The Ageing Population

Britain, like most Western industrialized countries, today has an ageing population. This simply means the average age of the population is getting higher, with a greater proportion of the population over retirement age, and a smaller proportion of young people.

The high birth and death rates of the nineteenth century meant that the majority of the population was young – people didn't live long enough to grow old! The decline in the death rate and increased life expectation has meant that more people are living longer, and more are reaching old age.

However, the decline in the birth rate has meant that fewer children are being born as well, and this has changed the overall age structure of the population. For example, in 1901, about 33 per cent of the population were under age 15, 63 per cent were between the ages of 15 and 65, and only about 4 per cent were over 65. In 1996, about 21 per cent were under 16, 63 per cent were between 16 and 64, and 16 per cent were over 65. This changing age structure of the population is shown in the pyramids in figure 16.6, and figure 16.7 shows the growing numbers of the elderly.

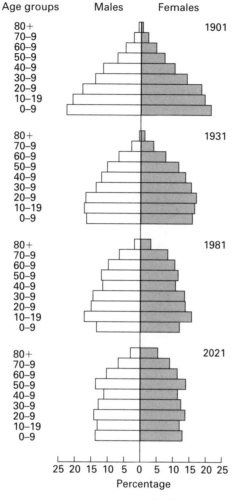

Age and sex distribution

Figure 16.6 The ageing population: Great Britain, 1901–2021
Source: Social Studies Review

The growing proportion of elderly people in the population creates a growing burden of dependence, or an increasing dependency ratio. This simply means that an increasing number of old people have to be supported by a decreasing proportion of the working population. This could mean higher taxes on those working to pay the costs of benefits for the elderly, such as the costs of income support payments for board and lodging of elderly people in residential and nursing homes. Figure 16.8 summarizes the processes involved in the ageing population, and some of the consequences are outlined below.

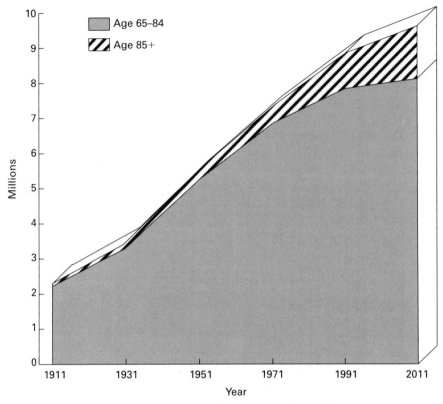

Figure 16.7 The growing numbers of the elderly: United Kingdom, 1901–2011
Source: Data from Office of Population, Censuses, and Surveys

ACTIVITY

Look at figure 16.6 on the previous page and answer the following questions:

1 About what percentage of females were in the 80+ age group in 1931?
2 About what percentage of males were aged between 20 and 29 in 1981?
3 By approximately how much did the percentage of females in the 70–9 age group increase between 1901 and 1981?
4 What evidence is there in figure 16.6 that women live longer than men?
5 Explain briefly how figure 16.6 shows that Britain has an ageing population.

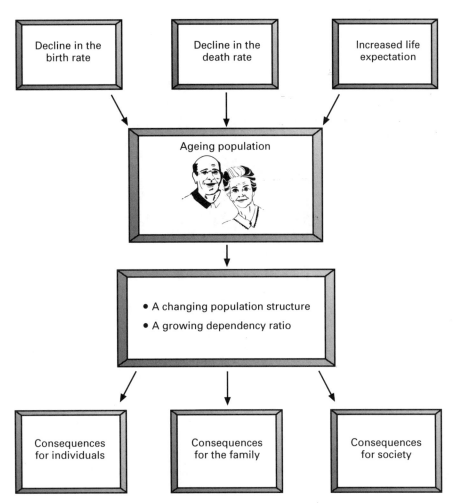

Figure 16.8 The causes and consequences of an ageing population

Some consequences of an ageing population

Consequences for individuals
- Enjoyment of retirement, with more time for leisure interests and activities, and more time to spend with grandchildren.
- Loss of income from work, possibly leading to poverty if on an inadequate pension.
- Loss of status obtained from work.
- Loss of social contacts with workmates and friends, and growing isolation and loneliness as friends and partners die.
- Deterioration in health, and growing dependence on others.
- Fear of crime, especially as television and newspapers are often the

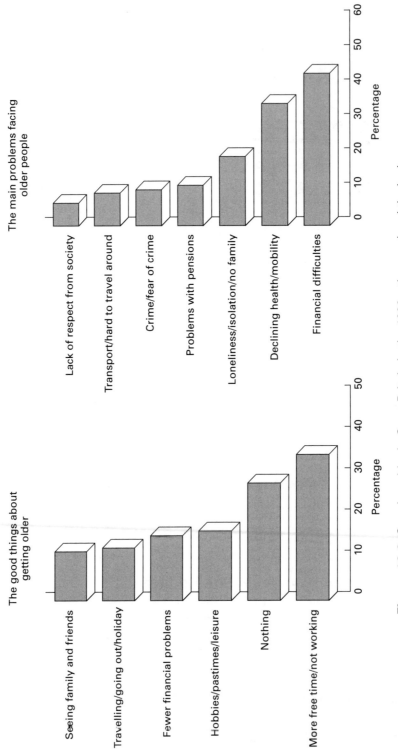

Figure 16.9 Growing older in Great Britain in the 1990s: the good and the bad
Source: Data from *The British Gas Report on Attitudes to Ageing 1991*

main source of information for the housebound elderly, and the mass media often give an exaggerated view of how much crime there is.

Consequences for the family

- Elderly relatives can help with childcare and babysitting, and maybe financially (especially in the middle class).
- Emotional strain and overcrowding if an elderly, and possibly infirm, relative moves in with his or her child's family. This might cause conflict between couples, or between children and grandparents.
- Problems for planning holidays and moving for work or promotion caused by the care needs of an elderly dependant.
- Financial hardship, as people may increasingly face having to support not just themselves and their children, but also their parents and possibly grandparents too. Loss of income may result if one partner has to give up work to care for elderly dependants on top of the financial burden of extra food and heating bills.
- Difficulties (like stress) for relatives who have to devote large amounts of time to caring for infirm or disabled elderly relatives.

Consequences for society

- An increased burden of dependency. This may mean more taxes on the working population to pay for higher levels of government spending on welfare benefits, health, and social services. Nearly half of all benefit spending goes to elderly people – 43.7 per cent in 1995–6 – and without welfare reforms, this is expected to keep on rising. An alternative approach involves cutting pensions and services to the elderly, or charging for services that were formerly free.
- Less money available for other areas, such as schools.
- Pressures on the NHS, such as cash shortages and longer waiting lists for treatment, as the elderly suffer more illness, particularly long-term illnesses.
- More poverty, as the elderly often fall below the poverty line.
- Housing shortages as people occupy their homes for longer.
- Youth unemployment and fewer promotion opportunities at work, as more people survive and work until retirement age.
- More day centres and day hospitals, both to care for the elderly and to provide respite care (facilities to enable relatives looking after elderly infirm relatives to have some time off).

A British Gas report on ageing in Britain in 1991 asked a representative sample of retired people over the age of 55 about what they thought were the good things about getting older in Britain in 1991, and what they thought were the main problems facing older people. Figure 16.9 shows the results of the survey.

ACTIVITY

Study figure 16.9 on page 424 and the section on 'Some consequences of an ageing population':

1 Explain fully two problems for society of an ageing population, and the possible consequences of these problems.
2 When elderly and infirm relatives move in with their adult children, it is usually the female who gives up paid work. Why do you think this is?
3 Look at figure 16.9:
  (a) What percentage of retired people thought there was nothing good about getting older?
  (b) What was the main problem most retired people faced in getting older?
  (c) What percentage of retired people thought lack of respect from society was a main problem of getting older?
4 Why do many of the elderly live in poverty?
5 What welfare services are available to help the elderly? List all those you can think of, explaining in each case the kind of help provided.
6 If you have, or were to have, an elderly parent, grandparent, or great-grandparent living with you, what advantages and problems are or might be created for family life? Discuss these with others if you are in a group.

Migration: Immigration and Emigration

A further influence on Britain's population size and composition has been migration. Migration to and from Britain has usually occurred because of 'push' factors, such as poverty, unemployment, or persecution, and 'pull' factors, such as the search for jobs and a higher standard of living, more political freedom, and joining relatives.

The pattern of migration

The peak period of immigration in the nineteenth century was in the 1830s and 1840s, when over half a million Irish fled the effects of the potato famine in Ireland. The Irish still remain the single largest immigrant group in Britain. The peak periods of emigration from Britain were in the 1880s and the first quarter of the twentieth century, when many left to go to places in the British Empire.

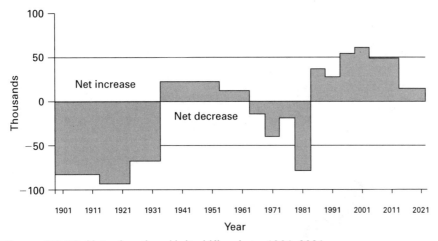

Figure 16.10 Net migration: United Kingdom, 1901–2021
Source: Data from *Annual Abstract of Statistics 1997; Population Trends*, no. 87

In the twentieth century, there were two peak periods of immigration. During the 1930s and up until about 1945, several hundred thousand refugees fled to Britain from Europe to escape the effects of Nazi occupation and persecution. In the late 1950s and 1960s, widespread immigration from the black Commonwealth (mainly India, Pakistan, and the West Indies) was actively encouraged by the British government, which sent out recruiting teams to these countries to solve labour shortages in unskilled and poorly paid occupations in Britain. Large-scale black immigration has been effectively ended by a series of racist Immigration Acts since 1962. These have taken away many of the rights to residence in Britain of black British people living in former British colonies, while at the same time preserving those of white people.

Overall, the pattern of net migration shows that from about 1870 to the 1930s there were more emigrants than immigrants; that is, a net loss of population through migration. In the periods between about 1931 and 1951, and 1955 and 1962, immigration exceeded emigration (that is, a net gain). In the 1960s and 1970s, more people left the country each year than entered it, but since the 1980s more people have entered the country than have left it. Figure 16.11 shows the overall origins and destinations of migrants between 1974 and 1995.

URBANIZATION

Urbanization is the process of the movement of people from rural (country) areas to urban areas (towns and cities), with the corresponding growth in towns and cities, which become the major centres of population in a society. An urbanized society is one where most of the population live in towns and cities.

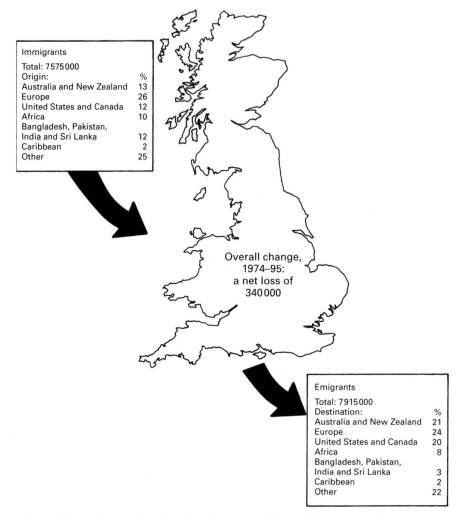

Immigrants

Total: 7575000
Origin:	%
Australia and New Zealand	13
Europe	26
United States and Canada	12
Africa	10
Bangladesh, Pakistan, India and Sri Lanka	12
Caribbean	2
Other	25

Overall change, 1974–95: a net loss of 340000

Emigrants

Total: 7915000
Destination:	%
Australia and New Zealand	21
Europe	24
United States and Canada	20
Africa	8
Bangladesh, Pakistan, India and Sri Lanka	3
Caribbean	2
Other	22

Figure 16.11 International migration into and out of the United Kingdom: 1974–95

In Britain, urbanization really began with the beginnings of industrialization in the late eighteenth and early nineteenth centuries. For example, in 1800 about 15 per cent of the population lived in towns and cities, and by 1900 this had increased to about 77 per cent of the population of England and Wales. In 1991, about 76 per cent of the population of Britain lived in urban areas, with about one-third of the population concentrated in seven large conurbations (large, densely populated urban areas including a number of towns). These conurbations are Greater London, Greater Manchester, Merseyside (around Liverpool), Strathclyde (around Glasgow), Tyne and Wear (around Newcastle upon Tyne), the West Midlands (around Birmingham), and West Yorkshire (around Leeds).

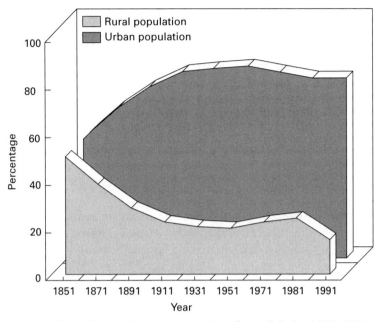

Figure 16.12 The urban and rural population: Great Britain, 1851–1991

The Reasons for Urbanization

Urbanization is linked to two basic factors: the mechanization of agriculture and the industrialization process. The movement to larger farms and the increasing mechanization of agriculture reduced the number of farm workers required. In the absence of any form of social welfare, these rural unemployed generally had no alternative but to seek work in the towns and cities. Industrialization in the nineteenth century led to the development of industrial centres in urban areas, and people moved to these centres for employment.

De-urbanization

Since the 1960s, there has been a gradual reversal of the process of urbanization, with a decline in the population living in cities. Between 1961 and 1981, for example, the population of the six largest conurbations fell by about two million. This movement of people away from living in cities towards the suburbs and new towns (like Milton Keynes) is known as **de-urbanization** or urban dispersal.

429

Why has de-urbanization occurred?

- Industrial firms have moved from the cities. This is because land prices, rent, and rates tend to be higher in city areas, and firms can cut costs by moving out. This has been assisted by central and local government incentives in terms of rent and rate concessions for firms which relocate in rural areas or in new towns.
- Improved road networks and fast rail services have enabled industry to operate just as efficiently outside the cities, and have also enabled people to commute to work rather than having to live within walking or cycling distance. The increase in private and company car ownership has helped in this.
- People have moved to get a better environment and cheaper housing. Often life in the suburbs and in new towns is generally more pleasant than in the cities. With the move towards more home-ownership, house prices in the more pleasant areas of cities are too expensive for many people, and housing is more modern and generally cheaper in the suburbs and new towns. There are usually more parks and open spaces, newer leisure facilities, and less noise and pollution there. General costs of living are lower, and there also tend to be fewer social problems like crime, vandalism, and violence in these areas.
- As firms have left the cities, employees following these firms can cut down travelling time and costs in getting to work.
- Many inner-city slum areas have been redeveloped, and this has often meant the people living there have been rehoused in large new social (council and housing association) housing estates in the suburbs or in new towns.

ACTIVITY

1 People often move around the country today, and there may be people in your school or college class, your neighbourhood or workplace, who have recently moved to your area. Do a small survey of these people, finding out (a) why they left the area they came from, and (b) why they chose to move to your area.

2 On the basis of your findings, what seem to be the principal factors influencing the movement of people around the country?

The inner cities have often been flashpoints of social conflict
Photo: Sean Smith, *Guardian*

The Inner Cities

The inner cities have undergone a rapid decline in recent years as firms either close down or move out to the suburbs and new towns. Often the only people left in the inner cities are those who can't afford to move out, such as the old, the unemployed, and low-paid unskilled and semi-skilled workers. Many inner-city residents are among the most deprived sections of the population in Britain. These areas have proven to be 'flashpoints' of social conflict, with riots breaking out in the 1980s in the St Paul's area of Bristol, the Toxteth area of Liverpool, the Southall, Brixton, and Tottenham areas of London, the Handsworth area of Birmingham, and other inner-city areas.

The inner cities have become centres of deprivation and flashpoints of conflict for a number of reasons.

Poverty and unemployment

Unemployment is particularly high in the inner cities. Many of the sorts of work which are available for inner-city residents without paying expensive travelling costs have been declining. Traditional industries such as docking, shipbuilding, textiles, and clothing have been disappearing,

431

partly because of cheaper foreign competition, and new firms have not opened up in these areas. The demand for semi-skilled and unskilled labour has in any case been declining with increasing mechanization. A lack of government investment in these areas has meant that little has been done to halt this decline.

Poor housing

The inner cities are likely to have the worst and oldest housing, with fewer facilities, more overcrowding, and a higher level of rented accommodation (often at exorbitantly high rents for the quality of the accommodation) than other areas. Tenants often can't afford to look after their homes properly, and private landlords frequently refuse to do so. Even owner-occupiers may have few extra resources to maintain their homes adequately.

Crime

Those who can afford to move out of the inner cities have done so, and only the poor are left. Petty crime is more likely as a necessity for surviving daily life. The redevelopment and slum clearance that have gone on have broken up extended kin networks and traditional communities, and this has weakened informal social controls. The anonymity this creates means delinquency and 'street crime' are therefore more common, as people can get away with them. This rise in the crime rate is frequently fuelled by police activity, as the inhabitants of inner-city areas fit their stereotype of potential criminals. Policing is therefore heavier in these areas, which may cause resentment among those living there, and consequently more confrontations with the police.

Racism and racial tension

Some inner-city areas have high concentrations of ethnic minorities, since they are often among the poorer sections of the population and live where they can best afford. The white population in such areas may scapegoat these ethnic minorities by blaming them for their problems of housing and unemployment, which may create racial tension. There is also evidence of racism in the police force, especially in the Metropolitan Police in London, and this often generates hostility and resentment among black people against the police for harassing them, for example by stopping and searching them without good cause.

Poor schools

Schools in inner cities are often in dilapidated buildings. There is frequently a high turnover of teachers in such schools because of the stress caused by having to deal with the complex social problems they encounter in the classroom. Parents do not have the money to provide support for the schools, as parents do in many middle-class areas.

General social problems

The inner cities are more likely to have a concentration of other general social problems, as a result of the stresses and strains caused by the accumulation of the points mentioned above. For example, the inner cities have higher levels of family breakdown and deprived lone-parent families, drug addiction, drug abuse, and prostitution than found in other areas.

Some attempts have been made to redevelop and improve the inner cities in recent years, but often these have not resolved the underlying problems. For example, the redevelopment of London's Docklands in the late 1980s simply meant a massive increase in property prices, and a takeover of the area by highly-paid young professionals. Such redevelopment means life for the remaining local residents is made ever more expensive and difficult to cope with. Often these residents are forced to move out by such circumstances, and the 'problem' simply moves elsewhere.

CHAPTER SUMMARY

After studying this chapter, you should be able to:

- Explain why governments need to collect information on population trends.
- Define the key terms used in the study of population.
- Explain the factors which influence the size of a country's population.
- Explain why the death and infant mortality rates have fallen in Britain, and why life expectation has increased.
- Explain sex differences in life expectation.
- Explain why the birth rate has fallen in Britain.
- Describe and explain the causes and some consequences of an ageing population.
- Explain briefly the reasons for immigration and emigration.
- Explain why urbanization and de-urbanization have occurred in Britain.
- Identify and explain the major problems of the inner cities.

KEY TERMS

birth rate	immigration
death rate	infant mortality rate
demography	life expectation
dependency ratio	migration
dependent age groups	net migration
dependent population	population projections
de-urbanization	sex ratio
emigration	urbanization
general fertility rate	

PROJECT SUGGESTIONS

1 Using secondary sources (see chapter 18) – such as the census – give an account of the major features of the population of your area, including the balance of the sexes, age distribution, ethnic origins, and occupational composition.

2 Interview a sample of elderly people (over retirement age) asking them about the advantages and disadvantages/problems of being elderly. Figure 16.9 earlier in this chapter may give you some ideas for a questionnaire. Compare your findings with those in figure 16.9.

HEALTH AND ILLNESS

17

KEY ISSUES IN THIS CHAPTER

- What is meant by 'health', 'illness', and 'disease'?
- The medical and social models of health.
- Becoming a health statistic.
- Medicine and social control: the sick role.
- How society influences health.
- The food industry.
- Social class, gender, and ethnic inequalities in health.

In Britain, more people are suffering and dying prematurely of preventable diseases than perhaps ever before. We hear more and more stories of people with cancer, heart disease, asthma, and eczema. If progress towards a civilized society can be measured by the health of a nation, we might sometimes be forgiven for thinking Britain is going in reverse. And if the health of the population is a measure of social justice, then Britain is as divided now as it has ever been. But it is not simply the hand of nature or fate that makes us sick. Poor health and premature death are not random lightning bolts that strike us out of the blue. Disease and premature death are not evenly or randomly distributed throughout society. Official statistics reveal a pattern of social class, gender, and ethnic inequalities in health. These differences in disease and death provide strong evidence that sickness and health are not simply matters of fate or bad luck, but a product of the society in which we live.

While the message has been that medicine can cure us, all the major advances in health occurred before medical intervention. In Britain, the elimination of the killer infectious diseases of the past, such as TB, pneumonia, flu, cholera, typhoid, and diphtheria, all took place before the development of modern medicine. It was social changes such as better diet, clean water supplies, sewage disposal, improved housing, and

Getting healthier is important to many people today – but what makes us unhealthy in the first place?
Photo: Ted Fussey

general knowledge about health and hygiene that improved health, rather than medical improvements like antibiotics and vaccines which proved less effective because of malnutrition. This is shown most noticeably in the Third World, where the major advances in health have come about as a result of simple preventative measures such as clean water and sewage control.

Given the newspaper stories we read about medical breakthroughs, 'miracle cures', organ transplants, and so on, we would expect doctors and nurses soon to be out of business, as the health of the population improves. Surprisingly, perhaps, the opposite is the case. The financial demands of the NHS have rocketed, and more and more people are going into hospital, or are on long waiting lists.

WHAT IS MEANT BY 'HEALTH', 'ILLNESS', AND 'DISEASE'?

The definitions of 'health', 'illness', and 'disease' are no simple matters. What counts as health and illness varies between different groups within a single society, such as between men and women, and between societies. Views of acceptable standards of health are likely to differ widely between the people of a poor African country and Britain. Even in the same society, views of health change over time. At one time in Britain,

mental illness was seen as a sign of satanic possession or witchcraft – a matter best dealt with by the Church rather than by doctors. Similarly, what were once seen as personal problems have quite recently become medical problems, such as obesity, alcoholism, hyperactivity in children and smoking.

There is no simple definition of illness, because for pain or discomfort to count as a disease it is necessary for someone to diagnose it as such. There are also subjective influences on health: some of us can put up with or ignore pain more than others; some feel no pain; and many of us will have different notions of what counts as 'feeling unwell'.

ACTIVITY

1   Write your own definitions, with examples, of 'health', 'illness', and 'disease'. Discuss, with examples, what your definitions might mean for promoting health and eliminating disease.
2   Try to think of ways in which your view of 'being healthy' might differ between (a) a rich country like Britain and a poor African country, and (b) a person who lives in poverty in Britain compared with a wealthy member of the upper class.

Health is probably most easy to define as being able to function normally within a usual everyday routine.

Disease generally refers to a biological or mental condition, which usually involves medically diagnosed symptoms.

Illness refers to the subjective feeling of being unwell or ill-health. It is possible both to have a disease and not feel ill, and to feel ill and not have any disease.

ACTIVITY

The United Nations World Health Organization defines health as 'a state of complete physical, mental, and social well-being, and not merely the absence of disease or infirmity'. Some have argued that this definition goes far beyond a realistic definition of health, as it implies not simply the absence of disease, but also a personally fulfilling life.

1 Discuss how the World Health Organization might view the health of the long-term unemployed in Britain.
2 Using the World Health Organization's definition, how might 'good health' differ between (a) people who live in a poor African country and those who live in modern Britain, and (b) people in Britain who live in an isolated village in the country and those who live in a town?
3 Discuss the view that 'good health is simply a state of mind'.

THE MEDICAL AND SOCIAL MODELS OF HEALTH

As seen above, there are different meanings attached to 'health'. There are two main approaches, arising from different views of what the causes of ill-health are. These are often referred to as the medical and social models of health.

The Medical Model of Health

This has two main features.

- Disease is seen as mainly caused by biological factors, and recently by personal factors such as smoking and diet. The sick person is treated in the same way as a car that has broken down. People become objects to be fixed by 'body mechanics' (doctors).
- The causes of ill-health are seen as arising either from the moral failings of the individual (such as smoking too much or not getting enough exercise) or from random attacks of disease. This is a bit like blaming car breakdowns on poor maintenance and lack of proper servicing, or on bad luck.

The Social Model of Health

This model differs in two ways from the medical model.

- A strong emphasis is placed on the social causes of health and ill-health, and on how society influences health.
- Health and illness are not seen simply as medical or scientific facts. A choice exists whether people see themselves as ill or not, and those with power can choose whether or not to classify someone as ill. In most cases, 'those with power' means doctors and other medical experts.

BECOMING A HEALTH STATISTIC

The process of becoming ill is not as simple and straightforward as it might seem. People may respond to the same symptoms in different ways. While some may seek medical help, others may choose to ignore their symptoms. They may look for alternative non-medical or less serious explanations for them: bronchitis may become simply a 'smoker's cough', and possible brain tumours may be dismissed as 'headaches'.

For people to be labelled as 'sick' – and to be recorded as a health statistic – there are at least four stages involved:

1 Individuals must first recognize they have a problem.
2 They must then define their problem as serious enough to take to a doctor.
3 They must then actually go to the doctor.
4 The doctor must then be persuaded that they have a medical or mental condition capable of being labelled as an illness requiring treatment.

ACTIVITY

1 List all the factors you can which might influence each of the four stages on the previous page, which lead some people to visit the doctor and others not to. For example, in stage 1, you might consider a person's ability to continue her or his responsibilities to friends and family, pressure from relatives, friends, and employers, etc. Draw on your own experiences of what makes you decide whether you are ill, and whether or not to go to the doctor's.
2 Discuss in a group what you think the most common influences on going (or not going) to the doctor might be.

MEDICINE AND SOCIAL CONTROL: THE SICK ROLE

Social control is concerned with maintaining order and stability in society. Sickness is really a form of deviance. When people are ill, they generally want to avoid normal responsibilities because these are too demanding or stressful. The **sick role** – the pattern of behaviour associated with someone who is ill – is an escape route for the individual. This is because, when you are sick, you can fairly abandon normal everyday activities, and often others will take over your responsibilities.

Allowing individuals to 'opt out' into the sick role is potentially dangerous because the smooth workings of society may be upset if too many people adopt it. Imagine a school or factory where the teachers, students, managers, or workers were always off ill!

Doctors play a key role in the social control of the sick by acting as gate-keepers of entry to the sick role, and preventing people becoming hypochondriacs and skiving on the grounds of illness. For example, they can stop people taking more than a few days off work on the grounds of illness by refusing to issue sick notes.

Features of the Sick Role

Rights

- Depending on the illness, individuals are excused normal social activities (for example, they are excused school or work). This requires approval by others such as teachers, employers, and family members.

The doctor often plays a key role in this process, by diagnosing the person as 'really ill', and issuing sick notes.

- Individuals are not seen as personally to blame for their illness: relatives, friends, and doctors are often very critical of those they do see as responsible for their own illness. Excessive drinking often doesn't get much sympathy the morning after!

Obligations

Individuals have an obligation to want to 'get well'. When necessary, they are expected to seek and accept medical help and cooperate in their treatment. In other words, sick people are expected to do what the doctor orders, and they cannot expect sympathy and support if they don't try to get well. Even if people don't want to call in the doctor because they don't see their illness as serious enough to do so, they are still expected to stay in bed or take it easy in an effort to recover.

HOW SOCIETY INFLUENCES HEALTH

The list you will make in the next activity may show you a number of ways that social factors influence health. That health is the product of

441

society rather than simply of biology or medicine is shown by historical evidence that patterns of disease change over time. Changes which occurred during the nineteenth century and the first half of the twentieth century illustrate this well.

ACTIVITY

Make a list of as many environmental, political, social, and economic factors affecting health as you can think of, such as unemployment, pollution, or poor housing. Explain in each case how the factors you identify might influence health.

Improvements in Health during the Nineteenth and Early Twentieth Centuries

In the nineteenth century, adult and child mortality started to fall, and since then there has been a large and rapid population increase. For a long time this was thought to be due to the development of medicine. However, it is now agreed that it was due to a number of social and economic changes and the general improvement in living standards. These changes included:

- *Public hygiene.* The movement for sanitary reform and public hygiene in the nineteenth century helped to develop a clean and safe environment and higher standards of public hygiene. Pure drinking water, efficient sanitation and sewage disposal, and paved streets and highways all helped to reduce deaths from infective diseases.
- *Better diet.* Being well fed is the most effective form of disease prevention, as shown in the Third World today, where vaccination programmes are not as successful as they should be because children are poorly nourished. The high death rates of the past were mainly due to hunger or malnutrition, which led to poorer resistance to infection. The nineteenth and early twentieth centuries saw improved communications, technology, and hygiene making possible the production, transportation, and import of more and cheaper food. Wages improved, and higher standards of living meant better food and better health.
- *Contraception.* This led to smaller families, making possible a better diet and health care for children. This also improved the health of women, who spent less time child-bearing.

442

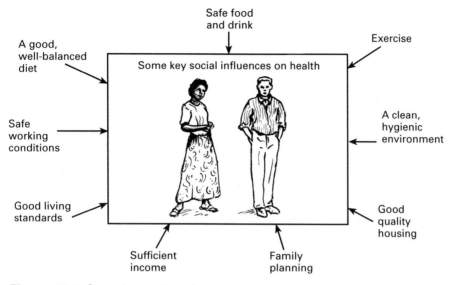

Figure 17.1 Some key social influences on health

- *Housing legislation.* This increased public control over standards of rented housing, which helped to reduce overcrowding and the spread of infectious diseases between family members.
- *The war effort.* During the First World War (1914–18) unemployment was virtually eliminated. As part of the war effort, rents were controlled, food rationing was introduced, and minimum wages were established in agriculture. The resulting decline in poverty cut childhood deaths, especially among the families of unskilled workers in urban areas.
- *General improvements in living standards.* Higher wages, better food, clothing, and housing, laws improving health and safety at work, reduced working hours, and better hygiene regulations on the production and sale of food and drink all improved health.

All the above suggest that good health is more the result of government policy decisions and of economic development than simply of individual initiative or medical intervention.

The New 'Disease Burden'

The infective diseases of the nineteenth century were often called the 'diseases of poverty', since most victims were malnourished and poor. These have been replaced by 'diseases of affluence' – a result of eating too much poor-quality food, a lack of exercise, smoking and drinking too much, and so on.

A well-balanced diet is necessary for good health, and the lack of one makes people more vulnerable to disease. Despite the wealth of modern industrial societies, there is a problem of malnutrition in the form not of too little food, as you find in less developed countries, but of too much of the wrong sort. As a result, advanced industrial societies experience health problems rarely found in simpler rural societies. The new 'disease burden' includes obesity, and degenerative (worsening) diseases like cirrhosis of the liver, certain cancers, heart disease, respiratory diseases, diabetes, stomach ulcers, and varicose veins. These kill or disable more people than they did in the past, and many more people are becoming chronically ill for longer periods in their lives than they did in the past.

What are the causes of these new diseases?

It is generally accepted that the causes of these new diseases of affluence are mainly social and environmental, and therefore preventable. Public concerns over the food supply have been rising. There were major scares over BSE ('mad cow disease') in beef in the 1990s, and the linked human equivalent CJD (Creutzfeld-Jakob disease) had killed twenty-three people in Britain up to September 1997. *E. coli* food poisoning outbreaks in 1996–7 killed twenty people, and many worry about genetically engineered foods. Between 1982 and 1997, cases of food poisoning serious enough to be reported to a doctor rose by 600 per cent. Some doctors have linked the rise of asthma to poor diet, with insufficient fruit and vegetables. The rise in heart disease has been blamed on factors such as smoking, stress, an inactive life style (too many couch potatoes!), and a diet high in fats but low in fibre. A 1997 British government report, *Nutritional Aspects of the Development of Cancer*, estimated that up to 70 per cent of cancer cases were linked to the type of food people ate. Diet was seen as ten times more important than the effects of job-related causes and of smoking on all cancers.

THE FOOD INDUSTRY

The British are now eating a more highly processed diet than at any time in history. We consume a whole range of factory-produced food, which is often low in nutritional value and may well be harmful to health because of additives like flavourings, colourings, and preservatives. Highly processed 'junk food' reinforces the trend towards a high-sugar and high-fat diet which is low in vitamins, minerals, protein, and fibre. Why do

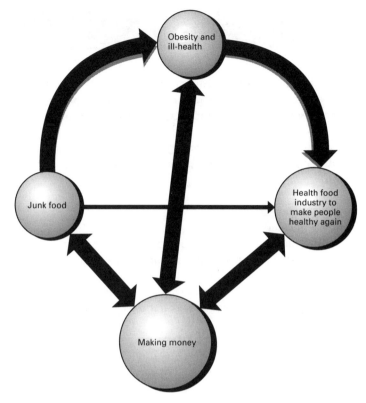

Figure 17.2 The food industry's triple whammy: making money and food production

Photo: Ted Fussey

445

people have unhealthy diets, and why are unhealthy foods allowed to be produced?

The activity above may have made you aware that many mass-produced foods are of poor quality.

The response to criticisms of the Western world's unhealthy diet is the 'health food' industry. Its products are more expensive, such as whole-meal bread and organic vegetables, and the food and drugs industry makes a lot of money through its marketing of 'healthy' foods, dietary supplements, and vitamins. The slimming industry – to offset the effects of obesity-producing junk food – is itself very big business. Vegetarianism and fitness centres have become money spinners, and we can now buy every manner of food which is 'low-calorie', 'slimline', 'low-fat', 'high-fibre', 'sugar-free', and so on. Health itself has become a product for companies to sell in a big way, while continuing to produce those products which often contribute to the original ill-health.

INEQUALITIES IN HEALTH

The following section quotes statistics on health. However, like the crime statistics discussed in chapter 10, some of these statistics should be treated with care (though it is hard to argue with deaths!).

Health statistics may be inaccurate because:

- They depend on people persuading doctors they are ill, and are therefore simply a record of doctors' decision-making.
- Doctors may diagnose illnesses incorrectly, reflecting the state of the doctor's knowledge – and therefore recorded illnesses may not be accurate. For example, there may have been many AIDS deaths recorded as pneumonia, etc., before doctors 'discovered' AIDS.
- Not all sick people go to the doctor, and not all people who persuade doctors they are ill are really sick.
- Private medicine operates to make a profit, and therefore is possibly more likely to diagnose symptoms as a disease.

Social Class Differences in Health

Official statistics reveal massive class inequalities in health. Nearly every kind of illness and disease is linked to class. Poverty is the major driver of ill-health, and poorer people tend to get sick more often and to die younger than richer people. Those who die youngest are people who live, on benefits or low wages, in poor-quality housing and who eat cheap, unhealthy food.

A 1995 Department of Health report noted that if everyone were as healthy as the middle class, there would have been 1500 fewer deaths a year among children under age 1, and 17 000 fewer deaths among men aged 20–64.

In contemporary Britain:

- The death rate in class V (unskilled manual workers) is about twice that of class I. A person born into social class I (professional) lives, on average, about seven years longer than someone in social class V.
- About twice as many babies are still-born or die in the first week of life in unskilled families than in professional ones. In the first year of life, nearly twice as many children die among unskilled workers as in class I. The risk of dying before the age of 5 is twice as great for a child born into social class V as for social class I.
- Men and women in class V are twice as likely to die before reaching retirement age as people in class I. About 90 per cent of the major causes of death are more common in social classes IV and V than in other social classes.

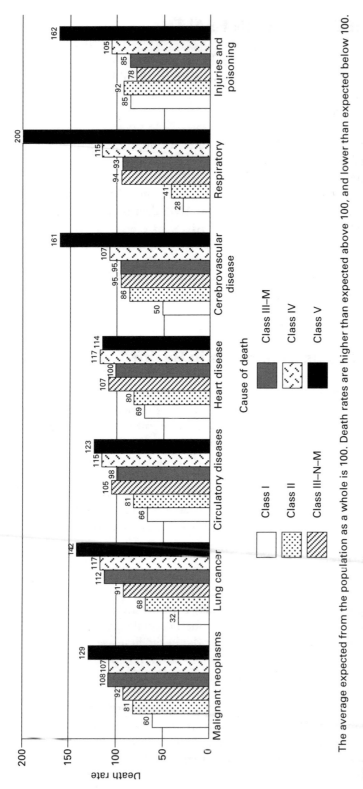

The average expected from the population as a whole is 100. Death rates are higher than expected above 100, and lower than expected below 100.

Figure 17.3 Mortality (1976–89) of men aged 15–64 at death, by cause of death and by their social class in 1971
Source: Data from *Population Trends 80*, Summer 1995

- Lung cancer and stomach cancer occur twice as often among men in manual jobs as among men in professional jobs, and four times as many women die of cervical cancer in social class V as in social class I.
- Working-class people, especially the unskilled, go to see doctors far more often and for a wider range of health problems than people in professional jobs.
- Semi- and unskilled workers are more likely to be absent from work through sickness than those in professional and managerial jobs. Long-standing illness is around twice as high among unskilled manual workers as for class I professionals.
- All of the above are worse for the long-term unemployed and other groups in poverty.

These patterns of sickness and death provide strong evidence that it is society and the way it is organized that influences health, rather than simply our biological make-up.

ACTIVITY

Study figure 17.3:

1 Which disease shows the greatest difference in deaths between social class V and social class I?
2 Which disease shows the smallest difference in deaths between social class I and social class V?
3 Which social class shows the lowest deaths from lung cancer?
4 Identify two trends shown in figure 17.3.
5 Which social class for deaths from what disease is exactly in line with the number expected from the population as a whole?
6 Refer to the box on the characteristics of people aged 16–64 on the next page, and suggest reasons why each of the groups identified might be more likely to consult their GPs than other groups.

The characteristics of people aged 16–64 who are more likely than most to consult their doctor

In urban areas
Council property tenants
In other rented accommodation
Widowed and divorced
Living alone
Adults with young children
Social classes IV and V
Construction, service, and industrial occupations
Unemployed
Ethnic minority group
Smokers

Source: Adapted from *Morbidity Statistics from General Practice 1995* (OPCS Fourth National Study)

The inverse care law

Social class differences in health are made worse through inequalities in the NHS. The inverse care law suggests that health care resources tend to

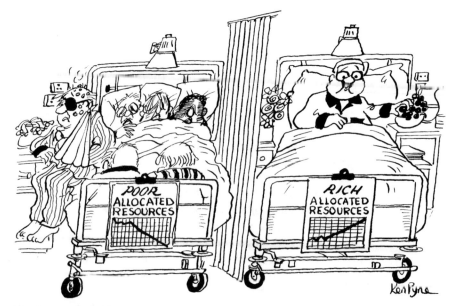

The inverse care law

ACTIVITY

1 How does the cartoon opposite illustrate the inverse care law?
2 Suggest reasons why people in more deprived areas are more likely to suffer from poorer health and get worse health care than those in richer areas.

be distributed in inverse proportion to need. This means that those whose need is least get the most resources, while those in greatest need get the least. For example, poor working-class communities tend to have the most overcrowded facilities in the NHS as poorer people suffer more ill-health, and yet they don't get the extra money spent on them that they need. Poorer people whose need is greatest therefore get less time with their GPs, and hospital waiting lists are longer than in more prosperous areas.

Explanations for social class inequalities in health

There are two main types of explanation for social class inequalities in health.

The cultural explanation

The cultural explanation suggests that those suffering from poorer health have different attitudes, values, and lifestyles which mean they don't look after themselves properly. Examples of this might include smoking too much, using too much salt or sugar, eating junk food, or not bothering to take any exercise.

The material explanation

The material explanation suggests that those suffering poorer health lack enough money to eat a healthy diet, have poor housing, dangerous or unhealthy working conditions, live in an unhealthy local environment, and so on.

Figure 17.4 identifies a range of possible factors which might explain health differences.

451

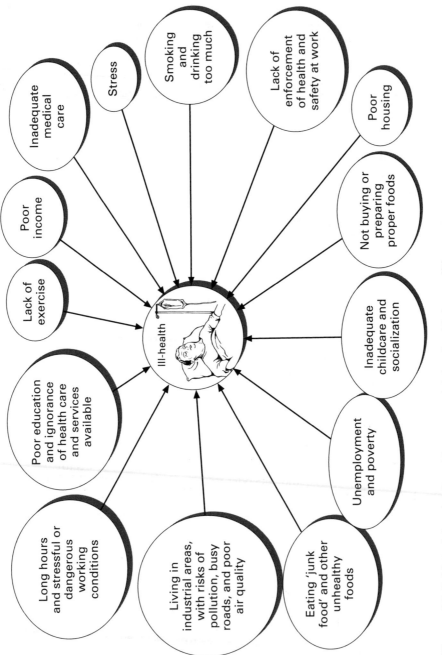

Figure 17.4 Material and cultural factors explaining health inequalities

ACTIVITY

Figure 17.4 suggests a series of points which contribute to social class inequalities in health. Study figure 17.4 and answer the following questions:

1 Divide the explanations into 'cultural' and 'material' ones.
2 Suggest ways each point might explain class inequalities in health.
3 Suggest other reasons of your own for social class differences in health.
4 Do you think cultural or material explanations (or a bit of both) are better in explaining health inequalities? Give reasons for your answer.

Gender Differences in Health

As well as a pattern of social class differences in health, there is also a big difference between the health of men and women. At all ages, women's death rates are much lower than men's. Men's death rates are almost double those of women in every class and on average women live five years longer than men. Almost two-thirds of deaths before the age of 65 are male. After age 65, there are almost twice as many women as men in the population. (Some reasons for this are discussed in chapter 16 on population.)

Are women healthier than men?

The answer is 'yes' if we use only the indicators of death rates and life expectancy. However, statistics show that men, who in general die younger, don't seem to experience as much ill-health as women, who live longer. Women are the major users of health care services and apparently get sick more often than men.

Compared to men, women:

- Go to the doctor about 50 per cent more often between the ages of 15 and 64.
- Report more head and stomach aches, high blood pressure, and weight problems.
- Consume more prescription and non-prescription drugs.
- Are admitted to hospital more often and have more operations.
- Go to see doctors about conditions like insomnia, tension headache, and depression (which are often labelled as 'psychiatric problems') about twice as often.
- Receive far more prescriptions for tranquillizers, sleeping pills, and anti-depressants.
- Are off work with reported sickness more often and spend more days in bed.

Why do women apparently suffer more sickness?

- *Stress.* Many women suffer a double burden of being both low-paid workers and responsible for housework and childcare. In many cases this involves having to manage limited household budgets with pressure to make ends meet, and a long day with little time to relax.
- *Poverty.* In low-income households, it is usually women who go without to ensure other family members get enough to eat. Women are therefore more likely to suffer the effects of poverty more directly than men.
- *Domestic labour* (housework). Domestic labour is rarely fulfilling (for further discussion on this, see chapter 6 on women). Depression may be linked to the unpaid, repetitive, unrewarding, low-status nature of housework, in a society where only paid employment carries any status. The high accident rates at home might be influenced by the isolated nature of housework.
- *Socialization.* Women are socialized to express their feelings and talk about their problems more than men. Since women are generally the ones who 'manage' family health matters, they are often more aware of health and health care matters. Women may therefore be more willing than men to report physical and mental health problems. The higher

rates of recorded illnesses among women could then be due not necessarily to greater health problems than men's, but to women's greater willingness to admit to problems and to take them to doctors. While women go to doctors for prescribed drugs like tranquillizers, men opt for non-prescribed drugs like alcohol. Men's higher death rates may simply be because they bottle everything up until it is too late.

- *Different diagnoses*. Due to gender roles, it may be that doctors are more likely to see symptoms reported by women as mainly mental, while men's are seen as physical. Women are therefore more likely to be diagnosed as depressed or suffering from anxiety than men. Until recently, women had a much higher chance than men of being institutionalized in mental hospitals.

ACTIVITY

1 Refer to the activity on pp. 439–40 about the four stages, and suggest reasons why women might be more likely to end up as a health statistic than men.
2 Discuss the explanations suggested above for women apparently suffering more sickness than men. Do you think women really do suffer more ill-health, or do you think they are simply more open and honest about it than men?

Ethnic Differences in Health

Social class and gender are not the only important social inequalities in health, and there are also some differences between ethnic groups. Afro-Caribbeans seem more biologically vulnerable to developing sickle cell anaemia (a blood disease), and they are more likely to be compulsorily admitted to mental hospitals. Rickets (which can lead to difficulties in walking) is found more commonly in the Asian community. This is probably due to vitamin D deficiency arising from less exposure to sunlight due to the Asian style of dress, and from aspects of the Asian diet. This diet may also explain higher levels of obesity.

Ethnic minority groups may also find some doctors unwilling or unable to respond to their particular cultural problems and needs. Access to health care may be made more difficult as much health care literature is still not translated into ethnic minority languages.

However, many of the health problems of some ethnic minorities arise for the same reasons as social class inequalities. Racism in society means some ethnic minority groups are more likely to find themselves unemployed, or working for long hours in low-paid jobs in hazardous and unhealthy environments, and living in poor housing.

CONCLUSION

This chapter has shown that 'health', 'illness', 'disease', and inequalities in health are very much products of society rather than simply of biological factors. Social and economic life has major influences on the patterns of illness and death. So long as inequalities of wealth, income, education, occupation, and social privilege continue, so will inequalities in health.

CHAPTER SUMMARY

After studying this chapter, you should be able to:

- Explain what is meant by 'health', 'illness', and 'disease'.
- Identify and explain the difference between the medical and social models of health.
- Suggest the reasons why some people may seek medical help while others may not.
- Explain what is meant by the 'sick role', and identify the rights and obligations of it.
- Identify and explain a range of social factors which influence health and disease.
- Identify some problems with health statistics.
- Explain social class, gender, and ethnic inequalities in health.

KEY TERMS

disease	illness
health	sick role

PROJECT SUGGESTIONS

1 Carry out a survey among men and women to find out when they were last ill enough to take time off work, school, or college, when they last visited the doctor, and how many times a year they visit the doctor. See if there are any differences between men and women. You could also do the same type of survey to identify any differences between social classes or ethnic groups.
2 Using secondary sources (see chapter 18), try to find out whether there are differences in the health of people in various areas of your city or county or in the country as a whole, for example between richer and poorer areas. Draw on the material in this chapter to try to explain your findings.

18 DOING SOCIOLOGICAL RESEARCH

> ### KEY ISSUES IN THIS CHAPTER
>
> ■ Quantitative and qualitative data.
> ■ Primary and secondary sources.
> ■ Social surveys.
> ■ Observation.
> ■ Doing your own research: coursework.

As has been seen throughout this book, sociology is concerned with a wide range of issues in social life, spanning the continuing existence of poverty, the influence of the mass media on our views about the world, the things that make work interesting or not, and how the very centre of our personalities is constructed through socialization into gender roles. The interests and concerns of sociologists are not that different from those of most people in society. However, what makes the views of sociologists different from those likely to be aired in a pub, in the canteen at work, or in other daily situations where views get exchanged is that sociologists try to provide evidence to back up what they say. This evidence is collected from a variety of sources and through the use of a number of research methods. In this section, we will examine the types of data (or information) sociologists collect, the range of sources used, and the methods sociologists use to collect their own information.

QUANTITATIVE AND QUALITATIVE DATA

Quantitative data is anything that can be expressed in statistical or number form or can be 'measured' in some way, such as age, qualifications, or

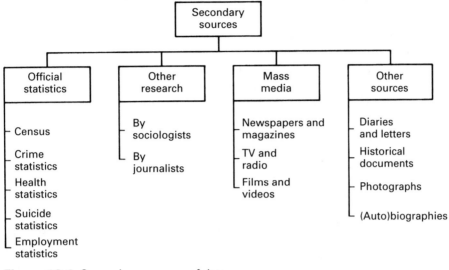

Figure 18.1 Secondary sources of data

income. Such data is usually presented in the form of statistical tables, graphs, pie charts and bar charts. There is more about interpreting statistical data in the appendix.

Qualitative data is concerned with people's feelings about some issue or event, and tries to get at the way they see things. Such data is normally in the form of the sociologist's describing and interpreting people's feelings and lifestyles, often using direct quotations from the people studied.

This data may be gathered from either primary sources or secondary sources.

PRIMARY AND SECONDARY SOURCES

Secondary sources of data are those which already exist. **Secondary data** has already been collected by others. Figure 18.1 shows a range of secondary sources which might be used by sociologists in carrying out research.

Because the existing data required for research may be unreliable or may simply not have been collected, sociologists often have to collect their own data from primary sources. **Primary data** is that which is collected by sociologists themselves – it only exists because the sociologist has collected it. Such information is usually obtained by carrying out a social survey or by participant observation (these will be discussed shortly).

The Advantages of Secondary Sources

Secondary sources have the main advantage that the material is readily available and so is cheap and easy to use. There is no need to spend time and money collecting data, and some data, such as that provided by the census, would be impossible for an individual to collect. In some cases, secondary sources may be the only sources of information available in an area, such as in historical research, and sociologists may therefore have no alternative but to use them.

The Problems of Secondary Sources

Secondary sources do present problems for use in sociological research. The information may be unrepresentative, and therefore may not apply to the whole population. For example, before the beginning of compulsory education in Britain in 1880, it was mainly only the well-off who could read and write, and so it was mainly they who left documents behind them.

The information may be inaccurate in some way and therefore unreliable or misleading. It may be forged or biased, contain errors or be exaggerated. Newspaper reports, for example, are notoriously unreliable as sources of evidence, as discussed in chapter 9.

Official statistics

Sociologists very often use official statistics, which are those produced by the government, in their research, such as those on crime, unemployment, and health. Such statistics must be treated very cautiously by sociologists. Chapter 10 showed the problems involved in using the official crime statistics as evidence of the real extent of crime. Two further examples of the possible inaccuracies of official statistics are shown by those on unemployment and health.

Unemployment statistics

Unemployment statistics have a number of limitations. According to the Unemployment Unit, the method of calculating unemployment statistics has been changed about thirty times since 1982, with each change creating a drop in the numbers counted as unemployed. Unemployment figures only include those signing on at job centres and eligible for benefit. They therefore exclude married women, people who have retired early, those reluctantly staying on at school or college because there are no jobs, those on government training schemes, and those working part-time because

ACTIVITY

Read the following passage and then answer the questions:

Suicide is, by definition, the death of a person who intended to kill him or herself. The problem for coroners is they can't ask dead people if they meant to kill themselves, so they can only guess at the truth by looking for 'clues' in the circumstances surrounding the death. Atkinson has suggested there are four main factors which coroners take into account when deciding whether a death is a suicide or not.

● Whether there was a suicide note.
● The way the person died, for example by hanging, drowning, or a drug overdose. Death in a road accident rarely results in a suicide verdict.
● The place the death occurred and the circumstances surrounding it; for example, a drug overdose in a remote wood would be more likely to be seen as a suicide than if it occurred at home in bed. A coroner might also consider circumstances such as whether the person had been drinking before taking the drugs, and whether the drugs had been hoarded or not.
● The life history and the mental state of the dead person, such as her or his state of health, and whether the victim was in debt, had just failed exams, lost her or his job, got divorced, and was depressed or not.

Coroners do not always agree on the way they interpret these clues. For example, Atkinson found one coroner believed a death by drowning was likely to be a suicide if the clothes were left neatly folded on the beach, but another coroner might attach little importance to this.

1 How is suicide defined in the passage?
2 Why do you think coroners attach such importance to suicide notes?
3 Suggest two reasons why the presence or absence of a suicide note might be an unreliable 'clue' to a dead person's intention to die.
4 Suggest ways relatives and friends might try to persuade a coroner that a death was not a suicide but an accident.
5 On the basis of the evidence in the passage, suggest reasons why (a) some deaths classified as suicides may have been accidental, and (b) some deaths classified as accidents may in fact have been suicides.
6 With reference to the evidence in the passage, suggest reasons why a sociologist should be very careful about using official statistics on suicide as a record of the real number of suicides in society.

there are not enough full-time jobs. This problem of the inaccuracy of unemployment figures was shown by the 1971 census, in which about 40 per cent more people reported themselves as unemployed than official unemployment figures showed.

Health statistics

A further example of the problem of using official statistics is shown by health statistics. These can be inaccurate because they depend on people persuading doctors they are ill, and the statistics are therefore simply a record of doctors' decision-making. Doctors may diagnose illnesses incorrectly, and therefore recorded illnesses may not be accurate. For example, there may have been many AIDS deaths recorded as pneumonia or another illness before doctors 'discovered' AIDS. Recent research has suggested that deaths from AIDS may have occurred in the 1950s in Britain, although the disease was not really 'discovered' until the 1980s. Finally, of course, not all sick people go to the doctor, and not all people who persuade the doctor they're sick are actually so – some may be malingerers or hypochondriacs.

The above discussion of unemployment and health statistics, and the discussion in chapter 10 of crime statistics, show that when sociologists use such secondary data, they must be very aware of its limitations, and approach it with care.

SOCIAL SURVEYS

Surveys involve the sociologist in systematically gathering information about some group of people. This is done by questioning them using questionnaires and interviews.

The Survey Population

One of the first steps in any social survey is the selection of the group of people to be studied. This group is called the **survey population**. The choice of survey population will depend on the *hypothesis* which the sociologist is investigating. For example, a hypothesis like 'teachers treat males more favourably than females' might mean the survey population would include all pupils and teachers in a particular school.

If the survey population is small, such as a class of college students, it may be possible to question everyone in it. In some cases, because the organization doing the research has enough time and money, it may be

---

A **hypothesis** is an idea which the sociologist guesses might be true, but which has not yet been tested against the evidence.

possible to investigate everyone even in a very large survey population. For example, the government has the resources to survey the entire population of the United Kingdom in the census every ten years – at a cost of £135 million in 1991. Such costs are way beyond the reach of most sociologists and market research organizations, and because of cost and time, most surveys are limited to studying a sample of the survey population.

Sampling

A **sample** is simply a small group drawn from the survey population. It is a way of making general statements about the whole survey population based on the responses of only a small percentage of the total survey population.

If the results obtained from the sample are to be used to make generalizations about the whole survey population, it is important that the sample is *representative*. Sociologists obtain representative samples by using various sampling methods.

A **representative sample** is one that contains a good cross-section of the survey population, such as the right proportions of people of different ethnic origins, ages, social classes, and sexes. The information obtained from a representative sample should provide roughly the same results as if the whole survey population had been questioned.

Methods of Obtaining a Representative Sample

1 Drawing up a sampling frame

A **sampling frame** is simply a list of names of all those included in the survey population from which the sample will eventually be selected; for example, the names of all schoolchildren in a school taken from registers, or doctors in a town. A commonly used sampling frame is the Electoral Register, which includes nearly all the names and addresses of adults over the age of 18 in Britain who are eligible to vote in elections. Doctors' lists of patients are also commonly used as sampling frames, as most people are registered with a doctor.

The choice and completeness of the sampling frame are very important if the results obtained are to be generalized to the whole survey population.

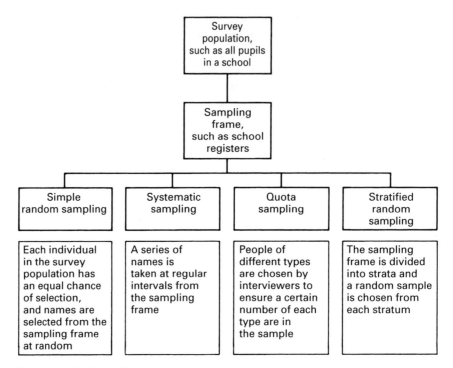

Figure 18.2 Sampling methods

For example, a telephone directory would be an unreliable sampling frame if we wanted to select a sample which was representative of the entire adult population, as it only contains those on the telephone and excludes those who may not be able to afford or want a telephone, or who are ex-directory and therefore not included in the phone book.

2 Deciding on the sample size

The size of the sample will depend on the amount of time and money available. However, if the sample is too small the results obtained may not be representative of the whole survey population. The ideal size of a sample is that at which the results obtained won't be made much more accurate by increasing the size of the sample.

3 Deciding on a sampling method

A sampling method is the process by which the sociologist selects representative individuals from the sampling frame to question. There are a number of sampling methods used by sociologists to try to gain a representative sample.

Simple random sampling

Simple random sampling means that every individual in the survey population has an equal chance of being picked out for questioning. For example, all names are put in a hat and enough names picked out to make up the required sample size. This is most commonly done by numbering all the names in the sampling frame and then getting a computer to select enough numbers at random to make up the size of sample required.

The problem with this method is that, purely by chance, the random sample may not be representative of the survey population. For example, there may be too many people of one sex, of one age group, or who live in the same area.

Systematic sampling

Systematic sampling is a method where names are selected from the survey population at regular intervals until the size of sample is reached. For example, every tenth name in the sampling frame is selected.

Quota sampling

Quota sampling is a method where interviewers are told to go and select people who fit into certain categories according to their proportion in the survey population as a whole. For example, an interviewer may be asked to question thirty men and women over the age of 45. The choice of the actual individuals chosen is left to the honesty of the interviewer (unlike other sampling methods where actual named individuals are identified).

Stratified random sampling

Stratified random sampling is a way of attempting to avoid the possible errors caused by simple random sampling. In this case, the sampling frame is divided into strata (layers) or sub-groups relevant to the hypothesis being investigated, such as groups of a similar age, sex, ethnic group, or social class, and a random sample is then taken from each sub-group. For example, in a survey of doctors, we may know from earlier research that 8 per cent of all doctors are Asian, and so the sociologist must make sure 8 per cent of the sample are Asian. To do this, the sociologist will separate out the Asian doctors from the sampling frame of all doctors, and then take a random sample from this list of Asian doctors to make up the 8 per cent of the sample of all doctors. In this way, the final sample is more likely to be representative of all doctors in the survey population.

Examples of simple random, systematic, and stratified random sampling

Survey population 400 students in a school
50 per cent are male and 50 per cent are female.
This information would be known from earlier research, such as school records.
In each group, 75 per cent are white and 25 per cent are black.

Sample size 10 per cent (40)

A simple random sample

To obtain a simple random sample:

1 Draw up a sampling frame: a list of the names of the 400 students in the survey population.
2 Pick out 40 names at random.

A systematic sample

To obtain a systematic sample:

Pick out every tenth name from the sampling frame until 40 names are collected.

The possible problem with these random and systematic samples is that, purely by chance, they might consist of too many males or females or too many black or white students. If this happened, the sample would be unrepresentative of the survey population, and therefore the survey results would give biased, inaccurate, and unrepresentative results. Stratifying the sample can avoid this problem.

A stratified random sample

To obtain a stratified random sample, complete the following stages:

1 Draw up a sampling frame (list of names) of the 400 students in the survey population.
2 Divide this sampling frame according to the way the survey population is made up. We know 50 per cent are male and 50 per cent are female, so divide the sampling frame into two.
3 We know that 25 per cent of males and females are black, and 75 per cent are white, so divide *each of* these sampling frames into two.
4 Now take a 10 per cent random sample from each sampling frame. This produces a sample made up like the one here.

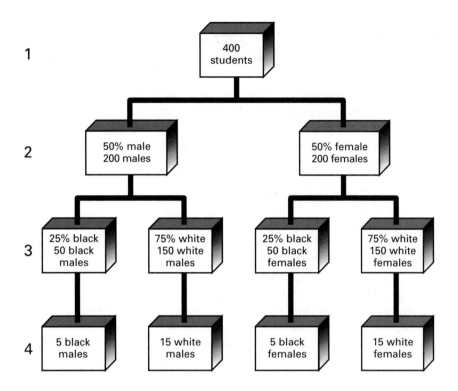

This stratified random sample should be representative of the sex and ethnic character-istics of the entire school population, as these features of the survey population are now certain to be included in the 10 per cent sample.

Stratified random sampling has the advantage of being much more repre-sentative than simple random sampling, because all the characteristics of the survey population are more certain to be represented in the sample.

By using one of the above sampling methods, the information provided by the sample can be generalized with great accuracy to the whole survey population. For example, opinion polls on the voting intentions of elec-tors often produce extremely accurate predictions of the outcome of gen-eral elections from questioning only about two thousand voters.

ACTIVITY

1 In each of the following cases, suggest both a hypothesis you might wish to test and how you might obtain your sampling frame.

- The attitudes of family doctors (GPs) to changes in the NHS.
- The attitudes of football supporters to soccer hooliganism.
- The reasons why few female school-leavers in a town go on computer courses at a local college.
- A survey of young mothers.
- A survey of old age pensioners.
- The opinions of adults in your neighbourhood about how they will vote in the next election.

2 Buneaton College has 3000 full-time students, and 6000 part-time students. Half of the full-time students are women, and three-quarters of the part-time students are men. You want to do a survey among students at Buneaton College. You haven't the time or the money to question every student, so you need to take a 10 per cent sample. In order to make this as representative as possible, you have decided to use a stratified random sampling method.
   (a) Explain how you would select this 10 per cent sample.
   (b) Give the actual numbers of the different groups in the survey population which will be included in your sample.

Research Methods Used in Surveys

There are two main methods which are used in social surveys to collect data: questionnaires and interviews.

Questionnaires

Most surveys involve the use of a questionnaire of some kind. A questionnaire is a printed list of questions to be filled in either personally by the *respondent* (the person answering the questions) or by an interviewer. All respondents answer exactly the same questions.

There are two main types of questionnaire: the pre-coded questionnaire and the open-ended questionnaire.

Questionnaires should be phrased in straightforward, everyday language

The pre-coded questionnaire

The pre-coded questionnaire involves the individual being asked a number of pre-set questions with a limited number of multiple choice answers. The person filling in the questionnaire will tick off the answer. A typical question might be 'Do you think wages should be paid for housework?' with available answers being Yes/No/Don't know. The problem with this type of questionnaire is that it does not allow respondents to explain their views fully or to develop their answers. An example of a pre-coded questionnaire (to be carried out by an interviewer) is shown in figure 18.3.

The open-ended questionnaire

Like the pre-coded questionnaire, the open-ended questionnaire usually has a number of pre-set questions, but there is no pre-set choice of answers. This allows respondents to write their own answer or dictate it to an interviewer.

An example of an open-ended question is: 'What is your opinion of the present government?' Such questions give respondents scope to express their own views. Such a questionnaire may form the basis for an unstructured interview (see below).

In a survey, both pre-coded and open-ended questions may be combined in the same questionnaire.

Newspaper survey

Conduct the interview politely. Ask questions clearly. Do not give extra emphasis to any words. Use only the words that are underlined. Mark the answer given by putting a circle round the appropriate code number.

Good morning/afternoon/evening. I am conducting a survey on newspapers and I would be grateful if you would help me by answering some questions.

		Code
A	Sex of respondent: Male Female	 1 2
B	Estimated age of respondent: 16 or under 17–21 22–40 41–60 61 or over	 1 2 3 4 5
C	Would you please tell me which of the following categories best describes your occupation: (show list) Professional/senior manager Manager in business Administrator/clerical Self-employed/business owner Manual Housewife Student Retired Unemployed Other	 1 2 3 4 5 6 7 8 9 10

Question		Code	Route
Q.1	Do you read a daily morning newspaper every day 4–5 times a week 2–3 times a week once a week less than once a week never?	 1 2 3 4 5 6	 Q.2 Q.2 Q.2 Q.2 Q.2 Classify
Q.2	Do you usually read: all the newspaper most of it part of it or just glance through it?	 1 2 3 4	 Q.3 Q.3 Q.3 Q.3
Q.3	Which newspaper or newspapers do you read? Sun Star Independent Mirror Telegraph Financial Times Mail Guardian Others (please Express Times write in)	 1 5 9 2 6 10 3 7 11 4 8	 Q.4 Q.4 Q.4 Q.4
Q.4	Where do you usually get most of your news about what's going on in Britain today? Is it from: Newspapers Television Radio Other (specify) Don't know?	 1 2 3 4 5	 Q.5 Q.5 Q.5 Q.5 Q.5
Q.5	Which of the following do you think gives the most truthful account of the news: Newspapers Television Radio Don't know?	 1 2 3 4	 Q.6 Q.6 Q.6 Q.6

Figure 18.3 Example of a pre-coded questionnaire conducted by an interviewer
Note the instructions given to the interviewer at the top of the questionnaire. These seek to ensure objectivity and consistency between different interviewers.

Designing a questionnaire

To design a successful questionnaire, you should follow these rules:

- It should be clearly laid out and well printed, and instructions for completing it should be easily understood by the respondent. The questionnaire should be easy to follow and complete.
- Questions should only be asked which the respondents are likely to be able to answer accurately. For example, people can only give opinions on things they know about and can remember accurately.
- The number of questions should be kept to the minimum required to produce the information. Respondents may be unwilling to spend a long time answering questions, or might stop answering the questions seriously.
- Questions should be simple and direct, and able to be answered briefly.
- Questions should be phrased in simple, everyday language so they are easily understood by the respondent. Technical words and 'jargon' should be avoided as the respondents may not understand the question. For example, a question about 'marital status' should be avoided – it is better to ask if someone is married, single, or divorced.
- Questions should be unambiguous, and their meaning quite clear. For example, a question like 'Do you watch television often?' is a bad question because people might interpret 'often' in different ways – it is better to specify actual time periods such as 1–2 hours a day, 3–4 hours a day, and so on.
- 'Leading' questions which encourage people to give particular answers should be avoided – otherwise the respondent might feel he or she is expected to give a particular answer. This might then produce invalid (or untruthful) answers.
- Pre-coded questionnaires should provide enough alternative answers to apply to all the respondents. There should be an opportunity for the respondents to give a 'Don't know' answer.

The postal questionnaire

A postal questionnaire is one which is sent to the respondents through the post with a pre-paid envelope for the reply. The respondents fill in the form themselves.

A key problem with postal questionnaires is that often people don't bother to return them. The percentage returning them may sometimes be only 20–30 per cent of the sample, and this may mean the results obtained may be inaccurate, biased, and unrepresentative. For example, those not replying might have answered differently from those who did reply, and those replying may be more educated, be interested in the topic being investigated, or have some 'axe to grind'.

To try to overcome the problem of non-response, postal questionnaires often have covering letters from well-known individuals or organizations, or offer free gifts, and other rewards. A reply-paid envelope is essential if the questionnaire is not to be dropped into the nearest waste-paper basket!

ACTIVITY

1 The following questions, which are intended to be filled in by the respondent, all have at least one thing wrong with them. In each case, describe what is wrong with the question and re-write the question in a more correct or more appropriate way.

(a) Do you watch television:

    1–2 hours a night?
    2–4 hours a night?
    4–6 hours a night?

(b) Don't you agree sex before marriage is wrong?   YES/NO

(c) Don't you think you should vote Labour if there were a general election tomorrow?   YES/NO/ DON'T KNOW

(d) Which recommendation of the Government Road Safety Committee regarding the change in the upper speed limit on class A roads and motorways do you support?

(e) Are you happy with your washing machine?   YES/NO/ DON'T KNOW

(f) Do you have joint conjugal roles in your household?   YES/NO/ DON'T KNOW

(g) Which social class do you belong to?

(h) Do you bonk with your partner a lot?   YES/NO

(i) Are you a good driver?   YES/NO/ DON'T KNOW

(j) Do you read newspapers:

    A LOT?
    QUITE A LOT?
    OFTEN?
    SOMETIMES?
    A BIT?
    NOT MUCH?
    NEVER?

2 Do you think any of the questions above in their present form would be either unlikely to be answered or answered dishonestly? Give reasons for your answer.

The strengths and limitations of postal questionnaires

Strengths

- Fairly cheap compared to paying interviewers.
- Large numbers of people over a wide geographical area can be questioned.
- Results are obtained quickly.
- People have more time to reply than when an interviewer is present, so more accurate answers may be obtained.
- Questions on personal, controversial, or embarrassing subjects are more likely to be answered than if they are asked by an interviewer.
- The problem of interviewer bias is avoided.
- Answers are easy to compare and put into statistical form (numbers and percentages) – for example, '87 per cent of women questioned said they had to do all the housework.'

Limitations

- Non-response, leading to unrepresentative, biased results.
- Extra questions cannot be asked or added, to get the respondents to expand or explain themselves more fully. The depth of information is therefore limited.
- With pre-coded questionnaires, the limited range of questions and answers may mean the researcher isn't getting at what the respondent really thinks.
- The wording may be confusing to the respondent, and the questions therefore misunderstood. There is no interviewer present to explain the question if necessary.

Interviews

Questionnaires are often carried out by an interviewer. There are two main types of interview: the structured or formal interview and the unstructured or informal interview.

The structured or formal interview

The structured interview is based on a pre-coded questionnaire. The interviewer asks the questions and does not probe beyond the basic answers received. It is a formal question-and-answer session.

The unstructured or informal interview

This type of interview is based on an open-ended questionnaire, or simply

Interviewers may not always get the cooperation they hope for . . .

. . . especially if they choose the wrong moment

a list of topics the interviewer wishes to discuss. The interviewer will ask the respondent open-ended questions which may trigger off discussions or further questions. The interviewer will try to put the respondent at ease in a relaxed, informal situation and encourage him or her to express his or her feelings and opinions. This means the interviewer can obtain much greater depth of information than is possible in a structured interview or in a postal questionnaire. It is a bit like a TV chat show.

Interviewer bias

A major problem with interviews, particularly unstructured ones, is that of **interviewer bias**. Interviewer bias is the way in which the presence or behaviour of the interviewer may influence in some way the answers given by the respondent. There is always the possibility that the respondent might adapt his or her answer according to the status, class, ethnicity, age, sex, speech, accent, tone of voice, style of dress, or behaviour of the interviewer. The interviewer may give the impression of wanting to hear a certain answer, and the respondent may try to impress the interviewer by giving answers she or he thinks the interviewer wants to hear and would approve of, rather than giving her or his real opinions.

Interviewer bias is a serious problem, as it could mean that respondents do not give answers which they really believe, and therefore the results of the survey may be unreliable. To overcome interviewer bias, interviewers are trained to avoid giving any impression of approval or disapproval based on their own opinions and feelings about the answers they receive. They should give the impression of polite indifference to the answers received.

The strengths and limitations of interviews

Strengths

- It is the best way of getting questionnaires completed – the problem of non-response found with postal questionnaires is much rarer. Skilled interviewers can persuade people to answer questions.
- There is more flexibility than with postal questionnaires – questions may be explained and, except with pre-coded questionnaires, extra questions can be asked and more detail obtained.
- Unstructured interviews allow the respondent to be more open and honest, and therefore more accurate information about the respondents' attitudes, values, and opinions can be obtained.
- Unstructured interviews enable the ideas of the sociologist to develop during the interview, and the interviewer can adjust questions and change direction as the interview is taking place if new ideas and insights emerge. By contrast, structured interviews have already decided the important questions.

Limitations

- Interviews are more time-consuming and costly than postal questionnaires – interviews are often slow and interviewers have to be paid. Many more people can be questioned with a postal questionnaire for the same cost.
- Because interviews tend to be slow and expensive, often only a small number can take place – this means the sample size is often small, and therefore risks being unrepresentative of the survey population.
- Interviews tend to be artificial situations, and there is no way of knowing whether what people say in an interview is what they really believe or how they behave in real life.
- The success of interviews depends heavily on the skill and personality of the interviewer, especially in unstructured interviews; for example, in getting people to answer questions that produce useful information and in keeping the conversation going.
- There is a risk of interviewer bias, leading to inaccurate results.

ACTIVITY

Consider the following situations, and in each case:

1 Suggest possible ways in which interviewer bias might occur.
2 Suggest what might be done to help remove the bias.

- A white person being questioned by a black interviewer about his or her racial attitudes.
- An adult interviewing pupils in a school.
- A British person interviewing a French person about her or his attitudes towards the English.
- An adult interviewer asking teenagers about their attitudes to glue-sniffing or other drug abuse.
- A well-dressed, middle-class sociologist asking gypsies questions about their lifestyle.
- A middle-class interviewer asking lower-working-class people about their attitudes to social welfare payments.
- A female interviewer asking a married or cohabiting couple about how household tasks are divided between them.
- An interviewer asking questions on birth control techniques.
- An older woman asking questions of a young mother about the way children should be brought up.
- An interviewer who is a committed Christian asking questions about religious belief.

The Stages of a Survey

Before carrying out a large-scale survey, it is important to carry out a **pilot survey**. This is a trial run of the final survey, using fewer people than the final sample. Its purpose is to iron out any problems which the researcher might have overlooked. For example, some questions may be unclear, some of the sample may have died or moved away, or there may be problems with non-response or non-cooperation by respondents.

After the pilot survey is completed, the results are reviewed, any necessary changes are made, and the main survey can then proceed. The stages of a survey are shown in figure 18.4.

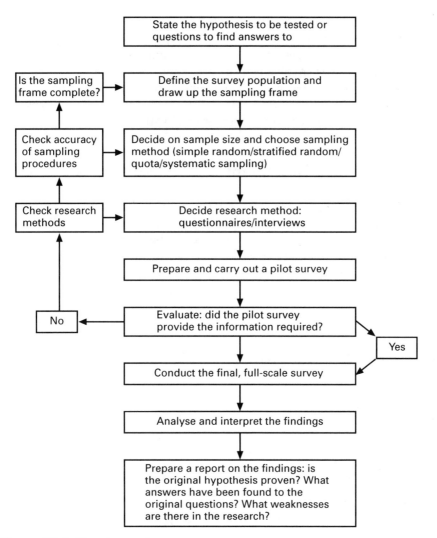

Figure 18.4 The stages of a survey

OBSERVATION

Apart from surveys, sociologists also collect data by observation. There are two main kinds of observation: non-participant observation (or direct observation) and participant observation.

Non-Participant Observation

The researcher observes a group or situation without taking part in any way. This has the advantage that the sociologist can study people in their 'natural setting' without their behaviour being influenced and changed by the presence of the researcher. For example, a researcher may observe people queuing in a supermarket to see how impatient they get. However, observation without involvement in the group means it is often not possible to understand what is really happening, or to find out more by asking questions. Therefore sociologists more often join in with a group to observe it. This is known as participant observation.

Participant Observation

Participant observation is a very commonly used observation technique. In this method, the researcher actually joins in the group or community she or he is studying. The researcher tries to become an accepted part of the group and to learn about the group as a member of it. For example, the sociologist may spend time as a mental patient in a hospital, join a gang, live as a gypsy or as a 'down and out', spend time in prison, or teach in a school.

The strengths and limitations of participant observation

Strengths

- The sociologist gains first-hand knowledge of the group being studied. She or he sees the world through the eyes of members of the group. This provides much more detail and depth than other methods like questionnaires and interviews.
- Questionnaires and interviews tend to provide information only at one point in time. Participant observation takes place over a long period and can therefore give a much fuller account of a group's behaviour.
- With other methods, the sociologist has already decided on a hypothesis, which affects what questions are asked and therefore what is found out. With

Limitations

- It is very time-consuming and expensive compared to other methods, as it involves the sociologist participating in a group for long periods.

- Because only a small group is studied, it is difficult to make generalizations.
- It depends a great deal on the personality of the investigator and his or her ability to fit in with the group.
- There is a danger of the researcher becoming so involved with the group and developing such loyalty to it that he or she may find it difficult to stand back

participant observation, interesting new ideas to explore may emerge during the research itself and the sociologist may discover things she or he would not even have thought of asking about.

- Participant observation may be the only possible method of research. For example, a criminal gang is hardly likely to answer questionnaires or do interviews for fear of the consequences, and a group like gypsies may well see an interviewer as 'official' and prying, and may fear harassment by councils, police, and other official bodies. By adopting a *covert* role – keeping her or his identity secret – the researcher may be able to investigate such groups. Even if the group knows who the researcher is (this is known as an *overt* role), the researcher may, after a time, win the trust of the group.

- People can be studied in their normal social situation, rather than in the somewhat artificial context of an interview or questionnaire.

and report his or her observations in a neutral way.

- There is no real way of checking the findings of a participant observation study. There is no real evidence apart from the observations of the researcher, and what one researcher might regard as important may be missed or seen as unimportant by another.

- There may be a problem of gaining the group's confidence (getting into the group) and maintaining it (staying in), especially if criminal and other deviant activities are involved. What does the researcher do if a group involves itself in criminal activities like theft, drug-dealing, or acts of violence? Failure to take part may result in the group's loss of confidence and trust, and the effective end of the research.

- The presence of the researcher, if she or he is known to the group as a researcher (an overt role) may change the group's behaviour simply because they know they are being studied.

- With a covert role, the researcher has to be very careful when asking questions, in case her or his real identity is revealed or people become suspicious. This may limit the information obtained.

ACTIVITY

1 What does the cartoon above suggest might be some of the difficulties involved in a participant observation study of a gang?
2 Many participant observation studies have been concerned with the study of various forms of deviance, such as homosexual groups or drug users. Suggest ways you might get in touch with and be accepted by such a group to study it, and outline any difficulties you might have with staying in the group.

ACTIVITY

1 According to figure 18.5, which method of data collection involves the largest number of respondents?
2 Which method has the highest level of personal involvement of the researcher with the respondents?
3 Which method, apart from observational methods, provides the most qualitative data?
4 Imagine you have three months to carry out a small-scale research project on one of the following issues, using both primary and secondary sources:

  - The difficulties facing the elderly.
  - The opinions of adults in your neighbourhood about how they will vote in the next election.

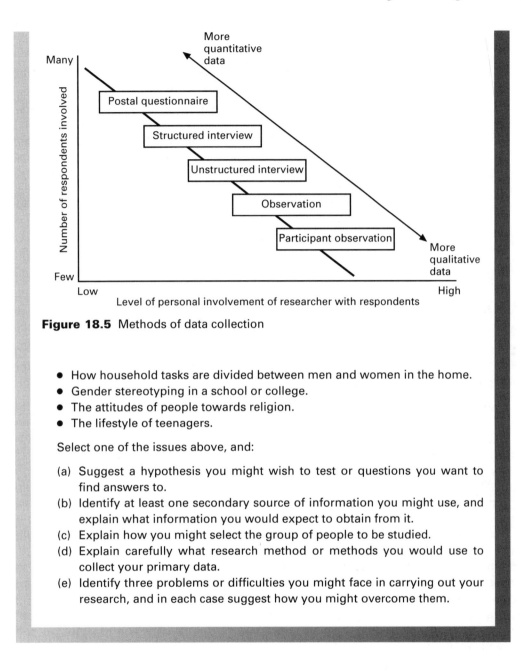

Figure 18.5 Methods of data collection

- How household tasks are divided between men and women in the home.
- Gender stereotyping in a school or college.
- The attitudes of people towards religion.
- The lifestyle of teenagers.

Select one of the issues above, and:

(a) Suggest a hypothesis you might wish to test or questions you want to find answers to.
(b) Identify at least one secondary source of information you might use, and explain what information you would expect to obtain from it.
(c) Explain how you might select the group of people to be studied.
(d) Explain carefully what research method or methods you would use to collect your primary data.
(e) Identify three problems or difficulties you might face in carrying out your research, and in each case suggest how you might overcome them.

In an actual piece of research, sociologists will probably use a variety of methods to collect the data they require. The methods chosen will be influenced by the questions or hypothesis being investigated, the information required (whether quantitative or qualitative), the scale of the research, and the time and money available to complete it. Figure 18.5 illustrates the relationship between some of these factors.

DOING YOUR OWN RESEARCH: COURSEWORK

As part of GCSE and many other introductory sociology courses, some form of coursework or project work has to be carried out. This coursework component is usually a small-scale piece of research into an area of sociology related to the syllabus.

One of the most important factors in successfully completing coursework is to keep research small-scale and manageable, to choose a topic you're interested in, and to recognize the limited time and resources available. Marks are awarded for the quality of the research and not simply quantity – a short (but not too short!), well-executed project is far better than a long rambling one.

The ethics of research

The ethics of research are concerned with morality and standards of behaviour when you carry out your research. When you are doing a survey or other types of research for your project, you should bear the following points in mind.

- You should adopt research methods which take into account the sensitivities of respondents. For example, it would not be appropriate to ask about attitudes to abortion in a hospital maternity ward where women may be having babies or have suffered miscarriages.
- You should report findings accurately and honestly.
- You must make sure the physical, social, and mental well-being of people who help you is not negatively affected by your research. You should be aware of the possible consequences of your work, and guard against harming those who help in your research. For example, do not disclose information given in confidence which might get the person into trouble, or cause him or her embarrassment.
- You should respect the anonymity, privacy, and interests of those who participate in your research. Do not identify them by name, or enable them (or an institution) to be easily identified.
- As far as possible, your research should be based on the freely given consent of those studied. You should make clear what you're doing, why you're doing it, and what you will do with your findings.

If in doubt, ask your teacher or lecturer for further advice.

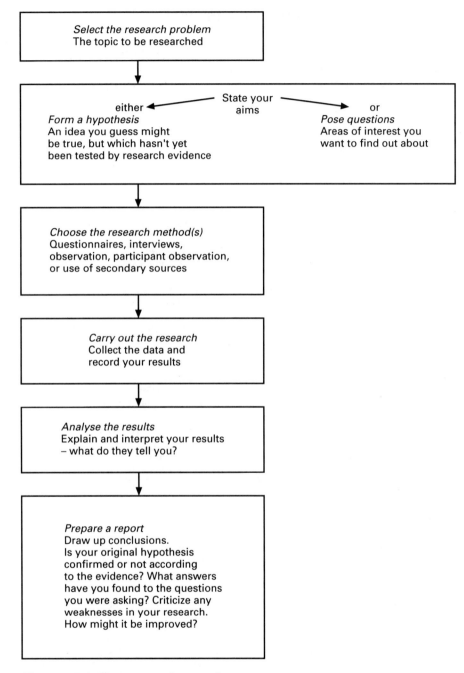

Figure 18.6 The stages of research

Planning a Project

In planning and carrying out a project, the sampling techniques and research methods discussed in this chapter should be applied. A successful project should follow the stages of research shown in figure 18.6.

You should also follow these guidelines:

- If information was collected from a sample of people, you should explain how you selected your sample. Was it representative? (It usu-

---

1 Has your project got a *title page*, with a *project title*, *your name*, *centre number*, and *candidate number*?

2 Does your project contain a clearly and fully explained *aim* (what you set out to do and why) or a *hypothesis* (a 'guess' about what you expect to find, with an explanation of why)?

3 Does your project use one or more *sociological methods* (for example, questionnaires, interviews, or observation/participant observation, and/or use of secondary sources?

4 Do you fully discuss *why* you chose the research method you did, explaining why this was the most suitable method for what you were investigating (your aim or hypothesis)? Do you explain the advantages/disadvantages of this method compared to using other methods for what you were investigating? Does your project contain a sample questionnaire, etc.?

5 If you selected a *sample* of people to investigate, do you explain *why* you selected them, *how* you selected them (what *sampling method* you used), and why you chose this method as the most suitable?

6 Are your research findings and the sources of information you used relevant to what you said you were going to investigate in your aim/hypothesis?

7 Does your project deal fully with all the aims you set yourself? Do you describe and explain fully all the evidence you collected? Do you explain what your findings show – in confirming and/or disproving your aims/hypothesis?

8 Does your project contain:

- numbered pages?
- a table of contents (with page numbers)?
- clearly separated chapters (for example, Aim/Hypothesis, Research method, Sample selection, Findings, Conclusions, Evaluation, Bibliography)?
- a clearly planned layout (does it follow a sensible order)?
- good grammar and spelling (if in doubt, use a dictionary!)?
- a bibliography–a list of the books, statistics, etc., you used, with their authors, publishers and dates?

9 Does your project have an *evaluation* – clear conclusions drawn from your research, indicating what you have found out, whether your aims have been achieved (and if not, an explanation of why not) or whether your hypothesis has been proven/disproven (and if not, an explanation of why not)? What are the limitations and weaknesses of your research and the methods you used? How might it have been improved? What are its strengths? Does your project have any interesting insights?

If it is all complete–hand it in!

Figure 18.7 Your project checklist

ally won't matter if it is unrepresentative, so long as this limitation of the research is explained in the conclusion.)

- You should give convincing reasons for the method(s) you chose, explain why they were particularly suited to the aims of your research and why the method you chose was more suitable than other methods you might have used, and give a clear description of how the information was collected.
- Your report should include:
  — A table of contents.
  — Clearly marked chapters.
  — Good layout.
  — Clear language.
  — The use of relevant diagrams and illustrations, with any pie charts, graphs, tables, photographs, or cassette or video tapes being clearly labelled and referred to in the text.
  — A list of books and sources you used – this is known as a bibliography.

Figure 18.7 gives a project checklist, based on the Southern Examining Group's GCSE sociology exam, for you to use.

Suggestions for possible projects are included at the end of each chapter in this book, except chapter 1 and this chapter, but you can usually choose any topic which interests you, so long as it is relevant in some way to the syllabus you are following.

CHAPTER SUMMARY

After studying this chapter, you should be able to:

- Explain the difference between quantitative and qualitative data.
- Explain, with examples, the difference between primary and secondary sources of data, and their advantages and disadvantages.
- Explain the various methods sociologists use to obtain representative samples.
- Outline the stages of a survey.
- Describe and explain the use of questionnaires, interviews, and non-participant and participant observation in sociological research, and explain their various strengths and limitations.
- Outline the stages a sociologist would go through in carrying out a piece of research.
- Carry out a small-scale piece of research of your own, using the various sources, sampling techniques, and research methods covered in this chapter.

KEY TERMS

hypothesis

interviewer bias

pilot survey

primary data

qualitative data

quantitative data

sample

sampling frame

secondary data

survey

survey population

APPENDIX: READING STATISTICAL DATA

The evidence that sociologists use in their research comes in a variety of forms, but often consists of statistical data presented in the form of tables, graphs, bar charts, pie charts, and various combinations of these. These often prove difficult for newcomers to sociology to understand. This appendix is designed to introduce you to the use and interpretation of these forms of data, and give you practice in doing so. This should make it easier to read the tables and figures appearing in this book, and construct your own should you wish.

STATISTICAL TABLES

When confronted with a statistical table, you should first read carefully the heading of the table – this will tell you what subject the statistics refer to. Tables generally show the relationship between two or more factors, and the key thing to note is what the statistics refer to – whether they are in actual numbers or percentages and what units the numbers are in. For example, the numbers might be in thousands or millions or they might be in the form of numbers per thousand of the population.

Table A1 is taken from a major source of official government statistics, *Social Trends*, which is published annually. The data in this table will be used to show the variety of ways in which statistical evidence can be presented.

Table A1 on divorce shows the relationship between a number of factors (shown in the left-hand column) and how these have changed over time (the dates shown along the top row). Notice that:

- The table refers to the different countries making up the United Kingdom. There are references to England and Wales, Scotland, Northern Ireland, Great Britain, and the United Kingdom.
- There are three ways in which the figures are expressed:
  — 'Petitions filed', 'decrees nisi granted', 'decrees absolute granted', and 'estimated numbers of divorced people who had not remarried' are expressed in *thousands*.

Table A1 Divorce: 1961–1989

	1961	1971	1976	1981	1984	1985	1986	1987	1988	1989
Petitions[a] filed (thousands)										
England and Wales										
By husband	14	44	43	47	49	52	50	50	49	50
By wife	18	67	101	123	131	139	131	133	134	135
Total	32	111	145	170	180	191	180	183	183	185
Decrees nisi[b] granted (thousands)										
England and Wales	27	89	132	148	148	162	153	150	155	152
Decrees absolute[c] granted (thousands)										
England and Wales	25	74	127	146	145	160	154	151	153	151
Scotland	2	5	9	10	12	13	13	12	11	12
Northern Ireland	–	–	1	1	2	2	2	2	2	2
United Kingdom	27	80	136	157	158	175	168	165	166	164
Persons divorcing per thousand married people										
England and Wales	2.1	6.0	10.1	11.9	12.0	13.4	12.9	12.7	12.8	12.7
Percentage of divorces where one or both partners had been divorced in an immediately previous marriage										
England and Wales	9.3	8.8	11.6	17.1	21.0	23.0	23.2	23.5	24.0	24.7
Estimated numbers of divorced people who had not remarried (thousands)										
Great Britain										
Men	101	200	405	653	847	918	990	1047	–	–
Women	184	317	564	890	1105	1178	1258	1327	–	–
Total	285	517	969	1543	1952	2096	2248	2374	–	–

[a] A petition is a request to a court to grant a divorce.
[b] A decree nisi is the stage before the divorce is finalized.
[c] A decree absolute is the final divorce, representing the legal termination of the marriage.

Source: Social Trends 21 (HMSO 1991)

— 'Divorces where one or both partners had been divorced in an immediately previous marriage' are expressed in *percentages*.

— 'Persons divorcing' are expressed as '*per thousand* married people' (this is known as the divorce rate).

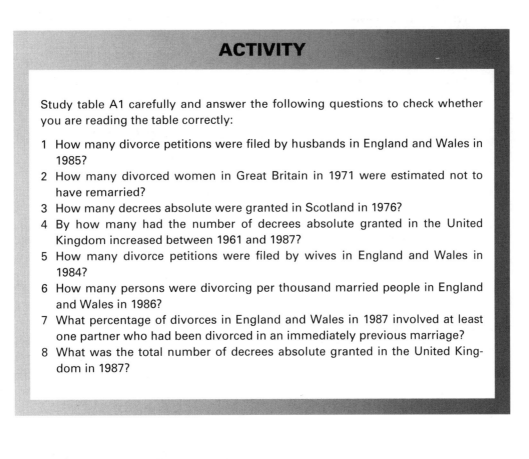

ACTIVITY

Study table A1 carefully and answer the following questions to check whether you are reading the table correctly:

1. How many divorce petitions were filed by husbands in England and Wales in 1985?
2. How many divorced women in Great Britain in 1971 were estimated not to have remarried?
3. How many decrees absolute were granted in Scotland in 1976?
4. By how many had the number of decrees absolute granted in the United Kingdom increased between 1961 and 1987?
5. How many divorce petitions were filed by wives in England and Wales in 1984?
6. How many persons were divorcing per thousand married people in England and Wales in 1986?
7. What percentage of divorces in England and Wales in 1987 involved at least one partner who had been divorced in an immediately previous marriage?
8. What was the total number of decrees absolute granted in the United Kingdom in 1987?

DESCRIBING A TREND

When interpreting statistical data, you will often be expected to describe a trend, or how the pattern shown changes over time. In describing a trend, you should normally give the starting figure and date and the finishing figure and date, and state whether the figure has increased or decreased, and by how much.

For example, with table A1 you might be asked: 'What trend is shown in the number of decrees absolute granted in the United Kingdom between 1961 and 1989?' Your answer might take the form: 'The number of decrees absolute has increased by 137 000, from 27 000 in 1961 to 164 000 in 1989' (the figure of 137 000 being obtained by subtracting the figure of 27 000 in 1961 from 164 000 in 1989).

ACTIVITY

Using table A1, practise describing the following trends:

1 What trend is shown in the number of persons divorcing per thousand married people in England and Wales between 1961 and 1989?
2 What trend does the table show in the number of decrees nisi granted in England and Wales in the period covered by the table?
3 Comparing the number of petitions filed by husbands and wives in England and Wales between 1961 and 1989, what *three* trends are shown?

GRAPHS

Statistics are commonly presented in the form of graphs. These show the relationship between two factors and how they change over time. These are shown on the vertical and horizontal axes, which are labelled to show what they represent. Trends can be immediately spotted by studying whether the line rises or falls between two dates. It is always important to note what the figures on the axes refer to – numbers, percentages, dates, and so on.

Figure A1, using the data given in table A1, illustrates how the number of decrees absolute granted in the United Kingdom has changed over time. Notice how the horizontal axis gives the date and the vertical axis gives the number of divorces (in thousands).

ACTIVITY

Using figure A1:

1 How many decrees absolute were granted in 1971?
2 About how many decrees absolute were granted in 1985?
3 What trend is shown in the graph?
4 Using the data given in table A1, practise drawing your own graph to illustrate the changing number of persons divorcing per thousand married people in England and Wales between 1961 and 1987. Make sure you label the axes correctly and put a title on your graph.

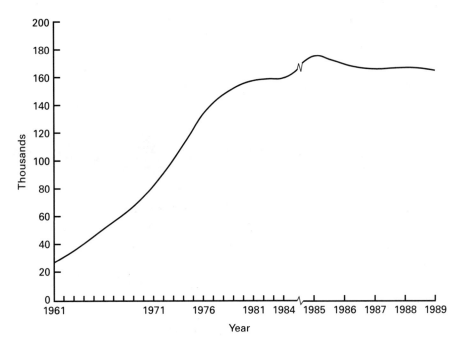

Figure A1 Decrees absolute granted: United Kingdom, 1961–89

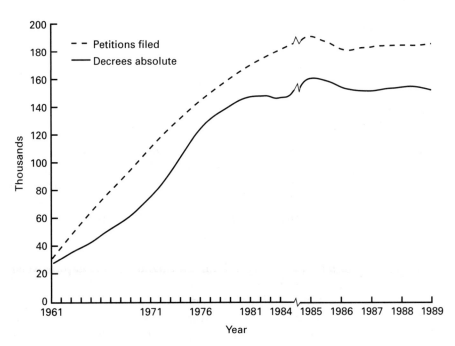

Figure A2 Divorces: England and Wales, 1961–89

Graphs may have more than one curve on them to show more information, and this is useful for making comparisons. For example, figure A2 shows that both the number of petitions filed for divorce and the decrees absolute granted (in thousands) have increased over time, and it is easy to see at a glance that there are large differences between them.

ACTIVITY

What does figure A2 on the previous page show about the number of divorce petitions compared to the number of decrees absolute granted over the period covered by the graph? How might you explain this difference?

Cumulative Graphs

Sometimes graphs may show how a total figure is made up by adding one set of figures to another. This is called a cumulative graph, as the figures 'build up' to the total. This is illustrated in figure A3, using the data from table A1 on 'petitions filed for divorce by husbands and wives in England and Wales'.

In figure A3:

- The top line shows the total number of petitions filed for divorce.
- The bottom line shows the number of husbands filing petitions.
- The space between the two lines represents the number of wives filing petitions.

By subtracting the number of husbands (the bottom line) from the total (the top line), it is possible to calculate the number of wives filing petitions. For example, in 1981, there was a total of about 170 000 petitions filed (point A), with 47 000 by husbands (point B). The number of wives petitioning for divorce is therefore about 123 000 (A minus B).

It is immediately obvious from looking at the graph that:

- Far more wives petition for divorce than husbands, as the gap between the top line and the bottom line is much wider than the gap between the bottom line and the horizontal axis.
- The gap between the curves widens over time, showing that the number of wives petitioning for divorce has grown at a faster rate than that of husbands seeking divorce.

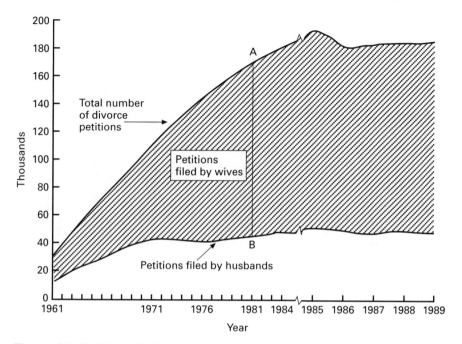

Figure A3 Petitions filed for divorce by husbands and wives: England and Wales, 1961–89

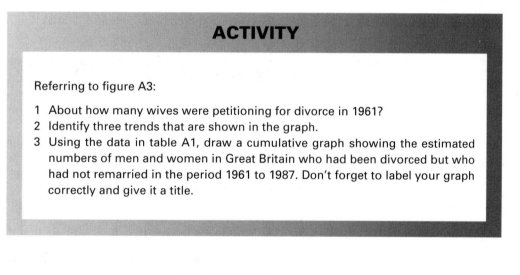

ACTIVITY

Referring to figure A3:

1 About how many wives were petitioning for divorce in 1961?
2 Identify three trends that are shown in the graph.
3 Using the data in table A1, draw a cumulative graph showing the estimated numbers of men and women in Great Britain who had been divorced but who had not remarried in the period 1961 to 1987. Don't forget to label your graph correctly and give it a title.

BAR CHARTS

Bar charts are another very commonly used way of presenting data and showing comparisons and trends in a visually striking way. Bar charts are constructed in much the same way as graphs, but columns are used instead of lines.

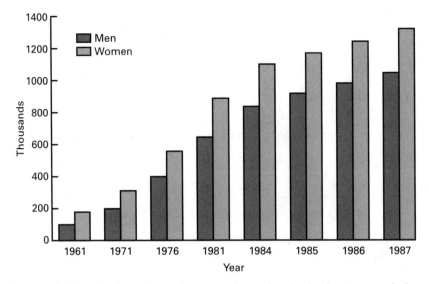

Figure A4 Estimated numbers of divorced people who had not remarried: Great Britain, 1961–87

Figure A4 shows a bar chart comparing the estimated numbers of divorced people in Great Britain who had not remarried between 1961 and 1987.

ACTIVITY

Referring to figure A4, answer the following questions.

1 About how many divorced women were estimated not to have remarried in 1985?
2 About how many divorced men were estimated not to have remarried in 1971?
3 Identify two trends shown in the chart.

Cumulative Bar Charts

Bar charts may, like graphs, be cumulative and show how totals are made up. Compare figure A4 with figure A5, in which exactly the same infor-

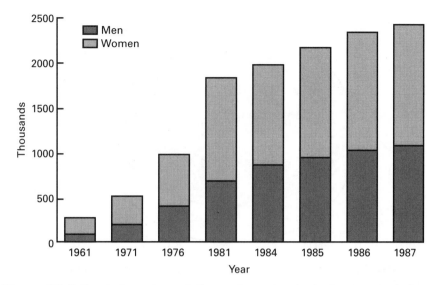

Figure A5 Estimated numbers of divorced people who had not remarried: Great Britain, 1961–87

mation is presented in a different form (note, however, that the scales on the vertical axes differ between the two).

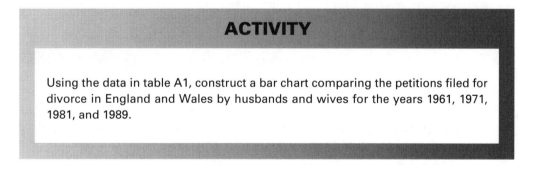

ACTIVITY

Using the data in table A1, construct a bar chart comparing the petitions filed for divorce in England and Wales by husbands and wives for the years 1961, 1971, 1981, and 1989.

PIE CHARTS

Pie charts present data by dividing a circle into sectors, with the size of each sector being proportional to the size of the item it represents. Pie charts are very effective in showing statistics in an easily digestible and striking way. For example, using the data given in table A1, the number of divorce petitions filed by husbands and wives in England and Wales in 1989 might be presented as in figure A6.

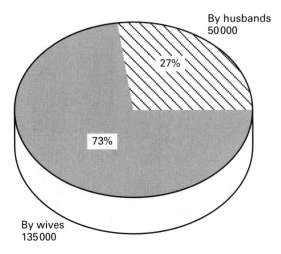

By husbands
50 000

27%

73%

By wives
135 000

Figure A6 Petitions filed for divorce by husbands and wives: England and Wales, 1989

ACTIVITY

Draw a pie chart illustrating the way your 24-hour day is divided up between school/college work or paid employment, travelling to and from work, leisure activities, domestic jobs in the home, and sleeping and eating.

Throughout this book there are many examples of statistics presented in a variety of forms, often with activities to develop your understanding of them. You should not simply ignore them, but try to read and interpret them. They often contain important information which will help you to understand the text better.

GLOSSARY

Words in **bold type** within entries refer to terms found elsewhere in the glossary.

Absolute poverty. Poverty defined as lacking the minimum requirements necessary to maintain human health. (See also **relative poverty**.)

Affluent worker. Well-paid manual worker.

Agenda-setting. The list of subjects which the mass media choose to report and bring to public attention.

Alienation. A lack of power and satisfaction at **work**.

Anomie. Confusion and uncertainty over social **norms**.

Anti-school sub-culture. A set of **values**, attitudes, and behaviour in opposition to the main aims of a school.

Arranged marriage. A marriage which is arranged by the parents of the marriage partners, with a view to background and status. More a union between two families than two people, and romantic love between the marriage partners is not necessarily present.

Authority. Power which is accepted as fair and just.

Automation. Production of goods by self-controlling machines with little human supervision.

Bigamy. Where **monogamy** is the only legal form of marriage, the offence of marrying a second partner without first getting divorced.

Birth rate. The number of live births per 1000 of the population per year.

Blue-collar workers. Manual workers.

Bourgeoisie. Class of owners of the **means of production**.

Caste system. A stratification system (see **social stratification**) based on Hindu religious beliefs, where an individual's position is fixed at birth and cannot be changed.

Class consciousness. An awareness in members of a **social class** of their real interests.

Classic extended family. A family where several related **nuclear families** or family members live in the same house, street or area. It may be horizontally extended, where it contains aunts, uncles, cousins, etc., or vertically extended, where it contains more than two generations.

Closed society. A stratification system (see **social stratification**) where **social mobility** is not possible.

Coercion. Rule by violence or the threat of violence.

Communes. Self-contained and self-supporting communities, where all members of the community share property, childcare, household tasks, and living accommodation.

Communism. An equal society, without **social classes** or conflict, in which the **means of production** are the common property of all.

Compensatory education. Extra educational help for those coming from disadvantaged groups to help them overcome the disadvantages they face in the education system and the wider society.

Conjugal roles. The **roles** played by a male and female partner in marriage or in a cohabiting couple.

Consumption property. Property for use by the owner which doesn't produce any **income**, such as owning your own car.

Craft production. The production of goods by hand tools.

Culture. The language, beliefs, **values** and **norms**, **customs**, **roles**, knowledge, and skills which combine to make up the 'way of life' of any society.

Culture of poverty. A set of beliefs and **values** thought to exist among the poor which prevents them escaping from poverty.

Customs. Norms which have existed for a long time.

Dealignment. In voting, no clear alignment (matching up) of particular social classes with one of the two main **political parties**. In particular, the working class (see **social class**) is no longer clearly aligned with the Labour Party, nor the middle class with the Conservative Party, and most voters no longer show loyalty to a party according to their social class.

Death rate. The number of deaths per 1000 of the population per year.

Democracy. A form of government where the people participate in political decision-making, usually by electing individuals to represent their views.

Demography. The study of population.

Dependency culture. A set of **values** and beliefs, and a way of life, centred on dependence on others. Normally used in the context of those who depend on welfare state benefits.

Dependency ratio. The proportion of the population which is dependent (see **dependent population**) compared to those who are working.

Dependent age groups. The under 16s, who are at school, and the over 60s (women) and 65s (men), who are retired.

Dependent population. That section of the population which is not in **work** and is supported by others, such as those in full-time education, pensioners, and the unemployed.

Deskilling. The removal of skills from **work** by the application of new machinery which simplifies tasks.

De-urbanization. The movement of people away from towns and cities.

Deviance. Failure to conform to social **norms**.

Deviancy amplification. The process by which the mass media, through exaggeration and distortion, actually create more crime and **deviance**.

Deviant career. Where people who have been **labelled** as deviant (see **deviance**) find conventional opportunities blocked to them, and so they are pushed into committing further deviant acts.

Deviant voter. Someone voting against the **political party** representing the interests of her or his **social class**.

Dictatorship. A form of **totalitarianism** where **power** is concentrated in the hands of one person.

Disease. A biological or mental condition, which usually involves medically diagnosed symptoms.

Division of labour. The division of **work** into a large number of specialized tasks, each of which is carried out by one worker or group of workers.

Divorce rate. The number of divorces per 1000 married people per year.

Domestic labour. Unpaid housework, including cooking, cleaning, childcare, and looking after the sick and elderly.

Ecumenical movement. A movement which seeks to achieve greater unity between different Christian churches.

Educational Priority Areas. Areas which face a range of social problems, such as poverty and unemployment, in which schools are given extra money and teachers to help children overcome difficulties at school arising from their home backgrounds.

Elaborated code. A form of language use involving careful explanation and detail.

The language used by strangers and individuals in some formal context, like a job interview, writing a business letter, or a school lesson or textbook. (See also **restricted code.**)

Elite. A small group holding great **power** and influence in society.

Embourgeoisement. The idea that, with higher wages, the working class (see **social class**) are becoming part of the middle class. The opposite of **proletarianization.**

Emigration. The movement of people out of a country or area on a permanent basis.

Endogamy. Where marriage must be to a partner of the same **kinship** or social group.

Equality of educational opportunity. The principle that every child should have an equal chance of doing as well in education as his or her ability will allow.

Ethnic group. A group of people who share a common **culture.**

Ethnicity. The shared **culture** of a social group which gives its members a common identity in some ways different from other groups.

Ethnic minority group. A social group which shares a cultural identity (see **culture**) which is different from that of the majority population of a society.

Ethnocentrism. A view of the world in which other **cultures** are seen through the eyes of one's own culture, with a devaluing of the others. For example, school subjects may concentrate on white British society and culture rather than recognizing and taking into account the cultures of different ethnic communities (see **ethnic groups**).

Evangelicalism. A form of Christianity involving a fundamentalist (see **fundamentalism**) belief in the Bible and a commitment to preaching the Christian gospel.

Extended family. A family grouping including all kin (see **kinship**). There are two main types of extended family: the **classic extended family** and the **modified extended family.**

False consciousness. A failure by members of a **social class** to recognize their real interests.

Feminist. Someone who believes that women are disadvantaged in society, and should have equal rights with men.

Feudalism. A closed (see **closed society**) system of stratification (see **social stratification**) based on land ownership and legal inequalities.

Floating voter. A voter with no fixed political opinion, nor a committed supporter of any **political party.**

Folk devils. Individuals or groups posing an imagined or exaggerated threat to society.

Fundamentalism. A return to the literal meaning of religious texts.

Gate-keeping. The media's refusal to cover some issues.

Gender. The culturally created differences between men and women which are learnt through **socialization.**

Gender role. The pattern of behaviour which society expects from a man or woman.

General fertility rate. The number of live births per 1000 women of child-bearing age (15–44) per year.

Glass ceiling. An invisible barrier of discrimination which makes it difficult for women to reach the same top levels in their chosen careers as similarly qualified men.

Health. Being able to function normally within a usual everyday routine.

Hidden curriculum. Attitudes and behaviour which are taught through the school's organization and teachers' attitudes but which are not part of the formal timetable.

Hypothesis. An idea which a researcher guesses might be true, but which has not yet been tested against the evidence.

Illness. The subjective feeling of being unwell or unhealthy.

Immigration. The movement of people into a country or area on a permanent basis.

Income. The flow of money which people obtain from **work**, from their investments, or from the state.

Infant mortality. The death of babies in the first year of life.

Infant mortality rate. The number of deaths of babies in the first year of life per 1000 live births per year.

Integrated conjugal roles. Roles in marriage or in a cohabiting couple where male and female partners share domestic tasks, childcare, decision-making, and income earning.

Inter-generational social mobility. A way of measuring **social mobility** by comparing an adult's present occupation with that of the family she or he was born into (usually measured against the father's occupation). It therefore shows how much **social class** mobility there has been between two generations.

Interviewer bias. The answers given in an interview being influenced or distorted in some way by the presence or behaviour of the interviewer.

Intra-generational social mobility. A way of measuring **social mobility** by comparing a person's present occupation with her or his first occupation. It therefore shows how much mobility an individual has achieved within her or his lifetime.

Inverse care law. In relation to the welfare state, the suggestion that those whose need is least get the most resources, while those in the greatest need get the least resources.

Kibbutz. A community established in Israel, with the emphasis on equality, collective ownership of property, and collective child rearing.

Kinship. Relations of blood, marriage, or adoption.

Labelling. Defining a person or group in a certain way – as a particular 'type' of person or group.

Laws. Official legal rules, formally enforced by the police, courts, and prison, involving legal punishment if they are broken.

Liberation theology. A Christian doctrine mixing **Communism** and Catholicism, and supporting the poor and oppressed in their fight for freedom.

Life chances. The chances of obtaining those things defined as desirable and of avoiding those things defined as undesirable in a society.

Life expectation. An estimate of how long people can be expected to live from a certain age.

Master status. The dominant status of an individual which overrides all other characteristics of that person, such as that of an 'ex-con'.

Matriarchy. Power and **authority** held by women.

Matrilineal descent. Property or title passing through the female side of the family.

Matrilocal residence. Where, on marriage, the husband is expected to live with or near his wife's family.

Means of production. The key resources necessary for producing society's goods, such as factories and land.

Mechanization. The process where production of goods by hand is replaced by machinery.

Meritocracy. A society where social positions are achieved by merit, such as educational qualifications, talent and skill.

Migration. The movement of people from one country or area to another.

Modified extended family. A family type where related **nuclear families**, although living apart geographically, nevertheless maintain regular contact and mutual support through visiting, the phone, and letters.

Monogamy. A form of marriage in which a person can only be legally married to one partner at a time.

Moral panic. A wave of public concern about some exaggerated or imaginary threat to society, stirred up by exaggerated and sensationalized reporting in the mass media.

Neo-local residence. Where, on marriage, the couple are expected to live away from both sets of parents.

Net migration. The difference between the number of people entering a country (immigrants) and the number leaving (emigrants) in a given period.

News values. The **values** and assumptions

held by journalists which guide them in choosing what to report and what to leave out, and how what they choose to report should be presented.

Norms. Social rules which define correct behaviour in a society or group.

Norm-setting. The process whereby the mass media emphasize and reinforce conformity to social **norms**, and seek to isolate those who don't conform by making them the victims of unfavourable public opinion.

Nuclear family. A family with two generations, of parents and children, living together in one household.

Objectivity. Approaching topics with an open mind, avoiding bias, and being prepared to submit research evidence to scrutiny by other researchers.

Open society. A stratification system (see **social stratification**) in which **social mobility** is possible.

Parity of esteem. The intention that the three types of school in the **tripartite system** should be of equal status.

Patriarchy. Power and **authority** held by men.

Patrilineal descent. Property or title passing through the male side of the family.

Patrilocal residence. Where, on marriage, the wife is expected to live with or near her husband's family.

Peer group. A group of people of similar age and status with whom a person mixes socially.

Perinatal death. Still-births and deaths within the first week of life.

Pilot survey. A small-scale practice **survey** carried out before the final survey to check for any possible problems.

Political party. A group of people organized with the aim of forming the government in a society.

Politics. The struggle to gain **power** and control in a society or group, by getting in a position to make decisions and implement policies.

Polyandry. A form of marriage in which a woman may have two or more husbands at the same time.

Polygamy. A form of marriage in which a member of one sex can be married to two or more members of the opposite sex at the same time.

Polygyny. A form of marriage in which a man may have two or more wives at the same time.

Population projections. Predictions of future changes in population size based on past and present population trends.

Positive discrimination. Giving disadvantaged groups more favourable treatment than others to make up for the disadvantages they face.

Poverty line. The dividing point between those who are poor and those who are not. There is no official poverty line in Britain today, but income support/supplementary benefit level and 50 per cent of average income are both used.

Power. The ability of people or groups to exert their will over others and get their own way.

Pressure groups. Organizations which try to put pressure on those with **power** in society to implement policies which they favour.

Primary data. Information which sociologists have collected themselves. (See also **secondary data**.)

Privatized nuclear family. A **nuclear family** unit which is separated and isolated from wider kin (see **kinship**) and the community, with members spending time together in home-centred activities.

Productive property. Property which provides an unearned **income** for its owner, such as factories, land, and stocks and shares.

Proletarianization. The process of decline in the pay and conditions of sections of the middle class (see **social class**), so they become more like the working class. The opposite of **embourgeoisement**.

Proletariat. The class (see **social class**) of workers, who have to work for wages as they do not own the **means of production**.

Proportional representation. A voting system where the number of representatives elected accurately reflects the proportion of the votes received.

Qualitative data. Information concerned with the meanings and interpretations people have about some issue or event.

Quangos. Quasi-autonomous non-government organizations. Bodies which are financed by public funds, whose leaders are appointed by the government, but are not elected by or accountable to the public.

Quantitative data. Information that can be expressed in statistical or number form.

Race. Humans classified into different groups according to physical characteristics, like skin colour.

Racial discrimination. When **racial prejudice** causes people to act unfairly against a racial group (see **race**).

Racial prejudice. A set of assumptions about a racial group (see **race**) which people are reluctant to change even when they receive information which undermines those assumptions.

Racism. Believing or acting as though an individual or group is superior or inferior on the grounds of their racial (see **race**) or ethnic (see **ethnic group**) origins.

Reconstituted family. A family where one or both partners have been previously married, and they bring with them children of a previous marriage.

Relative poverty. Poverty defined in relation to a generally accepted standard of living in a specific society at a particular time. (See also **absolute poverty**.)

Restricted code. A form of language use which takes for granted shared understandings between people. Colloquial, everyday language used between friends, with limited explanation and use of vocabulary. (See also **elaborated code**.)

Role conflict. The conflict between the successful performances of two or more **roles** at the same time, such as worker and mother.

Role model. Patterns of behaviour which others copy and model their own behaviour on.

Roles. The patterns of behaviour which are expected from individuals in society.

Sample. A small representative group drawn from the **survey population** for questioning or interviewing.

Sampling frame. A list of names of all those in the **survey population** from which a representative **sample** is selected.

Sanction. A reward or punishment to encourage social conformity.

Scapegoats. Individuals or groups blamed for something which is not their fault.

Secondary data. Data which already exists and which the researcher hasn't collected her or himself. (See also **primary data**.)

Secularization. The process whereby religious thinking, practice, and institutions lose social significance.

Segregated conjugal roles. A clear division and separation between the **roles** of male and female partner in marriage or in a cohabiting couple.

Self-fulfilling prophecy. People acting in response to behaviour which has been predicted of them, thereby making the prediction come true. Often applied to the effects of streaming in schools.

Serial monogamy. A form of marriage where a person keeps marrying and divorcing a series of different partners, but is only married to one person at a time.

Sex. The biological differences between men and women.

Sex ratio. The proportion of males to females in the population, expressed as the number of males per 1000 females.

Sexism. Prejudice or discrimination against people (especially women) because of their sex.

Sexual division of labour. The division of **work** into 'men's jobs' and 'women's jobs'.

Sick role. The pattern of behaviour which is expected from someone who is classified as ill.

Social class. An open (see **open society**) system of stratification (see **social stratification**) consisting of broad groups of people (classes) who share a similar economic situation, such as occupation, **income**, and ownership of **wealth**.

Social control. The process of persuading or forcing individuals to conform to **values** and **norms**.

Social institutions. The organized social arrangements which are found in all societies.

Socialization. The process of learning the **culture** of any society.

Social mobility. Movement of groups or individuals up or down the social hierarchy.

Social stratification. The division of society into a hierarchy of unequal social groups.

Sociology. The systematic (or planned and organized) study of human groups and social life in modern societies.

Status. The amount of prestige or social importance a person has in the eyes of other members of a group or society. *Ascribed status* is status which is given to an individual at birth and usually can't be changed. *Achieved status* is status which is achieved through an individual's own efforts.

Status frustration. A sense of frustration arising in individuals or groups because they are denied **status** in society.

Status group. A group of people sharing a similar social standing and lifestyle.

Stereotype. A generalized, over-simplified view of the features of a social group, allowing for few individual differences between members of the group.

Sub-culture. A smaller **culture** held by a group of people within the main culture of a society, in some ways different from the main culture, but with many aspects in common.

Survey. A method of gathering information about some group of people by questioning them using questionnaires and interviews.

Survey population. The section of the population which is of interest in a **survey**.

Symmetrical family. A family where the **roles** of husband and wife have become more alike (symmetrical) and equal.

Tactical voting. In an election, where supporters of a **political party** which has no chance of winning vote for another party which is not their preferred choice, in the hope of defeating the predicted winning party.

Totalitarianism. A system of government where society is controlled by a small powerful group or an individual, and ordinary people lack any control over government decision-making.

Tripartite system. The system of secondary education established in 1944 in which pupils were selected for one of three types of secondary school according to their performance in the 11+ exam.

Underachievement. The failure of people to achieve as much as they are capable of.

Underclass. A social group who are right at the bottom of the **social class** hierarchy, who are in some ways cut off or excluded from the rest of society.

Urbanization. The movement of population from rural (country) areas to urban areas (towns and cities), which become the major centres of population in a society.

Value freedom. The idea that the beliefs and prejudices of the sociologist should not be allowed to influence the way research is carried out and evidence interpreted.

Values. General beliefs about what is right or wrong, and the important standards which are worth maintaining and achieving in any society.

Wealth. Property which can be sold and turned into cash for the benefit of the owner.

White-collar workers. Non-manual clerical workers, sales personnel, and other office workers, whose work is non-professional and non-managerial.

Work. The production of goods or services that usually earns a wage or salary, though housework remains unpaid.

INDEX

Using the Index

If you are looking for general topics, it is probably best to refer first to the contents pages at the beginning of this book. If you want to find a particular item of information, look it up in this index. If the item is not listed, then think of other headings it might be given under: the same information is often included several times under different headings. This index only includes the main references found in the book, rather than every single occurrence of the theme, and it is sensible to check the largest references first, such as pages 152–9 before 147, 148 and 177. The chances are that what you're looking for will be in the largest entry, and this will save you time wading through a lot of smaller references.

Page numbers in **bold** refer to items in the glossary.